Marketing and the Internet

Marketing and the Internet
Conceptual Foundations

Eloise Coupey

Virginia Polytechnic Institute and State University

Upper Saddle River, NJ 07458

Library of Congress Cataloging-in-Publication Data

Coupey, Eloise.
   Marketing and the internet / Eloise Coupey.
      p. cm.
   Includes bibliographical references and index.
   ISBN 0-13-016975-7
   1. Internet marketing.   2. Internet.   3. World Wide Web.   I. Title.
HF5415.1265 .C68 2001
658.8′4—dc21
00-048333

Senior Acquisitions Editor: Whitney Blake
Assistant Editor: Anthony Palmiotto
Editorial Assistant: Melissa Pellerano
Media Project Manager: Cindy Harford
Senior Marketing Manager: Shannon Moore
Marketing Assistant: Katie Mulligan
Production Manager: Gail Steier de Acevedo
Production Editor: Maureen Wilson
Permissions Coordinator: Suzanne Grappi
Associate Director, Manufacturing: Vincent Scelta
Manufacturing Buyer: Natacha St. Hill Moore
Cover Design: Bruce Kenselaar
Cover Painting: © Pierre Coupey
               Notations 15
               Oil/beeswax on canvas
               100″ × 90″
               1995
               Collection of the artist, Vancouver
Full-Service Project Management: BookMasters, Inc.
Printer/Binder: Maple Vail

Prentice Hall

10 9 8 7 6 5 4 3 2
ISBN 0-13-016975-7

To William, Katy, and Mark

Brief Contents

SECTION FIVE: EXTENDING THE FRAMEWORK OVER TIME:
EXCHANGE RELATIONSHIPS IN THE INTERNET
ENVIRONMENT

Contents

SECTION FIVE: EXTENDING THE FRAMEWORK OVER TIME: EXCHANGE RELATIONSHIPS IN THE INTERNET ENVIRONMENT

Preface

The Internet has become an increasingly popular and versatile tool for marketing. Often touted as a revolutionary force for business, it is rapidly becoming a fundamental and often necessary vehicle for communications and transactions between marketers and consumers. Its benefits may become more pronounced, however, as the range of innovative possibilities for marketing is recognized and leveraged to develop coherent and effective marketing strategies. As a result, it is important to recognize and understand the implications of the Internet not only as a marketplace, but also as a set of tools and opportunities for conducting a wide variety of marketing activities that do not involve product-related transactions (e.g., marketing research, customer service).

Successful strategies for Internet marketing integrate the capabilities of the Internet with aspects of the marketer's resources, constraints, and objectives, and with the consumer's needs and expectations. Because the Internet is a dynamic environment for marketers, it is often difficult to know what types of strategies are likely to be effective, and when, and why. Simply looking at what marketers have done in the past may not be sufficient in the swiftly moving environment of the Internet. The ability to understand and predict what practices will work, and why, can be enhanced by using theory to integrate ideas and to generalize them to anticipated situations. The Internet is a new environment for many companies, however, and research to develop theoretical insight and guidance is at an equally early stage of development. That's why this book was written.

This book is designed to provide you with the conceptual foundations you need to understand the implications of the Internet as an environment in which marketing activities are conducted. By having a general picture of the Internet and its interaction with marketing activities, it is easier to envision possible outcomes of strategic actions that incorporate use of the Internet's capabilities as marketing tools. In addition, knowledge of the fundamental concepts that describe the impact of the Internet on marketing actions and outcomes can be generalized to guide strategy development in future states of the Internet that presently exist only in our imaginations. In other words, this book is intended to help you develop the knowledge and skills you need to operate effectively within the exciting and opportunity-laden environment of the Internet.

SECTIONS OF THE BOOK

To enable you to develop the skills necessary to understand and integrate Internet technology and characteristics into marketing strategy, this book incorporates marketing theory with Internet reality to address issues in determining and selecting market segments and formulating the marketing mix. The book contains five main sections. Section One presents the conceptual framework used to organize the text, and it provides an overview of the unique marketing environment embodied in the Internet. For instance, while most marketing texts emphasize the perspectives and influences of consumers, marketers, and policy makers, this text also includes a discussion of the influence of technology on the nature of the interactions between the other three perspectives. In Section Two, we look at the exchange relationships that exist within the Internet environment, from each of the key perspectives. Contrasts are noted between the nature of the relationships in traditional marketplaces and the Internet marketplace, and the implications of these contrasts are discussed.

With Section Three, we integrate the four perspectives and the framework components of the earlier sections to examine the influence of the Internet environment on marketing strategy. In Section Four, we apply the framework to consider the implications of the Internet for marketing action. Topics covered include marketing research, online business models, and marketing mix issues. The final section, Section Five, of the text extends the framework to examine ways in which marketers can foster relationships with the Internet. For example, we address the role of the Internet in business-to-business exchanges.

LEARNING TOOLS

Learning how to use the Internet effectively as a marketing tool means that you need to learn two different but related bodies of knowledge. First, you need to have available to you the body of information that presently exists about characteristics of Internet marketing. Second, you need to have available to you the skills you will need to keep abreast of changes in the Internet environment.

To make the acquisition of these skills more manageable, this text includes several types of learning tools. For example, to build on skills you have previously acquired for marketing in venues other than the Internet, the issues discussed in this text are described, where possible, in terms of their similarities to or differences from marketing in other environments. In addition, real-world examples of companies and organizations using the Internet to market goods or services are provided to illustrate key issues throughout the text.

At the end of each chapter, a review section is provided to help you determine whether you have mastered sufficiently the skills and topics provided in the text. If you have an interest in a particular topic that you would like to explore in greater depth, the list of suggested readings at the end of each section is intended to serve as a research resource.

The companion Web site to this book is an added resource for learning about marketing and the Internet. The site provides illustrative examples of many of the issues covered in the text, as well as up-to-date links to interesting, pertinent material online. For instructors, the site contains class outlines and presentation materials, as well as exercises and suggestions for developing students' understanding of the topic. A test bank with a variety of test formats is also available.

Acknowledgments

The process of writing a book about marketing and the Internet bears remarkable similarities to the topic. Dramatic and rapid changes, vast opportunities and pitfalls, and the need for coherent structure and approach to guide thinking and action have made the effort a challenge and a pleasure. One of the most pleasant activities is the opportunity to reflect on the thinking and writing process, and to recognize the people who have provided motivation, guidance, and encouragement.

I wrote this book not just because I'm an academic and we write, but because I am a teacher. My students provided the motivation for this text, and their patience, feedback, and encouragement are especially noteworthy. The students in my MBA and undergraduate classes in the spring 2000 semester deserve individual recognition: Meredith Alexander, Aline Almeida, Maeve Anderson, Brian Bedder, Tracie Bertsch, Elizabeth Blanchard, Kristina Boardman, Price Booker, Travis Boyer, Lisa Buco, Jerry Cai, Kelly Carrico, Shawn Cobb, Allyson Cochran, Eric Copen, Michael Dawson, Michael Doyle, Brand DuBose, Maureen Feldmann, Brian Freeman, Ryan Froman, Chris George, Poorvi Gohel, Brett Hale, Rasheedah Hamidullah, Reno Harnish, Mandee Hazard, Justin Hembree, Abbie Hickman, Mike Hill, Drew Horton, Andrew Hood, Tony Ibarra, Eric Jacobson (a.k.a. Hokie Bird), Jennifer Kilinski, Zack Kovolenko, Ryan Labrecque, Kate Lerch, Reid Limpert, Jon Lloyd, Nathan Lowe, Jennifer McNamara, Stuart Mease, Tom Mesquit, Matt Miller, Jason Moss, Suvit Nopachai, Erin North, Eric Powell, Jeff Puzenski, Carolina Quintero, Fabian Quintero, Venkat Ramaswamy, Kristin Reed, Hugo Rousset, Michael Schaefer, Henning Schueler, Yook Yeong Seock, Grant Shaklee, Dan Sheehan, Mike Sierakowski, Nick Sorensen, Anna Sparks, Missy St. John, Brandon Stinnett, Jane Thompson, Ankur Tiku, Holly VanMiddlesworth, Jennifer Walawender, Tamara Wayne, Chris Woronka, and Whitney Zivan.

In addition, Erin Sandgathe—research assistant and future professor—provided invaluable feedback and encouragement. Her willingness to plow through every draft chapter and her ability to provide thoughtful, constructive criticism made the process more enjoyable than it would have been without her help.

I would also like to thank Mark Jones and David Brinberg, as well as the following reviewers, for insights and suggestions, and the occasional reality check. I value their comments, and I hope that my recognition of their input is apparent in the improvements to the text that resulted from their effort:

Ken Williamson, James Madison University
Patrali Chatterjee, Rutgers University
James Zemanek, East Carolina University
Catherine Campbell Griffioen, University of Maryland University College
Judy Strauss, University of Nevada–Reno
Karen James, Louisiana State University–Shreveport
Nabil Tamimi, University of Scranton
Rajeev Batra, University of Michigan

The people at Prentice Hall deserve many thanks, too. For the opportunity to write the book, and for supportive guidance throughout the process, I thank Whitney Blake and Bill Beville.

Thank you all, very much!

Eloise Coupey

SECTION ONE

Developing a Conceptual Framework for Marketing and the Internet

The Internet has the potential to influence all aspects of buying and selling. In addition to providing marketers with a new environment for marketing activity, it facilitates exchange activities in traditional marketplaces. This section provides an overview to the study of marketing and the Internet. In Chapter 1, the impact of the Internet on marketing activity is described by considering the relationship between marketing and technology. For instance, developments in technology provide marketers with new ways to transmit information about products and their benefits. The Internet is a technological development that increases the options for marketing communications. Placing marketing and the Internet within a historical context of technology, rather than thinking about the Internet as an isolated phenomenon, builds the base for understanding the opportunities and difficulties associated with marketing and the Internet in contrast to capabilities for marketing prior to the Internet.

Because the Internet environment is growing and changing rapidly, strategies for integrating the Internet into marketing activity must be flexible: capable of being adapted as the medium evolves. In Chapter 2, a framework is presented to organize elements of marketing in the Internet environment. The Internet environment for marketing is described as exchanges between consumers, marketers, and policy makers. Building on the marketing and technology basis of Chapter 1, we also include exchanges that involve a technology perspective. The framework provides a "big picture" understanding of the goals and activities of different sets of people in the Internet environment, and the effect of the Internet on marketing processes in creating exchange.

CHAPTER 1

Introduction to Marketing and the Internet

FOCUS AND OBJECTIVES

This chapter characterizes the importance of the Internet as an influence on marketing activity. Key topics include the historical relationship between technology and marketing, and the implications of this relationship for marketing and the Internet. The origins and growth of the Internet and of the World Wide Web are reviewed.

YOUR OBJECTIVES IN STUDYING THIS CHAPTER INCLUDE THE FOLLOWING:

- Understand the need for the study of marketing and the Internet.
- Recognize the relationship between marketing and the Internet as an outgrowth of the relationship between marketing and technology.
- Develop familiarity with the history of the Internet and the World Wide Web.
- Recognize the need to integrate traditional marketing concepts into the study of marketing and the Internet.
- Be able to differentiate between online marketing and electronic commerce.

The Internet has become an increasingly popular and versatile tool for marketing. Frequently touted as a revolutionary force for business, it is rapidly becoming a fundamental and often necessary vehicle for communications and transactions between marketers and consumers, and between businesses. Its benefits will become even more pronounced, however, as the range of innovative possibilities for marketing is recognized and leveraged to develop coherent and effective marketing strategies.

Despite its relatively recent introduction into the day-to-day life of most American consumers, the Internet has grown dramatically, rapidly outpacing projected use in terms of the number of users worldwide. For instance, an average of user surveys compiled in 1999 by Nua Internet Surveys projected a worldwide user population in 2000 of 250 million people. By March of 2000, however, similar surveys indicated a user population of 304 million. Also underscoring the un-expected growth, online sales have consistently exceeded predictions. In 1995, ActivMedia projected 1998 sales in the neighborhood of $46 million. A Forrester Research survey placed estimates at the end of 1998 at $8 billion. By the end of 1999, Forrester Research gauged online consumer spending at $18.1 billion.

Companies that use the Internet to market their products come in all types and sizes, ranging from multinational corporations to home-based entrepreneurial busi-nesses. Marketing applications of the Internet are equally varied. For example, a com-pany might use the Internet merely as a tool for effecting standard business practices, such as using e-mail to handle catalog requests. Another company might make its entire product line available through an Internet site, as well as through traditional means. This approach is used by retailers such as Barnes and Noble, a book retailer, and Wal-Mart. Yet other companies might market their products solely through a virtual storefront on the Internet, as do Furniture.com and Amazon.com. The types of online activities are influenced by the goals of the company, and by its experience with Internet technologies.

WHY MARKETING AND THE INTERNET?

The Internet penetrated popular awareness in the last decade of the twentieth cen-tury. In spite of concerns about the privacy and security of information, such as credit card numbers, and fears about the reputability of online vendors, consumers have increased the frequency and amount spent on Internet-based purchases. Marketers have developed business models designed to take advantage of the op-portunities provided by the Internet medium—both for creating and offering new products, and for finding new ways to sell existing products.

So what makes marketing and the Internet worth an entire book? This question can be answered by understanding the impact of technology on marketing, and of marketing on technology. It is difficult to characterize the development of market-ing as we know it today without acknowledging the impact of technological devel-opment on marketing practices. In addition, although marketing has often adapted to developments in technology, it has also influenced the course of the develop-ment. The current emphasis of the Internet as a technology for commerce reflects the symbiotic nature of the relationship between technology and marketing.

An Abbreviated History

Marketing activities have existed for thousands of years. Early societies relied on barter and exchange methods in local marketplaces, reflecting the need to trade perishable goods (refrigeration had not yet been invented) and the absence of a money economy (banking cabbages and chickens is difficult). With the develop-ment of money economies, marketing activities became increasingly sophisticated; the ability to save money for a purchase lengthened consumption planning horizons and created the opportunity for financial arrangements of credit and interest.

The Industrial Revolution in the later part of the nineteenth century had a profound impact on marketing. The mechanization of many previously manual processes enabled the mass production of products; items that were once in scarce supply now existed in abundance—and at lower prices. Technological developments such as the automatic loom and the electric light facilitated mass production in factories, while the invention of the air brake and steel rails combined to provide train systems that were critical to widespread distribution of products.

With the supply in place, the next requirement for a vital marketing environment was demand. The introduction of technologies that enabled new ways to reach and communicate with consumers fueled the development of a consumer economy with knowledge and interest in available, mass-produced products. Prior to the beginning of the twentieth century, the primary avenues for making consumers aware of products were face-to-face communications or print, typically in the form of newspapers. Both methods had limitations. Face-to-face interactions were costly and time consuming. Printed communications ran the risk of missing their target, or of becoming too rapidly outdated.

Mass Communication and Demand

In the 1920s, radio became a common vehicle with which marketers could tout their wares to large audiences of consumers. The RCA Corporation formed the NBC Radio Network in 1926. This network enabled one source to broadcast content to several stations at the same time. The popularity of many of the broadcast radio shows, such as "Amos 'n' Andy" and "The Lone Ranger," made them desirable outlets for commercial messages. By the mid-1930s, known as the "Golden Age of Radio," approximately one-third of all radio shows were sponsored by companies. These companies used the shows as forums for advertising their products. The technology behind radio offered advantages over previous ways to deliver marketing communications. Salespeople and newspapers are geographically limited; radio broadcasts are less limited. By advertising on radio networks, marketers could reach audiences that stretched across the country, creating widespread awareness of brands and stimulating demand for these national brands.

Digital Artifact 1.1

Elapsed time for technologies to reach 50 million users: telephone, 40 years; radio, 38 years; cable television, 10 years; the Internet, 5 years.

(*Source:* **Netscape CEO Jim Barksdale, as reported in** *PC Magazine,* **November 4, 1997.)**

The advent of television in the 1930s complemented marketers' ability to reach national audiences by enabling them to include visual information about products in their advertising. The technology for television transmissions was largely developed during the 1920s, but it wasn't until 1939 that RCA introduced its fully electronic television to the American public. The first television ad was aired in 1941, by WNBT–New York. The commercial was a ten-second live pitch for the Bulova Watch Company.

Adoption of the television was slowed by World War II. Development and production, not just of television sets, but of many consumer goods, was halted to increase production of war materiel. The war effort spurred research that led to new products and technologies for their production. These inventions were greeted by an American public flush with money saved during wartime, and pent-up demand due to the scarcity of many products.

The market economy moved quickly forward. To illustrate the speed with which television technology was adopted, consider that in 1946, only 6,000 televisions were in American homes. This number increased to 3 million by 1948, and to 12 million by 1951. The only major change to the technology that enabled television was the introduction of color in 1952—an innovation that was not fully supported by the major broadcast networks until the mid-1960s!

From an Industrial Economy to a Digital Economy

Since the 1960s, techniques to create digitized, rapidly transmittable information have led to a shift from an industrial economy to a **digital economy.** The adoption of the personal computer reflects the shift to a digital economy. Similar to the growth of the mass media of radio and television, personal computers have been adopted rapidly. By 1995, 36 percent of Americans owned computers. That number increased to 43 percent in 1998, and to 65 percent by the end of 1999. Even more dramatic has been the acceptance of the technologies that enable the Internet. In 1995, only 14 percent of the U.S. population used the Internet. Results of a 2000 poll conducted by Harris Interactive indicated that more than 50 percent of U.S. households have Internet access, and that 90 percent of these households are active online.

In the early and middle years of the twentieth century, the widespread electrification of America and the construction of the interstate highway system provided the necessary infrastructure for an industrial economy. In recent years, however, the emphasis has shifted from "industry" to "information" as information networks provide a new infrastructure for a digital economy that is characterized by the importance of networked intelligence in the form of digitized information.

The critical element of this shift is the means for transmitting the digitized information. Satellites, wireless technologies, and networked computers are all capable vehicles for transmission, and all are components of what has been termed "the Information Highway." Best known to most people, however, is the Internet, which is a network of networks that enables high-speed digital communications.

Many marketers have focused on the Internet as an interactive media to inform consumers about their products and services and, in many cases, to sell products and services online. **Interactive media,** such as the medium represented by the Internet, enable flexible communications in real time between marketers and consumers, by technological means, such as computers. This interactivity differentiates the Internet from the communications technologies of television, radio, and print, traditionally used by marketers. In addition, interactivity enables marketers to tailor information to meet the needs of different customer targets. This **personalization** is based on the two-way communication between consumer and marketer, which is made possible by the Internet.

The Internet as Just Another Technology

Technology and marketing have coexisted—generally to the benefit of each—for hundreds of years. In this sense, the Internet is merely the most recent technology for the delivery of marketing. The importance of understanding the role of the Internet for marketers, however, lies in recognizing how the technologies that underlie the Internet enable marketers to change the way they carry out marketing activities.

One way to begin to understand the implications of the Internet for marketing is to consider how past technologies have changed the nature of the interactions between marketers and consumers. We can summarize the history of the relationship between marketing and technology as a timeline, as depicted in Figure 1.1.

FIGURE 1.1 Marketing and Technology Have a Long Relationship.

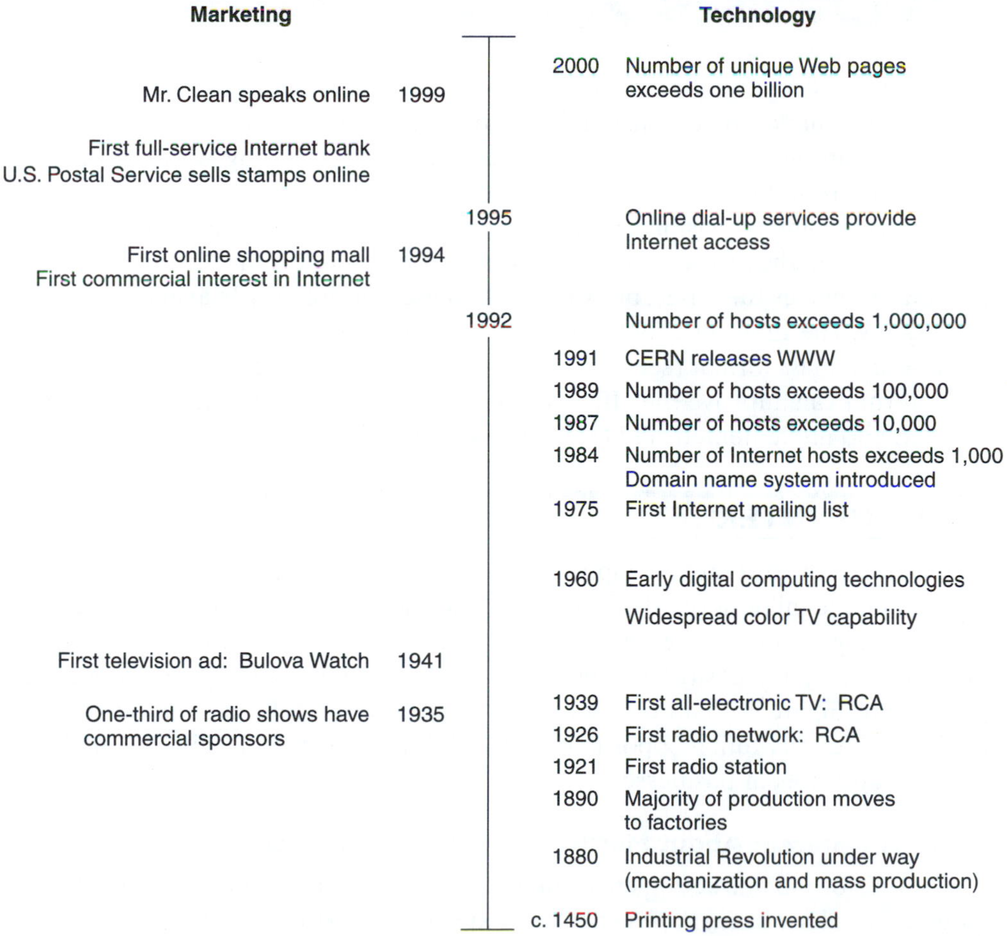

Marketing		Technology
	2000	Number of unique Web pages exceeds one billion
Mr. Clean speaks online 1999		
First full-service Internet bank U.S. Postal Service sells stamps online		
	1995	Online dial-up services provide Internet access
First online shopping mall 1994 First commercial interest in Internet		
	1992	Number of hosts exceeds 1,000,000
	1991	CERN releases WWW
	1989	Number of hosts exceeds 100,000
	1987	Number of hosts exceeds 10,000
	1984	Number of Internet hosts exceeds 1,000 Domain name system introduced
	1975	First Internet mailing list
	1960	Early digital computing technologies
		Widespread color TV capability
First television ad: Bulova Watch 1941		
	1939	First all-electronic TV: RCA
One-third of radio shows have 1935 commercial sponsors	1926	First radio network: RCA
	1921	First radio station
	1890	Majority of production moves to factories
	1880	Industrial Revolution under way (mechanization and mass production)
	c. 1450	Printing press invented

The Spiral of Communications Characteristics

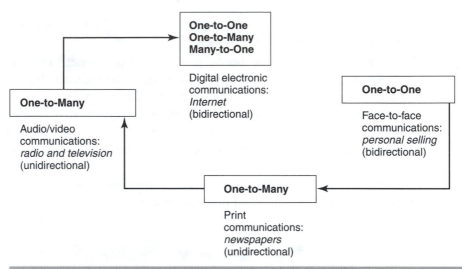

FIGURE 1.2 The Full-Circle Effect of Technology on Marketing Capability.

Next, consider the types of interactions that the technology enabled. For instance, early marketing emphasized one-to-one, face-to-face interactions between the seller and the buyer. With advances in technology, starting with the development of the printing press by Gutenburg in the fifteenth century, and progressing through radio and television, marketers were able to target larger, more dispersed audiences. With the introduction of the Internet as a tool for marketing, the shift in capabilities comes full circle, but with advantages not previously available through technology. The Internet enables marketers to communicate not only one-to-one, but also in a mass format (see Figure 1.2). In addition, the technologies that define the Internet can improve the efficiency with which marketing activities can be developed and implemented, and the richness of the content of the activities.

WHAT IS THE INTERNET?

On one level, the **Internet** is simply a means of communication between consumers, marketers, and millions of other organizations. The Internet enables people to tailor the way they communicate, whether with just one person or with an entire target market, quickly and easily. The ready accessibility of one-to-many communication, pictured in Figure 1.3 and once only available through television, radio, or print media, creates marketing opportunities that did not exist with traditional media for all types and sizes of businesses.

What Is Different About Marketing With the Internet?

The nature of the marketing environment enabled by the Internet means that the scope and nature of marketing activities are more flexible. For example, with the

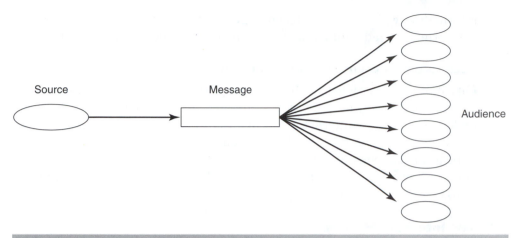

FIGURE I.3 One-to-Many Communications Can Reach Broad Audiences.

Internet as the tool for communication, physical boundaries become less important in the execution of a transaction than they are for other, more traditional forms of marketing exchange.

> *Digital Artifact 1.2*
>
> **86.55 percent of documents on the Web are in English.**
>
> (*Source: www.inktomi.com/webmap/, 2000.*)

Suppose that you are interested in selling the furniture produced in your factory in North Carolina. By advertising your product on the Internet, you gain the attention of a potential client in Bangkok, Thailand. Although you must still face the difficulties associated with transferring the furniture, post-transaction, halfway around the world, the physical distance exerts a minimal effect in the negotiation of the deal.

From your perspective as the marketer, you can provide information about your product more efficiently to your customer than you could if you had to create a hardcopy brochure or catalog. It means that you can react to competitive forces, adapting flexible elements of your marketing mix to stay ahead of the competition.

In addition, the Internet is a more interactive medium than many traditional marketing venues. This interactivity means that you can communicate in real time with your customer though your Web site to provide specific, desired information. Such reciprocal, tailored communication may result in more efficient and satisfying transactions—characteristics that are important for developing long-term relationships with customers.

In summary, the Internet offers marketers several benefits that are not available with traditional vehicles for marketing. The Internet enables marketers to create flexible information displays, to provide a greater range and depth of information with interactive technology, and to combine the modalities of television, print, and radio into a single presentation of video, text, and sound.

Technological Characteristics of the Internet

On a more complex level, the Internet is a product of advances in science, and it can be described largely in terms of its technological components. It is not necessary to understand how the Internet works in order to make use of it as a marketing tool: similar to the notion that you do not need to know what makes a car run in order to be a car salesperson! A brief description of the technical evolution of the Internet may, however, help you better understand its capabilities and limitations, as well as some of the more prevalent jargon.

The Internet's History

The Internet is a network of computer networks, as shown in Figure 1.4. *Internet* is a contraction of the words, *international* and *network;* networks of computers around the world are connected to each other, enabling rapid transmission of data from point to point. The computers in a single **network** are each linked to a **server,** which is a large computer that manages the communications for a network. The Internet is primarily a network of these servers, in which communication is accomplished by fiber optic cables, satellite transmissions, phone lines, microwave, and Ethernet lines. A brief history of the development of the Internet is useful for explaining some of the network's characteristics.

FIGURE 1.4 The Internet Is a Network of Networks.

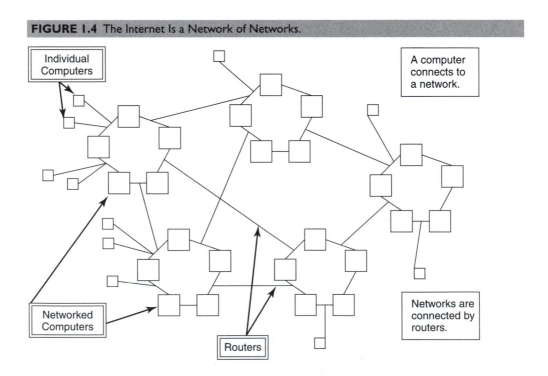

Individual Computers

A computer connects to a network.

Networked Computers

Networks are connected by routers.

Routers

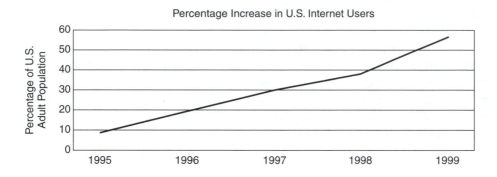

Source: Harris Interactive (*www.harrisinteractive.com*)

FIGURE 1.5 The Internet Is Adopted at an Increasingly Rapid Pace.

Developed under the sponsorship of the Defense Department's Advanced Research Projects Agency (ARPA), the Internet was envisioned as a decentralized network of computers, with some duplication, or redundancy, between computers. The logic was straightforward. In the aftermath of World War II, including the development of the atomic bomb and the increasing tensions of the Cold War, the government became concerned about the vulnerability of a single, centralized computer system.

In 1969, the network, then called ARPAnet, became a reality when two nodes were linked. A node is a computer connected to a network. The nodes can communicate by exchanging packets of information, in which chunks of information are forwarded across computers to the network address on the packet. These packets, which may take different network paths to reach the address, are reassembled at the destination computer.

By 1989, the National Science Foundation had replaced the Defense Department as the chief source of support for the network of networks, renamed NSFnet. This new network, designed to link together five supercomputers, served as the backbone of what is now known as the Internet. Originally intended to facilitate research and communication within the scientific community, the Internet has grown to include networks and users across a wide variety of backgrounds and interests. This growth can be attributed in large part to the rapid increase in popularity of personal computers. Figure 1.5 illustrates the phenomenal growth rate of the late 1990s.

INTEGRATING PEOPLE AND TECHNOLOGY: THE RISE OF THE WORLD WIDE WEB

From its origins as a high-tech tool for facilitating communications between scientists, the Internet has evolved into a communications medium of far greater accessibility to people around the world. This evolution, which reflects the large-scale adoption of the technology, can be attributed to the development of the **World Wide Web,** often called simply "the Web," or "WWW."

The Web is a network of electronic documents, called Web pages, that may be in text, graphic, and even audio or video formats. The documents are integrated through **hyperlinks.** Hyperlinks enable the user to acquire desired information by moving from one page to another through links in a flexible sequence. Information organized and connected by hyperlinks is called **hypertext.** The hypertext approach makes it possible to present information in ways that are more intuitive and user friendly than the original form of the Internet.

The growth of the Web is reflected in the variety of types of Internet users. The Internet uses the **domain name system** (DNS) as a form of address for users. The domain names provide users with a way to describe a particular Internet site without having to know the Internet Protocol address, which may be a number of up to twelve digits. The DNS domains indicate different types of Internet users, providing structure and organization to the growing medium. For example, users who are affiliated with an academic institution are designated by "edu" in the address. Commercial affiliations are denoted by "com." Simply knowing the domain can tell you something about the affiliation of the person behind an electronic communication. Figures 1.6 and 1.7 show the characteristics and popularity of various domains.

The rapid increase in the number of Internet users and domains has been mirrored by the growth in the commercial domain. Figure 1.8 illustrates the dominating role of .com hosts. In fact, since the first widespread interest in the Internet as a vehicle for commerce in 1993, the number of .com domain hosts has exceeded that of any other domain continuously from 1995 to the present. The importance of the commercial domain for the Internet is reflected in the rapid increase in sales, and in online advertising revenues. Statistics that describe this growth are shown in Figures 1.8 and 1.9.

FIGURE 1.6 Top-Level Domains in the United States.

Domain Label	Characteristic Domain User	Example
.com	Commercial, for-profit organizations	Barnes & Noble Bookstore (*barnesandnoble.com*)
.net	Network resource organizations and gateways	Internet Alaska (*alaska.net*)
.edu	Educational organizations	Virginia Tech (*vt.edu*)
.gov	Government organizations	Argonne National Lab. (*anl.gov*)
.mil	Military organizations/branches	Air Force (*af.mil*)
.org	Not-for-profit organizations	Girl Scout Council (*gsusa.org*)

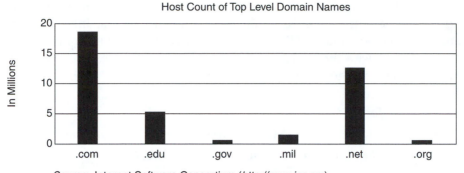

Source: Internet Software Consortium (*http://www.isc.org*)

FIGURE 1.7 .com Hosts Outnumber Any Other Host.

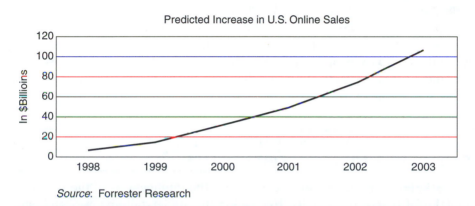

Source: Forrester Research

FIGURE 1.8 Online Sales Continue to Increase.

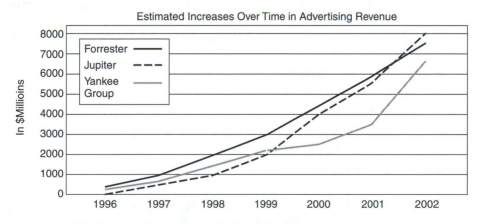

Source: As Compiled by Nua Analysis (*http://www.nua.ie*)

FIGURE 1.9 Yearly Online Advertising Revenues Show Rapid Growth.

These statistics indicate the increasing importance of the Internet to marketers, and they underscore the need to understand how to use the Internet to best advantage. In the remainder of this text, we will cover a wide range of topics designed to provide you with the background knowledge and abilities needed to integrate the marketing activities with Internet capabilities.

Digital Artifact 1.3

The first registered domain, Symbolics.com, was assigned on March 15, 1985.

(*Source:* **Hobbes Internet Timeline at** *www.isoc.org.*)

In this book, we focus on the Internet as the means for transmitting information. At present, more people are familiar with the Internet than with other methods of digital transmission. It is this familiarity and adoption of the technology that has led to the high levels of **interconnectivity,** reflected in the amount of communication between people via the Internet, that makes the Internet an important component of marketing strategy.

It is necessary to keep in mind, however, that the Internet is merely one way to move information. Given the rate and extent of technological change, it is likely that other means for communicating digitally will quickly become valuable components of effective business strategies.

INTEGRATING MARKETING AND THE INTERNET: OLD CONCEPTS, NEW OPPORTUNITIES

For marketers, it is important to understand the implications of the Internet environment for marketing activity. To develop this understanding, we can begin with the fundamental components of the marketing process undertaken by most businesses. The American Marketing Association has adopted a definition of **marketing** as, "the process of planning and executing the conception, pricing, promotion, and distribution of ideas, goods, and services to create exchanges that satisfy individual and organizational objectives."[1] This definition delimits several activities critical to the success of the company. The activities can be classified simply as either strategic planning or marketing planning.

Digital Artifact 1.4

In 1999, shoppers spent an average of $1,225 online. Sixty percent of online shoppers spent at least $500.

(*Source:* **Ernst & Young.**)

Strategic planning provides the company with the big picture of what it would like to do and how it plans to do it. The "what it would like to do" is formulated as a clearly

---

[1]Peter D. Bennett, *Dictionary of Marketing Terms* (Chicago: American Marketing Association, 1998).

defined and attainable set of business objectives that will enable the business to accomplish its mission. These objectives might include the definition of the product or service to be offered and the position the company would like to acquire within the competitive environment. Determining "how to do it" necessitates analysis of the opportunities and threats in the marketing environment, as well as the strengths and weaknesses of the business. This **environmental scanning** affects the business's ability to meet its mission objectives.

The Internet contains vast amounts of information about products and companies. Strategic planning may involve scanning information obtained from the Internet to determine whether a window of opportunity exists for a new product or service. In addition, Internet searches can be conducted to obtain information about potential redundancy in a product concept, about the features available in competing products, and about the number of competing products, and even about the marketing campaigns for brands, including the pricing, promotional, and distribution options.

Strategic planning establishes general objectives for the business. Of course, input from marketing is necessary to ensure that the goals for the business are feasible and desirable. With its objectives clearly established through strategic planning, the business can focus more narrowly on marketing planning. **Marketing planning** is the development of a set of activities that will enable the business to meet its strategic objectives with regard to a particular product or service.

The Internet can also be used to define and develop aspects of the marketing planning process. For instance, target markets can be determined and analyzed with help from the Internet. As for strategic planning, the Internet can be tapped as an information resource. In addition to serving as a rich source of market information about marketers and consumers, the Internet can be used to gain new insights. By using the Internet as a tool for conducting surveys, a marketer can conduct market research quickly, and potentially at a lower cost, than by more traditional methods, such as mail or phone surveys.

The formulation, execution, and evaluation of marketing plans requires a host of activities that are generally lumped together as aspects of marketing management. **Marketing management** includes oversight of target market selection, marketing strategy development, marketing program planning, and marketing activity implementation. Each of these components introduces unique opportunities for integrating marketing and the Internet.

Digital Artifact 1.5

Online retail sales exceeded $5.3 billion in the first quarter of 2000, without including online travel services, ticket agencies, and financial brokers. Total retail sales were estimated at $748 billion.

(*Source: www.census.gov/mrts/www/current.html.*)

Of interest for marketers is the fact that information on the Internet can be posted, or put on the Internet, not just by the business who markets the product, but by anyone with sufficient interest, ability, and resources to do so. With this capability, marketers have access not only to marketers' descriptions and product claims, but also to consumers' reactions to the offerings. This information can be used to guide strategy selection, such as whether to enter a particular market, or whether—and how—a differentiation strategy should be adopted.

Aspects of developing and implementing marketing programs can also leverage the Internet to enhance the prospects for a successful product or service offering. The benefits of Internet use extend beyond its ability to serve as a resource for acquiring information; the Internet can also serve as a means for transmitting desired information by a company. For example, in addition to information about its product on a company-created Web site, a company can provide information through links with other sites, as with ads or hyperlinks that guide the user to the company site.

The activities in Figure 1.10 represent a subset of the possible ways in which the Internet may influence how we approach and conduct the activities associated with the marketing process. In some cases, the influence of the Internet may even affect whether the traditional activities are relevant. For instance, promotion efforts associated with the production of product information brochures may become less important for a company that can effectively use the Internet to reach and inform its target market about the benefits of its products.

The importance of the Internet is not limited to its implications for marketing. Just as the marketing function is only one part of developing and maintaining a successful commercial venture, the Internet often plays a vital role in the types of activities carried out both within and between other functions of commercial organizations. In the following section, we will consider the role of Internet technologies and marketing within the broader context of electronic commerce.

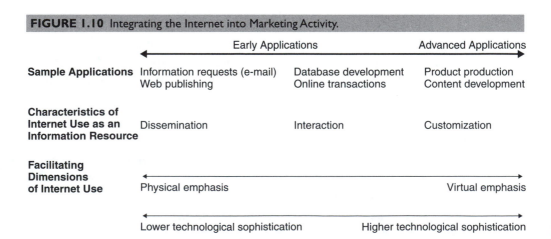

FIGURE 1.10 Integrating the Internet into Marketing Activity.

	Early Applications		Advanced Applications
Sample Applications	Information requests (e-mail) Web publishing	Database development Online transactions	Product production Content development
Characteristics of Internet Use as an Information Resource	Dissemination	Interaction	Customization
Facilitating Dimensions of Internet Use	Physical emphasis		Virtual emphasis
	Lower technological sophistication		Higher technological sophistication

MARKETING EFFORTS AND ELECTRONIC COMMERCE

Business strategies that include the Internet are often characterized as electronic commerce. **Electronic commerce** is a label that encompasses a wide variety of business activities, including those activities most typically associated with marketing. Because electronic commerce is often described simply as the completion of buying and selling transactions online, it is easy to confuse marketing and electronic commerce. In this text, electronic commerce is defined more broadly as the sets of activities undertaken by organizations to enable and facilitate the buying and selling of goods and services through electronic, paperless, information systems technologies (see Figure 1.11). Marketing is viewed as a subset of activities that may be conducted within the more general realm of electronic commerce.

Origins of Electronic Commerce

Electronic commerce had its start in corporations and banks, largely as a means of facilitating aspects of business by computerizing business practices to facilitate in formation exchange. Two early applications of electronic commerce were **electronic data interchange (EDI)** and **electronic funds transfer (EFT).** These activities within and between companies were desirable because they decreased the impact of constraints such as time and place. Information could be communicated rapidly and in flexible formats to improve communications within a company.

Electronic commerce is quickly becoming a goal for many companies, as they seek to complete purchase transactions and fund transfers over computer networks, and to conduct exchange activities related to new commodities within the digital medium, such as electronic information. Electronic commerce is more than just a shift from traditional commerce to a digital environment; it enables new products and new types and forms of transactions and businesses.

FIGURE 1.11 Marketing Activities as a Subset of E-commerce Activities.

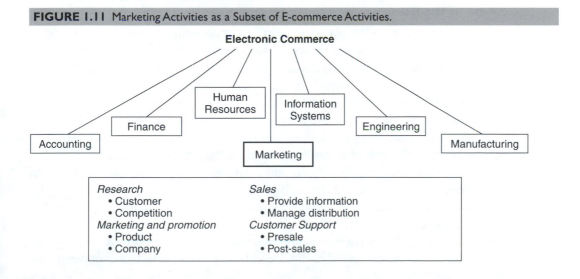

The Changing Face of Electronic Commerce

Early applications of electronic commerce were focused on within-business and business-to-business uses. This focus is changing to include and emphasize the growing importance of a consumer orientation. The changing emphasis is made possible through the concurrent growth and compatibility of Internet technology and structure, growth of computerized business practices, and spread and adoption of digital information.

This synergy enables electronic commerce to perform as a system comprised not only of revenue-generating transactions, such as buying and selling goods and services, but also of revenue-supporting transactions, such as sales support and customer service. As a result, electronic commerce not only facilitates communications within a company, but between a company and its consumers, as through customer service, any time, any place. It is this set of capabilities—more and more frequently directed toward consumers—that makes the Internet a desirable component of marketing strategy.

ABOUT THIS BOOK

Successful strategies for Internet marketing integrate the capabilities of the Internet with aspects of the marketer's resources, constraints and objectives, and with the consumer's needs and expectations. This book is intended to serve as an illustrative introduction to the array of issues related to using the Internet as an integral component of a successful marketing strategy. The primary objective of the text is to provide you with the knowledge and the ability to develop the skills needed to develop effective marketing practices for the Internet, and to remain on the cutting edge of developments in technology and their role in establishing effective marketing practices.

Sections of the Book

To enable you to develop the skills necessary to understand and integrate Internet technology and characteristics into marketing strategy, this book incorporates marketing theory with Internet reality to address issues in determining and selecting market segments and formulating the marketing mix. The book contains five sections. Section One provides an overview of the unique marketing environment embodied in the Internet. For instance, while most marketing texts emphasize the perspectives and influences of consumers, marketers, and policy makers, this text also includes a discussion of the influence of technology on the nature of the interactions between the other three perspectives. In subsequent sections, we will build on a framework that emphasizes the four key perspectives—consumer, marketer, technology developer, and policy maker—and their interactions to explore the impact of the Internet on marketing activity.

In Section Two, the perspectives are examined in depth to provide you with a clear understanding of the role of each perspective in the Internet environment. The goal is to enable you to predict future activity in each of these areas, and to understand the implications of this activity for marketing action that incorporates the Internet.

With Section Three, we put the perspectives together, by building on the basic framework from Section I, to consider the impact of the Internet environment on marketing strategy. We begin with a general, theoretical description of businesses within the Internet environment, and then we consider the implications of the Internet for marketing planning. This section serves as the basis for Section Four, in which we look at the role of the Internet in implementing marketing strategy. We examine the impact of the Internet on aspects of marketing management, including marketing research and the formulation of the marketing mix.

In Section Five, we extend our basic framework to examine the impact of the Internet on the interactions between companies who conduct business-to-business marketing activities. In the final chapter of the text, we examine ways in which marketers can leverage the Internet to maintain and extend interaction with people in each of the perspectives identified by the basic framework.

Learning Tools

Learning how to use the Internet effectively as a marketing tool means that you need to learn two different but related bodies of knowledge. First, you need to have available to you the body of information that presently exists about characteristics of Internet that are useful for marketing. Second, you need to have available to you the skills necessary to keep abreast of changes in the Internet environment.

To make the acquisition of these skills more manageable, this text includes several types of learning tools. For example, to build on skills you have previously acquired for marketing in venues other than the Internet, the issues discussed in this text are described, where possible, in terms of their similarities to or differences from marketing in other environments. In addition, real-world examples of companies and organizations using the Internet to market goods or services are provided to illustrate the key issues throughout the text.

At the end of each chapter, several review questions help you determine whether you have sufficiently mastered the skills and topics provided in the text. The section of thinking points is intended to stimulate thinking and discussion of issues related to the chapter material. If you have an interest in a particular topic that you would like to explore in greater depth, the suggested readings serve as a research resource.

Chapter Summary

The Internet offers marketers the opportunity to develop business strategies and to reach consumers in ways that traditional approaches to marketing cannot. It is an environment in which consumers and marketers can communicate more rapidly. Speed of communication is enhanced because traditional barriers of time and distance are minimized by the marketer's ability to create databases of product information, and by the consumer's ability to selectively obtain information.

The interactive medium may serve many functions including advertising and communications, and merchandising and distribution. The chief objective of this textbook is to provide you with a comprehensive introduction to the concept of using the Internet as one component in the development and implementation of effective marketing strategy.

REVIEW SECTION

Key Terms

- digital economy
- interactive media
- personalization
- Internet
- network
- server
- World Wide Web

- hyperlinks
- hypertext
- domain name system
- interconnectivity
- marketing
- strategic planning
- environmental scanning

- marketing planning
- marketing management
- electronic commerce
- electronic data interchange (EDI)
- electronic funds transfer (EFT)

Review Questions

1. What are the key differences between the medium for marketing created by the Internet and traditional media, such as television, radio, and print?
2. Describe the actual rate of growth of the Internet, compared to its predicted growth.
3. For what purpose was the Internet originally developed?
4. Describe the key differences between an industrial economy and a digital economy.
5. Name several advantages of electronic commerce for businesses and other organizations.
6. How is the World Wide Web different from the Internet?
7. What are the benefits of the domain name system?
8. Describe two ways that the Internet can be used to facilitate the development of
   a. strategic planning.
   b. marketing planning.
9. Explain the difference between marketing and electronic commerce.

Thinking Points

1. What opportunities and advantages do interactive media offer
   a. marketers?
   b. consumers?
2. What challenges and difficulties might interactive media create for
   a. marketers?
   b. consumers?

3. How might the original purpose for the development of the Internet affect its
   a. form?
   b. use for contemporary applications?
4. How might advances in electronic commerce influence the activities typically associated with marketing?
5. What does the rapid adoption of the Internet—following development of the World Wide Web—suggest is important for marketers who use the medium to market to consumers?
6. How might the marketing program of an organization that uses the Internet for planning differ from the program of an organization that does not use the Internet for planning?

Suggested Readings

1. *Where Wizards Stay Up Late: The Origins of the Internet,* by Katie Hafner and Matthew Lyon (New York: Simon and Schuster Inc., 1996).
2. *Marketing in the Cyber Age: The Why, The What, and The How* (chapters 1, 2, 3, and 6), by Kurt Rohner (New York: John Wiley & Sons, Inc., 1998).
3. *The Digital Economy* (chapters 1, 2, 4, and 7), by Don Tapscott (New York: McGraw-Hill Companies, Inc., 1996).
4. "History of the Web," by Shahrooz Feizabadi. In *World Wide Web: Beyond the Basics,* edited by Marc Abrams (Upper Saddle River, NJ: Prentice-Hall, Inc., 1998).
5. "The Electronic Marketplace Metaphor: Selling Goods and Services on the I-Way," Part 3 in *Internet Dreams,* edited by Mark Stefik (Cambridge, MA: The MIT Press, 1997).

CHAPTER 2

A Framework for Integrating Marketing and the Internet

FOCUS AND OBJECTIVES

This chapter presents a framework for thinking about marketing and the Internet. The framework emphasizes the relationships between people who wish to conduct exchanges of resources, such as goods, information and money, in the Internet environment. The framework integrates the perspectives of consumers, marketers, technologists, and policy makers and serves as a basis for examining the impact of the Internet on exchanges between the perspectives.

YOUR OBJECTIVES IN STUDYING THIS CHAPTER INCLUDE THE FOLLOWING:

- Understand the benefits of using a framework to organize thinking.
- Be able to describe the difference between exchanges and transactions, and their roles in marketing.
- Learn the basic types of resources that can be exchanged on the Internet and what factors guide their exchange.
- Understand the role of relationships as vehicles for resource exchanges.
- Be familiar with a general framework that integrates resource exchanges and relationships to describe an Internet environment for marketing.

Bay.com, an online auction company, was begun by Meg Whitman and Pierre Omidyar to facilitate exchanges of Pez candy dispensers between collectors. Today, the company has a customer base of more than 3.8 million, brand recognition by 32 percent of adult Americans, and more than two million products for sale that will never be handled by company employees.[1]

The history of eBay.com illustrates the nature of the Internet as an environment for marketing. For instance, technology plays an important role in eBay's continued growth. The networked communications and graphics capabilities of the Internet

---

[1]"eBay vs. Amazon.com," *BusinessWeek* (May 31, 1999).

make it possible for ordinary consumers to exchange goods with each other through person-to-person auctions, rather than buying from marketers. The company enables interaction between consumers, and these interactions are the basis for the auction-based, dynamic pricing model that contrasts with the fixed price approaches typically found in traditional, offline markets.

The vast array of products that can be placed for auction, as well as the anonymity of the online environment can create problems. For instance, attempts by eBay members to auction a human kidney,[2] stocks, and fraudulent Beanie Babies have invited the attention of government agencies. Although these types of issues attract attention and sometimes require changes to the way that eBay conducts business, eBay's members are loyal users, often spending more than two hours a week at the Web site.

The characteristics that describe eBay highlight the unique capabilities of the Internet as a venue for marketing activity, as well as the different sets of people whose interactions influence online exchange. In Chapter One, we saw how the technologies that make up the Internet can influence the nature of the marketing environment, as well as the ways in which marketing activities can be completed. In this chapter, we will develop a framework that will serve as the basis for our discussion of marketing activity in the Internet environment. We will use this framework to examine the ways that exchanges are carried out, with an emphasis on the different partners in the exchanges. The relationships between these partners define the marketing environment of the Internet and suggest opportunities for marketing activities that are not available in a traditional marketplace environment.

This chapter is divided into two sections that reflect these different, though related, objectives. We begin with a general framework to reflect the exchange of resources between participants in the marketing environment. Then we discuss the resources that can be exchanged between partners in the framework. The framework will serve as the basis for organizing the subsequent chapters of this book. The main objectives of this chapter are (1) to describe the framework and its benefits for understanding how to use the Internet as a marketing tool, and (2) to use the framework to illustrate the unique applications and influences of the Internet for marketing.

WHY DO WE NEED A FRAMEWORK?

A **framework** provides a way to organize many different topics, each related to a central purpose. In addition, the framework can be used to specify the relations between different elements it contains. As a result, with a framework we can systematically and thoroughly examine a wide array of relevant topics in a manner that might otherwise seem disconnected or incoherent.

---

[2]The kidney received a high bid of $5,750,100 before the auction was shut down by eBay.

FRAMEWORK OBJECTIVES

Our framework is designed to meet several objectives. In addition to describing the focus and direction of the rest of this book, it is also intended to spur your thinking about the ways that the introduction of the Internet may influence marketing. It would be impossible to imagine all of the ways that Internet influences might occur; the topic is a broad one, and the environment is changing so rapidly that new possibilities arise daily. Thus, the framework can be used to suggest avenues for possible effects of Internet influences on marketing, and the implications of these influences, without being limited to the present state of technology. Taking a dynamic perspective to integrating the Internet and marketing will help you to adapt marketing activities effectively as the Internet marketing environment continues to evolve.

The Framework's Basic Premise

Our framework is based on the idea that marketing involves processes of exchange between two parties. **Exchange processes** occur when parties negotiate with a goal of reaching an agreement. While the process of reaching an agreement reflects exchange, however, the fulfillment of the exchange process is called a **transaction.** The goal of a transaction is that the parties receive something they value from the other party in the exchange. Any time a consumer hands over money to receive a product from a marketer, a transaction has taken place (see, for example, Figure 2.1).

Marketing as Exchange

The concept of marketing as exchange is fundamental to many descriptions of marketing activity. For example, an introductory text for marketing states that, "Marketing occurs when people decide to satisfy wants and needs through exchange."[3] In addition, exchange is described as the ". . . act of obtaining a desired product from someone by offering something in return."[4]

These definitions of marketing as exchange emphasize several characteristics of the marketing process that are relevant for the development of our framework. First,

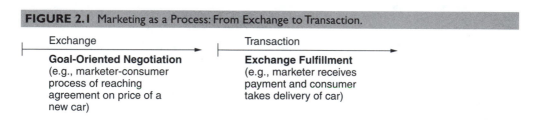

FIGURE 2.1 Marketing as a Process: From Exchange to Transaction.

Exchange	Transaction
Goal-Oriented Negotiation (e.g., marketer-consumer process of reaching agreement on price of a new car)	**Exchange Fulfillment** (e.g., marketer receives payment and consumer takes delivery of car)

---

[3]Philip Kotler and Gary Armstrong, *Principles of Marketing,* 6th ed. (Upper Saddle River, NJ: Prentice-Hall, Inc., 1994), p. 8.
[4]Ibid.

an exchange implies the involvement of two parties. Second, the willingness to participate in the exchange process suggests that each participant has something to gain from the exchange, and that each participant believes that the other participant has something to exchange that would provide the desired benefit. Simply put, exchange is a two-way street.

THE GENERAL FRAMEWORK

Our framework describes the marketing environment that is created and influenced by the advent of the Internet in commercial activities. The different elements of the framework are presented in Figure 2.2.

In Figure 2.2, Agent A and Agent B are the central figures in the exchange environment. The exchange environment consists of the exchange processes that flow between the active agents. The upper path from A to B reflects the marketing actions initiated by A that will affect B. The lower path, from B to A, is the reverse circumstance.

Suppose that Agent A is a consumer and Agent B is a marketer. The upper path that links the agents reflects a consumer-marketer relationship in which the consumer's actions influence the marketer. For example, a product complaint initiated by the consumer may lead the marketer to recall all recently manufactured products that are affected. The lower path also reflects a consumer-marketer relationship, but in this instance, the marketer's actions influence the consumer. This direction is illustrated by the situation in which a marketer develops a mix designed to appeal to a certain target market.

Our framework allows us to consider the ways in which the effects of integrating marketing and the Internet may be different for the various types of exchange relationships. For example, the ability to post information on the Internet about a product might take a different form when posted by a marketer for consumers than when posted by a disgruntled consumer for other consumers, or for the marketer.

FIGURE 2.2 An Exchange-Based Framework for the Internet Environment.

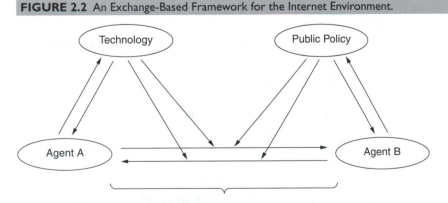

The Central Exchange Environment

This latter idea illustrates the importance of considering the implications of both directions of the exchange process. Although we could simply talk about two partners in a relationship, we would lose much of the ability to understand how the exchange process provides unique opportunities for marketing when combined with Internet capabilities. As a result, an important aspect of this framework is its emphasis on exchange as a process that reflects the influence of both parties on each other. In addition, the framework enables us to describe how the results of marketing actions and influence attempts may differ, depending on the originator of the process.

Digital Artifact 2.1

Approximately 90 percent of college students in the United States have access to the Internet.

(*Source:* **Forrester Research, 2000.**)

The framework also reflects the ways in which policy makers and technologists influence the types of exchanges that may occur between marketers and consumers. While marketers and consumers create the exchange environment, policy makers and technology developers alter the exchange environment. These alterations are observed when the technology or policy activities constrain or facilitate the types of behaviors that consumers and marketers can carry out in the central exchange environment.

The influence that policy makers and technology developers exert is itself the result of exchange processes, as between consumers and policy makers, or between marketers and technology developers. For example, widespread miscomprehension by consumers of a possible product hazard may lead policy makers to introduce regulations that require marketers to provide additional information about product use. As a result, the relationship between consumers and policy makers influences the exchange environment that exists between the marketer and the consumers. The effect of the consumer and policy maker exchange is on the flow of information from the marketer to the consumer.

Another example illustrates the effect of the marketer and technology relationship on the central exchange environment. A marketer might work with a technology developer to create a capability for assessing competing product offerings. For instance, the exchange might result in a software tool for the Internet that searches online resources for comparable, available products. The information provided by the created technology enables the marketer to alter elements of the marketing mix to differentiate the offering, to create a set of benefits desired by targeted consumers. A marketer-technologist exchange may result in a product alteration to meet segment needs, a price reduction, a description of the product that emphasizes benefits desired by consumers, or even a reconfiguration of the channels through which the product reaches consumers.

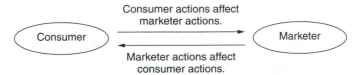

FIGURE 2.3 Bidirectional Exchange in the Central Exchange Environment.

Marketers and Consumers: The Central Exchange Context

Marketers and consumers comprise the central exchange relationship. Their actions may directly affect each other, and without the participation of both parties, there would be no marketing environment.

The idea of bidirectional communications, shown in Figure 2.3, can be described with reference to the partners who comprise the relationship. In addition, the nature of the relationship may also depend on where the communication originates, that is, with the marketer or with the consumer. Possible relationships include marketer-consumer, marketer-marketer, consumer-marketer, and consumer-consumer.

The marketer-consumer relationship is familiar to us as the typical interaction that results in the exchange of a consumer's money for a marketer's product. The marketer-marketer relationship reflects the exchange processes of many business-to-business transactions, a topic we will examine in detail in Chapter 13. A consumer-marketer relationship exists when consumers serve as the information resource for marketing research, as when a marketer seeks consumer input to develop a new product or to define target market segments. Consumer-consumer relationships exist when information about a marketer's offering is communicated through word-of-mouth or referral networks. The types of activities that may result from the particular types of these relationships are depicted in Figure 2.4.

FIGURE 2.4 Relationships in the Central Exchange Environment.

	Originating Agent	
	Marketer	Consumer
Receiving Agent Marketer	Business-to-business transactions	Product complaint Request for product information
Consumer	Product transactions Marketing research	Word-of-mouth Referral network Online bulletin boards

Policy and the Marketing Environment

As Figure 2.2 suggests, the role of policy makers and technology developers in the Internet environment differs from that of marketers and consumers in the central exchange environment. Although they are important influences, policy makers and technologists are not central to the existence of marketing activity. The primary importance of policy makers and technology developers is their ability to affect the nature of the environment in which exchange processes occur between consumers and marketers, as by regulating the environment or by enabling new capabilities in the environment.

To illustrate the nature of policy influence on the environment, think about sales of alcohol or other adult products. Policy makers routinely place constraints, in the form of restrictive regulations, on the ways that marketers of these products can make them available to consumers.

Most marketing texts emphasize the marketer-consumer relationship, and the effect of a public policy perspective on that relationship. We can incorporate these three perspectives into our framework and consider the set of exchange relationships that may occur between them. The relationships are illustrated by the triad in Figure 2.5.

To illustrate the exchange processes between the perspectives, suppose that a substantial number of consumers (in their roles as Agent A) decide to launch a protest against a particular industry. They file lawsuits against manufacturers and marketers, and demand that the industry be regulated. To this end, they communicate with policy makers, providing them with information to support their position. The policy makers respond by increasing restrictions on the manner in which the marketers in the industry can make the product available. The end result of this exchange between consumers and policy makers is the constraint placed on marketers that alters the central exchange environment. The effect is represented by the arrow from the policy maker to the path from Agent B to Agent A.

The exchange relationship between consumers and marketers can be influenced by the relationship between consumers and policy makers in a variety of ways. For example, voting behaviors result in the election of politicians and political administrations that appoint policy makers and formulate the agendas for regulatory agencies, thus influencing the nature of the exchange environment.

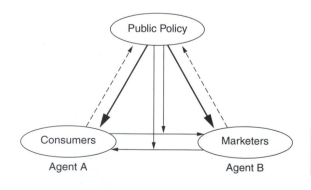

FIGURE 2.5 A Traditional View of the Marketing Environment.

Marketers can also interact with the policy entity to influence the central exchange environment. If Agent B is a marketer, the path from B to the policy entity may reflect a lobbying effort by the marketer, or by a consortium of marketers in an industry, to influence the regulatory climate. The lobbying effort may lead to a decrease in restrictions on the activities that marketers can undertake, or in the way that they can carry out the activities. For instance, effective lobbying pressure may open up new options for promotion (e.g., doctors on television).

Technology and the Marketing Environment

The relationships that exist between consumers, marketers, and policy makers in traditional marketing contexts also exist in a context in which the Internet plays a role. In addition to the issues addressed in the exchanges between the three traditional perspectives, however, the Internet introduces a new set of issues. These issues can be represented as exchanges between consumers and marketers and the developers of the technologies that make the Internet environment possible. These relationships are represented as another triad (Figure 2.6) in our general framework.

The introduction of the Internet into marketing planning can be compared to the effects of other technologies when they were new. For instance, the rapid adoption of the television after its introduction to the American public in the 1950s provided marketers with a new medium for marketing activity. As we saw in Chapter 1, the important point is that the role of technology for marketing is not new. Rather, the changes to the context in which marketing activities occur are new and deserve attention. The nature of the changes introduced by the Internet is different, however. Radio and television enabled people to hear and see information in a mass communication format. Once the basic technology was in place for each innovation, other enhancements to the basic technology made the products more effective and economical, but they did not drastically affect the core benefits of the originally introduced technologies. The Internet is different. It is characterized by rapid and ongoing technological change. These changes not only improve existing capabilities, but they often add new capabilities. The push for these changes is frequently guided by the relationship between agents in the Internet environment. With the commercial interest as a dominant focus for Internet development, we

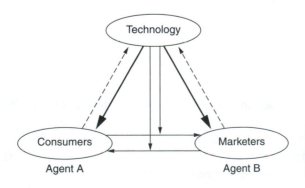

FIGURE 2.6 The Internet Environment Introduces a Technology Perspective.

need to understand how the relationships between marketers, consumers, and technology developers guide changes to the Internet environment.

Digital Artifact 2.2

Approximately 760 U.S. households sign up for Internet access every hour.

(*Source:* **The Industry Standard (citing Nielson Media Research) and The Internet Index, #25.)**

The marketer-technology relationship is evident in the development of technology and applications for technology specifically designed to enable marketers' goals in the central exchange environment. For example, a marketer who has Internet software developed to provide consumers who visit a Web site with an interactive product demonstration is using the marketer-technology relationship to further marketing strategy goals.

The consumer-technology relationship is seen in the development and adoption of technical standards and software tools that facilitate consumers' use of technology for marketing-related purposes. For instance, user-friendly interfaces to the computer medium provide consumers with easier access to marketers' information on the Internet. In addition, intelligent agents can help consumers manage search and use of the available information once they have access to the network. **Intelligent agents** are software tools designed to facilitate aspects of information use for decision making, such as searching for specific types of information, storing the results of searches, and constructing displays of stored information to make consumers' comparisons between brands and products more manageable.

RELATIONSHIPS AS VEHICLES FOR EXCHANGE

The types of relationships described in Figures 2.2, 2.5, and 2.6 influence the nature of exchange between partners in the relationships. To understand how relationships affect exchange processes, we begin this section with a brief discussion of the characteristics of relationships, and then we consider the nature of the exchanges between partners in the different relationships.

Relationships 101

A relationship can be described in terms of the goals it serves, the general characteristics of the relationship, and the partners in the relationship.

Goals of Relationships

Relationships make it possible to achieve several different goals. One goal is to manage uncertainty and dependence. For example, developing loyalty to a particular brand or company can reduce uncertainty about product experiences on the part of a consumer. From the marketer's point of view, consumer loyalty also reduces uncertainty about the likelihood of a repeat purchase.

In the marketing environment of the Internet, reducing uncertainty is an important goal for marketers. Research results indicate that consumers prefer to make online purchases from companies with a familiar offline, or **bricks-and-mortar,** presence. Retailers with only an online presence were perceived to be less dependable and trustworthy.[5] Companies with a combined online and offline presence are often described as **clicks-and-mortar** companies.

A second goal is to decrease the costs associated with the exchange activities. For example, extended interaction between a marketer and its customers provides the marketer with increased knowledge of the customers' preferences and needs. This knowledge can be used to reduce customers' search costs when a marketer can tailor product information to provide only the information of value to its customers. Marketers can use the Internet to automate the collection and storage of customer preferences, thus reducing exchange costs for both partners. For instance, Amazon.com can track users' search and transaction habits to provide information about product offerings that appear to match customer needs. Knowledge of consumers' needs is also used to guide product development and positioning. As the preceding examples indicate, a single relationship can address more than one goal.

Digital Artifact 2.3

The White House Web site came online in 1993.

(*Source:* **Hobbes Internet Timeline at** *www.isoc.org.*)

Features of Relationships

Relationships are described by the extent to which they exhibit four characteristics. One characteristic is the reciprocal exchange between partners; a relationship involves a bidirectional transfer of resources. A second characteristic of a relationship is that the activities undertaken by the partners are purposive; that is, the partnership has meaning for each partner. Relationships are also described by the amount of activity that occurs in the relational exchange. Multiple activities may occur. A fourth characteristic reflects the idea that the set of activities is a process; developing and maintaining a relationship that meets the needs of both parties is an interaction over time, rather than a set of separate transactions.

These characteristics provide us with a way to gauge relationships in order to guide marketing action. For instance, a marketer who recognizes that a relationship is in the later stages of development can tailor interactions with the relationship partner to maximize mutual benefit. The phrase, "the honeymoon is over," illustrates the link that exists between the age of a relationship and behavior—perhaps only too well!

---

[5]These conclusions are drawn from a March 2000 survey of 1,548 U.S. consumers by BrandForward, Inc. A similar conclusion is reached by Greenfield Online, based on an April 2000 survey of 3,000 respondents in which 43 percent expressed highest comfort levels with clicks-and-mortar retailers.

Types of Relationships

Relationships for conducting marketing activity take many different forms. For example, a company may form a relationship with a favored supplier to procure parts. That same company may also work to develop a relationship with particular distributor, or even with the end-consumer. As part of its public relations agenda, the company might maintain a partnership with a nonprofit organization to meet mutually beneficial objectives. Marketers work with technology developers to produce new products and marketing capabilities. Policy makers interact with marketers and consumers to determine the appropriate regulatory structure of the central exchange environment. Consumers develop exchange relationships with each other, in order to convey information or products. Common across the different partnerships, however, is the process of relational exchange. **Relational exchange** refers to the activities by which partners establish, develop, and maintain patterns of cooperative interaction that enable each partner to meet its objectives. As summarized in Figure 2.7, the primary sets of partners in our exchange framework have representative exchange activities that define and differentiate them from the other perspectives.

Now we are ready to take a closer look at the types of exchanges that can occur between different combinations of people.

What Is Exchanged?

The idea of marketing as a set of exchange-based transactions may seem simple and quite obvious. To make things more complicated, consider the variety of types of exchanges that can occur. While we can quickly bring to mind examples in which

FIGURE 2.7 Activities of Exchange Parties.

	Marketers	*Consumers*	*Policy Makers*	*Technologists*
Stage I	Develop marketing opportunities, based on observed and stated consumer needs	Assess needs and survey product offerings	Maintain market balance between consumers and marketers	Determine need for technology development
Stage II	Determine and implement product strategy	Compare and evaluate alternative offerings	Introduce regulation that promotes fair trade and competition between marketers	Develop infrastructure via hardware and software
Stage III	Communicate opportunity to target segment/s	Participate in transaction	Monitor effect of introduced regulation	Develop applications for infrastructure via hardware and software
Stage IV	Participate in transaction	Consume product	Adjust policy	Refine and augment product

money is exchanged for goods or for services, people often carry out other types of exchanges. For instance, producing and making available a new product based on input from consumers is a form of exchange. The consumers and the marketers have transacted an exchange of information about needs and wants. Word-of-mouth between consumers and negotiations between consumers and salespeople are also forms of informational exchange. The existence of different types of exchanges means that we need to develop a framework that includes not only the relationships that exist to enable exchanges, but also the array of things that can be exchanged.

RESOURCES AS THE BASES FOR EXCHANGE

Exchange involves the transfer of something between two parties. In order to make the exchange happen, that "something" has to be valued by the other party in the exchange process. The next step in understanding the exchange process is to determine what we mean by "something." That is, what is it that gets exchanged? How can we describe the focus of the exchange process?

One approach is to think of the objects of the exchange process as resources. **Resources** are defined as anything that can be transacted between two parties. From a marketing point of view, this definition is intuitively appealing; we are used to the idea of a transaction as the exchange of money for a good or a service. The concept of exchanging monetary assets for commodities has been examined in detail by economists, and it has served as a useful way for examining many issues related to economics, such as saving behavior, and the determination of fairness in exchange.

If we look back at the history of marketing, however, it quickly becomes evident that marketing exchanges have not always involved money. In the days (or years, or centuries) before money economies existed, people acquired necessary goods and services through barter and exchange activities. People traded goods for other goods, services for services, and even goods for services. Money, while a familiar resource for marketing exchange, is just one of several types of resources.

Digital Artifact 2.4

The average number of Internet activities by individual users is 7.2.

(*Source:* **Internet and Society report, from the Stanford Institute for the Quantitative Study of Society.)**

Taking an even broader view of resources that can be transacted between two people, consider the resources that are often exchanged in relationships. For example, suppose you are presented with a description of a set of activities that consists of washing dishes, doing laundry, making beds, and sweeping floors. These activities comprise a set of services related to cleaning. For what resource might they be exchanged? One reasonable guess is that the exchange is one of service for money—the activities are to be completed by a housekeeper as a part of an employment agreement. Alternatively, the activities might be those routinely associated with being a homemaker. In this case, the exchange might be a transfer of service for love, or for the status associated with responsibility.

The idea of different types of resources and that these resources can serve as the bases for exchange has been formalized as **resource theory.** Resource theory was developed by social psychologists to provide a general framework for describing the sets of resources, and the relationships between the types of resources, that capture the variety of exchanges between people.

Resource Theory and Exchange Processes

Resource theorists classify resources into six categories: money, goods, services, information, status, and love. Each of these six types of resources has been studied in great detail by researchers. For example, as noted earlier, economists have focused on money and commodities as the bases of exchange. In contrast, some psychologists have examined human needs, such as status and affiliation. For instance, researchers have focused on the effect of the Internet as a surrogate for emotional and social interactions.[6] The results suggest that the experience of using the Internet constitutes a resource that replaces the need for some amount of social interaction. The different sets of resources were integrated into one comprehensive framework by Uriel Foa, a psychologist who described what we recognize as resource theory.

One characteristic of resource theory is that the types of resources can be organized in a perceptual space defined by two dimensions. One dimension is the extent to which the resource is concrete or abstract. For instance, a good is more concrete than love. The second dimension reflects the amount of specificity, or focus on a particular person, in the resource. This dimension, called particularism, is illustrated by the difference between money and love. Money is a universal type of resource; you can exchange it with anyone. In contrast, love—for the majority of people—is specific in nature. We don't walk around expressing generic love for everyone around us. Although **concreteness** is focused on the nature of the resource (e.g., its tangibility), **particularism** emphasizes the importance of people as agents in the exchange process. A spatial illustration of the relationships between resources is shown in Figure 2.8.

In the figure, the distance between resources tends to reflect the likelihood that the resources will be seen as reasonable exchanges. In this perceptual closeness, resources that are more similar to each other are more likely to be exchanged than resources that are less similar. For example, we can easily think of situations in which money is traded for a good, or a good for a service, or money for information. It is more difficult, however, to find situations in which money is traded for love. The table in Figure 2.9 provides illustrative examples of exchanges between resources. Can you think of any other examples of resource exchanges in the table?

---

[6]Robert Kraut et al., "Internet Paradox: A Social Technology that Reduces Social Involvement and Psychological Well-Being," *American Psychologist* (September 1998).

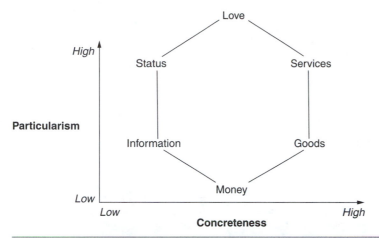

FIGURE 2.8 Foa's Resource Theory Provides Structure to Resource Exchanges.

Another insight from resource theory is that exchanges are influenced by context. For example, breakfast served to you on a tray with a flower in a bud vase might engender exchange expectations of a hug or a kiss from a spouse, but probably not from a waiter! The ability to influence the likelihood of exchange has implications for how marketers can induce purchase by positioning products to match situations. For instance, a cell phone can be marketed to professionals as a way to obtain status through improved job performance. For parents, a cell phone can be marketed as a way to stay in touch with children.

In summary, resource theory makes several predictions about the nature of resource exchange. First, it suggests that resources that are perceived to be similar will tend to be exchanged more often than resources perceived to be dissimilar. Second, resource theory emphasizes the importance of the context for an exchange, and it predicts that exchanges of identical resources will not always be viewed as equally acceptable (e.g., a kiss for a waiter, instead of a tip). These predictions can be used to understand how people effect exchanges within the Internet environment, and the implications of these exchanges for marketing activity.

Resource Theory and the Internet

When we consider the Internet as an aspect of the marketing environment, many of the concepts associated with resource theory are relevant. Each type of resource is reflected in Internet use. For instance, information is readily available from many online sources, and goods and services of all types are increasingly available. In addition, companies can derive status from a .com presence, and people can fulfill needs for affection and affiliation through online personal ads, support groups, and chat rooms.

The dimensions of concreteness and particularism can also be extended to the Internet environment. The concreteness dimension continues to reflect the extent to which resource benefits can be described and experienced in the virtual environment. Particularism also has its Internet analog. The extent to which a resource

Resource	Money	Goods	Services	Information	Status	Love
Money	Currency Exchange	Buying a hamburger	Getting a haircut	Buying a newspaper	Joining a country club	
Goods		Trading beads for Manhattan	Au pair for room and board			Engagement ring
Services			Building a Web site in exchange for landscape maintenance		Providing professional services (e.g., doctors and lawyers)	Running errands for a parent
Information					Espionage, Annual performance review at work	
Status					Socializing at an elite club	"Trophy" spouse
Love					Celebrities and fans	Support groups

FIGURE 2.9 Resource Exchanges Take Many Forms.

is targeted toward a specific individual can be described as **personalization.** A re-interpretation of resource theory for the Internet is given in Figure 2.10.

Resource Theory and Marketing Opportunity on the Internet

Now we consider the implications of resource theory for the role of the Internet in marketing. We can use resource theory to look for exchange opportunities that either may not exist in traditional marketplaces, or that may have other ways in which they can be enacted. For example, we can trace the history of resource exchanges on the Internet to determine whether untapped possibilities exist. By following the path of exchange development over time, we can anticipate where other possible exchange opportunities may be created.

In the commercial domain, one of the first applications of the Internet was to transfer funds from one institution to another. This process of electronic funds transfer (EFT) is a form of exchange. As interest in the Internet as a commercial medium increased, companies began to use the Internet as a way to exchange information about products with other businesses and with consumers. Online catalogs were developed, as was **brochureware,** the simple posting of a brochure in its traditional form on a Web site. Sales of goods and services followed rapidly on the heels of informational exchange.

Note that the pattern with which resource exchanges were undertaken on the Internet follows the basic predictions of resource theory. Information and goods, both closer to money than services are to money, tended to be the earliest adopted forms of exchange on the Internet. In addition, exchanges between similar resources have tended to occur earlier in the marketing environment of the Internet than exchanges between more distant resources. For instance, nonmonetary exchanges

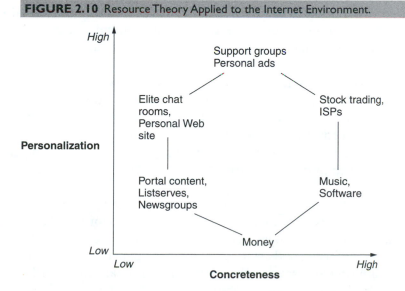

FIGURE 2.10 Resource Theory Applied to the Internet Environment.

between information and status are reflected in the provision of content to Web sites with high traffic, in return for name recognition and status. This status, in turn, can be exchanged for money, as when an advertiser secures advertising space on the Web site where the content is made available, and a portion of the revenue is returned to the content provider.

Digital Artifact 2.5

Eleven million U.S. consumers will be first-time Internet shoppers in 2000.
(*Source:* **CyberAtlas, 2000, citing a report by Forrester Research.**)

This pattern of created resource exchanges suggests that marketers can use resource theory to uncover marketing opportunities. Marketers can look for opportunities presented by novel resource exchanges, leveraging the infrastructure of the Internet to add value to the exchange process. For example, the Internet makes it possible for two parties to carry out a nonmonetary exchange that provides value for each, while still providing revenue to a third party. These capabilities have resulted in new products and in new business models that we will examine in subsequent chapters.

Chapter Summary

Marketing can be described as a collection of activities intended to foster exchange. In this chapter, we have examined the role of the Internet as an environment for marketing exchange. We began be developing a framework to describe the presence of four key perspectives in the environment—consumers, marketers, policy makers, and technology developers. Consumers and marketers comprise the central exchange environment, and their interactions result in bidirectional exchanges. Policy makers and technology developers exert an indirect influence on the central exchange environment; their activities alter the nature of the marketing environment.

Relationships serve as the vehicles for effecting exchange. We described relationships in terms of their goals, their characteristics, and their participants. Relationships serve goals of decreasing uncertainty and reducing costs, as well as providing direction for meeting needs. They are bidirectional, purposive, and involve multiple activities and interaction over time. Relationships may be formed between people within and between each of the four perspectives in the exchange environment of the Internet.

Resources are the basis for exchange activities; people conduct exchange processes to obtain desired resources. We used Foa's resource theory to characterize resource exchange. Foa's theory suggests that six types of resources are exchanged: money, information, services, goods, status, and love. Exchanges are more likely to occur between more similar resources than between dissimilar resources. Implications of resource theory for the detection of marketing opportunities in the Internet environment were discussed.

Resource theory guides our understanding of how people trade or exchange resources in order to obtain needed resources. With our exchange framework, we can incorporate the idea of resource exchanges between people in the marketing environment, and we can describe the types of exchanges that are possible by considering the reasons why the exchange relationships may exist.

Combining Resources and Relationships: Looking Ahead

When the four perspectives—marketers, consumers, technologists, and policy makers—are integrated into a single model, we arrive at the general exchange framework depicted in Figure 2.2. This framework lays out the different relationships that characterize many aspects of marketing, and the role of the Internet as a technological force in the development of marketing planning. In the remaining chapters of this textbook, we will use the framework to integrate the different factors that affect the success of marketing activities involving the Internet.

In the next four chapters, we will take a closer look at each of the four perspectives in the exchange environment of the Internet. The environment creates opportunities and poses challenges for growth and success that are unique to each perspective. This uniqueness is due to differences in the goals that motivate the exchanges between perspectives.

REVIEW SECTION

Key Terms

- framework
- exchange processes
- transaction
- intelligent agents

- bricks-and-mortar
- clicks-and-mortar
- resources
- resource theory

- concreteness
- particularism
- personalization
- brochureware

Review Questions

1. Distinguish between the concepts of exchange and transaction.
2. What four key interest groups may be involved in exchanges in the Internet marketplace?
3. What goals do relationships address?
4. What are the four basic characteristics of relationships?
5. Explain the difference between Foa's *particularism* and our reinterpretation to *personalization*.
6. Explain how the pattern with which resource exchanges were undertaken on the Internet follows the basic predictions of resource theory.

7. How does the Internet influence our traditional view of the marketing environment?
8. From a marketing perspective, what are the benefits provided by intelligent agents?
9. If the key role of marketers and consumers is to create the exchange environment, what is the key role of policy makers and technology developers?

Thinking Points

1. How is a framework useful for understanding marketing activity within the Internet environment?
2. Why is it necessary to distinguish between the concepts of exchange and transaction?
3. How is the exchange/transaction distinction useful for describing the development of a relationship between two parties?
4. Using the framework developed in this chapter (Figure 2.2), develop examples of exchange processes for each of the four key parties (e.g., consumer-marketer, marketer-technologist).
5. How can we use resource theory to explain and predict exchange over the Internet?
6. What unique influences does the Internet environment exert on exchange processes?

Suggested Readings

1. *Resource Theory: Explorations and Applications,* by Uriel G. Foa, John M. Converse, and Edna B. Foa (San Diego: Academic Press, 1993).
2. "The Once and Future Craftsman Culture," by Les Alberthal. In *The Future of the Electronic Marketplace,* edited by Derek Leebaert (Cambridge, MA: The MIT Press, 1998), pp. 37–62.
3. "A Store as Big as the World," by Walter Forbes. In *The Future of the Electronic Marketplace,* edited by Derek Leebaert (Cambridge, MA: The MIT Press, 1998), pp. 63–90.
4. "Advertising in an Interactive Environment: A Research Agenda," by Eloise Coupey. In *Advertising and the World Wide Web,* edited by David W. Schumann and Esther Thorson (Mahwah, NJ: Lawrence Erlbaum Associates, Publishers, 1999), pp. 197–215.
5. *Internet Culture,* Parts One and Two, edited by David Porter (New York: Routledge, 1996).

SECTION TWO

The Framework in Depth: Perspectives on Marketing and the Internet

Consumers, marketers, technology developers, and policy makers all play vital roles in the marketing environment of the Internet. In this section we take an in-depth look at each of the four perspectives represented in the exchange framework of Chapter 2. The overarching goal of this section is to help you understand how the Internet affects the activities of individuals in each perspective. As a general objective, it is important to understand when, how, and why the Internet can foster or inhibit exchange processes within and between each perspective, in order to recognize opportunities and pitfalls for marketing activity.

In Chapter 3 we consider the impact of the Internet environment on the exchange activities conducted by consumers to obtain resources. Marketers can identify new product and customer opportunities by understanding the types of resources sought by consumers, as well as the ability to make those resources available with the Internet. Problems in taking advantage of opportunities can be reduced by knowing how the Internet affects consumption processes such as information processing and decision making.

The Internet affects how marketers market. In Chapter 4, we consider the influence of the Internet from the marketer's perspective. For instance, the Internet can provide benefits obtained from changing the structure of marketing activity, such as emphasizing the importance of different types of marketing personnel. In addition, the Internet alters the processes for marketing activity, both within and outside the marketing organization.

Technological advances resulted in the creation of the Internet. For marketing and the Internet, however, it is the ongoing interactions between people who develop technology and the other perspectives in our framework that influence marketing activity. In Chapter 5, we look at the impact of technology on the exchange activities that take place between perspectives in the Internet environment.

Marketers' actions are governed by regulatory policy. Because the Internet is a new and novel environment for marketing, many regulatory issues are undecided, while still others are unknown. As a result, it is important for marketers to understand how policy decisions are made, and to be able to recognize the factors that create situations that necessitate regulation. Public policy in the Internet environment is the focus of Chapter 6.

CHAPTER 3

Consumers and the Internet Environment

FOCUS AND OBJECTIVES

The focus of this chapter is on the relationships that exist between consumers and the consumption environment of the Internet. Building on the framework for resource exchange presented in Chapter 2, we consider the effects of the Internet environment on consumer behavior. Demographic and psychological characteristics of online consumers provide a basis for assessing the impact of the Internet on the ways in which consumers conduct exchange relationships to acquire money, goods, services, status, information, and love.

YOUR OBJECTIVES IN STUDYING THIS CHAPTER INCLUDE THE FOLLOWING:

- Develop familiarity with characteristics of typical online consumers and their consumption activities.
- Understand the nature of Internet effects on consumption as a function of exchange processes and relationships.
- Recognize the facilitating and inhibiting effects of the Internet environment on consumers' ability to carry out resource exchanges.
- Identify opportunities for marketing activity based on knowledge of resource exchange theory.

Have you ever wondered what people were thinking and feeling as new ideas and inventions, such as automobiles and televisions, changed their lives? Now is your opportunity to find out. The Internet represents a technological change capable of influencing many aspects of how we all live. As a medium for communications, the Internet can be used to interact not just with marketers, but with other consumers, colleagues, friends, family, politicians—anyone with a network connection and the desire to communicate.

From a marketing perspective, the changes in consumer behavior that may be caused or enabled by the Internet must be examined to understand the opportunities and issues they raise for marketing planning and strategy implementation. After all, consumers are a necessary and important element of the central exchange environment. To understand just how important consumers are, consider the increase in consumers' use of the Internet for consumption purposes.

Consumers are accepting the Internet as an integral component of the marketing environment at a much faster rate than predicted by experts, including marketing researchers and technology watchers. Consumers' use of the Internet is shifting from using the technology mainly to obtain information about goods and services to an increasing emphasis on purchasing these goods and services via the Internet.

As recently as the mid-1990s, Internet-effected transactions consisted mainly of computer equipment and software, and books. Today, it is possible to search for—and find—virtually any item that exists in the traditional marketplace, as well as a host of newly spawned goods and services that reflect our fascination with and adoption of the medium.

As in traditional markets, consumer behavior on the Internet is far more than just buying products that satisfy wants. Consumers can search for information about companies and their products, communicate with marketers and with other consumers who have similar consumption goals or experiences, and even establish online communities and organizations devoted to praising or criticizing the activities of a marketer. One of the key differences between traditional consumer activities and consumption via the Internet, however, is the role that the Internet itself plays, as an influence on the nature of consumer behavior.

Digital Artifact 3.1

Twenty-nine percent of people who spend more than 10 hours a week on the Internet spend less time shopping at stores.

(*Source:* **Internet and Society report, from the Stanford Institute for the Quantitative Study of Society, 2000.**)

As an environment for consumption, the Internet can provide opportunities for obtaining resources, and it can constrain the availability of resources. Efforts to obtain needed resources often involve exchanges between parties in the environment. Resource exchanges form the basis for relationships that are mutually beneficial.

The Internet environment can influence the types of exchanges that are carried out by making it possible to acquire resources that are less feasible in traditional marketplace settings. For example, imagine how difficult it would be to find out what other people with tastes and values similar to yours thought about a particular product, such as a new car. Short of incidental word-of-mouth, getting these opinions could amount to carrying out a full-scale marketing research project! On the Internet, however, this information is readily available through bulletin boards and newsgroups (e.g., via Usenet). The Internet environment influences the types of exchanges people make, and the types of relationships formed to get resources.

The rapidly changing pace of the marketspace environment—in terms of technology and people's response to technology—suggests a need for marketers to understand how to anticipate and adapt to likely changes in the consuming public. Because the Internet can be used to facilitate communications between marketers and consumers, and even to tailor the nature of communications and product offerings to more directly address consumer needs, marketers must have detailed and up-to-date information about potential consumers and their needs.

What factors can explain the appeal of the Internet as a virtual marketplace for consumers? In this chapter, we will examine the nature of consumer behavior in a marketspace environment. We will consider the ways in which people attempt to acquire resources, given environment characteristics. By focusing solely on the actions of consumers in our exchange framework, we can obtain detailed insights and knowledge of the interaction between consumers and the Internet, and the implications of this interaction for marketing.

Digital Artifact 3.2

Twenty-five million 2- to 17-year-olds have Internet access in the United States. Mothers are online too—16.4 million of them.

(*Source:* **Grunwald Associates, 2000.**)

We will begin with a description of the online consumer population. This description will provide a general characterization of the population members in the consumer component of our framework. With the demographic introduction completed, we will shift to a more detailed examination of consumers in the online environment, by considering the types of resource transactions they complete.

DESCRIBING ONLINE CONSUMER BEHAVIOR

Descriptive research relies on demographics and psychographics. **Demographics** are useful for answering questions such as, "who is buying on the Internet?" and "how frequently do people complete online transactions?" and "what products are most likely to be purchased via the Internet?" **Psychographics,** a combination of demographics and psychological dimensions that reflect consumers' beliefs and opinions about consumption-relevant activities, can be used to obtain insights about when consumers might use the Internet to make purchases, and for what types of purchases. A list of demographic and psychographics variable can be found in Figure 3.1.

For example, a psychographics survey can be used to develop a strategy for providing post-purchase service to consumers. Knowledge of purchasers' past activities and usage patterns for the product can be combined with information about their perceptions of product risks and performance, as well as general knowledge of their service expectations. This rich set of information can then be used to predict which types of consumers are likely to experience need for follow-up service, and the forms of service that may be most beneficial to the consumer.

Demographic	*Psychographic*
Age	Religious values
Education	Social values
Income	Personality traits
Gender	
Marital status	
Occupation	

FIGURE 3.1 Describing Online Consumers with Demographic and Psychographic Variables.

Demographics and psychographics have a long history of frequent and helpful application in marketing. Given the novel character of the Internet as both a component of marketing strategy and as a venue for consumption, it is not surprising that demographics and psychographics have received early and sustained attention as research tools in the new medium. Both areas are useful for discerning and evaluating potential segments of consumers in terms of their reactions to marketing strategies that include the Internet.

DESCRIPTIVE RESEARCH AND INTERNET-RELATED CONSUMPTION

Recent research has provided us with descriptions of Internet consumers, in varying levels of demographic and psychographic detail. Ongoing surveys of Internet use are one source of this information. For instance, the GVU surveys at the Georgia Institute of Technology, conducted twice annually from 1994 through 1998, can be used to track changes in the numbers and characteristics of consumers, and of the types of products and services they purchase through the Internet. Many commercial research firms also publish data about Internet uses and users.

Another source of descriptive information about consumers is obtained from academic researchers, who integrate demographics with psychological features to develop profiles of Internet consumers. This type of psychographic research is often conducted with a goal of being able to predict longer-term changes in consumption patterns and reactions to product offerings on the Internet.

We can use the results of a wide variety of survey methods to understand consumption on the Internet. For instance, we know that a typical consumer on the Internet is a man in his mid-thirties, with a professional job, college education, and an annual income of $58K. Of course, in order to make this information more useful, we also need to know what the typical Internet user *does* on the Internet, and how he does it.

What about all of the other people who use the Internet? Marketers would overlook many marketing opportunities if they failed to recognize the diversity of the online population. Information about Internet use is widely available, with an equally wide range of content and quality. Getting a clear picture of the people and their online activities involves careful evaluation of multiple data sources and methods for data aggregation.

Although the need to know the characteristics of a particular online population may differ by product type, company needs, or strategic marketing objectives, several demographic variables can provide a big picture of the online world. For instance, we can look at where people are using the Internet, and for what purposes (e.g., home or work). We can also look at Internet usage and its relation to geographic location.

Figure 3.2 summarizes Internet user statistics from a variety of online sources, including the GVU surveys, Nua, Inc., Cyberdialogue, eMarketer, and Forrester Research. The statistics describe aspects of the who, what, where, and when of online consumption. Keep in mind, however, that all figures are estimates, and that they are based on often differing methods of data collection.

To better understand online consumers, we can also obtain information about lifestyles, such as the activities and hobbies typically engaged in by online and offline consumers. A 1999 survey of 85,000 randomly selected adults in the United States, conducted by Scarborough Research, combined demographic data with lifestyle data to develop profiles of three categories of consumers: "e-shoppers" (online shoppers, 18 and over); "wired but wary"; and "unwired." E-shoppers are adults who make purchases online. Wired but wary consumers use the Internet, but not for shopping. The unwired have no Internet access. In general the unwired segment is less active in lifestyle activities, such as sports; travels less, and has lower incomes and education levels. The wired but wary segment is similar in many respects to the e-shopper segment, but tend to use the Internet for e-mail, rather than for the wider array of informational purposes (e.g., financial and medical services, games, and news) of e-shoppers. The reasons people shop online are summarized in Figure 3.3.

Now that we know who the consumers are—at least in general descriptive terms—it is time to take a closer look at the types of behaviors they carry out, as well as the ways in which exchanges are influenced by the marketspace environment.

FIGURE 3.2 Characteristics of Internet Use in the United States.

Who?	*What?*	*Where? (locally)*	*When? (usage)*	*Experience*

Gender
 • 48% female
 Income
 • 10%, $100K+
 • 30%, $50K–
   100K
 Age
 • average 35
 Education
 • 60% college
	Online Activities
	 • 42% shopping
	 • 65% enter-
	   tainment
	 • 54% work
	 Online Buying
	 • 1 Books
	 • 2 CDs
	 • 3 Software
	 • 4 Hardware
	 • 5 Travel
	 • 6 Clothing
	 • 7 Hobbies
		Home
		 • 62%
		 Work
		 • 32%
			Frequency
			 (times/day)
			   1–4 (42%)
			   5–8 (17%)
			   9+ (27%)
			 Duration
			 (hours/week)
			   7–9 (15%)
			   10–20 (32%)
			   20+ (26%)
				1–3 years (45%)
				 4–6 years (27%)
				 7+ years (9.5%)

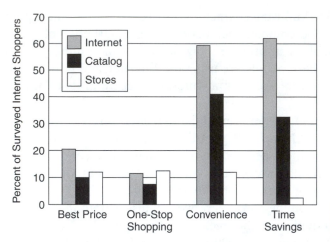

Source: Andersen Consulting (2000)

FIGURE 3.3 Why Do People Buy Online?

UNDERSTANDING ONLINE CONSUMER BEHAVIOR

Our examination of consumer behavior is organized in terms that will be familiar from Chapter 2. First, we can think about consumer behavior in terms of *transactions;* consumers fill needs by acquiring *resources* that enable them to thrive in their *environments.* Second, success in obtaining resources is affected by *environmental factors.* The environment may create opportunities for resource acquisition, and it may place constraints on resource acquisition. Third, the ways in which the environment affects the ability to consume resources may lead to the formation of *exchange relationships.*

If you have studied consumer behavior—whether as a formal part of your education or by simply thinking about your personal activities—you probably noticed that many of your actions were influenced by internal characteristics, and not just by environmental factors. For instance, people are affected by their past experiences, their peer groups, and their motivation. These influences may lead consumers to seek out particular resources, such as a certain product category (e.g., a beach vacation for spring break), or a particular brand (e.g., Daytona Beach, instead of Miami Beach).

The psychological factors that affect consumer behavior comprise a large part of most description of consumer behavior. For the Internet environment, however, they are not sufficient to explain why people seek the resources they do, or how they go about getting those resources. To develop a more complete understanding of online consumer behavior, we need to include internal, psychological factors into a more general model of behavior that also incorporates the environment and its effects on consumption. In addition to thinking about the joint influences of psychological and environmental factors on resource consumption, it is important to think about the ways in which the interaction of these factors influences the type of relationships that people form to carry out resource exchange processes. This approach is reflected in Figure 3.4.

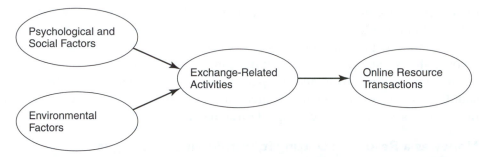

FIGURE 3.4 Consumer Behavior Is Influenced by Characteristics of the Consumer and the Environment.

In the following sections, we will examine the types of consumer behavior that are observed in the consumption environment of the Internet. We will organize our effort in terms of the resources that people seek to acquire. In addition, we will look at the role of the Internet as an environment that facilitates and constrains resource consumption, and at the ways in which internal, psychological influences on behavior are affected by the characteristics of the Internet environment. Figure 3.5 depicts the ways that the Internet environment may affect consumer behavior, by facilitating or inhibiting resource availability, exchange processes, and exchange relationships.

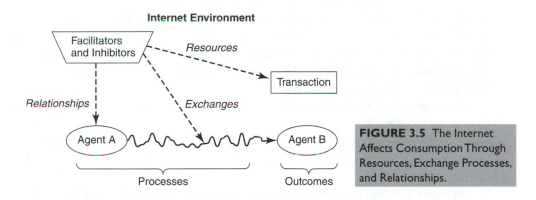

FIGURE 3.5 The Internet Affects Consumption Through Resources, Exchange Processes, and Relationships.

RESOURCES IN THE INTERNET ENVIRONMENT

Now we are ready to look at each of the six types of resources that people try to obtain. Before we plunge in, however, a couple of caveats should be noted. First, when we talk about resources and consumer behavior, we are not just talking about objects of marketing activity. Resources can be obtained in many nonmarketing ways. Think about consumption in a general sense. That said, however, the exchange-related behaviors that people carry out in order to consume resources can provide opportunities for marketing activity far beyond the simple selling of goods and services to meet needs.

Second, when we talk about resources, keep in mind that the value of a resource is somewhat subjective; that is, what it means to one person may be notably different from what it means to another person. As a result, we are interested in understanding the ways in which resources have meaning for consumers, and how marketers can create or encourage desired meanings.

Money as a Resource: Getting It, Transferring It, Using It

As one of the six basic resources in Foa's resource theory, money is characterized by its position, relative to the other resources, as the least person-specific resource. That is, money is universal; it can be acquired from a wide number of sources, without changing its inherent value. It can also be traded to others, in exchange perhaps, for other desired resources. Economists refer to this readily exchangeable quality as **fungibility.**

The Nature of Money

We are all used to thinking about money in terms of coins and bills. In addition, we are increasingly familiar with forms of money that are less tangible, such as transfers through ATMs, using bank checks and debit cards, and even phone cards and credit cards. Each of these different ways of using money may influence the meaning of the resource to consumers. To illustrate the idea that the form of money may affect its meaning, think about what happens when you go to a casino (not, of course, that we are recommending that you do so in order to verify this example), or play in a friendly game of poker. In many cases, you exchange money for chips in order to begin playing. One advantage of the chips is that they facilitate play; it is easier to make bets and collect winnings with only a few categories of value (e.g., red chips, blue chips, white chips), than it is with all different denominations of cash. But is this the only reason for chips?

Another effect of the changed form, from money to chips, is that it separates the meaning of money from its actual, physical nature. As a result, it may be psychologically easier to part with chips, in placing bets, than to part with cash. The implications of different forms of money as a resource can be extended to the Internet environment.

In order to effect online transactions that involve money, businesses need a digital form of cash. Several different ways to implement online monetary exchanges already exist, and plans for alternative forms are imminent. For example, the "old-fashioned" use of credit cards is prevalent. In addition, some companies have introduced payment forms and money transfer that involve **cybercash,** or **digital cash.** These forms of money can be stored in online accounts and transferred digitally to other online accounts. The central idea is that the form of money on the Internet is often quite different from money forms available in traditional, physical marketplaces. The various money forms have both advantages and disadvantages, as indicated in Figure 3.6.

Types of Electronic Money		
	Electronic Checks (e.g., CyberCash, NetCheque)	*Smartcards and Stored Value Cards (SVCs)*	*Electronic Cash (electronic tokens or notational money, e.g., eCash, CyberCoin, NetCash)*
Advantages	Familiar form for consumers Readily transferred across networks for automatic crediting and debiting	Integrated processing chip enables multiple functions (e.g., as credit, debit, or cash cards) Not limited to online commerce	Customer anonymity (Digicash) Security through encryption Ready transferability
Disadvantages	Expensive and time-consuming to process Primarily used only in the United States	Security concerns (e.g., broken encryption, counterfeit cards) Unclear regulation	Requires foresight; customer must stock electronic wallet Some forms do not protect anonymity

FIGURE 3.6 Forms of Electronic Money Differ in Advantages and Disadvantages.

One issue for online marketing is whether the form of money affects its meaning to consumers. If so, will consumption behaviors be affected? Are the uses of money online systematically different from uses in marketplace environments? These questions lead to consideration of the ways in which the online environment may facilitate or inhibit exchanges that involve money.

Spending Money in the Online Environment

Getting and using money online may differ from offline behaviors in several ways. First, the difference in tangibility may affect consumers' consumption behaviors. That is, because it is possible to negotiate exchanges and carry out transactions without ever seeing the money, the value of the resource may be less salient than in other exchange environments. As a result, consumers may be less averse to using money in the Internet environment than spending it in traditional environment, such as handing cash to a cashier, writing a check to a landlord, or signing a credit card receipt in a restaurant.

The implications of separating the meaning of money from its physical nature go even farther. For instance, for some types of exchanges you are more likely to be happy about giving up your money than others. Researchers have found that people often have systems of **mental accounting,** in which they establish internal, cognitive accounts that reflect a budget plan. For example, a set of mental accounts might include one for entertainment (movies, eating out), living expenses (food, rent, utilities), educational expenses (books, supplies), and transportation expenses (car payment, insurance). In general, unexpected hits to the budget are more likely to be viewed as undesirable events than are budgeted, planned-for debits. For instance, a speeding ticket would be seen as an undesirable and unexpected use of money that messes up the budgeting system. In contrast, an anticipated Valentine's

Day dinner at a nice restaurant with a pleasant companion would constitute a desirable use of financial resources.

Extending these ideas to the online environment provides several insights. First, people may be more willing to part with money when it is made less tangible, as with digital transfers. Second, the concept of resource tangibility may be differently applicable for different types of exchange situations. That is, some types of transactions may benefit more from the online transfer of money than other types. When the transaction is desired, people may prefer to enjoy the actual act of the transaction—giving up the money is not painful. In contrast, when the transaction is not desired, it may be better to be able to make the payment in a digital form, rather than in a salient, physical form. Less tangible forms of transfer may not only increase the likelihood and frequency of the transaction, but also the consumer's satisfaction with the exchange. In sum, the Internet environment, which separates the meaning of money from its physical being, may facilitate exchange and transaction for unexpected transactions and for undesirable, or aversive transactions. It may, however, inhibit the completion of transactions in which the meaning of the resource exchange provides the consumer with pleasure (e.g., buying a gift for a close friend).

To this point, we have considered issues of how people might transfer money online, and how their willingness to use money in a transaction might be helped or hindered by characteristics of the online medium. Equally important, however, are some of the novel ways in which the Internet environment makes it possible for people to get money. The Internet abounds with opportunities that vary widely in their legitimacy and in their potential payoff.

An innovative business approach makes it possible for people to surf the Internet and make money while doing so. For example, a company can use a site to register a users who wish to benefit from **net-surfing,** moving through Web sites in search of interesting or useful content. The users provide some personal demographic information and agrees to accept advertising content on their screens while using the Internet. Their surfing behaviors are tracked and recorded. The users are compensated for the advertising they choose to view. If users sign up other users, they get a percentage of the revenue received by the other users. This approach is similar to the viewbar-driven provision of advertising to registered users by AllAdvantage.com (see Figure 3.7).

The businesses behind these types of sites make money in several ways. One is by combining the user's demographic profile with those of others who register for the service. That information serves as a user database that can be made available, for a price, to interested companies. In addition, the Internet usage patterns of registered users can be aggregated as marketing research data and sold to interested companies. In short, the user obtains a resource by providing a service—Internet usage behavior—that would not be possible without the existence of the Internet environment. This type of opportunity, combined with the increasing frequency of similar, information-based ways to obtain money on the Internet, underscore the importance of understanding the role of information as a resource.

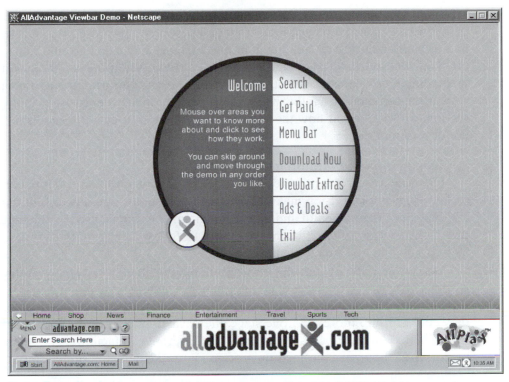

FIGURE 3.7 Users Earn Money by Viewing Ads Via the Viewbar.

Information as an Online Resource

One of the most important benefits of the Internet is its ability to function as an information resource. From its initial inception as a vehicle for communication, the Internet has grown into a vast repository of information—of all types and for all purposes.

The Nature of Information

We can think about the role of information as a resource to be consumed, and consider the impact of the Internet on people's ability to get the resource, by classifying online information into two categories. First, information may be used solely for its own sake; that is, information can provide benefits simply by being consumed. For example, people read online content to keep abreast of world events, to learn about topics of interest, and to be amused and entertained. In this type of resource acquisition, getting the information is the desired goal of the exchange: it is itself a product.

In addition, information can be used as a means to an end. In this situation, we can characterize the information resource as a service designed to facilitate some other transaction, whether online or not. For instance, people may obtain information from a variety of Internet sources about a contemplated purchase, such as a new car. Information acquired from online sources may also provide a service to a consumer, such as calculating monthly mortgage payments given different levels of income and down payment, or showing consumers how they might look if they were ten pounds slimmer. In both of these latter uses of information as a means to an end, the common idea is that people get information in order to use it. In the next section, we will look at how the Internet environment affects the acquisition and use of information.

Using Online Information

One way to describe the role of information as a means to an end is to consider its importance for decision making. Whether a consumer's goal is to find the best car deal, or to plan a health and diet regimen, information is used as the input for the determination of what course of action to follow (e.g., buy the Volvo or the Yugo; find a diet to lose ten pounds).

We can describe the process for decision making in terms of stages. A decision is often characterized by stages of (1) information search, (2) evaluation, and (3) choice and consumption. While behaviors carried out by consumers may often seem as if they could fit into more than one stage, the basic depiction of decision making is robust across large amounts of research. The Internet can facilitate and inhibit behaviors in each stage of the decision process. Figure 3.8 depicts a simple stage model of decision making.

Information processing theories are often used to describe how consumers attend to, perceive, and comprehend information. Each of the aspects of information processing is important for developing a thorough understanding of how information available from the Internet, or through similar types of interactive, digital environments, may be received and interpreted by consumers.

Information Search Characteristics

Consumers often gather information to make a choice. Information search and acquisition processes are undertaken to form a **consideration set.** A consideration set is the set of alternatives known to the consumer, which may be appropriate for

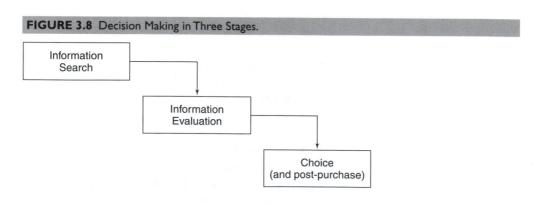

FIGURE 3.8 Decision Making in Three Stages.

consumption purposes. A consumer may form a consideration set based on past experience and familiarity with particular brands or features of brands. In addition, an alternative may be placed into the consideration set when the consumer becomes aware of it during the search process.

The Internet can influence the search process. The array of available information on the Internet, as well as the variety of search engines that can be used to weed through the information, can provide the consumer with larger numbers of alternatives to consider than would be available in a marketplace-based search. Thus, the Internet can facilitate information search.

The Internet can also make search difficult. The ability to obtain large amounts of seemingly relevant information may tax consumers' processing ability. Researchers have studied how people know when to stop acquiring information, and whether too much information can reduce decision quality. These areas of academic inquiry are often described as the **economics of information** and **information overload,** respectively.

Economics of information research suggests that people will continue searching for new information only as long as the benefits of each new piece are not exceeded by the costs of obtaining that information. The basic idea is that the expected benefits of each new piece of information decrease as the base of information already acquired grows. This notion makes intuitive sense if you think about reading classified ads in a particular product category. Even if the product is unfamiliar to you at first, as you read the ads, you begin to learn what features seem to be important, and what constitutes typical, good, and bad performance on those features. Remember the saying, "If you've seen one, you've seen them all"? After a while, little can be gained by continuing to search, but the costs of searching may remain. As a result, you stop searching.

The Internet facilitates search by changing the cost/benefit tradeoffs that people make in getting information. That is, as search costs decrease, consideration set sizes increase. Given limits to people's processing capabilities, however, larger amounts of information to consider may result in poorer quality decision, because it is harder to evaluate more alternatives. Research on information overload indicates that more information is not always better. A description of information overload is shown in Figure 3.9.

The Internet can facilitate the formation of a consideration set and reduce the possibility of information overload when consumers can use search tools to screen alternatives. **Search engines** and intelligent agents are two ways in which people can specify characteristics of the information to be returned from an automated search. These types of tools represent a range of abilities to customize search. Search engines (e.g., AltaVista and Lycos) use a variety of methods to search through and index Web pages. As the chart in Figure 3.10 illustrates, different search engines vary widely in the method and scope of their searches. Intelligent agents (e.g., Firefly) perform a similar, automated search, but they often build on the capabilities of search engines by incorporating knowledge of user preferences to conduct searches with greater detail and precision.

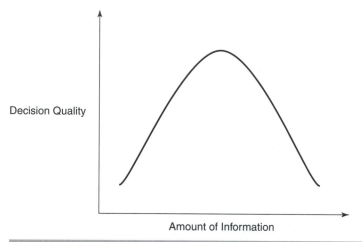

FIGURE 3.9 The Hypothetical Relation Between Information Load and Decision Quality.

The ability to customize a search may also result in a higher percentage of information that is appropriate for the user's purpose; that is, the quality of information may be higher. The tradeoff is that the more tailored the search, the greater the burden on the user to specify the criteria for the search. As a result, users with greater familiarity with the search tool, and with the search category, will tend to experience greater benefits than users with less familiarity.

Information Evaluation

Once the consumer has a set of information to consider, the next stage of the decision process is to evaluate the alternatives. In the evaluation stage, the consumer compares the options and applies some criteria to determine which option is

FIGURE 3.10 Search Engines Differ in Scope of Search.

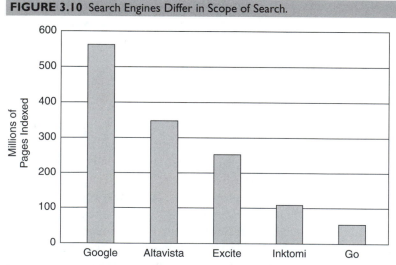

Source: Searchenginewatch.com (July 2000).

most suitable for the goal of the decision. Two areas of research are useful for considering how the Internet environment may interact with user characteristics to influence evaluation: (1) an effort/accuracy approach to decision making, and (2) decision heuristics. These areas are closely related, as they each address the issue of how consumers might structure the information in a decision in different ways at different times.

Decision structuring refers to the efforts of the consumer to create a representation, whether internally (i.e., it's all in your head) or externally (e.g., making notes), of the information acquired to make a decision. The ways that people structure decisions may be affected by what they know from past experience, such as "only look at Amazon.com, because they always have what I want." In addition, structure may be driven by situational factors, such as the number of items returned from an Internet search, or by a friend's enthusiastic recommendation (e.g., "You should check out Buy.com! They have everything!").

An **effort/accuracy approach** to evaluation is conceptually similar to the cost/ benefit idea of information search. The basic premise is that people trade off the cognitive effort they are willing to invest in comparing and judging the value of different alternatives against the quality, or accuracy, of the final decision result they would find acceptable. For decisions in which the consumer does not have prior knowledge about the best alternative (e.g., always read the *New York Times*), a consumer who puts little effort into a decision will tend to make decisions of lower quality. This concept has implications for consumers' levels of involvement and post-decision satisfaction. The idea of effort/accuracy tradeoffs is captured in Figure 3.11.

One way that consumers trade effort and accuracy in evaluating alternatives is by choosing among sets of decision heuristics. **Decision heuristics** are strategies for structuring, weighting, and editing sets of alternatives to meet decision goals, such as the desired amount of decision quality. Heuristics are shortcuts; they enable the user to eliminate information from consideration. For example, a simple heuristic of "only go to Yahoo!" for news and weather can reduce the effort that the user must invest in making the decision about which information sources to consider.

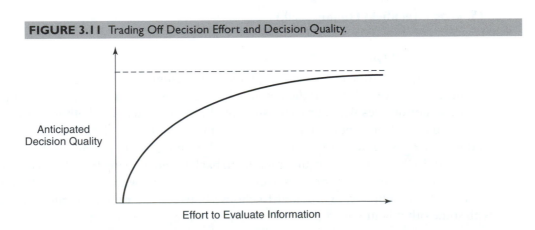

FIGURE 3.11 Trading Off Decision Effort and Decision Quality.

The Internet environment can affect the effort required to evaluate alternatives. As a result, it also influences the type of decision heuristics that consumers use. For instance, if the environment facilitates comparisons across different brands in a product category by making several brands available on one screen, then consumers may be more likely to use heuristics that examine more brands, thus resulting in better informed, and presumably higher-quality decisions.

Web retailers have begun to incorporate comparison capabilities into their sites. For example, Microsoft's eShop is an online collection of many retailers, including Blue Nile, Eddie Bauer, Toys R Us, and Amazon.com. Shopping tools on the site enable customers to compare information about a product across brands and vendors, and to specify searches for comparative information on particular features, such as price ranges and return policies. Assisted comparison shopping provides consumers with desired information in a structure that reduces the effort needed to evaluate the brands.

The Internet can also facilitate information evaluation when information is available in formats the consumers already know. For example, a consumer who has learned about a set of information by organizing her knowledge by attributes will find it easier to choose one alternative from among a set if the information is arranged by attributes. To illustrate this idea, think about a consumer who wants to decide on an online information service and wants one with financial news, sports, and technology developments. She could go through each source and try to figure out what content areas exist, and then determine which source is best for her needs based on which source offers the desired areas. This task would be easier, however, if the possible sources were arranged by whether they had a particular content section, such as sports scores, or financial news.

Digital Artifact 3.3

What attracts people to Web sites? Of 3,000 people surveyed, 66 percent said free goods or services, 47 percent said discounted prices, 43 percent are attracted by contests, and 39 percent by games.

(*Source:* **Greenfield Online, 2000.**)

Choice and Postchoice Processes

Once the evaluation process is completed, the consumer can use the results of the evaluation to make a choice. If the decision heuristic resulted in a clear winner, then the consumer decides whether to pursue the alternative, such as whether to accept the information from a particular vendor site or portal. In other situations, however, evaluative heuristics may not result in the clear discrimination of one alternative over the others. In this case, the consumer has to go back to the drawing board, and decide whether to begin the entire process over again (i.e., starting with search), whether to use a different heuristic, or whether to choose between the remaining alternatives with some other heuristic.

The Internet may affect consumers' willingness to revisit parts of decisions, largely by reducing the effort required to do so. A consistent finding in surveys of online shoppers is the perception that the Internet increases shopping convenience and decreases shopping effort. Of course, one characteristic of the Internet that may inhibit additional decision activity is the ease with which a once-visited source can be found again. The size and rapidly changing nature of the Internet's content base, combined with the variety of ways to search the content—ones that may provide different results—may increase the difficulty in getting back to a site previously visited. This problem can be particularly pronounced for decisions involving information that is novel, unique, or rarely used.

Consumers use bookmarks and browser histories to track and locate previously visited sites. Bookmarks, user-created records of sites, are stored in the browser on the user's computer. Marketers can encourage site visitors to bookmark a site to encourage and simplify repeat visits. Users can also review browser histories to retrieve information about visited sites, as shown in Figure 3.12. Because only a limited number of sites are stored, however, this approach is primarily of short-term benefit to the consumer.

FIGURE 3.12 Browser Histories Track User's Web Site Sequences.

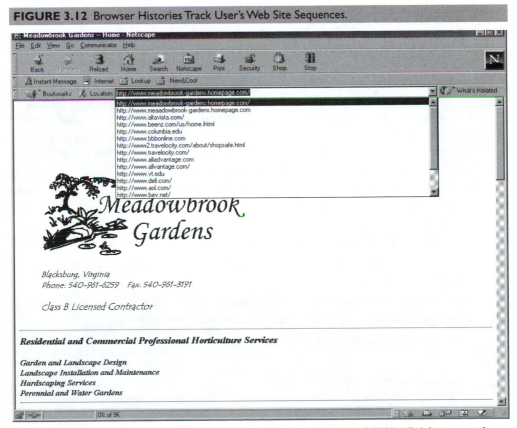

The Internet environment may also affect postdecision processes, such as satisfaction with the outcome, and confidence that the process for reaching that outcome was a good one. In decision situations where the costs of getting information are high, consumers may be satisfied with the result of a decision based on relatively little information. In the Internet environment, however, the ease with which consumers think they could have obtained additional information may lead them to be less confident about the choice just made. If acquiring and evaluating information proves difficult, given characteristics of the environment, the consumer may be dissatisfied, not only with the process for making a choice, but also with the transaction that resulted from the process.

These aspects of information and its use affect consumers' ability to acquire and use other Internet-based resources. In each of the remaining resources we will examine, information plays a role. For example, when we think of goods or services as forms of resource that can be obtained in the Internet environment, information about these resources is often consumers' primary way of gauging the desirability of the items in those sets of resources.

Getting the Goods Via the Internet

As the Internet continues to increase in popularity as a commercial medium, the amount and variety of goods available through the Internet also grows. Not all of the goods that are available, however, are provided by marketers who operate within traditional marketing models of making products that meet needs in order to effect exchange and transaction. Many goods that can be obtained through the Internet have been developed outside the recognizable boundaries of traditional marketing institutions. For example, the development of the MPEG music compression capability (MP3) has made it possible for people to obtain music in a digital format from the Internet. In many cases, the music is available free of charge (a source of great consternation to companies in the music industry). Even though some cases clearly may become the focus of regulatory attention, goods are not simply something that must be acquired through an exchange with a marketer, as the result of a transaction of financial resource. The Internet can enhance and inhibit people's ability to effect exchanges of goods, by enabling not only new types of goods, but also by opening up possibilities for establishing new relationships for effecting transactions of goods.

Digital Artifact 3.4

Consumers like to participate in online auctions. Forty-four percent of online consumers visited auctions sights to browse or buy in 1999.

(*Source:* **Greenfield Online, 2000.**)

The Nature of Goods Online

Goods are often described as one of three types: search, experience, or credence. How a good is categorized is determined by the ability of the goods' attributes to provide information to a consumer about the likely benefits that would be obtaining by consuming the good—before the good is consumed. In simpler terms, how much could you tell about how well a good will meet your needs, based just on information about the product's features?

Search goods generally convey the benefits of consumption through their attribute descriptions. In other words, if you searched for the information, you would understand the nature of the good and assess whether it is right for you. Computer equipment tends to be a good example of a search good. You can learn alot of information about the computer's features, and then determine whether the features meet your needs.

In contrast, experience goods can only be evaluated in terms of their appropriateness for you after you have consumed them. Swimsuits are an example of an experience good. All of the product details about cut, color, components, and cost will not tell you whether you will be happy in the suit. Of course, for some goods, once the initial experience is over and you know what is acceptable, the good may become a search good in the future. That is, the quality can be assessed after one use.

Credence goods are items for which quality cannot be easily assessed, even after consumption. For some credence goods, quality can be based on the advice of other, more knowledgeable consumers. Consider the purchase of an expensive bottle of wine. Even though you might have a lot of information about the age, vineyard, winery, bottling, and storage of the wine, you still cannot really know whether the wine in that particular bottle will be good. Even after you drink the wine, and although you may have been satisfied, you may still not be confident in your ability to assess the wine's quality.

These different categories of goods also apply to the Internet. In addition, goods that can be obtained via the Internet can be described in terms of their ability to be provided in a digital format. That is, goods can be characterized by the extent to which they can be obtained entirely through the Internet, or indirectly through the Internet and delivered from a physical location. Goods that can be delivered in a digital form are called **soft goods,** while goods that require physical delivery are called **hard goods.** We can integrate the three types of goods with the notion of digital versus physical goods to look at the ways in which the Internet may affect the ability to acquire desired items.

Environmental Effects on Obtaining Goods

By combining the three types of goods with the physical/digital distinction, we have six different types of goods. These types are shown in Figure 3.13. Of course, as already mentioned, examples of each type of good may be available through the

FIGURE 3.13 Characterizing Goods in the Internet Environment.

| Form of Good | Type of Good | | |
	Search	Experience	Credence
Physical	Computer hardware, Car	Clothing, Flowers	Wine
Digital	Software	MP3 (music)	Books

Internet. Obviously, however, you cannot get physical products over the Internet, but it can facilitate the process of obtaining goods as a resource through offline channels. We are interested in understanding the way in which the environment of the Internet affects the types of goods consumers can acquire, and how they go about getting those goods.

For search goods, the Internet can facilitate consumers' ability to obtain attribute information that can be used to assess the quality of the good. As with the use of the Internet as a source for any type of information, however, the readiness with which information can be obtained may be a double-edged sword. We saw in the previous section that large amounts of information, often available through an Internet search, may have a damaging effect on decision quality. Because the effects of information search, and the factors that lead to these effects, are of central importance for search goods, the same constraints and opportunities for information as a resource apply, in large measure, to search goods.

One difference between digital search goods and physical search goods may be a shortened time between the decision to acquire the good and the consumption of the good. Search and experience may often be more closely related for digital goods than for physical goods. As a result, consumers may encode in memory more information about the evaluative aspects of consumption than the specific attribute values that describe the product. One implication of this effect is that advertising designed to trigger retrieval of attribute-specific information may be less effective for digital search goods than for physical search goods.

Experience goods provide a challenge for quality assessment, both online and offline. In both cases, difficulty stems from the need to provide consumers with a situation in which the benefits of the product can be sufficiently understood. For example, in a physical environment, such as a clothing store, the clothing can be tried on, and the effect on appearance or comfort analyzed. In a virtual environment, however, sensory knowledge of the experience is limited. Even with new technologies that provide simulations of users trying on clothes, the tactile sense that tells you whether the clothing is comfortable is missing.

One approach for experience goods is to try the good first in an offline setting, and then use the Internet to obtain the good when it is needed subsequently. This approach works for durable goods, with product characteristics that are consistent and predictable over time.

Credence goods, for which quality may be difficult to assess even after consumption, provide a unique set of opportunities for consumers and for marketers. Credence goods depend on the formation of a set of beliefs about the quality of a product. As a result, simply being able to obtain information about the good, or even trying the good may not be enough to lead a consumer to believe that he or she can confidently assess the quality of the good. In cases where a consumer has access to other people's beliefs about the quality of a good, quality assessment may be simplified. In traditional marketplaces, credence goods are often evaluated through product testimonials by credible spokespersons.

The ability to rely on the expertise of other consumers to gauge the quality of a credence good is made easier by the Internet environment. For instance, recommendations of books at Amazon.com can be perused to see whether other people, whose reading tastes might resemble yours, thought a book was good. In addition, online vineyards often provide expert recommendations about wine selections.

The Internet environment also facilitates communications between consumers through **brand communities,** or collections of consumers whose basis for interaction is the common experience or appreciation of a particular brand. The shared history of the members of a brand community may lend credence to a brand, even in the absence of a long history of use, or of acquired expertise, on the part of any one community member. The communications capabilities of the Internet may enable people to share information, as through e-mail, bulletin boards, and newgroups, so that collective word-of-mouth is a surrogate for individual knowledge or experience.

In sum, the traditional bases for differentiating types of goods may be altered by the Internet environment. Experience goods may become more like search goods, given the ability to obtain simulated product experiences. Learning the opinions of knowledgeable consumers may make up for a consumer's own lack of knowledge or expertise about a product.

Some benefits of the Internet environment may often be offset, however, by the issues that arise when the features of the environment make it possible for experience and credence goods to be evaluated as search goods. Limited information processing capacity, or even just the limits on the effort a consumer wishes to invest in examining a wide array of search goods may introduce new concerns about how the quality of goods is determined.

Several of the issues and characteristics related to the consumption of goods on the Internet are also relevant for services. We can look at how goods differ from services to understand the implications of the Internet for both types of resource consumption.

Services and the Internet

Services differ from goods in several ways. One simple difference for many people is that goods tend to be tangible, while services tend to be less tangible. That is, goods are things you have, and services are events that happen to you. Both are sought-after resources because they provide benefits. Another difference between goods and services is the extent to which each type of resource tends to be specific to the consumer. Remember the dimension of particularism that was used to describe resources in Foa's resource theory? Services, even when they are widely available and fairly standardized in intent and execution, are still more personalized in their consumption than are many goods.

Other dimensions used to describe services include inseparability, heterogeneity, and perishability. **Inseparability** refers to the idea that the service cannot be separated from its consumption, or from its provider. Unlike goods, which can be produced, stored, and then consumed, the service does not really exist until it is consumed. **Heterogeneity** refers to the variation that may exist because a service is performed by different people in different places at different times. In addition, the higher degree of particularism may also lead to increased heterogeneity of services. **Perishability** stems from the intangible nature of services, and reflects the idea that services cannot be stored in warehouses. Services that are underconsumed at the time they are produced are a loss to the provider, unlike goods that can be stored for later sale.

Think about getting a haircut. Inseparability is present because the service cannot exist without the stylist, and it does not exist for you until your hair is actually cut.

Have you ever had a haircut you didn't like? The interaction between the skills of the stylist and the unique characteristics of your hair results in service heterogeneity. In addition, even if no one walks into the salon on a day that it is open, the owner incurs the costs of having the stylist available. If more people come in than can be clipped, and the salon owner turns them away, then revenue potential is lost. Hence, perishability is reflected in the underconsumption or in the overcapacity demand for the stylist's efforts.

The Internet has the potential to change the influence of each of these characteristics for services that can be obtained online. Let's look at the market for online services, and then at the effect of the environment on the nature of services.

The Nature of Internet Services

The Internet services area is one of the fastest growing segments of Internet resources, increasing 71 percent in 1998 alone. Market estimates for Internet services in 1998 were about $4.6 billion, just in the United States. Based on a projected compound annual growth rate of 60 percent, industry analysts and market research firms have tended to converge on a projection that the overall services market will surpass $78 billion by 2003.

What types of services are being consumed through the Internet? The Internet has provided consumers not only with new ways to obtain familiar services, but also with entirely new services. Some examples of familiar services include news services, such as the customized content available through portals like Yahoo! and America Online, as well as stock and financial services (e.g., eTrade). Other services include health-related information, online education, weather reports (see Figure 3.14), and professional services, such as tax and accounting applications. In addition, companies have begun to investigate the potential of online customer service, for goods and services purchased in online or traditional outlets.

Some of the services that have acquired an online presence would not be possible without the development of other, entirely new services that enable their existence. For example, internet service providers (ISPs), such as CompuServe and AOL, have formed and grown as the result of the high demand for Internet access and functionality. These types of resources reflect the consumption of one resource that is necessary to consume other online resources.

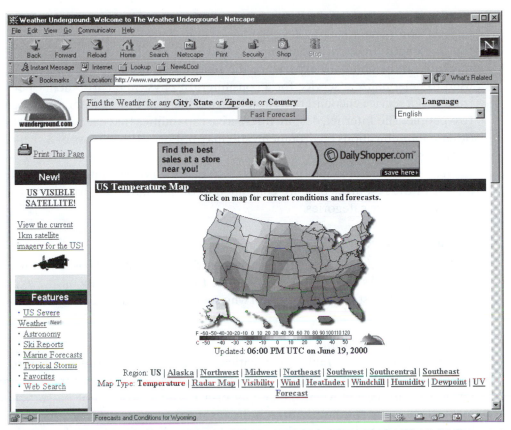

FIGURE 3.14 Consumers Obtain Local Weather Forecasts Via the Internet.

Environmental Effects on Service Consumption

The Internet blurs the distinction between goods and services. For instance, goods that can be transacted via the Internet are far less tangible than many goods in traditional marketplaces. In addition, the types of services that are available through the Internet are often sufficiently automated that the consistency of their provision is high. For instance, an automated tax preparation advisory service can rely on a database of accumulated expertise that may be greater than the ability of any single provider. In addition, the database nature of the input for the service maintains the quality of the potential service output.

A related effect of the online transmission of services is that they may tend to be less distinguishable from goods in terms of heterogeneity. Finally, the ability to automate the provision of many online service offerings (e.g., through intelligent agents) means that online services often do not face the same concerns of over- and underconsumption as do services that exist in the physical marketplace.

While many types of services can be obtained through the Internet, the digital nature of the environment does have its drawbacks. Clearly, some types of services just cannot be obtained through the Internet: for example, anything that includes a physical component, such as dry cleaning, or dental work. More subtle, however, are the challenges for service consumption that arise due to constraints of the digital medium on the ability to experience the service. For instance, the Internet can be used to personalize a service for a consumer. In physical environments, personalization of a service encounter often stems from the face-to-face interaction between two people. The Internet, despite interactive capabilities that exceed those of many other communications environment, still may not provide richness of a real-world, interpersonal situation.

The human interaction that is central to many service situations is also characteristic of the resources that are consumed to obtain status and love—the last two of Foa's resource categories.

Status as a Resource

Status is the relative esteem, prestige, or regard of an individual based on the evaluation of others. As such, status is a resource that depends heavily on the exchange processes that exist between a person who seeks status, and the persons from whom it is sought.

The Nature of Status

Status refers to the rank or evaluation of one person, relative to a comparison group of peers. **Scarcity** is often the motivating factor behind status. In economic terms, scarcity occurs when the supply of a resource would not be sufficient to meet the demand for the resource, if the resource were available free of charge. In human terms, scarcity means that we tend to accord status to people who demonstrate an ability to obtain larger amounts of limited, desirable resources than we do. In many cases, status reflects power; the possession of a resource that can be traded for other resources, such as money, can enable a person to control situations and exchanges in ways that would not be possible without the initial resource. For instance, millionaires can make large donations to have buildings named after them.

Facilitating Effects of the Internet

The Internet influences how people maintain or increase status by enabling them to obtain scarce resources, and by providing ways to indicate exclusivity. In terms of scarcity, the environment may make it easier for people to acquire resources that serve as a basis for obtaining status. For example, the Internet has created an opportunity for new goods and services, creating in the process, a new class of Internet millionaires.

The expression of status through exclusivity is facilitated by Internet characteristics that enable people to extend circles of peers. With this medium, one may be more likely to find people who share sets of values and accomplishment related to those values. The interaction between similarly accomplished people provides reciprocal benefits in terms of respect and status (see Figure 3.15). The exchanges

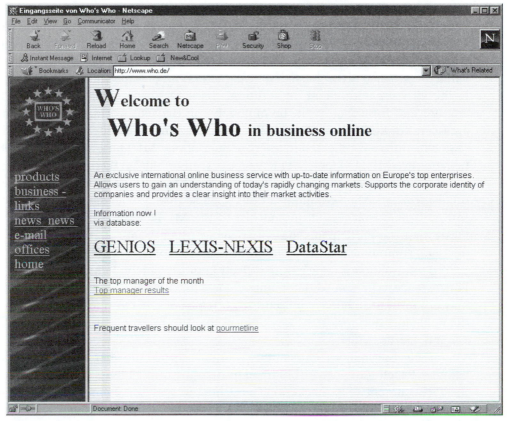

Source: Reproduced with permission of Who's Who Edition GmbH. Copyright © 2000. All rights reserved.

FIGURE 3.15 Conveying Status Through Exclusivity.

that enable interaction can occur through newgroups and online bulletin boards, and can be further fostered through focused, personal, e-mail communications.

The nature of the Internet makes it possible for people to present information about themselves that supports, creates, or reflects a status-worthy image. For example, the ease with which Web sites can be created, combined with the ability to produce, alter, and disseminate digital content, makes the Internet an easy way to present information about oneself to promote a desired image, consistent with exclusivity.

The Internet also enables people to acquire status through exclusivity even in the absence of achivements related to traditional values. The ability to obtain status through the Internet environment—even when it does not reflect real-world accomplishment—is related to the saying, "On the Internet, nobody knows you're a dog." The Internet can create the opportunity for anonymity; that is people can invent new selves, managing the impressions of themselves that they create for others, in order to acquire status.

For example, on the Internet, people can create fictitious personae to participate in fantasy existences, such as those of multi-user dungeons (MUDs). These characters may often reflect the desire to fulfill a need for belonging and status that is unmet in the real-world, day-to-day existence of the user in a society that places value on personal accomplishment. Characters can obtain skills and acquire power in the virtual environment. In addition, characters can acquire possessions of an amount and form that might be impossible in the real world. The importance of amassing "things" in a material culture where status is accorded by command over scarce resources is reflected in the comment of one MUD user about why she participates in a MUD, "I feel like I have more stuff on the MUD than I have off of it."[1]

People can also manage the impressions they provide of themselves through other forms of online communications, such as through newsgroup discussion and Internet relay chat (IRC). In contrast to the MUD setups, in which everyone is aware that the participants are role-playing, other forms of Internet-based interpersonal communications may inhibit the user's ability to determine whether presented information is an accurate reflection of the person behind the information. For instance, a person who communicates with others in an ongoing chat may or may not present an honest or accurate portrayal of self. Despite the motivation and the behaviors that result, the key point is that the Internet can facilitate the acquisition of status.

Finally, the highly technical environment of the Internet can serve as a new venue in which status can be obtained by demonstrating high levels of skills in using the environment (e.g., hackers). Thus, the Internet serves as a source of status through exclusivity, by introducing a new way for people to demonstrate accomplishment in the form of mastering aspects of the online environment.

Inhibiting Effects of the Internet

The Internet may also inhibit the expression of status. Research indicates that in relationships where status levels are different, interaction tends to be initiated by the person with higher status. The meaning of status is reflected in the ways in which members of a society generally tend to adhere to the unwritten rule that the person with higher status guides the tone of an interaction. Consider, for example, the difference in reactions that you might encounter in the following situations:

Your boss speaks first: *"I'd like to get your advice on how I should've handled that last client. Any suggestions?"*

Versus

You speak first: *"I think you blew it with that last client, Boss. I have some suggestions about how you could've handled it."*

With the Internet, hierarchical communications patterns that reflect status may be decreased; the impersonality of the medium may lower the barriers that

---

[1]As reported by Sherry Turkle in "Virtuality and Its Discontents," *The American Prospect* (Winter 1996).

inhibit some communications. The Internet may also influence other, subtle ways in which status is reflected in interpersonal communication. The ease and speed with which e-mails can be sent, for instance, may lead to less attention to the details that differentiate a traditional memo to a boss, and a traditional memo from a boss. In addition, the anonymity of computer-mediated communications may also result in decreased use of titles and forms of respect that are typically associated with status.

The characteristics of the Internet environment that foster or inhibit people's ability to obtain status exert a similar effect on the ability to acquire the last of Foa's six resources—love. In some cases, the Internet may even facilitate exchanges of status for love (e.g., via online personal ads). Although the environmental factors that influence resource acquisition may be similar, however, the basic motivation behind the need for the two types of resources, as well as the ways in which the resource needs are satisfied, are often quite different.

Love as a Resource

In real-world interactions, emotional resources are typically available through relationships that have as a primary goal the shared satisfaction of emotional needs. These relationships include marriages and friendships, and community and social organizations. In general, the emotional dimensions that characterize these relationships are included in theories of love. As a result, we will focus on the idea of love as a resource, and the role of the Internet in the acquisition of love.

The Meaning of Love

Three dimensions that have been used to describe relationships are intimacy, passion, and commitment.[2] The types of love that exist are described as different combinations and intensities of the dimensions. **Intimacy** refers to the feeling of love for someone else, rather than the feeling of being "in love." Intimacy generally reflects a deep liking and trust for someone, based on the belief that meaningful thoughts and feelings can be shared. Good friendships tend to exhibit high levels of intimacy.

Passion, in contrast, is the feeling of being "in love." It is an arousal state, in which a person may experience euphoric feelings, as well as high levels of uncertainty and anxiety about whether the love is reciprocated. Because uncertainty tends to be reduced with longer-term interactions that provide intimacy, as well as information about the other person's feelings, passion is usually more intense, relative to the other dimensions, earlier in a relationship.

Commitment involves the desire to nurture the relationship, often by doing things that please the other person. Although commitment is often reflected by contractual obligations, such as marriage, the meaning of commitment revolves around the idea of doing what is necessary to maintain the relationship. In general, commitment means putting the other person's needs first.

---

[2]Robert J. Sternberg, "A Triangular Theory of Love," *Psychological Review,* 93, pp. 119–135.

If we think about the different combinations of dimensions that can occur, we can immediately recognize some familiar types of relationships. For example, high intimacy combined with low passion and commitment indicates a friendship, but not one that is likely to endure a long separation (such as moving away after college). In contrast, high intimacy and high commitment indicate a more lasting friendship. Love of the sort that fascinates many poets and authors of romantic novels, is characterized by high intimacy and passion, but not a lot of staying power. Passion by itself is infatuation (e.g., love at first sight), while passion and commitment without intimacy constitutes a sort of "puppy love," or crush-type relationship. A relationship with high levels of all three dimensions is known as consummate love. In general, consummate love is assumed to be a sought-after goal, although in many situations other types of relationships may be both desired and obtained.

For our purposes, the Internet can serve as a way for people to initiate relationships of the different sorts, and as a way to nurture a variety of relationships.

Digital Artifact 3.5

Teenagers' primary purpose for online activity is communication. Eighty-three percent of teenagers in NFO's Interactive Panel say they use the Internet for e-mail. Forty percent use chat rooms, and 31 percent send electronic greeting cards.
(*Source:* **PricewaterhouseCoopers, 2000.**)

Love in a Digital World

Little is yet known about the ability of the Internet to serve as a way to obtain emotional fulfillment. Numerous attempts, however, have been made to create digital analogs of real-world means for fulfillment. For example, support groups exist online for an enormous variety of human needs and conditions. The groups have organized around the need to provide emotional support along a particular need or dimension (e.g., for parents of children with leukemia; for Native Americans). These types of groups serve as a means for people to express and receive intimacy. Shared experiences that increase the perception of intimacy may be facilitated by the relatively anonymous nature of the exchange environment. These types of groups do not tend to exhibit high levels of commitment; in many cases, the groups are characterized by a continually shifting membership.

Some forms of online relationships do exhibit both intimacy and commitment. The history of WELL, one of the earliest online communities, illustrates the way in which emotional resources can be derived from the online community for a variety of relationship types and needs. WELL originated in the mid-1980s as a way for people, largely based in the Bay area of California, to share interests and concerns about life issues. Rapidly, however, the interactions resulted in friendships that extended far beyond the ostensible purpose of the community interaction. In one case, community resources were mobilized to obtain medical treatment and transportation home for a former community member suffering from a dangerous form of hepatitis contracted while in India.

Companionate relationships (i.e., high intimacy and commitment) are also facilitated on a more individual level, as through the ability to communicate rapidly and easily with e-mail. This characteristic may enhance both intimacy and commitment. In addition, Web sites that enable people to send jokes and humorous messages on topics of shared interest foster intimacy, as do greeting card sites.

The Internet also fosters other types of relationships. For instance, a person in a passion-only relationship, complete with high uncertainty about the feelings of the other person, may be reassured or redirected by information from an online astrologer about the shape of the future. A person seeking a relationship can turn to online dating services, in the hopes of finding consummate love. Failing that, consumers can find commitment-only relationships with foreign nationals who seek American spouses.

Although the Internet environment can facilitate exchanges that enable participants to acquire emotional resources, researchers have raised concerns about the effect of the online environment on emotional well-being. Some research suggests that high levels of online involvement may actually reduce well-being, by decreasing the amount of interpersonal interaction and communication. In addition, the Internet may inhibit the quality of emotional exchange. Limits to the range of interpersonal communications cues, such as facial expressions, body language, and tone of voice, suggest that the Internet is better suited for informational communication than for emotional communication.

Chapter Summary

In this chapter, we have focused on the interaction between consumers and the Internet environment. Our goal was to develop our understanding of how the ways in which consumers seek to obtain necessary resources are facilitated or inhibited by characteristics of the Internet as a medium for consumption.

Following an overview of online consumer demographics, we considered each of the six resources delimited by Foa's resource theory. Starting with a general description of the nature of each resource, we moved to an examination of the resource in the digital environment. Similarities and differences between online and offline forms of the resources were considered, as were the nature of exchanges through which the resources can be obtained. The role of the Internet as a facilitating or inhibiting force on consumers' effort to obtain the resource was discussed.

REVIEW SECTION

Key Terms

- demographics
- psychographics
- fungibility
- cybercash
- digital cash
- mental accounting
- net-surfing
- information processing
- consideration set

- economics of information
- information overload
- search engines
- decision structuring
- effort/accuracy approach
- decision heuristics
- soft goods
- hard goods
- brand communities
- inseparability
- heterogeneity
- perishability
- status
- scarcity
- intimacy
- passion
- commitment

Review Questions

1. How does the Internet environment influence the types of exchanges that are carried out?
2. What factors can explain the appeal of the Internet as a virtual marketplace for consumers?
3. Discuss the differences between demographics and psychographics.
4. What is the profile of the average Internet user?
5. From a resource exchange perspective, how does using chips rather than money affect gambling behavior?
6. What is one advantage of using the Internet to search for information? What is one disadvantage?
7. Explain the effort/accuracy approach to decision making.
8. What different categories of goods are available to Internet consumers?
9. What three dimensions can be used to differentiate services from goods?
10. How does the Internet environment enable people to acquire status? Love?

Thinking Points

1. Profiles of Internet users are often based on data aggregated from a number of sources. What issues does this aggregation raise for marketers who attempt to use these data for segmentation and forecasting purposes?
2. Demographic variables can provide a broad description of consumers in a marketplace. Why is it often desirable to augment demographic insights with analysis of psychological factors?
3. Why is it necessary to describe Internet users? That is, why are they likely to differ from consumers who do not use the Internet for consuming goods and services? What are some of the implications of these differences for marketing activity?
4. The Internet can facilitate or inhibit consumers' resource exchanges by affecting the types of resources, types of exchange processes, and types of relationships that are available. What are some types of exchanges that exist in a marketspace environment that do not exist in traditional marketplace environments? What aspects of the resource exchange differ most markedly? How?
5. The Internet provides consumers with novel consumption opportunities, as well as novel ways to conduct exchanges and transactions (e.g., digital cash). How might the novelty of the Internet environment influence the ways that consumers evaluate goods and services? What are some of the advantages and disadvantages of this novel environment for consumers?

6. What do the differences between goods and services suggest about the relative ease with which consumers might adopt the Internet as a source of goods, versus services? That is, services are often perceived as more highly variable in quality than goods. How might the provision of services via the Internet affect this type of perception?

7. Foa's resource theory suggests that resources more similar to each other are more likely to be viewed as reasonable candidates for exchange. What are some types of resource exchanges that can be facilitated with the Internet, using the Internet to minimize perceived distances between resources?

Suggested Readings

1. "Some Consequences of Electronic Groups," by Lee Sproull and Samer Faraj, and "Netiquette 101," by Jay Machado. In *Internet Dreams,* edited by Mark Stefik (Cambridge, MA: The MIT Press, 1997).

2. "Consumer Behavior in the Future," by Jagdish N. Sheth and Rajendra S. Sisodia. In *Electronic Marketing and the Consumer,* edited by Robert A. Peterson. (Thousand Oaks, CA: Sage Publications, Inc., 1997).

3. "Evaluating the Potential of Interactive Media Through a New Lens: Search versus Experience Goods," by Lisa R. Klein. *Journal of Business Research, 41* (1998), pp. 195–203.

4. "Kiddie Kash," by Rebecca Vesely. *Business 2.0* (May 1999), pp. 24–26.

5. "Social Impact of the Internet: What Does It Mean?" by Robert Kraut, Sara Kiesler, Tridas Mukhopadhyay, William Scherlis, and Michael Patterson. *Communications of the ACM, 41,* 12 (1998), pp. 21–22.

CHAPTER 4

Marketers and the Internet Environment

FOCUS AND OBJECTIVES

This chapter is focused on the relationship between marketers and the Internet environment. Characteristics of marketing activity online are described, and the influence of the Internet on the nature of marketing activity is considered in terms of its effect on company structures and processes. The Internet is described as an environment that creates challenges and opportunities for marketers. Marketing responses to challenges are addressed by considering ways in which marketers can identify opportunities to meet strategic objectives, given consumers' goals for resource exchange.

YOUR OBJECTIVES IN STUDYING THIS CHAPTER INCLUDE THE FOLLOWING:

- Develop familiarity with characteristics of companies involved in e-commerce.
- Understand the implications for marketers of differing levels of Internet integration into marketing activity.
- Recognize potential effects of the Internet on the ways that companies organize themselves for business, and on the processes for marketing action.
- Identify major sources of challenges and opportunities for marketers in the Internet environment.

For marketers, the Internet is a new and rapidly changing environment for selling goods and services. It is nearly impossible to ignore the growing popularity of the Internet for business applications. Business periodicals and newsletters devote much column space to the benefits of using the Internet to conduct business; Internet services are touted in television, radio, and print media; Web sites are increasingly replacing more traditional promotional activities; and new companies with the .com suffix appear daily. These examples are only a fraction, however, of the total population of companies who operate within the Internet environment. Many companies make use of the Internet for aspects of marketing other than to sell goods or services online.

The ability to use the potential of the Internet for marketing can be enhanced by having a clear understanding of how the Internet affects marketing processes and practices. The type and function of the various exchange relations that exist in the marketspace environment imply changes to the *types* of marketing activities that companies can execute. In addition, the digital environment makes possible changes in the *ways* that traditional marketing activities can be carried out. Before determining which activities to pursue, and how to use the Internet to pursue them, however, you must be able to determine which activities will enable the company to achieve its strategic objectives.

In this chapter, we will examine the exchange relations from the perspective of the marketer. What does the availability of the Internet mean for developing marketing strategy and the actions needed to implement the strategy? How do the relationships that exist, either directly or indirectly, between marketers and consumers, technology developers, and policy makers, affect the formulation of effective strategy? The ability to answer these questions will provide you with the insights needed to develop appropriate goals for organizations who wish to incorporate the Internet into marketing activity, and to understand the characteristics of marketing activity that use the Internet to achieve goals.

We begin with a general characterization of businesses in the central exchange environment of the Internet. Then we consider the effect of the environment on the ways that businesses carry out their marketing activities. In the last section of this chapter, we build on the idea of resource consumption to illustrate some of the ways in which the Internet enables marketers to address strategic marketing objectives.

MARKETERS IN THE MARKETSPACE

Several descriptors can be used to characterize the types of companies that conduct marketing activity in the Internet environment. We will look at three of these descriptors to get a bird's eye view of the marketing environment: (1) .com versus traditional companies, (2) types of products sold online, and (3) types of customers online.

A Company Focus

To use a simple descriptor, we can divide the marketing world into .com companies and non-.com companies. Recent reports by research analysts indicate that the number of .com companies is increasing at a rapid rate, more than doubling each year from 1997 through 1999. Many of these companies are **pure-player companies;** that is, all their transaction activities are conducted via the Internet. Ebay and Amazon are examples of pure players—companies with no physical, brick-and-mortar retail presence. ActivMedia Research estimated that retail sites online accounted for 71 percent of revenue generation in 1998.

A Product Focus

While a .com dichotomy provides some descriptive information about the impact of the Internet on the formation of new companies, it is an incomplete description. Many companies have hybrid strategies that combine Internet capabilities with traditional marketing methods to achieve marketing goals. These companies may derive substantial revenues from Internet-based transactions, in addition to sales in traditional marketplace structures. Thus, we can segment companies by the types of products or services they emphasize. The chart in Figure 4.1 illustrates the main categories of goods and services that provide revenue through Internet-based transactions.

A Customer Focus

A drawback with the product focus is that it tends to emphasize online sales of goods and services to individual consumers. Of course, this approach leaves out an important segment for marketing—the business consumer. As a result, we need to consider a descriptive dimension that reflects this segment. For example, a company might emphasize a **business-to-consumer (B2C)** approach, such as selling a product or service to a single person who will be the end user of the item (e.g., compact discs from Buy.com). Alternatively, a company may have a **business-to-business (B2B)** focus that targets sales of products or services to organizations that will use them for conducting aspects of their business operations.

The relative impact of the business-to-consumer and business-to-business distinction can be seen in terms of the revenues projected for each segment. As Figure 4.2 shows, the revenue potential for B2B goods and services dramatically outpaces that projected for the B2C segment. We will take a closer look at the impact of the Internet on business-to-business marketing in Chapter 13.

A major reason for the anticipated growth is the need to develop the infrastructure for electronic commerce activities. For example, a company might carry

FIGURE 4.1 A Product Focus Illustrates Differences in Online Retail Demand.

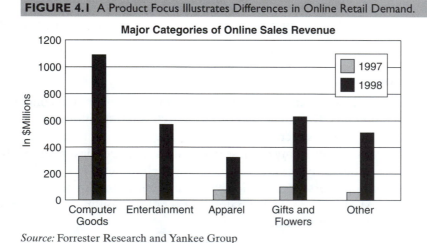

Source: Forrester Research and Yankee Group

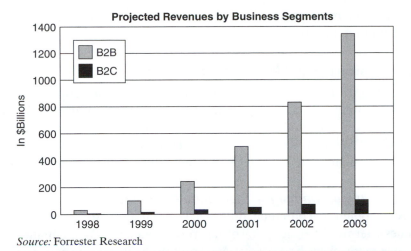

Source: Forrester Research

FIGURE 4.2 A Customer Focus Illustrates the Importance of the B2B Market.

out its marketing activities in a traditional manner, with the exception of developing a Web site from which customers can obtain product information and order products. The software and technological capabilities that make these activities possible are referred to as **front-end applications.** In addition, the company might decide that using the Internet offers benefits to complete other business activities, such as maintaining databases of customer queries for sales leads, and coordinating budget development and activity. These types of electronic commerce applications—invisible to the ordinary end user—are called **back-end applications.** Back-end applications are the key factor in the rate with which the infrastructure for electronic commerce is predicted to grow. They are also the primary source of projected revenue in the business-to-business sector. (See Figure 4.3.)

Each of the three dimensions we have considered provides complementary information about the role of the Internet on the focus of marketing activity. Because much of the Internet's influence, however, may not be centered on online sales, we

FIGURE 4.3 Types of Internet Software Applications.

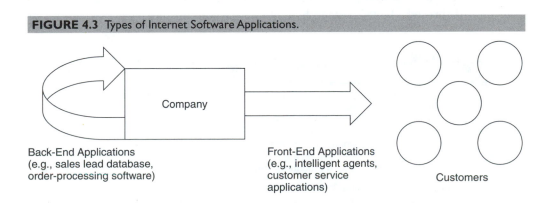

Back-End Applications
(e.g., sales lead database,
order-processing software)

Front-End Applications
(e.g., intelligent agents,
customer service
applications)

Customers

need a way to describe more generally the nature of the interaction between marketers and the Internet environment.

Describing the Company and Internet Interaction

Two concepts reflect the nature of the relationship between a marketing entity and the Internet environment. The first approach is a **continuum of electronic commerce** that captures the range of levels of involvement of a company in electronic commerce activities. The second concept, **netcentricity,** is a measure that quantifies a company's involvement in electronic commerce as a function of online activities.

An Involvement Continuum for Electronic Commerce

The electronic commerce continuum proposed by eMarketer provides a way to describe companies in terms of their adoption of electronic commerce. The continuum consists of four stages, in which each successive stage reflects the increasing pervasion and influence of electronic commerce on the company's activities. The continuum is presented in Figure 4.4.

In Phase I, involvement with electronic commerce is limited to familiarity with the Internet, and use of the Internet, by the company's employees. Phase I is characterized by little or no formal expectations on the part of company of how tasks will be conducted using the Internet. Instead, the Internet is used on the employees' initiative, as to facilitate coordination and communication through e-mail. Typically, a company has passed through Phase I when most of the senior employees regularly use the Internet.

Phase II reflects a shift from internal, company use of the Internet to an external, consumer-oriented focus. In this phase, the company uses the Internet as a way to communicate features and benefits of its products or services. A company has passed through Phase II when its Internet presence is more than a simple **brochureware** presentation of the company.

Moving from maintaining an online presence to actually consummating transactions online reflects a Phase III level of business involvement on the Internet. In Phase III, typical accomplishments include the ability to use the Internet's interactive capabilities to complete sales and to provide online service. A company that has passed through the third stage has integrated the consumer orientation of Phase II

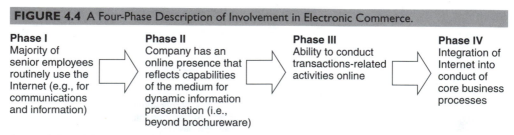

FIGURE 4.4 A Four-Phase Description of Involvement in Electronic Commerce.

Phase I
Majority of senior employees routinely use the Internet (e.g., for communications and information)

Phase II
Company has an online presence that reflects capabilities of the medium for dynamic information presentation (i.e., beyond brochureware)

Phase III
Ability to conduct transactions-related activities online

Phase IV
Integration of Internet into conduct of core business processes

Source: Adapted from eMarketer, 1999.

with internal processes used to effect transactions, thus building on the employee acceptance of electronic commerce in Phase I.

In the final phase, the integration of electronic commerce in the business is complete. At the end of Phase IV, the company's core processes are linked with electronic commerce applications. In this phase, the front-end applications that create an interface between company and customer are augmented by back-end applications that enable the company to function smoothly in the Internet environment.

In general, smaller companies tend to move more rapidly through the continuum. This effect occurs because smaller companies are often more flexible in structure, and thus able to adapt to change more readily than larger companies.

Of course, it is important to note that being at a later stage is not necessarily more desirable than being in an earlier stage. For some types of companies, a Phase II presence may be the most beneficial level of electronic commerce involvement (e.g., an ice cream shop). For other companies, competitive competency may only be achieved through complete integration of electronic commerce into all aspects of business function (e.g., a digital music provider).

Digital Artifact 4.1

Three out of five U.S. companies are involved in e-commerce, and an additional 20 percent intend to become involved. Involvement has affected the organizational structures of 25 percent of the businesses surveyed.

(*Source:* **Nua Internet Surveys, Inc., April 2000, citing the National Association for Business Economics.**)

Netcentricity: Quantifying Involvement

Another way to characterize the impact of the Internet on the ways that companies do business is by looking at the company revenues. Netcentricity is the percentage of revenues due to online activity as a portion of the total revenues earned by a company. It is used as a way to quantify the extent to which a company has adopted electronic commerce—especially Phase III in the continuum—as a way of doing business. In the aggregate, we can look at netcentricity to determine which types of companies and industries tend to move most quickly toward online activity, and to compare the extent of such activity. The graph in Figure 4.5 is based on reports of netcentric activity by 1,296 companies.

UNDERSTANDING THE INTERNET'S INFLUENCE ON MARKETING

The involvement continuum and netcentricity are useful ways to describe Internet adoption by businesses; however, they still provide an incomplete picture of the Internet's influence. To develop a broader understanding of how the Internet affects marketing practice more generally than just sales, we can also look at the effects of

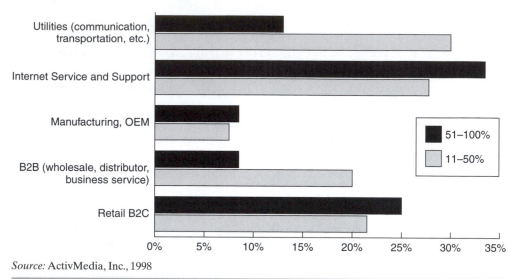

Source: ActivMedia, Inc., 1998

FIGURE 4.5 Netcentricity Differs Widely, Depending on Business Type.

the Internet on the structure of the company and its processes for marketing. These two aspects of Internet effects reflect descriptive insights into what companies look like, and what companies do, in the Internet environment.

Effects of the Internet Environment

The Internet environment affects the way that companies organize themselves for business activity. Two ways in which the characteristics of the environment have affected business structure are (1) decentralization of processes, thus changing the nature of traditional business functions, and (2) changes to hierarchical business structures.

Internet Effects on Company Structure

The connectivity of the Internet makes it possible for people to work at remote locations, yet still share information almost instantaneously. As a result, working in the same, central location is often less necessary for getting work done. Although it is still necessary to maintain central stores of information, as in the form of databases, the same technological capabilities that make the databases possible also make it possible for multiple people to make use of the central information—adding to it and retrieving from it—from different locations.

The Internet also increases the ability of company employees to coordinate activity across the different functions (e.g., marketing, sales, engineering, accounting). Being able to communicate directly and efficiently with people in other functions eliminates the need for many traditional hierarchies intended to oversee and control the flow of information from one person to another. That is, while hierarchies, or chains of command, served an important cost-reducing function previously, the decreased communications costs enabled by the Internet make such structures potentially less efficient than alternative structures that foster direct communication between employees.

One such approach is reflected in the use of teams, called platforms, for product development and marketing. The **platform approach** consists of cross-functional teams of employees, in which team members are empowered to make significant decisions about many aspects of the product. In addition, the team is given the responsibility for overseeing the processes that must be completed to produce a product that can be marketed successfully. This responsibility results in the hand-in-hand coordination and reliance of all team members.

This coordination often has two related effects. First, it increases the need for effective access to team-based digital applications for completing work activities. For example, Chrysler's ability to develop its new automobile models using shared, networked applications has been an important factor in the company's ability to move from concept to production and distribution more quickly than the competition.

Digital Artifact 4.2

Responsibility for developing and implementing e-commerce strategies is shifting from IT executives to marketing executives. In mid-1999, 28 percent of 1,300 organizations surveyed indicated that e-commerce was a marketing responsibility, up from 15 percent in early 1999. IT executives with e-commerce oversight dropped from 59 percent to 46 percent.

(*Source:* **Zona Research, 1999.**)

A second influence of the Internet on the environment in which marketers operate is the increasing shift toward integrated management structures in the workplace. For example, the ability to store and to communicate information, such as market research about consumer needs, through digital databases means that information can be entered by one person, but accessed by many. As a result, rather than each organizational function operating independently, the functions can be coordinated and processes can be standardized to create efficient processes for acquiring and sharing information that result in decreased errors (e.g., through flawed data entry). Of course, the flip side to this benefit is that if an error is entered, its impact may be large (and negative), because it is widely distributed.

Internet Effects on Company Processes

The Internet also influences the way in which companies carry out business processes. The effect of the Internet on the pace of marketing activity—and on many aspects of day-to-day productivity—has introduced the idea of Internet time into the popular lexicon. **Internet time** reflects the increased speed with which many types of tasks can be completed using the Internet. It also reflects the changes to expectations of what people can be expected to accomplish, given the capabilities of the interactive medium. People are expected to do more, and to do it better and faster, with the information and communications capabilities of the Internet.

This increase in performance expectations is illustrated by the reduction in intervals for product introductions in Internet-related industries. Cycles for new product and model introduction have tended to decrease. In the computer industry, for example, prior to the widespread adoption of the Internet by businesses, new models were introduced at an average rate of one model every 18 months. Expectations on the part of management and consumers have changed; to remain competitive, a company must now unveil a new model every four months. This increased pace is due in large part to **information acceleration:** an increase in the rate at which information can be compiled and transmitted via the Internet.

The Internet makes possible the use of **workflow software**, designed to streamline business processes that rely on document sharing and communications between business functions. At Lawrence Livermore National Laboratory, for example, the use of an Internet-based workflow system call "Zephyr" resulted in time savings of up to 90 percent. It also created substantial cost savings and improved product quality. In addition, the lab's ability to pay suppliers more quickly increased the number of vendors willing to work with the lab, thus creating greating competition and the potential for additional cost savings.

Facilitating Capabilities of the Internet

The changes to company structures and processes are reflected in the use of the Internet to meet performance expectations. That is, the Internet does not just cause things to change, it makes it possible for things to change. For instance, the Internet facilitates a decentralized structure and the formation of platform-based teams by enabling communications through customized networks. These networks, such as corporate intranets and extranets, reflect the role of the Internet as a force in changing the ways companies work.

Getting Work Done: Intranets and Outside Intranets

Intranets are local area networks that use the fundamental structure of the Internet to move information from place to place, but which are internal to the organization. These corporate networks provide managers with a means of disseminating information efficiently through the levels of the organization. Intranets can be used to facilitate data transfer across functions in the organization, thus streamlining the nature of traditional business practices. In addition, the communications capabilities of intranets can be used to foster interaction between employees. The form of these interactions may be hierarchical, with information flows upward or downward. They may also be horizontal, as through interactions between employees at the same level or rank.

Intranets are typically established to maintain the ability to carry out networked communications within an organization. The proprietary nature of corporate intranets is reflected in the efforts made by companies to develop networks that cannot be accessed by outside parties. The techniques for enhancing network security often involve the use of **firewalls.** Firewalls serve as barriers that block unauthorized access to a site on a network.

In some instances, however, companies may find it advantageous to allow an outside party some level of access to an intranet. **Outside intranetting** occurs when an organization provides access to the corporate intranet to a third party—someone outside the company. Outside intranetting is used when the interaction between members of the organization and the third party work together to accomplish a specific objective. For example, a company might provide a consulting engineer with access to its intranet to facilitate communications between marketing researchers and company engineers about the optimal design of a new product.

Outside the Company Walls: Extranets

When companies need to allow access to information by a set of users in distant locations, they can set up extranets. **Extranets** are wide area networks that operate much like the Web. They enable companies to overcome network limitations of size and distance that exist with intranets. Extranets can be designed so that access to the network can be protected, as with a password. They can be used for a range of business applications, such as linking suppliers and customers.

As is illustrated by the changes to companies' structures and processes, the rapidly changing environment of the Internet means that marketers must be prepared to manage a variety of new situations. Marketers must also be able to evaluate the nature of changes to the environment, and the speed with which they tend to occur, in order to predict and anticipate likely developments in the marketing environment. In the next section, we will consider several of the challenges that face marketers in the Internet environment.

CHALLENGES OF THE INTERNET ENVIRONMENT

The environmental factors of the Internet create challenges that must be addressed by marketers in order to succeed in the online environment. The changes that companies make to their processes and activities reflect **adaptivity.** Adaptivity refers to changes made by organisms to thrive as a population within their environment. Within the Internet environment, companies that do not change may not be able to compete effectively against other companies who recognize and respond to environmental factors.

The Internet is a dynamic medium—a reality that also presents a challenge to marketers. Unlike the advent of telephone service, or television, the Internet is a medium that continues to evolve and develop. This continuing development means that marketers must stay abreast of changes that will affect marketing practices. The fact that the Internet as a marketing environment is a work-in-progress means that marketers may exert increasing levels of influence in the subsequent development of the medium.

In traditional approaches to marketing, the need to adapt marketing activity is often characterized as the result of an inability to control one or more of five factors. These factors, often called the Five Cs, consist of company, channels, customers, competition, and conditions. These factors are ordered by the decreasing influence of the marketer; that is, a marketer is likely to have the most direct impact on the company, but a far less direct influence on general conditions, such as the rate of technological development.

In the Internet environment, the issue of adaptivity is a bit more complex. Not only must marketers deal with the same five factors that have always made marketing strategy an inexact science, now they must manage an additional influence—that of the Internet environment itself. The basic idea, as shown in Figure 4.6, is that the environment creates changes to the ways that the five factors reflect the influence of marketing activity. The marketer must be able to recognize the implications of these changes, and to adapt marketing strategy accordingly.

Environmental Effects on Company Structure and Function

We have already considered several of the ways in which the Internet environment may lead to changes to the structure and processes of companies. It is important to note, however, even though a company restructures its form and function, it has no guarantee that the outcomes of its effort will provide the desired ability to manage the environmental challenges—particularly if the competition adapts equally well!

The effect of the Internet on company structure is observed in the changes in percentages in employee growth rates for different segments of companies in the Internet economy. A study commissioned by Cisco Systems, Inc., and conducted by faculty at the University of Texas indicates that the number of people whose jobs are related to the Internet increased 36 percent from 1998 to 1999. The chart in Figure 4.7 illustrates the percent changes in growth for segments of companies with netcentric activity.

Growth measured in employee increases was greatest for the infrastructure segment, at 48 percent, and least for the intermediary segment, including portals and brokers, at 17 percent. The Internet commerce segment, which included business-to-business and business-to-consumer exchanges, increased 26 percent.

FIGURE 4.6 The Internet Necessitates Adaptive Marketing Behavior.

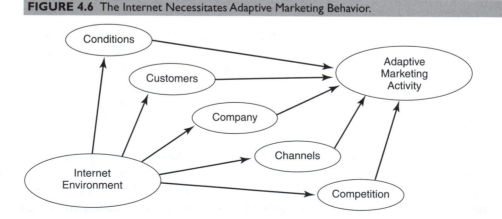

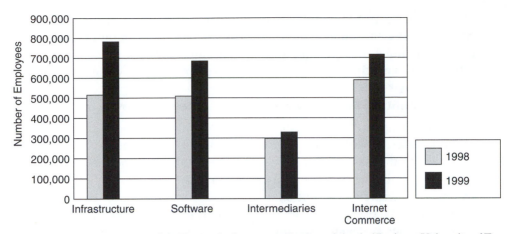

Source: The Center for Research in Electronic Commerce, Graduate School of Business, University of Texas at Austin

FIGURE 4.7 The Internet Economy Affects Employee Growth Rates.

While the Internet can provide benefits for companies in terms of new marketing opportunities and greater efficiencies in marketing processes, it also creates challenges for employee management. The results of a study by Greenfield Online, cited by eMarketer (2000), suggest that people do not limit their consumption of resources to nonwork hours. Employees play games online (21 percent), use online services to plan vacations (16 percent), look for information in the form of investment advice (16 percent), decide where to live (6 percent), look for love (3 percent), and download pornography (2 percent).

The potential for decreased employee productivity due to Web surfing has led many companies to institute employee surveillance programs to monitor Internet-related activities. **Employee Internet management software,** or EIM, was a $63 million business in 1999, and is expected to grow to a $562 million industry by 2004, according to International Data Corp.

Digital Artifact 4.3

Fifty-four percent of companies monitor employees' Internet connections, and 38 percent read employees' e-mail messages.

(*Source:* **CNN.com, July 11, 2000, citing the American Management Association.**)

While some EIM software tracks and blocks Internet activity, other forms allow employees to perform a variety of Web-based personal activities. The goal of this software, such as the employee portal provided by Abilizer Solutions, Inc., is to enable employees to carry out personal activities in a manner that does not negatively affect work performance.

Another solution to the time pressure, temptations, and increased expectations of employees created by the Internet is to provide them with the capability to work at home. Delta Air Lines and Ford Motor Company have each entered partnerships with PeoplePC that enables employees to buy personal computers and Internet access for nominal sums. Delta also provides employees with access to its corporate intranet, thus making it possible for employees to work anywhere, anytime.

Environmental Effects on Channel Structure and Power

For many companies, the Internet provides a new way to move goods to customers. In some cases, as with soft goods, the Internet itself can be used as a distribution channel. In other cases, as for hard goods, the Internet can be used to coordinate aspects of distribution, including inventory control and shipping scheduling. As we will see in Chapter 11, traditional structures for distribution can be altered. For some products, the changes enable the marketer to eliminate intermediaries, a process known as **disintermediation.** For other products, however, additional steps may need to be included. This process, termed **reintermediation,** is often observed in the Internet environment when intermediaries are added to manage the transmission of distribution-related information. These people are called **infomediaries.**

Marketers must determine the appropriate channel structures. In addition, they must also be able to meet the challenges created by the change from old channel relationships to new ones. New channel members must be identified and relationships forged in a way that does not hinder the flow of products from company to consumer.

Another challenge may arise when the environment shifts the nature of the power relationship that exists between the marketer and the channel member. For some situations, the Internet environment may increase the power of the marketer in the channel relationship. For example, a shift in power can occur when a marketer can negotiate a more favorable agreement with an existing channel participant who fears being eliminated in favor of an alternative, digital, distribution channel. In other cases, however, the channel member may be able to use the coordination capabilities of the Internet to consolidate warehousing and transportation needs, thus reducing dependence on any single marketer. In this instance, the marketer must adapt channel strategy to reflect the change in power.

Environmental Effects on Competitive Activity

The Internet creates challenges for marketers that stem from changes to the nature of competition. Several aspects of competition may be affected by the influence of the Internet on business activity. Among the effects are influences of information flow on (1) product development; (2) benefits of cooperation, versus competition; and (3) strategies for product consumption.

Internet time creates challenges for marketers in maintaining product quality and product differentiation. Shortened horizons for planning and producing new products mean that less time is available for product testing. Combined with the speed with which product information can be communicated and new product benefits can be observed, the shorter intervals between product introductions may result in decreased differentiation between products in a product category. As a result, the speed of product introductions needed to remain competitive can increase the importance of developing and maintaining a differential advantage, as well as the difficulty of accomplishing the differentiation.

The Internet environment also affects the benefits of cooperation. Changes to the nature of economic activity, such as moves toward market structures and the formation of business ecosystems, illustrate the viability of strategic alliances, rather than zero-sum approaches to competition. For example, the merger of America OnLine and Time Warner is a strategic alliance that eliminates the need for direct competition between the two companies in the online content market. Marketers must be able to identify opportunities for strategic alliances, and be prepared to delimit and defend the territorial arrangements.

Digital Artifact 4.4

Average percent increase in stock prices for pure players at IPO in 1999: 233 percent. (*Source: The Wall Street Journal*, December 27, 1999, and The Internet Index, #26.)

A third influence of the Internet environment on competition stems from the opportunities that arise in making products available for consumption. That is, with the Internet, a competitor can make the same product offering, but provide it in a way that differs from the traditional means of product consumption. The competitive challenge exists if the new form of consumption is deemed preferable by a significant proportion of current customers. For example, online trading, such as that popularized by E*TRADE and Ameritrade, provides consumers with the same service as that provided by Merrill Lynch: consumers can trade stocks. The difference is in the form of the service; the online firms enable consumers to complete their trades via the Internet. Once again, the competitive challenge enabled by the Internet underscores the importance of developing a defensible differential advantage, based on a clearly defined market segment.

Environmental Effects on Consumer Acquisition and Retention

The Internet is an information resource for consumers. For marketers, the Internet is a way to provide desirable information about their goods and services. Of course, the competition has the same opportunity. As a result, consumers are able to compare information across manufacturers and marketers with lower search costs than are encountered in many offline, traditional marketplaces. The information that consumers obtain may influence the attitudes they hold about brands, products, and companies. In addition, it may affect the behaviors they carry out, such as word-of-mouth, and purchasing. In general, more knowledgeable consumers tend to be more demanding consumers, in terms of product quality and service.

The importance of online information is illustrated by the results of a recent survey by CyberDialogue, a research organization. They found that 42 percent of the consumers they surveyed changed their impressions of a brand based on information obtained from the Internet. The sources most influential in stimulating changes to impressions were manufacturing sites (70 percent were influenced) and comparison sites (69 percent were influenced). The specific product categories that tended to be most influenced are shown in Figure 4.8.

These results are important even for marketers with little or no electronic commerce involvement. Suppose that you are an automobile dealer with absolutely no interest in the Internet. You are determined to sell cars the way you have always sold them: big holiday sales; year-end inventory clearance; tooth-and-nail negotiations between customer and manager. Unless you have a pool of customers equally determined to buy cars in the same way that you have always sold them, you may have a problem. Anybody can post information on the Internet, given the skills and equipment. This capability means that information about your product can be made available to consumers in ways over which you have no control. As a result, you must react to the effect of this information on your consumers.

Environmental Effects on Market Conditions

General market conditions, such as economics, politics, and climatic conditions, influence marketing activity. In the Internet environment, marketing activity is most directly affected by the climate of the central exchange environment. Recall that in Chapter 2, we examined the influence of technology and public policy on the exchange environment that exists between consumers and marketers. We can think of these groups as influences on political and economical conditions that, in turn, affect the activities of marketers. (To this point, weather and climatic conditions seem unperturbed by the popularity of the Internet.)

Although the Internet has existed for nearly 30 years, it is only within the last decade that marketers have focused their efforts on the marketspace medium. Technology's impact on economic conditions, however, is reflected in the fast growth in

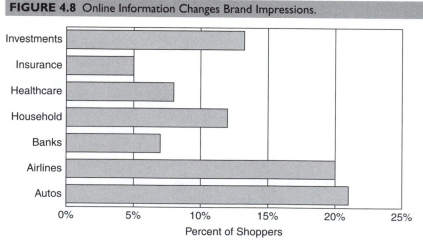

FIGURE 4.8 Online Information Changes Brand Impressions.

Source: CyberDialogue

the numbers of .com domains, and in the rapidly increasing rate of revenues related to the Internet.

The Internet was not developed with an eye toward facilitating marketing transactions, or for carrying out any of the activities typically associated with marketing exchange. As a result, marketers are faced with the need to learn how to use the technologies of the Internet, adapting business practices to make effective use of the structure and function of the digital environment.

The Internet also influences policy decisions, which themselves affect the actions that marketers can take. One challenge for marketers is the relatively undeveloped state of policy specifically directed toward use of the Internet in general, and as a venue for marketing. Issues for Internet policy, such as taxation, fraud, fair access, and copyright, are still surrounded by uncertainty about the extent to which they are concerns for the public, and about the appropriate ways to manage the situations that they create. For marketers, an evolving regulatory structure creates challenges for developing strategies that neither create nor are impeded by policy issues.

RESPONDING TO CHALLENGE: OPPORTUNITIES IN MARKETSPACE

The development of the Internet for purposes other than marketing means that many of its characteristics are not ideal for marketing situations. Marketers must be reactive in developing strategies that enable them to use the Internet for purposes unintended by its creators. In addition, marketers must be proactive in developing relationships that reflect the unique ways in which resources can be provided and obtained with the Internet. These goals are obtained by formulating strategic objectives, and by developing and implementing the strategies needed to attain them.

In this section, we will look at three strategic objectives and their implementation in the Internet environment: revenue, branding, and loyalty. Although marketers may, of course, establish other goals as bases for strategy, these three serve to illustrate the relationship between the Internet as a means of obtaining resources, and the Internet as a way to pursue marketing activities.

Strategic Objectives and the Internet Environment

We can characterize much of marketing activity as the attempt to achieve revenues, to develop a brand image, or to foster consumer loyalty. Many marketing efforts seek to address combinations of these objectives. The Internet creates opportunities for marketers to implement strategies to reach objectives that often differ from physical marketplace approaches. Let's look at three ways in which the Internet makes it possible for marketers to accomplish the strategic objectives.

Revenue and the Internet

To obtain revenue, one can always rely on the old standby: sell something to someone. The huge variety of goods and services available on the Internet illustrates the viability of this approach. With the Internet, marketers have access to global markets in which they can derive revenues from the same target segments as always, simply by adding new customers. In contrast, the wide reach of the Internet may also make possible new markets, characterized by new and different needs for an existing product, or even a new, related product.

In addition to the traditional transaction approach to revenue, however, the Internet provides new opportunities. Even though a transaction is still involved, the form of the transaction is often less clear-cut than in traditional, offline situations. For instance, marketers can gather information from consumers, as through tracking Internet search behaviors and user demographics, and then sell this information to other marketers. As a result, a consumer who may be visiting sites in order to complete transactions with the site's vendor may also be serving as the basis for an unrelated transaction that provides revenue for another marketer.

Branding and the Internet

The Internet also provides opportunities for branding. For example, a marketer can leverage consumers' needs and searches for different resources to create a brand image, even when the resource being sought is not the product offered by the marketer. For instance, consider a consumer who searches online for information about a new car. At each site visited, the consumer might encounter promotional material from another marketer, for a different product (e.g., stereo equipment, insurance policy, etc.). Of course, a traditional dealership might also make promotional information from other marketers available. Because the cost of search is higher, however, fewer consumers are likely to be exposed to the brand information.

Loyalty and the Internet

To foster consumer loyalty, marketers can use the Internet to provide information and services related to a product. In many instances, the Internet component may not provide revenue or alter brand perceptions. The availability of customer support at any hour, any day, may engender loyalty, however. With the Internet, customer support does not necessarily require interpersonal, interactive communications. Marketers can provide information about a host of typical issues in the form of frequently asked questions, or **FAQs** (see Figure 4.9). AllAdvantage.com combines FAQs with other forms of customer support, such as e-mail contacts, to provide customers with product information and assistance.

Strategic Objectives and Consumers' Resource Goals

We can look at the ways in which the Internet can be used to attain strategic objectives by considering examples in each of the six resource categories: money, information, goods, services, status, and love. The key point to remember is that the opportunities for marketers are based on consumers' needs for the resources. We will consider each resource in terms of the opportunities it provides for revenue, branding, and loyalty.

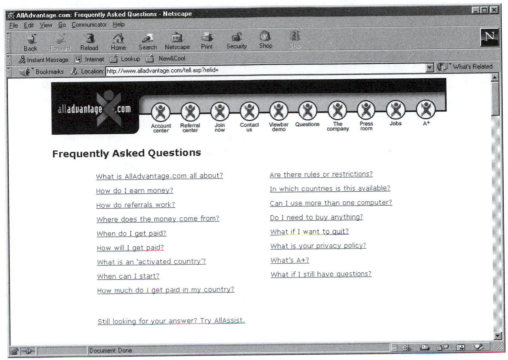

FIGURE 4.9 FAQ's Enhance Loyalty with 24/7 Customer Assistance.

Money and the Strategic Objectives

The surfing for cash opportunities provide a clear example of how consumers' need for money can be used to generate revenue. In this case, the consumer makes money by looking at information, and the marketer makes money by selling the surfing pattern and user demographic information.

Branding can occur directly, when the name of the company that is acquiring the information is provided on the user's screen. Of course, a company that places an ad on the screen through the surfing service provider may also be attempting to reinforce a brand image. For the surfing service company, branding occurs indirectly through company exposure to the user at payment time. Loyalty is also promoted through payment.

Information and the Strategic Objectives

When consumers seek information as a resource from the Internet, marketers can obtain revenue through pushed content and customized information presentation. For example, some companies enable customers to specify the types of information they want (i.e., the **channels,** such as financial news or sports scores). This information is then **pushed,** or delivered, to the customer at prearranged times, for a fee.

Online branding is often seen in information-rich sites. Companies sponsor sites, paying the site owner to mention the brand or company, and perhaps post the company's logo. High-content sites are desirable for sponsorships because consumers tend to revisit the sites to receive updated information, and because the density of content means that consumers tend to stay on the site longer, thus increasing exposure to the sponsoring brand.

Consumers' use of the Internet to acquire information also provides opportunities for marketers to encourage brand loyalty. When a marketer provides information through numerous media (e.g., television, newspaper, radio, and Internet), the consistency of the quality and format of the information across the contexts can reinforce consumers' perceptions of the product. For example, a news service that provides content in all media will encourage loyalty to that "brand" when the content is reliably high, no matter where the consumer acquires it.

Goods and the Strategic Objectives

The Internet enables marketers to obtain revenue through online sales of goods in two main ways. First, the Internet makes it possible to reach new customers (e.g., in distant markets where a marketing effort was not cost-effective prior to the Internet). Second, the Internet creates opportunities for new products (e.g., MP3).

Branding and loyalty can also be facilitated for goods on the Internet through the global reach of the Internet, and the ability to provide complementary services to support product use (e.g., customer service).

Digital Artifact 4.5

Thirty-eight percent of Web retailers are profitable.

(*Source: The Wall Street Journal,* **April 18, 2000, and the Internet Index, #27.**)

Services and the Strategic Objectives

Consumers' need to acquire services offers revenue opportunities for marketers when the services can be sold via the Internet for a fee: a direct transaction. For instance, several online services specialize in searching for and providing information about people. The customer provides information online (e.g., name, general location, age), and the service accepts a credit card number in order to initiate the search request. The results of the search are often provided to the user via e-mail. Revenues can also be obtained indirectly. A marketer can provide a service for free, and sell brand exposure for another marketer on the Web site.

Objectives of branding and loyalty are similar to those noted for goods. Marketers can use the Internet for service provision to demonstrate cutting-edge technical skills (e.g., for Web site development services), and to enable efficient, real-time interactions with consumers.

Status and the Strategic Objectives

When consumers seek status as a resource through the Internet, marketers can derive revenues from sales of luxury goods and services. For some products in which the target market is particularly small (e.g., for 50-foot luxury yachts), the Internet facilitates revenue generation by exposing the company's products to a wider range of potential consumers.

Branding can be accomplished by positioning and promoting a product online to indicate its exclusivity or scarcity. For example, providing potential consumers with easily observable information about the criteria for ownership or membership (e.g., income) communicates exclusivity.

Creating loyalty to a company and its offering through status can be accomplished by limiting the target set of consumers. Related to creating exclusivity, this approach means that a marketer can develop strategic alliances to market a status product, but that the alliances should be similar in terms of status connoted by the brands. In other words, advertising a Rolls-Royce on the K-Mart Web site may not only result in few sales, but it may also have the negative effect of reducing the status value of a Rolls-Royce.

Love and the Strategic Objectives

Leveraging love to attain strategic objectives provides marketers with many opportunities—after all, love is a many-splendoured thing, right? These opportunities reflect consumers' use of the Internet to acquire resources that demonstrate love, and resources that are means for obtaining love.

Revenues for resources that demonstrate love can be obtained through sales of items such as diamonds and flowers. For consumers who seek to acquire love, marketers can charge fees for dating services and astrological forecasts of romance possibilities.

Branding possibilities based on consumers' need to demonstrate love are reflected in the increasing prevalence of online bridal registry services. The bride selects a wish list of desired items from a single vendor, and then tells friends and family where to shop. To develop branding in cases where consumers seek love via the Internet, a marketer can identify and promote his products or services on sites that are likely to be visited, such as personal ads and dating services.

Marketers can use consumers' need to obtain love to promote brand loyalty. The foundation of loyalty and love based on commitment reflects the importance of time and the recognition of what the other party in the relationship deems important. As a result, marketing efforts that reflect the recognition of commitment will foster loyalty more effectively than those that fail to recognize the basis for the relationship. For example, an online jeweler might send anniversary reminders via e-mail to favored clients.

Chapter Summary

In this chapter, we have examined the role of the marketer in the exchange environment of the Internet. We began by considering several dimensions with which marketing entities in marketspace can be described, including product focus (e.g., product categories) and customer focus (i.e., business-to-consumer versus business-to-business). In addition, we used the concepts of electronic commerce involvement and netcentricity to develop additional insights into the relationship between marketers and the online environment.

To further our understanding of the Internet as an influence on marketing activity, we considered its effect on the ways companies structure themselves to take advantage of Internet capabilities. We also considered the effect of the Internet on the characteristics of processes that companies carry out.

The changes to structure and process underscore the need for companies to adapt to the Internet environment. The changes that companies make often reflect challenges to the effectiveness of previous marketing strategy. We looked at five different sources of challenges, and at the impact of the Internet on each source. These sources are company, channels, competition, customers, and conditions.

Marketers are used to adapting. Marketers make changes to products, and to the way they are presented, based on shifts in consumer preferences and on developments in technology that enable the production of products that satisfy needs. This concept is the essence of marketing. The Internet, however, not only introduces opportunities for product changes, but for changes to the processes for conducting marketing activity. These changes are not limited to the facets of marketing that are visible to consumers; the Internet may affect the basic processes by which companies operate to produce and distribute goods and services.

We examined the opportunities that can arise from the need to adapt. These opportunities are characterized by three different marketing objectives: (1) increasing revenues, (2) developing brand image, and (3) fostering consumer loyalty. We built on the resource needs elaborated in Chapter 3 to discuss the ways in which marketers can use the Internet environment to achieve strategic objectives. Marketing opportunities were illustrated by determining marketing actions related to specific strategic objectives, based on the types of resources sought by consumers, and by the way in which they attempt to obtain the resources using the Internet.

Looking Ahead

In Chapters 3 and 4, we looked at the characteristics and activities of the two main sets of people in the central exchange environment: consumers and marketers. These groups exert a direct and bidirectional influence on each other. In Chapters 5 and 6, we will continue to examine the relationships that exist in the marketing environment of the Internet, by looking at the influence of technology and policy on the exchange environment of marketers and consumers.

REVIEW SECTION

Key Terms

- pure-player companies
- business-to-consumer (B2C)
- business-to-business (B2B)
- front-end applications
- back-end applications
- continuum of electronic commerce
- netcentricity

- brochureware
- platform approach
- Internet time
- information acceleration
- workflow software
- intranets
- firewalls
- outside intranetting
- extranets

- adaptivity
- Employee Internet management (EIM)
- disintermediation
- reintermediation
- infomediaries
- FAQs
- channels
- pushed information

Review Questions

1. How is a pure-player company different from a traditional company?
2. Why is the predicted revenue potential greater for the business-to-business approach to online sales than for the business-to-consumer?
3. Distinguish between front-end and back-end applications.
4. Discuss the four phases of the continuum of electronic commerce.
5. What is netcentricity?
6. How does the Internet environment affect the way that companies organize themselves for business activity?
7. How are intranets different from extranets?
8. What five factors have been traditionally considered to be outside the realm of marketers' control?
9. Discuss the ways in which the Internet environment changes the approach to adapting to the Five Cs.
10. What three strategic objectives constitute the marketing focus? How can marketers use the Internet to achieve these strategic objectives?

Thinking Points

1. The marketspace can be described in terms of company type (e.g., pure-player vs. hybrid), product focus, or customer focus. Why are three different descriptions possible? How might the conclusions a marketer could draw about the online marketplace differ, depending on the perspective adopted?
2. What factors might affect the desirability of moving toward greater e-commerce involvement, as characterized by the four-phase continuum of involvement? That is, what characteristics of companies are likely to provide the greatest benefits from increasing integration of e-commerce into business practices?

3. The Internet can influence changes to business structures and processes. Consider the implications of adopting either a proactive or a reactive approach to implementing structural and procedural changes. What are the potential costs and benefits of each approach?

4. Marketing activity must adapt to changes in each of the Five Cs. How does the Internet environment necessitate adaptation? That is, what are possible effects of the Internet on each factor, and how might these effects create a need to adapt?

5. How can the Internet be used to facilitate adaptation to each of the Five Cs?

6. The Internet can be used in many different ways to meet strategic objectives of revenue, branding, and loyalty. Identify some of the ways in which strategies for reaching these objectives with the Internet differ from strategies that might be used in traditional marketing environments.

7. Does the Internet change the nature of these strategic objectives? That is, what differences distinguish how we think of branding and loyalty in marketspace, compared to marketplace views?

Suggested Readings

1. "Work Remade: An Electronic Marketplace Inside the Corporation," by David Braunschvig. In *The Future of the Electronic Marketplace,* edited by Derek Leebaert (Cambridge, MA: The MIT Press, 1998), pp. 177–205.

2. "Get the Right Mix of Bricks and Clicks," by Ranjay Gulati and Jason Garino. *Harvard Business Review, 78,* 3 (2000), pp. 107–114.

3. "Evolution of the Marketing Organization: New Forms for Turbulent Environments,"
by Ravi S. Achrol. *Journal of Marketing, 55* (October 1991), pp. 77–93.

4. "Twelve Themes of the New Economy," and "The Internetworked Business at Work," in *The Digital Economy,* by Don Tapscott. (New York: McGraw-Hill, 1996).

5. "How It Works," by Mohanbir Sawhney, Alicia Neumann, Kim Cross, Mark Leon, Sean Donahue, and Carol Pickering. Edited by Jeffrey Davis. *Business 2.0* (February 2000), pp. 112–140.

CHAPTER 5

Technology and the Internet Environment

FOCUS AND OBJECTIVES

In this chapter we examine the Internet environment from a technological perspective. In addition to creating the possibility for a marketspace, technology developers often work hand-in-hand with marketers to produce products and services that enable and enhance marketing activity. To understand the nature of the relationship between technologists and the marketing environment of the Internet, we briefly discuss the history and technological characteristics of the Internet. Then we examine the influence of technology on the relationships that exist in the exchange environment of the Internet.

YOUR OBJECTIVES IN STUDYING THIS CHAPTER INCLUDE THE FOLLOWING:

- Develop familiarity with the basic structure and terminology of the Internet.
- Understand the technological implications of the Internet as a communications channel for the end user.
- Learn the primary types of Internet access and their associated demographics.
- Recognize and understand the impact of technology on the of the end user's Internet experience.
- Identify implications of Internet technology for the marketer and the consumer perspectives.

In earlier chapters, we have described the Internet environment, and the marketers and consumers who carry out exchanges within the environment. We have considered the role of the Internet in making available to us an abundance of information, ease of communications, and wide varieties of goods and services.

Because the Internet has gained popularity and acceptance, and grown so rapidly, it is easy to forget that the Internet of today is vastly different from the

Internet of just 10 years ago. The technologies that have resulted in the arrays of networks and the software that make the networks useful are changing daily. The pace of these changes underscores the importance of recognizing the influence of technology on marketing activity in the Internet environment.

Despite the fact that the Internet was not developed for marketing purposes, it has been quickly adopted for commercial use. In order to facilitate marketing applications on the Internet, technologists have focused attention on the development of hardware and software that augment present capabilities and present new opportunities. These technological developments create the Internet environment in which marketers and consumers interact. As a result, it is important to understand the basic technology of the Internet.

A rudimentary knowledge of the technological aspects of the Internet is desirable for two main reasons. First, the technological characteristics of the environment impose constraints on what marketers and consumers can do in terms of exchange relationships. In addition, the technology can create opportunities for new marketing activities. Being aware of the ways in which technology can help or hinder marketing activity can improve the outcome of marketing action. Second, given the changing nature of the Internet as a marketing environment, it is useful to understand how technological factors have influenced the development of the central exchange environment, as a way to anticipate how they might affect subsequent changes. Being able to predict changes means that you can be proactive in developing marketing strategy, rather than having to react to unexpected situations by adapting existing approaches.

In this chapter, we will begin with a brief look at the nuts and bolts of Internet technology. Because it is such a complex area, a discussion of the history, challenges, and techniques that reflect the development of the present-day Internet is far beyond the scope of this text. Our goal is to describe enough of the technical underpinnings to illustrate the impact of technology on marketing practice, and to suggest some of the ways in which future technological development may alter current marketing activities.

We will begin by considering the technologies of the Internet as a channel to transfer information between points. We will then take a brief look at the channel components, and at some of the technological characteristics that make them work. The technical background will provide a basis with which we can consider the relationships that exist between technologists and other groups in the Internet environment.

Digital Artifact 5.1

Approximately 98 percent of the words in *Webster's English Dictionary* have been registered as domain names.

(*Source: The Wall Street Journal*, April 24, 2000, and the Internet Index, #27.)

THE TECHNOLOGY THAT MAKES THE INTERNET POSSIBLE

A common description of the Internet is that it is a "network of networks." Of course, networks existed long before the Internet was begun. Most of us are familiar with a number of different applications of networks, such as television and radio networks, and networks of friends and acquaintances.

What Is a Network?

The importance of a network becomes clear if you stop and think about what a network does. Typically, a network is a set of connections between otherwise discrete, separate entities, such as people or computers. People throughout history have joined together in communities in which networks of human interaction convey social values, daily events, and plans for activities that foster the well-being of the individual within the community, and the community within the larger environment.

Marketers have long counted on networks of consumers to spread favorable word-of-mouth about products. These **referral networks** are often fast, efficient means of communicating information. Suppose that one consumer tries a product, likes it, and recommends it to two friends. Then these two friends try it, like it, and each recommends it to two more friends. Next, the friends of the original friends try the product, like it, and . . . you get the idea! The number of people who may potentially be exposed to word-of-mouth information about the product grows rapidly. This phenomenon is often described as **viral marketing,** because the pattern of communication reflects the pattern with which an especially contagious virus might move through a set of interacting hosts.

The Internet is an important tool for viral marketing. The results of a study by Roper Starch Worldwide, released in June 2000, indicate that 8 percent of American Internet users are **e-fluentials.** E-fluentials are people who influence others' Internet-related behaviors. In offline environments, word-of-mouth tends to be spread from one person to two other people. E-fluentials disseminate information to an average of eight people. In addition, people are four times more likely to seek the advice of e-fluentials on business and technology issues than of average users.

The underlying concept behind the viral marketing technique is that people will interact with other people. The speed with which the information is disseminated depends on the nature of the network that exists between the people. The ultimate number of people exposed to the information depends on the size of the network. Although viral marketing describes a single direction of information flow in a network, networks are often characterized by repeated interaction between network members. This ability to interact contributes to the value of the network.

The size of the network also contributes to its value as a means of communication. To illustrate the relation between size and value, think about a simple network between two people. Assuming that neither is schizophrenic, the number of conversations that occurs between the two people is just one. If you add one more person to the network, you have the possibility of three conversations. Things get even more interesting if you add a fourth person, because now the potential is six conversations. The basic idea is that the more people you add to the network, the greater the value of the network as a means of transmitting information. In addition, the value of each additional person increases, because the number of conversation links introduced by the new person is greater than the number contributed by any prior entrant to the network. These ideas are illustrated in Figure 5.1, and are often referred to as Metcalfe's Law.

A Network of Networks

The idea of networking computers into what we now recognize as the Internet gained interest (and funding) in the 1960s, even though widespread implementation and adoption of the technology as a medium for marketing did not occur until the 1990s. The value of a network of computers through which scientific advances could be communicated lay in its ability to make computing resources, as well as research results, quickly and widely available. This capability meant that resources did not have to be duplicated, thus saving time and money.

A Distributed Network Architecture

The actual structure of the network that connected the earliest computers of the Internet (first known as ARPAnet, for Advanced Research Projects Association) reflects the point in history at which the networking effort occurred. During the Cold War, national defense efforts dictated the need for a decentralized network with redundant connections between points. This redundancy means that if any one connection is eliminated, as through an enemy attack, other connections can be used to complete a transmission. This type of network is called a distributed network. The difference between a centralized network and a distributed network is shown in Figure 5.2.

The value of a network can only be fully realized if all of the points connected by the network communicate in the same language. For the Internet, two aspects of communications "languages" are relevant. One is the way in which information is translated into a common tongue for all computers, and another is the way in which the information is moved between the networked computers, or the **Internet protocols** (IP).

FIGURE 5.1 Network Value Increases with Network Size.

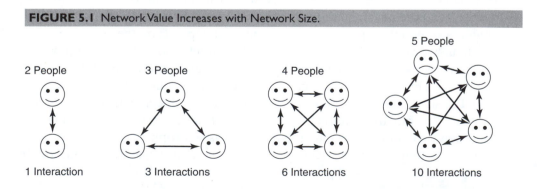

2 People — 1 Interaction

3 People — 3 Interactions

4 People — 6 Interactions

5 People — 10 Interactions

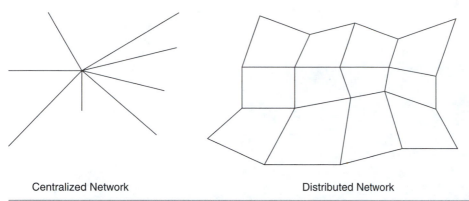

Centralized Network   Distributed Network

FIGURE 5.2 Network Structures Take Different Forms.

A Digital Language

The information being transmitted over a computer network is encoded in a **digital format.** This format is an alternative to sending a physical instance of an item (e.g., a sweater) or a physical analog of an item (e.g., a photo of a sweater). With a digital transmission, binary computer code transforms information into digital ones and zeros that, in unique combinations, serve as symbols for their physical counterparts. For instance, a 1 is represented as a 1, but the number 2 is a 10, while 3 is an 11. Applied similarly to letters, these combinations of 1s and 0s can be represented in a computer as the presence or absence of electrical signals. Although the earliest efforts to digitize information focused on letters and numbers, current techniques enable fast digitization of graphical images, such as photographs and pictures, as well as auditory signals, such as voices or music.

Information stored in a digital form is stored in **bits.** Digitization enables rapid transmission of bits across computer networks. Digital information is available through many sources. For example, digital cell phones and televisions transmit information. The same information can also be transferred over a computer network, such as the Internet. Figure 5.3 describes how images are digitized for transmission.

Moving Bits with Packets

Being able to digitize information means that a symbol or a whole idea, such as an image, can be broken up into parts. The bits are divided into **packets** (also known as **datagrams**), which are then sent out across the network. The network consists of many possible paths a packet could take, and the packets that make up a single message might travel by different routes. The packets wind up in the right place, and are reassembled in the proper order, because each packet leaves the originating computer with the Internet address from which it came, and the Internet address to which it should arrive.

An obvious question is that of how the computers on the network all know how to correctly read the address information, so that they can forward the packets properly. This problem is addressed by Internet protocols that enable computers to "talk" with each other. These protocols are agreed-on standards for encoding and

(255,0,0) (128,135,53) (126,137,55)
(255,1,4) (130,140,50) (128,141,53)
(255,3,7) (133,142,49) (131,152,51)

Above is the binary representation of the first column of the 3 by 3 matrix.

(11111111,00000000,00000000)
(11111111,00000001,00000100)
(11111111,00000011,00000111)

Above is the numeric (decimal) representation of a 3 by 3 block of "pixels" from the picture on the left.

Computers store images as an array of pixel values, where each pixel represents a color at a particular position in the picture. The image above is an array of 387 by 242 pixels. The pixel colors are typically represented as a combination of three colors, red, green, and blue. The color of a pixel is represented, therefore, by three values, one value each for red, green, and blue. For example, if a 3 by 3 block of pixels was extracted from the picture above, the (red, green, blue) values would look like those in the upper shaded box. The computer stores these color values, like all other data, in a binary representation as shown in the lower shaded box.

FIGURE 5.3 The Nature of Digital Information.

transferring information. On the Internet, TCP/IP stands for Transfer Control Program/Internet Protocol. The Internet Protocol contains the address information that tells a computer where to send the packet. The network protocols are standards for communication.

INTERNET TECHNOLOGIES AS A CHANNEL

With the ability to digitize information and to transmit it over a distributed network in packets, we have the foundation of the Internet. Numerous steps, however, make up the transmission process that gets information from the Internet to the computer of any particular user. In this section, we will look at the technological aspects associated with the channel of communications that constitutes the Internet.

When you sit down to read an e-mail or to look up information on the Internet, the part of the information channel most salient to you is probably the computer at your desk. The end user and the local computing equipment are the first component of the channel.

Of course, aspects of technology are also related to getting the information from the outside world (e.g., an e-mail from a friend at another university, or an order update from an online merchant) into your computer. We will consider the technologies by which information reaches the end user as a second component of a computer communications channel. A third component of our communications channel consists of the computing infrastructure that makes it possible to move information over the Internet. These three components are shown in Figure 5.4.

The User at the End of the Channel

Advances in technology have enabled developers to reduce the costs of producing sophisticated computing equipment, as well as the size of the equipment. In the 1950s, computers—used primarily for doing complex mathematical calculations—filled entire rooms. High levels of technical expertise were required to cajole intelligible output from the machines.

Over the years, the cost of technology has decreased and the capabilities of computing equipment have increased. These changes have made it possible for people to buy personal computers for home and work applications that would have been unimaginable just a few decades ago. The desire to own a personal computer, as well as the increasing affordability of the equipment, will result in sales of 45 million PCs in the United States in 2000 (eTForecasts). The demand for PCs is reflected in the year-to-year increase in the estimated number of homes with computers in the United States (see Figure 5.5).

From the end user's point of view, the technologies that are most relevant for effective Internet consumption tend to be those related to the quality of the Internet experience enabled by the personal computer. In terms of hardware, quality concerns include issues of **resolution** (clarity of screen images), **memory** (amount of computer storage), **speed** (rate at which the computer processes information), and **sound** (quality of audio data). For software, usage issues at the end-user level include concerns with the user-friendliness of the software, such as how easy the software is to install and learn to use. In addition, software concerns revolve around flexibility, or the extent to which the software makes it possible for the user to manipulate and produce content.

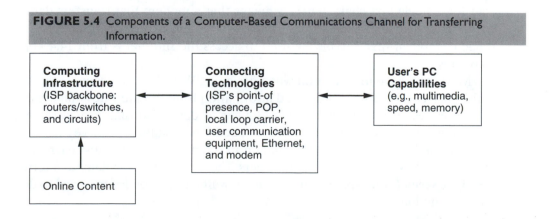

FIGURE 5.4 Components of a Computer-Based Communications Channel for Transferring Information.

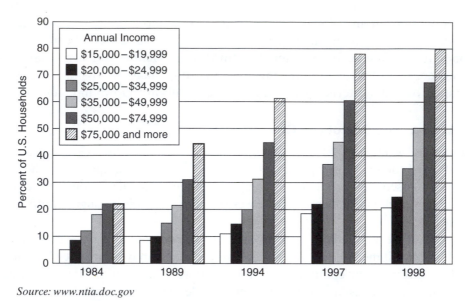

Source: www.ntia.doc.gov

FIGURE 5.5 Increases in the Number of Computers in the Home, Across Income Levels.

Access to Computer Communications

The quality of the Internet experience for the end user is also influenced by the technologies that bring the digital content to the desktop computer. For this purpose, two different classes of technologies are important: the equipment that transmits the content, and the service that provides access to the Internet.

Internet Connection: Equipment

The hardware options that enable a user to connect to the Internet differ in terms of connection speed and reliability. Most people connect to the Internet from home with a **dial-up modem.** Modems connect computers to the Internet through telephone lines. They vary widely in the speed with which they can transfer data. Speed is measured in bits per second, or bps, and it takes approximately 10 bits to transfer a single text character. This means that a modem that transfers data at a speed of 28.8 kbps can send a page of text in around two-thirds of a second. The range of modem speeds typically used to access the Internet is from 14.4 kbps to 56.6 kbps.

Marketers have to be careful when designing Web sites to recognize the speed with which consumers can download information from the site. Sites that are dense with graphics or animation may take longer to download than users are willing to wait, given the constraint of modem speed. The results of a survey conducted by ActivMedia suggest that $4.35 million in online revenue are lost each year to marketers whose sites frustrate consumers. These results are explained in terms of the **eight-second rule**—people are willing to wait eight seconds for a page to download, but no longer!

Other connection options tend to be more expensive than modems, and they are often not readily available in many areas. These options include **ISDN** lines, **DSL** lines, **cable,** and **wireless** (e.g., satellite) options. These technologies enable the user to transfer data from the Internet more quickly, and with fewer glitches in data transfer, than with standard modem technology. The chart in Figure 5.6 shows the reported connection speeds of a survey of nearly 3,000 users with different methods of Internet access.

Internet Connection: Service

The Internet operates much like a relay, or the Pony Express of the 1800s; data packets are transferred from computer to computer until they reach their destination. Connecting to the Internet works similarly. A user gets access to the Internet through an **Internet service provider (ISP),** which allows the user to connect to its computer, which is connected to other computers on the Internet. Many users connect to the Internet through online service companies, such as America Online and Compuserve. These companies not only provide Internet access, but also a host of other services and content. The table in Figure 5.7 indicates the popularity of various access services.

The Outside World

Internet service providers enable users to receive and transmit information from their own computers to other computers connected to the Internet. The computing infrastructure that makes possible the transfer of massive amounts of information every second depends on the availability of acceptable bandwidth. **Bandwidth** describes the speed with which information can be sent over telecommunications lines. It is measured in bits per second (bps). High bandwidth is similar to a large pipe: more stuff can be sent through it. The large amounts of bandwidth needed to connect the many Internet computers together are available from **backbone providers,** such as Sprint and MCI. These companies not only provide bandwidth, they may also run the services needed by many companies to carry out their Internet activities. These backbone providers are strategically located near areas of high bandwidth infrastructure (e.g., Washington, D.C.).

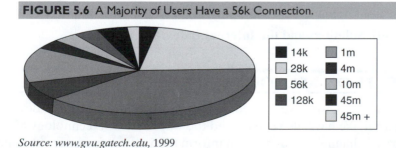

FIGURE 5.6 A Majority of Users Have a 56k Connection.

14k	1m
28k	4m
56k	10m
128k	45m
	45m +

Source: www.gvu.gatech.edu, 1999

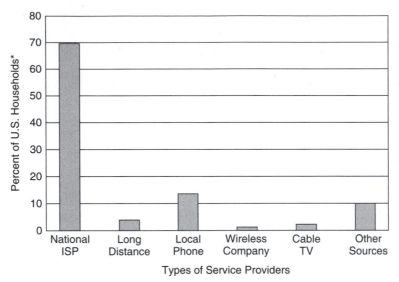

*Based on a sample of 48,000 households.

Source: www.ntia.doc.gov, 1999

FIGURE 5.7 Most Users Access the Internet Through National Service Providers.

A Unified Channel Structure

One outgrowth of the technological development in the Internet environment is the increase in strategic alliances and shared focus between the industries that provide computer-based communications. The content viewed by a user on a personal computer is made available by the development of digital communications technologies that in turn rely on the computing infrastructure. This process reflects the convergence of objectives and abilities in three key industries: content, communications, and computing. Alliances between companies in these areas often stem from the recognition of new opportunities for products and services (e.g., personalized content for users). In addition, the alliances, such as the formal merger of Time-Warner and America Online, represent strategic adaptation. Strategies for coexistence provide the companies—and industries—with competitive advantages for growth in the Internet environment.

Digital Artifact 5.2

Fourteen percent of domain names are purchased by consumers.

(*Source:* **Network Solutions and the Internet Index, #27.)**

CHANNEL EFFECTS ON RELATIONSHIPS

In the preceding sections, we have looked at the role of technology in the development of the Internet. We have also considered the ways in which technology affects the computer-based channel through which information moves from person to person. These investigations have focused solely on the role of technology in the Internet environment.

The effects of technology in the Internet environment can also be examined through the relationships between elements of the exchange environment. Three components of the set of relationships in the Internet marketing context are presented in Figure 5.8. We will consider the effects of technology on the central exchange environment that exists between marketers and consumers. In addition, we can examine the relationships that exist between technologists and marketers, and between technologists and consumers.

Technology and the Central Exchange Environment

We begin by considering the nature of the effect of technology on the central environment for exchange. This effect is illustrated by the two arrows in Figure 5.8 that drop from the technology node to the arrows that connect consumers and marketers.

Technology can influence the relationship between exchange agents in two different ways. First, technology can enable the exchange, by making it possible for the two agents to communicate. For example, with the Internet, a consumer can conduct a worldwide search for a particular product, establish contact with a vendor on the other side of the globe, negotiate an exchange, complete the transaction, and arrange delivery. Without the Internet, any or all of these activities might be impossible.

Second, technology can affect the nature of the exchange between the two agents. Suppose that the scenario we just considered could occur without the Internet. For example, an explorer—like Columbus—could sail from Europe to India in search of spices, conduct the negotiation and transaction, and bring the spices home. With the Internet, however, characteristics of the exchange can change dramatically. At a minimum, the time and human effort to conduct the search can be reduced. In addition, errors in the process may be reduced—like tripping over the New World in route to India. As a result, even when the Internet does not determine whether an exchange relation can exist, it can influence the nature of the relationship.

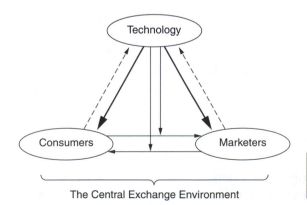

FIGURE 5.8 Technology Relationships in the Internet Environment.

These two situations illustrate the ways in which the technological environment can mediate or moderate the nature of the exchange relationship. These different effects are not unique to the Internet environment. Any time the interaction between two entities is affected by a third factor, one of the two effects is operative. In research terminology, these effects are referred to as **mediating effects** and **moderating effects.** A mediating effect occurs when the presence of a variable, such as technology, determines whether the relationship exists. In contrast, a moderating effect occurs when the presence of the variable affects the nature of the relationship, but does not determine whether the relationship exists.

Mediating and Moderating Effects of Internet Technology

Computing technologies provide the means by which marketers and consumers can connect in the Internet environment. In this sense, the Internet exerts a mediating influence on the relationship; without the Internet, relationship would not exist.

A **computer-mediated environment** is a link between agents that is characterized by information technology (e.g., the computer) and interactivity or the ability to restructure the information environment.

Because the information technology imposes a computing environment between the two people in the communication, we can distinguish between the effects of person interactivity and machine interactivity on the nature of the relationship. When we think about an interaction between two people, such as a salesperson and a consumer, we can describe the nature of the interaction in terms of **person interactivity.** That is, we can consider all of the signals and content transmitted by each person as a way to facilitate understanding of what is being communicated. When we put a computer in the center of the communication, we introduce the possibility for machine interactivity. **Machine interactivity** refers to the nature of the relationship between one of the agents and the computing environment. If a consumer has difficulty interacting with the computer environment and withdraws from the effort, a marketer's attempt to create an exchange relationship may be in vain.

The person-machine relationship may also affect the nature of the relationship that develops between the two human agents. In this sense, the effect of the computing environment serves to moderate the human relationship. As a result, the computer-mediated environment moderates the central exchange environment. Although it sounds complicated, the underlying notion is straightforward: the technology of the Internet environment may influence the ways that people interact through the Internet. The trickier part, for marketers and for researchers, is trying to figure out how to predict the nature of the Internet's influence.

The Salience of Technology

One factor that may affect the extent to which the computer-mediated environment moderates relationships and influences individual behavior is the salience of the computing environment to the user. That is, if the environment is unusual, unexpected, or necessitates changes to ordinary patterns of behavior, then it may occupy a more central position in a person's thoughts and actions. Because the Internet is a relatively novel environment for many people, it may receive greater attention and affect the nature of communications between agents more strongly than might other communications environments. As the Internet becomes a more typical venue for consumption, the effects of the technical environment on interaction may become less pronounced.

We can see how this might work by considering the reaction of young children to communications technologies. The immediate reaction of a toddler when handed a telephone with Grandma on the other end tends to be that of fascination with a new, talking toy. The next reaction is a perplexed look and a desire to get Grandma out of the receiver. A similar "how-do-they-do-that?" concern is raised when children acquire sufficient cognition to express curiosity about how the little people get into the television. Invariably, however, the novelty of the telephone and television as communications media decreases with familiarity until the technology is taken for granted and the medium is simply a vehicle for conveying and acquiring information.

One goal for developing technology is to make it easy for people to experience the computer-mediated environment, without the technology creating a barrier to the experience. Meeting this goal occurs when the salience of the technology is reduced, and the perceived experience of the environment is increased. In lay terms, this simply means that the objective is to make the communications experience via the Internet just like being there—wherever "there" may be.

To create computer-based environments that are the next best thing to being there, we need to understand the factors that affect perception of the environment. **Telepresence** is a concept developed to reflect the combined influence of technological factors and personal experience in the perception of the computer-based environment.

Telepresence in the Moderated Environment

The literal meaning of telepresence is reflected in its roots. "Tele," from Greek, means far off, while "presence" refers to nearness. A more complete description of telepresence is credited largely to Jonathan Steuer, who defined telepresence as "the extent to which one feels present in the mediated environment, rather than in the immediate physical environment." In other words, the perceived distance between the person and the environment being perceived is reduced or eliminated when telepresence is high.

In Steuer's description of telepresence, vividness and interactivity are two dimensions on which technological factors influence a person's perception of the environment. **Vividness** is "the ability of the technology to produce a sensorially rich, mediated environment." **Interactivity** is "the degree to which the user can influence the form or structure of the environment." Figure 5.9 illustrates the relationship between the two dimensions of telepresence, and the factors that create vividness and interactivity.

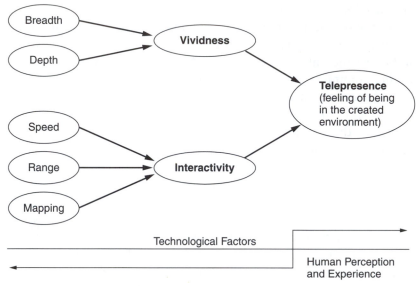

Source: Adapted from Steuer, 1992

FIGURE 5.9 Dimensions of Telepresence.

Vividness increases with **sensory breadth** and **sensory depth.** That is, the more senses that are involved in the perception of an experience, the more vivid the experience is perceived to be. For example, a mediated environment designed to convey information about a farmer's market would have greater sensory breadth if you could not only see the fruits and vegetables, but you could also touch and smell them. Sensory depth refers to the quality of the sensory experience: that is, the ability of the environment to convey the intensity of the sensory experience. In an online farmer's market, greater sensory depth would be achieved if the environment could actually provide the smell of fresh produce, rather than relying on words to convey the experience. Higher levels of vividness increase the reality of the perceived experience.

Interactivity is enhanced by three factors: speed, range, and mapping. Each of these factors is influenced by technological capabilities. **Interactivity speed** refers to rate at which the user's input affects the structure or form of the environment. For example, clicking on a menu of options in a Web site provides a new screen display. The faster the new screen appears, thus demonstrating the user's impact on the environment, the higher the level of perceived interactivity.

Range describes the size of the set of actions that a user could carry out to affect the nature of the mediated environment. Greater range is related to higher interactivity. A Web site that enables the user to pick and choose among several options or formats for viewing information would create stronger perceptions of interactivity than a "one-size-fits-all" graphical display.

The third factor that influences interactivity is mapping. **Mapping** refers to the extent to which the user's actions in modifying the environment correspond to changes in the environment. Early computer games required the user to work in a textual mode, typing in verbal commands to move through virtual rooms. Technological advances have made it possible to guide a virtual person through seemingly three-dimensional spaces by moving a joystick or by turning a wheel in the desired direction of travel. The improved match between the user action and movement within the environment increases perceived interactivity.

For marketers, the technological developments that increase interactivity and vividness can be tailored to create environments that increase the likelihood of telepresence. It is important to note, however, that while marketers can use technological factors to promote telepresence, the ultimate perception of the experience is subjective. That is, an environment that one person finds highly vivid and interactive might be perceived as hopelessly dull or frustrating to someone else. (This subjectivity of experience is the same reason for the wide variation in spectator reactions to televised golf games—from completely engrossed to utterly stupefied.)

Communications in Place and Time

The concept of telepresence captures the idea that people respond to situations, or environments, differently depending on the extent to which the environment is perceived to be distant or near. For marketing, forms of communications can be characterized as environments that differ in perceived distance. For instance, a salesperson may be standing right in front of you, or communicate with you by telephone.

We can consider the Internet, as well as traditional environments, as differing not only in terms of physical distance, but also in terms of time. The table in Figure 5.10 classifies technologically created communications environments by place and time. For each dimension, synchronicity indicates no distance, while asynchronicity indicates at least some distance.

An interesting characteristic of the computer environment of the Internet is that it is closer to a real-world, face-to-face encounter with another person than are many other forms of traditional marketing communications. One impact of technology on the marketing environment has been to bring the interaction between agents in the exchange environment full circle. Prior to the Internet, the most sensorially rich,

FIGURE 5.10 Time and Place as Dimensions of Communications Media.

Time	Place	
	Synchronous	*Asynchronous*
Synchronous	Face-to-face Internet	Telephone Live broadcast Live radio broadcast
Asynchronous	Notes Phonemail	Mail (letters, brochures) Prerecorded television Prerecorded radio

interactive environment between buyers and sellers existed in local marketplaces, with face-to-face interactions. Even though the Internet cannot provide exchange agents with the full complement of sensory stimulation, its potential for telepresence is greater than that of other media. In addition, shortcomings in sensory richness may be compensated by the ability of the Internet to facilitate a sense of being there—even when "there" is thousands of miles away.

Digital Artifact 5.3

The domain name *business.com* was bought in 1997 for $150,000. It was sold in 1999 for $7.5 million.

(*Source:* **Hobbes Internet Timeline at *www.isoc.org*.**)

The Technology and Marketer Relationship

The effects of Internet technologies extend beyond their influence on the central environment for exchange. The relationship between technology and marketing affects the types of marketing processes carried out by companies, as well as the types of products and services that can be provided. Technology is a basic force in determining the nature of the Internet environment; its effects serve in some ways to facilitate marketing efforts, and in others, to inhibit them.

Facilitating Effects on Processes

Internet technologies can increase the speed and cost-effectiveness of business processes. Two main categories of marketing applications illustrate the facilitating effect of technology: research processes and transaction-oriented applications. Both of these categories reflect the central importance of information to the marketing organization.

For research processes, the Internet enables marketers to gather information for primary and for secondary marketing research. Information from prospective consumers can be collected from online focus groups, chat rooms, and online surveys. Secondary data can be acquired from published data, as well as through online databases. We will look at the use of the Internet for marketing research in greater detail in Chapter 9.

The technologies of the Internet also make it possible for marketers to provide information, either to an end user or to other business partners as part of the value chain processes. For example, affiliate programs and technologies that enable marketers to provide targeted advertising lure consumers to Web sites. In addition, content management technologies can be used to create online catalogs of goods and services designed to meet the needs of targeted segments. At an even more individualized level, product configuration software allows consumers to customize products from an array of options. With a purchase decision made, technologies for money transfers streamline online transactions. All aspects of the process may be tracked, recorded, and used for future, personalized marketing activity by means of data-mining software.

Inhibiting Effects on Processes

Technology may also inhibit marketing activity. For instance, the rapid pace with which technology has changed the nature of the marketing environment may lead to hastened obsolescence of the very technologies that create benefits right now for marketers. This concern underscores several possible benefits for marketers of being a follower in technology adoption, rather than a leader.

First, decreasing costs of technological innovation may make it cost-effective to adopt a follower position. Second, as acceptance of online activities increases, both for marketers and for consumers, the opportunities for returns on online investments may also be higher for followers than for leaders. Third, strategic advantages may be obtained for followers who can benefit from a larger knowledge base of how to leverage specific online technologies, learning from the efforts—and mistakes—of leaders.

The Technology and Consumer Relationship

Consumers in the Internet environment are also influenced by and interact with technologists. As a general description, technological influences on consumer behavior can be classified as issues related to accessing the medium, and issues related to using the medium's content.

Interface Capabilities

The Internet user population has shifted from its early base of scientists and computer technologists to a broader base of mainstream users and commercial applications. The shift has created a need for technical development intended to create user-friendly interfaces between computers and the people who use them. Researchers who address this aspect of technology development typically work in the area of **human factors,** or **human-computer interface (HCI).** Much of the work conducted by researchers in this area deals with issues of machine interactivity, with an objective of decreasing the difficulty with which people can make use of computer technologies.

Resource Discovery

Technology development has also been focused on problems that arise when consumers attempt to use the Internet as an information resource. A key issue is resource discovery. **Resource discovery** refers to the results of the cognitive and behavioral processes people use to find information, to store and retrieve acquired information, and to customize information, using online resources.

Internet technologies make available vast information resources for consumers. Although information availability can facilitate the acquisition of desired information, the sheer mass of information to be searched can make the hunt for useful information difficult. As we learned in Chapter 3, users can be overloaded with information to the detriment of decision quality.

Current efforts to develop search technologies that can assist people in sifting through information have focused on the difference between browsing and searching behaviors. These behaviors differ in terms of the extent to which people can specify characteristics of the desired information before they initiate the search, with lower levels of specification usually observed for browsing. To develop useful search technology, the developers must understand the interaction between the structure of information in memory—how knowledge categories are organized—and the retrieval of stored information for use as a guide for online searching.

Digital Artifact 5.4

Lost productivity (6,882 person years) and sales opportunities due to computer viruses will cost U.S. businesses $266 billion in 2000.

(*Source:* **CyberAltas, 2000, citing a study by PricewaterhouseCoopers.**)

Technology and Security

Technology influences the activities of marketers and consumers in the exchange environment. While technology can facilitate exchange, it also raises issues for online marketing activity when technology is misused. Of particular importance for marketers is the potential for unauthorized access into databases and network systems. For example, marketers must manage concerns associated with the protection of consumer information online, such as credit card numbers and social security numbers.

Many companies store transaction-related information. If the information, such as a set of credit card numbers, in stored in a plain text file on a computer, it is readable by anyone with access to the computer. One solution is to encrypt the file.

Encryption is a software technique that enhances security by coding messages so that they cannot be read by anyone who does not have the ability to decode the message. Cryptographic methods have existed for thousands of years. Roman soldiers in Gaul used secret codes to communicate with commanders in Rome, developing battle plans and arranging logistics of supplies and legion movements.

The fundamental idea behind cryptography is much the same today as when it was developed. A message is encoded using a cipher, which is a set of rules that explains the transformation to the information in the message. The encoded message, or cipher text, can only be decoded by someone who knows how the information was altered.

As applied to the Internet, encryption is a little more complicated. While many forms of encryption are available, one of the more prevalent forms of Internet applications of cryptography involves the use of an algorithm and a key. The algorithm and key work together as a cipher to produce the encoded text. The two most frequently used forms of key-based encryption on the Internet are symmetric key encryption and public key encryption.

Encryption addresses issues of security and privacy. Both symmetric and public key encryption can enhance confidentiality, and hence privacy, by limiting access to the information in a message only to people who have the right key. In addition, public key encryption can be used to verify the identity of the message sender, thus enabling authentication. A message encrypted with a private key is similar to a digital signature; if the message recipient is confident that only the sender has access to the private key, then the message must have come from the sender.

A concern for companies who need secure transactions systems is that the methods used to secure the information can make it difficult to transfer information between businesses involved in the transaction (e.g., the selling company and the credit card institution). The potential for communications difficulty underscores the need for standard protocols that facilitate secure information transfer. In 1997, a consortium of major businesses and credit card companies, including Microsoft, Visa, MasterCard, and Netscape, introduced **SET, or Secure Electronic Transaction.** SET uses encryption and decryption methods to protect credit card information transferred through any online network.

Digital Artifact 5.5

Of 520 organizations surveyed, 60 percent reported unauthorized use of computer systems. The Internet was involved in 57 percent of these breaches.

(*Source:* **FBI/Computer Security Institute, 2000.**)

Chapter Summary

In this chapter, we considered the role of technology development on the nature of the Internet as an exchange environment. We started with the basics of networks and digital technology, and we characterized the transfer of data through the Internet to the end user as a computer-based communications channel. Three elements of the channel were described: end user, Internet access, and computing infrastructure.

We extended our examination of technology to include the relationships between the technological component of the Internet environment and other players in the environment. For instance, we looked at the influence of technology on the exchange environment that exists between consumers and marketers. This influence was described as a mediating influence when it operates as a link that makes possible the interaction between exchange agents. In contrast, the influence was described as a moderating influence when it changes the nature of the relationship between exchange agents.

The moderating influence of the computer environment was characterized as the combination of technological factors that increase or decrease telepresence. These factors were described as the general dimensions of vividness and interactivity. The communications environment created by Internet technology was compared with traditional communications media to illustrate the importance of telepresence in creating communications environments that increase realism.

We also considered the relationships between technology and marketers, and between technology and consumers. In each relationship, technology affects the types and quality of actions that can be conducted in the Internet environment.

REVIEW SECTION

Key Terms

- referral networks
- viral marketing
- e-fluentials
- Internet protocols
- digital format
- bits
- packets
- datagrams
- resolution
- memory
- speed
- sound
- dial-up modem
- eight-second rule

- ISDN
- DSL
- cable
- wireless
- Internet service provider
- bandwidth
- backbone providers
- mediating effects
- moderating effects
- computer-mediated environment
- person interactivity
- machine interactivity
- telepresence

- vividness
- interactivity
- sensory breadth
- sensory depth
- interactivity speed
- range
- mapping
- human factors
- human-computer interface (HCI)
- resource discovery
- encryption
- Secure Electronic Transaction (SET)

Review Questions

1. What benefits come from an understanding of the technological aspects of the Internet?
2. How is word-of-mouth communication related to our population ecology perspective?
3. What type of network structure characterizes the Internet?
4. What does TCP/IP stand for?
5. What technological problem, often experienced by end users, may result in millions of dollars of lost online revenue?
6. How can technology influence the relationship between exchange agents?
7. Distinguish between mediating and moderating effects.
8. What are the two key dimensions of telepresence?
9. What are some advantages of Internet technologies for marketers? What are some disadvantages?

Thinking Points

1. How does the concept of a network increase the value of the Internet as an outlet for marketing activity?
2. What is the importance of Internet communications standards, such as TCP/IP, for marketers?

3. Describe a scenario that illustrates the role of the Internet on the experience of a person using a computer to access the Internet as a mediating effect.
4. Describe a scenario that illustrates the moderating effect of the Internet in user interaction with the medium.
5. Consider the likelihood of telepresence in each of the following environments: telephone, television, radio, and Internet. How might the experienced telepresence differ in each environment? Why?

Suggested Readings

1. "Internetworking: Concepts, Architecture, and Protocols." In *Computer Networks and Internets,* by Douglas E. Comer (Upper Saddle River, NJ: Prentice Hall, 1997).
2. *Every Student's Guide to the Internet,* by Keiko Pitter, Sara Amato, John Callahan, Nigel Kerr, Eric Tilton, and Robert Minato (New York: McGraw-Hill, 1995).
3. "Defining Virtual Reality: Dimensions Determining Telepresence," by Jonathan Steuer. *Journal of Communication, 42,* 4 (1992), pp. 73–93.
4. "Thriving on Technology Change." In *Now or Never,* by Mary Modahl (New York: Harper-Collins Publishers, Inc., 2000).
5. "Cyber Crime," by Ira Sager. *BusinessWeek,* (February 21, 2000).

CHAPTER 6

Public Policy and the Internet Environment

FOCUS AND OBJECTIVES

This chapter looks at the role of the policy perspective in the marketing environment of the Internet. The recent development of the Internet, combined with its novel nature, raises issues for policy makers that are unique and often not well understood. In this chapter, we review the history and nature of public policy for marketing, and we consider several policy-related issues in the Internet environment. The overarching goal of this chapter is to describe the role and scope of policy, and to delimit areas that may be affected by regulatory decisions, thus influencing what marketers can do.

YOUR OBJECTIVES IN STUDYING THIS CHAPTER INCLUDE THE FOLLOWING:

- Identify the primary regulatory agencies that affect marketing activity and the Internet, and how they operate.

- Understand the implications of previous policy decisions for regulation of marketing activity in the Internet environment.

- Recognize major issues for policy makers from the marketer and the consumer perspectives.

- Identify likely types and outcomes of regulation for the major issues on marketing activity.

Imagine a marketplace with a huge variety of desired goods and services, and all the information you could possibly need to evaluate them to make your choice. The prices are good, because the market is competitive. In addition, it is likely that you won't have to pay a sales tax, if the vendor is out-of-state. Sounds like a dream: too good to be true? In the marketing environment of the Internet, this scenario becomes a reality for many consumers.

All of the opportunities, however, come hand-in-hand with a gaggle of potential problems. Suppose, for instance, that the array of goods and services includes illegal, unapproved products, or that the really great price you found is because the item is an inferior imitation—a fraud. Further, suppose that when you type your credit card information in the online form, the information is not adequately protected, and somebody else goes on a shopping spree. Now the dream becomes a nightmare. These issues, as well as a host of other concerns, are the daily focus of the organizations and agencies responsible for formulating, implementing, and enforcing public policy.

Regulatory policy is an important component of the marketing environment. It can affect the type and quality of resource that can be exchanged, by restricting or enabling the types of products and services that can be offered (e.g., weapons). In addition, regulatory policy can influence the way in which the exchange is conducted (e.g., prescription drugs). As a result, the impact of regulatory policy on marketing activity can be substantial. Policy makers can determine the success or failure of a company or even an industry through the effect of regulatory action on the exchange environment.

The Internet has led to the reconsideration of many of the laws and regulations that apply to traditional marketing environments. Even though it shares many characteristics of other media, the Internet—with its global reach and rapid, interactive transmission—has the potential to create new situations that are not clearly addressed by existing policies. In addition, where existing regulation does apply to the Internet, policy makers must address the issues that the sheer size and scope of the Internet raises for policy enforcement. In this chapter, we will look at the role of public policy in the marketing environment of the Internet. We will begin with a brief description of what public policy is, and where it comes from. Then we will consider the issues for policy that result from the various exchange relationships in the Internet environment.

GOVERNMENT AND REGULATORY POLICY

The government's regulatory policies are carried out by an array of federal agencies. These agencies are created through acts of Congress. The commissioners who guide the agencies' efforts are appointed by the executive branch of the government (i.e., the president). These agencies implement laws enacted by the legislative branch of government (i.e., the Congress). When attempts to enforce legislation are not successful, the agencies may pursue legal sanctions, thus involving the judicial branch of the government. The involvement of the three branches of government are summarized in Figure 6.1.

Aspects of Government Policy

Public policy is the area of regulation that most directly influences the interaction between marketing and the Internet environment. Public policy exists for two main reasons: (1) to protect consumers in the marketplace, and (2) to provide a fair environment for commercial activity among businesses. These goals can be described

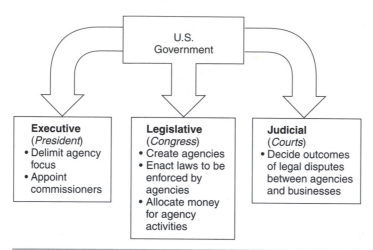

FIGURE 6.1 Roles of Government Branches in Public Policy.

as the more general objective of maintaining a balance between the interests of consumers and the interests of marketers.

Public policy also affects the marketing environment by fostering the development of infrastructures that enable exchange relationships to occur. For example, the development of a nationwide communications network was facilitated by regulatory policies that enabled widespread access to telephone service (i.e., through the Communications Act of 1934) and to television (e.g., through the Rural Electrification Act of 1936).

Agencies and Their Activities

Public policy is executed by a variety of government agencies. Agencies are created by Congress to oversee and implement legislation in specific areas of interest. The president appoints the commissioners who run the agencies. Although many of these agencies' activities involve enforcement of existing laws, other activities address issues that reflect the underlying spirit of the legislation. For example, an agency may institute a program of consumer education to try to protect consumers from developing incorrect beliefs that could lead to detrimental effects of product use. In sum, agencies are responsible for making sure that policies are carried out. Their activities may be reactive, as when they respond to violations of legislation, or proactive, as when an agency attempts to forestall a potential problem.

The sequence of policy activities shown in Figure 6.2 is reflected in several Internet-based situations. For instance, when several consumers complained that they had not received their earnings for participating in a car leasing program, the Federal Trade Commission began an investigation. After determining that the company's business was a pyramid scheme, the FTC took the case to court. A federal court ruled against the company. The Web site was shut down, the defendants were

FIGURE 6.2 Illustrative Path of Policy Actions.

barred from any other multilevel marketing activity, and they were ordered to pay $2.9 million to their customers.

Policy activity can also be initiated by the agency. For example, the Securities and Exchange Commission (SEC) became concerned about online trading when a series of television ads made trading look glamorous and profitable, with little mention of the risks involved. The SEC's 125–person Office of Internet Enforcement inspected Web sites of online brokerage firms and found that few provided adequate disclosure of risk. The agency sought to remedy the problem by sending a letter to each online brokerage, requesting them to provide better disclosure of potential pitfalls in online trading.

We can look at the specific mandates and scope of several agencies that exert a strong influence on the exchange environment of the Internet to better understand the role of public policy. (See Figure 6.3.) In the following section, we will focus on the Federal Trade Commission (FTC), the Food and Drug Administration (FDA), and the Federal Communications Commission (FCC). Of the many agencies, these three provide a representative overview of the intent and scope of regulatory policy that affects the commercial environment. The FTC regulates the operation of markets, the FDA regulates the products sold in the markets, and the FCC regulates the means by which information about commercial opportunities is disseminated.

FIGURE 6.3 Primary Regulatory Agencies in the Central Exchange Environment.

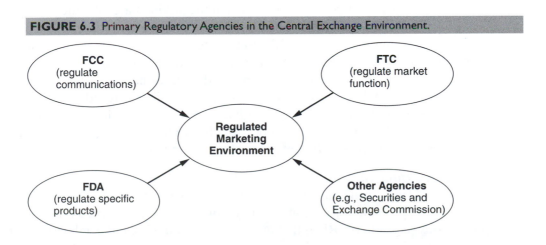

Federal Trade Commission

As its name implies, the FTC is directly concerned with the regulation of the exchange environment. Its overarching goal is to create a smoothly operating environment for trade. To this end, the FTC works to enforce antitrust laws designed to foster competition and fair trade. In addition, the FTC enforces laws that protect the interests of consumers in the marketplace.

The FTC also has two primary nonenforcement interests. Commensurate with its mandate, the FTC conducts research on the effects of trade practices on consumers and competition, and it makes the results of the research available to interested parties. As a result, the FTC can influence the development of policy, as well as its implementation. In addition, the FTC develops and provides educational programs intended to provide information for consumers and for companies about deceptive or fraudulent business practices.

The Internet has increased the FTC's workload; in 1999, the agency received 10,000 complaints about online auctions alone. To manage the increased activity, the FTC expanded the size of the staff devoted to Internet fraud to 79 people, or 23 percent of its staff—up from 14 people in 1996.

Issues have arisen that reflect each of the agency's mandates. For example, the FTC has scrutinized Amazon.com's practice of using its Alexa division software to monitor users' travels through Web sites for possible privacy concerns. In addition, the agency has assessed the timeliness of eToys' shipping, and decided to file suit against Toysmart.com for attempting to sell customer data when it guaranteed that it would not. In its nonenforcement arena, the FTC has published a proposal on the applicability of the law for advertising and selling on the Internet, and commissioned research on online privacy policies.

Food and Drug Administration

The FDA regulates products such as food, cosmetics, drugs, and medical devices. The agency's mandate is consumer protection. The FDA was formed through the Federal Food, Drug and Cosmetic Act of 1938 to exercise oversight of the production, distribution, and sales of its focal products to insure that the products are safe, and that appropriate types and amounts of information for their safe use are available to consumers.

The oversight responsibility of the FDA extends to the way that companies advertise their products on the Internet. For example, the FDA can, and has, taken formal action against companies that post misleading information on their Web sites. Although the FDA has not proposed a regulatory policy designed specifically for the Internet, its actions are consistent with the enforcement of legislation designed for print media. The multimedia nature of the Internet, however, presents the FDA with the issue of whether different types of legislation are needed.

Federal Communications Commission

The FCC was formed in 1934 as a result of the Communications Act. The commission is responsible for regulating communications in the United States and its possessions (e.g., Puerto Rico) that are conducted via wire, radio, television, satellite, and cable. An important goal of the commission is to develop and implement regulatory programs that result in the effective coordination and operation of the different types of communications systems.

The Internet is, in many respects, a convergence of several separate communications systems. The FCC must make decisions about whether regulation would help or hinder the development of the Internet as a medium characterized by converging communications technologies. Historically, the deregulation of telephone equipment, and the absence of regulation of phone service—beyond basic service—may have spurred the Internet's growth by fostering competition between companies.

Digital Artifact 6.1

As of February 2000, 65 percent of U.S. households had at least one computer. Fifty-five percent of the population had access to the Internet.

(*Source:* Internet and Society report, from the Stanford Institute for the Quantitative Study of Society.)

BRIEF HISTORY OF PUBLIC POLICY

The Internet environment provides a new arena for regulatory attention. It creates opportunities for new products and services. In addition, it serves as an information source for many products, and as a channel for acquiring the products. As a result, the FTC and the FDA also have an interest in marketing activity in the marketspace. Because the Internet can be accessed through cable, phone lines, or wireless sources, the FCC is also concerned with the application of legislation to the marketspace.

Despite much attention to the implications of the rapidly growing use of the Internet for marketing, many policy issues are still a source of debate. In addition, given the rate of technological change, other concerns may surface. One way to evaluate the potential for regulation and the nature of possible policies is by looking at how regulatory policy has developed historically. Even though the Internet may provide challenges and raise novel issues for policy makers, it is still subject to the same regulatory intentions and mandates that have guided policy development in the past.

Timeline of Regulation

Public policy often tends to be characterized as consumer protection. Even though consumer protection is clearly an important aspect of policy, as we saw in the descriptions of the three agencies, it is not the only objective they address. For the FTC and the FCC in particular, implementing legislation to maintain a fair, efficient, and competitive market environment has long been an important goal.

Our economic system operates under the fundamental economic premise that businesses should be allowed to grow and operate as freely as possible. This concept, known as a *laissez-faire* approach, translates literally from French as "to let do." Putting the concept in action translates functionally into the idea that fewer restrictions on the way that companies do business will result in a healthy, strong economy.

A laissez-faire approach to market regulation worked pretty well in the early years of the country. Companies tended to be small, and their influence tended to be local. As the country developed, however, so did business and industry. Companies increased in size and influence, often by swallowing other, smaller companies, or by squeezing weaker competitors out of the market.

By the last decades of the nineteenth century, the benefits of letting companies operate as they wished began to be outweighed by the costs of the practice. For instance, a powerful company could create a monopoly, thus limiting consumers' choices and potentially reducing product quality. These larger companies effectively curtailed the ability of smaller companies to compete fairly in the marketplace. To address the concerns, the government sprang into action. The Sherman Act of 1890 and the Clayton Act of 1914 were passed to foster fair competition.

The 1950s, 1960s, and 1970s were the decades most characterized by the introduction of legislation for consumer protection. Among the targets of regulation were flammable fabrics, food additives, toys, and information. The form and content of information provided to consumers was also affected by regulatory policy. For instance, suggested retail prices for cars were required, as were package sizes and labeling. Information about the cost of credit, as well as information about consumers' credit status were the subjects of legislation to protect consumers' rights.

The major regulatory activities that have affected the exchange environment between marketers and consumers are summarized in Figure 6.4. As you can see, policy that specifically focuses on the Internet is both relatively recent and scarce. Reasons for the dearth of Internet legislation include the newness of the medium for business activity, and the expectation that existing legislation will address many situations that arise in the online exchange environment. Government agencies have tended to take a wait-and-see approach, emphasizing the importance of industry self-regulation. In the following sections, we will consider the implications of existing legislation for marketing activity, and examine issues that may create additional legislation.

APPLYING POLICY TO THE INTERNET

Recall that in our exchange environment framework (Chapter 2), technology and policy exert an indirect influence on the central exchange environment. We can see this effect by considering the implications of the Telecommunications Act for the policy-marketer-consumer triad, shown in Figure 6.5.

The goal of providing universal service so that everyone has access to the Internet reflects an effect of policy on the central exchange environment. The two center arrows in the figure reflect this effect. Widespread access to the Internet means that

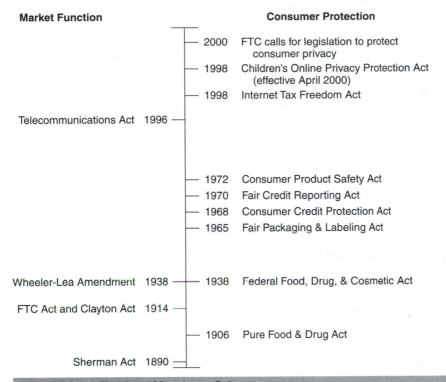

Market Function		Consumer Protection
	2000	FTC calls for legislation to protect consumer privacy
	1998	Children's Online Privacy Protection Act (effective April 2000)
	1998	Internet Tax Freedom Act
Telecommunications Act 1996		
	1972	Consumer Product Safety Act
	1970	Fair Credit Reporting Act
	1968	Consumer Credit Protection Act
	1965	Fair Packaging & Labeling Act
Wheeler-Lea Amendment 1938	1938	Federal Food, Drug, & Cosmetic Act
FTC Act and Clayton Act 1914		
	1906	Pure Food & Drug Act
Sherman Act 1890		

FIGURE 6.4 A Timeline of Regulatory Policy.

how people use the informational content, as in online resource exchanges, will become increasingly important for policy makers. Information-related policies may originate from either consumer or marketer actions, and policy decisions may affect consumers or marketer behaviors directly, or the exchange environment, indirectly.

One issue for policy makers is how people will use the information that is available on the Internet. Will marketers adhere to legislation that currently affects the way that product information can be presented, so that it is not misleading? If not, then the FTC and other agencies must determine whether different enforcement

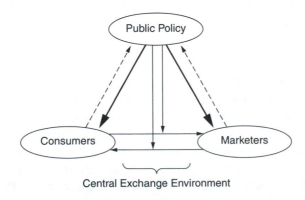

FIGURE 6.5 The Policy-Marketer-Consumer Triad.

policies are needed for the Internet environment, or even whether entirely new regulation is indicated.

Marketers' actions that deceive or harm consumers may result in investigation by a government agency. If the results of the investigation suggest that regulation is desirable, the agency may propose regulation that affects either the marketer directly, or the exchange environment more generally. Similarly, consumers' use of Internet-based information may lead policy makers to assess the need for regulation. For instance, the potential exposure of children to adult-oriented material, or to controlled products (e.g., alcohol and tobacco), may lead to the imposition of regulation that restricts the manner in which these products can be offered via the Internet. These situations are represented by the arrows that originate with consumers or marketers, travel through policy makers, and back to the central exchange environment.

The Issue of Universal Access

In 1996, Congress passed the Telecommunications Act. Because the act revamped policies pertaining to interstate communications networks, such as telephone and cable services, responsibility for implementing and enforcing the legislation fell to the Federal Communications Commission.

The Telecommunications Act addresses several aspects of how the Internet is likely to develop. For example, the act has as a key objective the provision of **universal service.** It means that any American who desires access to the Internet should be able to get it. In many cases, universal service is implemented by making sure that schools and libraries have access to telecommunications services. The policies associated with the act have implications for marketing activity that involves the Internet. These implications extend to market function issues via the digital network of the Internet, and to consumer protection issues in Internet use.

One concern for policy makers has been whether the Internet is a resource that is capable of creating a society of "haves" and "have-nots." That is, does the Internet provide benefits or create opportunities for users that cannot be obtained by nonusers? The polarizing effects of the Internet, which suggest that people with access tend to be characterized by demographics such as higher income and educational attainment have created a situation termed the **digital divide.** One objective of the Telecommunications Act was to reduce the socioeconomic gap between people with access to the Internet and people without access to the Internet, by making access widely available.

Access Issues for Universal Service

Regulation designed to guarantee universal access must address two separate issues: access and capacity. **Access issues** focus on *who* will be able to use the Internet, while **capacity issues** focus on *how* these people will be able to use it. That is, access refers to whether a person can connect to the Internet, while capacity refers to the capability of the user's equipment to dictate the form of the information encountered by the user. These terms illustrate the concern that Internet access does not always mean full ability to use the Internet. Even if everyone has Internet access, thus implying universal service, differences in computing capacity mean that people will experience the Internet environment differently.

Capacity Issues for Universal Service

Because capacity affects the computer-mediated environments in which consumers will obtain and process information—particularly for sites that rely heavily on graphics to communicate with consumers—the effects of different types of information environments on knowledge and decision behavior must be assessed prior to introducing regulatory policy. In addition, capacity issues mean that Internet regulation will have to be flexible enough to compensate for differences while still accomplishing regulatory goals.

Digital Artifact 6.2

Government involvement in online sales activity is not cheap. President Clinton asked Congress for $10 million to enforce regulation of online prescription drug sales (*Boston Globe*, December 28, 1999), while the Department of Commerce requested $3.5 million to track e-commerce (*The Wall Street Journal*, February 8, 2000).

(*Source:* The Internet Index, #26.)

Information Use and Internet Regulation

The issues for policy raised by capacity concerns tend to focus on how people will use information from the Internet. Information use issues fall into two categories. First, how will people's information-related behaviors be affected by the Internet? Second, how will these behaviors differ, if at all, from the behaviors typically observed in other information environments (e.g., radio and television)?

These categories are both important because policy makers have to determine whether regulating information on the Internet can be accomplished by simply transferring existing legislation, or whether entirely new policies must be developed. The task for policy makers is complicated. Even though current laws that regulate the provision of information, such as advertising, apply to the Internet, policy makers still must determine whether the Internet is more like radio or television, or both, or neither. Different media have different restrictions, and it is not clear which restrictions are most appropriate for the Internet environment. As one former FTC commissioner, Christine Varney, has noted, "[C]yberspace clearly represents a convergence of several technologies: telephones, broadcast media, and other media. Any advertising on the Internet is subject to current law on deceptive or fraudulent advertising. But whether cyberspace should be considered more analogous to print or broadcast media remains to be seen."[1]

---

[1]Quoted from *The Los Angeles Times,* Business Section (May 21, 1995), p. 1.

Understanding Internet Effects on Information Use

The wide variety and escalating amount of information available on the Internet suggests that policy makers will pay greater attention to regulatory concerns in the environment as time goes on. At present, the Internet is relatively unrestricted. Marketers can operate proactively to recognize and curtail actions that may be harmful to consumers. Failure to self-regulate effectively may lead to increased agency scrutiny and restrictive regulatory policy. Functioning proactively means that marketers have the same goals of understanding information use on the Internet as policy makers.

The Internet can influence information in several ways. For instance, the ready availability of information about a vast number of products may influence consumers' knowledge bases for product choices, including their perceptions of and attitudes toward goods and services. Because it affects the amount of information used to make decisions, this effect may lead to information overload, and perhaps to decreased decision quality.

In addition, the interactive nature of the Internet environment may influence the type of information that consumers include in decisions. For example, being able to easily acquire jazzy graphics and animated simulations may lead a consumer to disproportionately include information about a product that is offered in this form. Alternatively, long download times for a graphically intensive Web site may cause a consumer to ignore relevant information (remember the eight-second rule?).

Finally, the novelty of the computer-mediated environment may influence information use by serving itself as a persuasive characteristic of a decision situation. This situation occurs when a consumer incorporates an evaluation of the computer-mediated environment (CME) into a decision about a product, even though the evaluative information is completely irrelevant. The CME serves as a peripheral cue that may influence the product evaluation, or even the consumer's comprehension of the product's capabilities—even when the CME has no informational value.

These potential influences of the Internet on information use are described in the table in Figure 6.6. In the table, each concern is reflected as a level in which the Internet environment interacts with information use. Thus, at Level 1 the effect of the environment is least obtrusive, meaning that observed behaviors will tend to be more similar to behaviors observed with information use in traditional media. At Level 3, the interactive environment is highly obtrusive, and behaviors are predicted to differ most from those observed in traditional media.

The policy issues associated with universal access and information use reflect proactive efforts by government agencies, such as the FCC and the FTC, respectively, to understand and avert problems before they happen. In other areas, however, problems have already surfaced. In the next section, we will consider several policy issues that influence the nature of the direct exchanges between consumers and marketers.

Internet Influence on Information Processing	Description	Key Locus of Effect	Sample Theoretical Issues	Possible Outcomes/ Behaviors
LEVEL 1 *Minimal*	Internet enables information provision, but does not influence its form or content	On *amount* of information acquired and used in decision making	Information overload; decision heuristics for information acquisition and use	Objective decision quality may decrease, even though subjective perceptions of quality increase; frustration; decreased knowledge of key attributes
LEVEL 2 *Moderate*	Internet influences construction of form and content of information display	On *form* of information display used in decision making	Information display restructuring; information evaluation (heuristic use)	Ignore information that takes too long to acquire/ download; develop incorrect product category knowledge
LEVEL 3 *Extensive*	Internet influences information processing as a persuasive attribute independent of form and content	On *content* of information acquired and used in decision making	Attitudes and persuasion (e.g., peripheral cues; subjective norms)	Focus on vivid but peripheral cues, with decreased message comprehension; peer pressure leads to decreased or inaccurate product knowledge

Source: Reprinted from *Journal of Business Research, 41,* Don L. Cook and Eloise Coupey, "Consumer Behavior and Unresolved Regulatory Issues in Electronic Marketing," 1998, pp. 231–238, with permission from Elsevier Science.

FIGURE 6.6 The Internet Environment and Information Use.

POLICY AND EXCHANGE RELATIONSHIPS IN THE INTERNET ENVIRONMENT

When situations arise in the exchange environment that create the potential for regulation, policy makers must consider several issues before deciding on the nature of regulation. First, they must evaluate the costs and benefits of regulation. Who will be harmed—and how badly—if regulation is not enacted? In addition, will the benefits of regulation that will be experienced by some segment of society, such as consumers, outweigh the potential costs of restriction to another segment (e.g., marketers)?

A second issue for policy makers is the extent to which a behavior should be regulated. For instance, too much regulation within an industry may squash innovation and decrease the appeal of the industry for potential entrants to the market, potentially reducing product variety and quality for consumers, as well as competition between marketers. On the other hand, too little regulation might place consumers and smaller companies in jeopardy, at the hands of large corporations.

Once the extent of regulation is decided, policy makers must figure out the nature and the form of the regulation. Regulatory policy is best designed when it has benefits for marketers, thus reducing enforcement and compliance hassles, as well as being readily understood by consumers, thus increasing its efficacy.

The issues faced by policy makers as they decide whether to impose regulation, to remove regulation, or to do neither are summarized in Figure 6.7.

The issues in the following section arise from the nature of the Internet as an environment for marketing exchange, and they jointly affect consumers and marketers. To simplify discussion of the issues, however, they are grouped as issues that more directly affect marketers, and issues that more directly affect the well-being of consumers.

Issues of Market Function

From the marketers' perspective, three policy issues of interest are taxation, liability, and copyright. For taxation, we will consider the issues related to whether, and how, Internet purchases should be taxed. For liability, we will examine several is-

FIGURE 6.7 Public Policy as Decision Making.

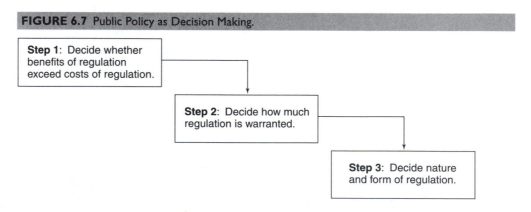

sues that focus on the marketer's responsibility in Internet-based exchanges. For copyright, we will look at concerns created for marketers by the digital nature of the Internet.

Taxation

Policy on taxation in the marketing environment of the Internet involves business taxes and sales taxes. **Business activity taxes** are assessed on companies in accordance with the tax policies of the company's location: a cost of doing business. **Sales taxes** are assessed on consumers' purchases according to the consumer's location.

For the Internet, tax policy is complicated in both situations, but for the same reason. The key question faced by policy makers is "Where is the company located?" Is a virtual presence, as at the end user's desktop computer, the same as a physical presence in the downtown shopping center? How the question is answered often depends on who is providing the response.

Business Activity Taxes   When a company opens a store in a local shopping mall, the company is required to pay the business taxes appropriate for the locale. This tax liability may include taxes for the town or city, as well as for the county and state. If the company opens another location, taxes must be paid in that new location, in addition to the taxes for the first location.

Now, what happens if the company opens a virtual storefront in an online mall? Offline marketers have argued that online merchants should be taxed as if the business had a physical presence, or **nexus,** at the point of online presence. Carried to an extreme, it means that an online marketer would have "stores" at every unique location from which its Web site was accessed! Taking the other extreme, some online vendors have argued that they do not fall within taxation guidelines; hence, they should be exempt from the tax regulations that apply to marketers in traditional environments.

For policy makers, developing policy on taxation means balancing the need to keep the fledgling Internet economy growing, while upholding the rights of marketers in the traditional, offline marketplace. Remember that one goal of market-related policy is to keep the playing field fair and competitive? One concern with the absence of a uniformly applied tax policy is that it potentially creates an unfair competitive advantage for companies who conduct their transactions online. Going back to our marketer-consumer-policy triad of Figure 6.5, we can see how a situation in which offline marketers' complaints of unfairness could lead to the imposition of tax policy that in turn affects the marketer-consumer exchange environment.

Sales Taxes   The topic of whether Internet purchases should be taxed in the same manner as offline purchases is of interest to consumers, as well as to competitors. For many consumers, buying products from the Internet is a better option than buying offline, because tax policy for the Internet is sufficiently murky that often no taxes are levied. For marketers, keeping the Internet free from tax policies applied to offline transactions means that online retailers have an implicit competitive advantage, in terms of price. Of course, as online sales grow in number and amount, the government faces the prospect of losing increasing amounts of tax revenue.

The boundaryless nature of the Internet, however, creates problems for determining how tax policy should be applied. States pass their own tax laws, as do locales within states. It means that there are more than 30,000 separate tax jurisdictions in the United States. At a minimum, transactions that occur within a state are subject to the tax laws of that state. For the Internet, however, which tax law applies? The law of the state in which the consumer lives? The law of the state in which the home office of the vendor is located? Or the law of the state from which the order was processed and shipped?

For situations in which the online transaction is between a vendor and a consumer in the same state, the state tax laws apply. A common practice for Internet vendors is to tell consumers to add on the appropriate tax percentage if the purchase will be delivered within the state. Some offline marketers have argued, however, that all purchases should be taxed at the appropriate rate of the state in which they are delivered, regardless of the source of the product or the location of the company. Countering this argument, some online marketers have taken the position that the state laws of the consumer do not apply. In this approach, the delivery is characterized as simply a posttransaction transfer of the product, rather than the actual consummation of the exchange process.

Another issue for tax policy on transactions is whether the online vendor should be responsible for collecting the appropriate taxes for the state to which the product will be delivered, similar to physical marketplace vendors. Online marketers have operated in a manner more like catalog merchants; in general, consumers are entrusted with the responsibility for determining the appropriate tax amount, and including it with payment. Offline marketers who feel that this practice creates an unfair advantage for online marketers would like to see regulation enacted that would require the online vendors to collect the sales tax.

These issues are complicated, and regulatory solutions are not likely to be different. The Advisory Committee on Electronic Commerce, formed by the Internet Tax Freedom group, provided a report to Congress in March 2000 that grapples with some of the issues. The committee members recommended a permanent ban of taxes on Internet access, and an extension of an existing moratorium on new Internet taxes, into 2006. Congress will use the report to help determine the nature of legislation regarding e-commerce taxes.

The moratorium does not limit the ability of local jurisdictions to apply existing taxes to Internet sales. Of concern for marketers is how to actually implement the calculation of taxes, given the wide variety of different tax structures. Tax collection software, like Taxware's Transaction Tax Server, can automate the tax process. The software calculates the tax, based on the mailing or billing address, provides the consumer with the charge, and forwards the tax information to the appropriate tax authority—all in real time, without slowing down the transaction or burdening the vendor.

> *Digital Artifact 6.3*
>
> **The longest domain name on the Web:** *http://www.tax.taxadvice.taxation.*
> *irs.taxservices.taxrepresentation.taxpayerhelp.internalrevenueservice.audit.*
> *taxes.com.*
>
> (*Source: www.inktomi.com/webmap.*)

Liability and Jurisdiction

The geographic vagueness of the Internet does not limit confusion to tax policy. It also influences policy-related concerns about marketers' liability. For example, if a consumer purchases a product through the Internet, and the product is unsatisfactory or causes harm, where does the consumer turn? The Internet creates an issue of jurisdiction. Suppose that the consumer decides to take legal action. Similar to the concern for company location in taxation, the issue is where the business is located. Does a virtual presence mean the same thing as a physical presence? Is the marketer liable wherever the consumer is, or in the place of the corporate headquarters?

Another set of policy issues related to liability concerns the marketer's responsibility for verifying customer information. For instance, is a marketer responsible for the harm done to those who misrepresents themselves to obtain a restricted product, such as underage consumers? On the Internet, it can be difficult to verify the age or identity of a consumer. In a face-to-face exchange, the marketer can assess the age of a prospective customer. In addition, identity can be checked by requesting a driver's license, photo identification, or by matching a signature on a charge slip to the signature on the credit card.

In marketspace, these protections are not available to the marketer. Even when the marketer adheres to the regulations that guide sales of any product, verification is difficult. This difficulty facilitates online credit card fraud by consumers, estimated at $400 million in 1999. Credit card fraud is particularly pronounced for products that can be consumed directly from the Internet, such as software, reaching rates as high as 30 percent.[2]

Marketers can use fraud detection systems to combat credit card fraud. For instance, neural network systems compare stored profiles of fraudulent transactions with new transactions to determine the apparent legitimacy of the transactions. Because these programs can cost many thousands of dollars, however, they are used by fewer than 5 percent of online sales sites. Online marketers use low-tech methods to verify transaction authority, such as checking the e-mail, phone, and home address provided by a customer.

Copyright in a Digital Medium

A third issue for policy makers and marketers is that of how to protect copyright in the Internet environment. The digital nature of the Internet makes it

---

[2]Data reported in *PC Week Online* (December 13, 1999), citing research by Meridien Research, Inc.

possible for marketers to provide products and information that can be digitized, such as software, music, and books, through Web sites. The same characteristics that facilitate their provision, however, also make it easy for unauthorized reproduction of the content. Although copyright laws developed to protect the creators of similar products in offline contexts apply to the Internet, policy makers are faced with the need to determine how best to enforce the laws in the marketspace.

Concerns raised by businesses in the music industry illustrate the challenges that Internet technologies pose for copyright enforcement. For example, **MP3** is a technology that enables digitized music to be stored in a format that compresses it to a small fraction of its initial, digitized size. This compression technique facilitates the ability to store and transfer music on the Internet. Organizations that provide MP3 files or that make it possible to obtain MP3 files through their Internet systems have been sued by the Recording Industry Association of America (RIAA), on the basis that the copyrights held by record labels are violated when pirated music is made available free of charge. In addition, Napster, peer-to-peer software that enables users to share music lists of MP3 files, has been sued by RIAA. Napster's defense is that it does not actually provide the music files, it merely provides the service that enables users—who presumably have paid for the music—to share them with other users. The resolution of these lawsuits will create precedents for the development and application of regulatory policy on copyright and intellectual property.

Digital Artifact 6.4

Universal Music sued MP3, citing concerns about its digital music service. In September 2000, Judge Jed Rakoff ruled against MP3.com, with potential damages of $25,000 for each Universal CD copied by MP3.com.

(*Source:* **Newsbytes, November 12, 2000.**)

Issues of Consumer Protection

Many of the laws and regulations that guide marketers' actions in exchange relationships with consumers are designed to address three main public policy goals: to eliminate some undesirable behavior, to protect some segment of society from harm, or to provide information necessary for making informed decisions. The laws and regulations currently in place were developed for marketers within the context of the traditional media of print, radio, and television. Policy makers must determine how these laws apply to the Internet. Some of the difficulties in developing or extending and applying regulatory policy to the Internet can be seen by looking at concerns with advertising on the Internet, and with issues of privacy.

Advertising Regulation and the Internet

In general, as suggested by the quote from former FTC commissioner, Christine Varney, legislation for traditional media are applicable to the communications medium of the Internet. Regulation of advertising takes three forms. These forms are product regulation, audience regulation, and method regulation.

Product regulation imposes restrictions on advertisements for products that have the potential for negative effects on consumption. For instance, alcohol and tobacco products are restricted in terms of where they can be advertised, and when. Both tobacco and alcohol must include health warnings. Cigarette ads can be placed in print media, but not on television or radio.

Some regulation, like the health warnings, can be readily applied to advertising these products on the Internet. Less clear, however, is whether these products, such as cigarettes, are allowed to be advertised on the Internet. Is the Internet more like print media, in which case the advertising would be permissible? Or is the Internet more like broadcast media, which would not allow the advertising?

Audience regulation has a goal of protecting vulnerable consumers, such as children. Although much of the regulation is self-regulation, voluntarily undertaken by the advertising industry, legislation does exist that regulates when certain types of ads can be aired on broadcast media to reduce children's exposure. In addition, regulation restricts the amount of advertising that can occur on television shows directed at children.

How do these regulations apply to the Internet? The Internet is not a typical broadcast medium. Its content can be accessed at any time. In addition, the Internet is not a passive medium, like radio and television. The audience interacts with the medium, collecting information and determining the amount and timing of exposure to Internet content. As a result, the time-based restrictions for traditional media do not transfer well to the Internet.

Method regulation is focused primarily on the prevention of deceptive advertising practices. For example, marketers may not lie about the quality or performance of their products. This restriction applies quite straightforwardly to the Internet. A concern arises, however, with how to enforce the regulation. The ease with which a marketer can post information, and change posted information, accompanied by the vast amount of information on the Internet, makes enforcement by federal agencies a mountainous task.

Another issue related to deceptive advertising is based on communications that do not explicitly make false statements, but which have as a result the creation of an inaccurate perception or belief by the consumer. As with more extreme forms of deception, the intent of existing legislation applies readily to the Internet. Of concern, however, is whether the nature of the Internet medium can contribute to the formation of incorrect beliefs. That is, even if a marketer presents information honestly and completely, and in the same amount as in other media, does the Internet affect the types of perceptions formed by consumers? More importantly, do these perceptions lead to inaccurate beliefs about the product? This concern is related to the information use issues at Level 3 of the framework in Figure 6.6.

Because potentially harmful products, such as alcoholic beverages, are available through the Internet, the idea that consumers might use information from the Internet differently from information obtained in traditional shopping environments is of interest to marketers and policy makers. In addition, products with safe-use concerns, such as the use of medical products, raise questions about how consumers will utilize information such as nutritional labeling or product warnings in the Internet environment.

Fraud and the Internet

Concerns with how to regulate the way marketers advertise their wares have increased as reports of fraud on the Internet have escalated. The National Consumers League has tracked reports of fraud related to Internet exchanges since 1996. They note a consistent increase in reported frauds, from 689 in 1996 and 1,280 in 1997, to 7,752 in 1998 and 10,660 in 1999. The top five reported frauds in 1999 were auctions (87 percent), general merchandise (7 percent), ISPs, or Internet access services (2 percent), computing equipment (1.3 percent), and work-at-home offers (0.9 percent). The chart in Figure 6.8 shows the exchange circumstance in which the reported fraud occurred, along with the way in which the victim was initially contacted.

Most of the reported frauds originated when consumers obtained the initial information about the exchange opportunity from a Web site. Far smaller percentages of fraud stemmed from initial e-mail contact. Keep in mind that these statistics may reflect only a fraction of actual online fraud incidents; some people may just take their losses without taking any action. It is also important to note that the reported incidents cannot always be verified. As a result, these numbers may be low, relative to actual instances of fraud, and the reported instances may overestimate the occurrence of fraud. Difficulties in obtaining accurate figures of problems are faced by agencies, such as the FTC, that often use information from consumer groups to determine whether to initiate regulatory reviews of individuals, companies, or industries.

FIGURE 6.8 Type of Fraud by Form of Initial Contact.

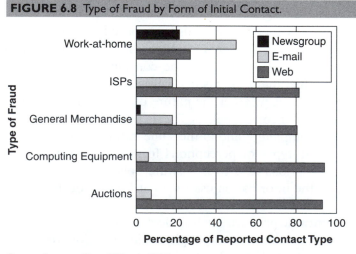

Source: Internet Fraud Watch, 2000

Protecting Consumer Privacy

When you type information into your computer to place an order, and send it to a Web site, how do you know who will have access to that information? When you browse the Internet, looking for a perfect gift for Mother's Day, how do you know whether your search has been electronically watched? These concerns are related to the more general issue of privacy on the Internet.

Many organizations collect information about us on a routine basis. For example, Internet service providers who manage user accounts gather personal data. Companies from which we purchase goods and services also collect various types of consumer profile information. When we use e-mail on company networks, systems administrators have access to information about e-mail traffic, and to the content.

In the United States, public policy restricts the collection of personal information and the creation use of computerized files only in the public sector—for government-related activities. The Privacy Act of 1974 and the Computer Matching and Privacy Protection Act of 1988 restrict the collection of personal data in several ways. For instance, the personal data can only be used for a specified purpose, and the person who is the focus of the data must be made aware that the data is being gathered. In addition, the government is not allowed to make the personal information available to anyone else. This type of regulation makes it possible for the government to collect and analyze information that provides benefits to society, while at the same time protecting the rights of the individual. The U.S. Census is an example of public sector collection of personal data.

Survey results provided by Market Facts TeleNation in January 1999 indicate that privacy is a substantial concern for many people. The survey tracked Internet users as well as nonusers, of whom 53 percent noted privacy as their main concern with online shopping. Respondents most concerned with privacy tend to be users with higher levels of income and education. These demographic characteristics are also associated with the largest percentage of Internet use, and of online shopping. As a result, the survey underscores the importance of privacy as a concern for marketers, as well as for policy makers.

To illustrate the reason for concern, suppose that you subscribe to an online health information service. To access the service, you type in an identifying password that can be linked back to your registration information. While you are searching for information about health-related topics of interest to you, a record is made of the areas of the Web site that you visit. This record is known as a **data-stream.** Who might be interested in acquiring this information from the health site? An insurance company, looking at you as a potential policy holder, might benefit from information that indicated health problems that might make you a poor insurance risk. In addition, an employer could make use of private, personal health information to decide whether to hire you. These situations, though extreme, underscore the reason for concern about Internet privacy.

Internet technology can be used to track users' search behaviors and preferences for a variety of reasons. Not all of the uses of tracking technologies threaten privacy. For example, cookies are often used to facilitate communication between a user and a Web server. A **cookie** is information in a text file that is sent to the user's browser (e.g., Netscape) by a Web server. The cookie can be used to store information, such as a user's registration and password for a particular site. The Web server can then read back this information when the user wants to return to that particular site. The user benefits by not having to retype all of the identifying information. Cookies can be used for online ordering systems, to remember what items a consumer has selected. They can also be used to provide customized site displays (e.g., just news and sports scores from MSNBC.com). Marketers also use cookies to track how many unique visitors have been to a particular Web site.

The information obtained from cookies can provide marketers with information about consumers' habits and preferences, including which ads a user is exposed to, and which ads a user acts on (i.e., click-through). This information enables marketers to tailor promotional information. In some cases, however, the potential for abuse is present. Information believed by consumers to be confidential may be transmitted to other vendors, or made available for uses unanticipated by the consumer. Consumers can disable cookies, but in many cases they may not be aware that cookies exist, or have the technical knowledge to change the browser settings to disable them.

The Federal Trade Commission investigates situations in which violations of privacy may have occurred, or in which they have the potential to occur. In 1998, the Children's Online Privacy Protection Act was passed. The law, which went into effect in April 2000, requires Web sites that obtain information from children to follow a set of rules vetted by the FTC. These rules require sites to obtain parental permission before transferring information obtained from or about a minor to a third party. In addition, children's sites must post privacy notices, and allow parents to prohibit the sale of personal information about a minor that was obtained for internal company use. The law mandates a fine of $11,000 per violation.

With regard to protecting the privacy of adults, the FTC has taken a watch-and-wait approach, focusing on investigation and observation. Their policy has, in effect, been to maintain the status quo of no regulation, letting companies and industries devise their own standards for privacy. The results of a study commissioned by the FTC and released in May 2000, however, may signal an end to self-regulation. The study results indicate that of sites with more than 39,000 unique visitors a month, only 20 percent protected consumers' privacy. The FTC has recommended to Congress that privacy legislation be adopted. Until legislation is passed, companies must develop effective forms of self-regulation to protect consumers.

Digital Artifact 6.5

In the 2000 State of the Union address, the number of times President Clinton mentioned the Internet: Six.

(*Source:* **The Internet Index, #26.**)

Privacy and Self-Regulation

Industry self-regulation has been a key force in efforts to reassure consumers that their privacy is protected. Companies issue privacy statements that outline how they will use information provided by consumers. In addition, organizations such as the Better Business Bureau Online (BBBO) and TRUSTe act as digital "seals of approval" to increase consumers' confidence in online exchanges of information.

The TRUSTe program is a nonprofit organization that reviews the privacy statements of participating companies to ensure that they meet goals of disclosure and informed consent. Companies are required to make available to site visitors a privacy statement that explains what information will be collected, how it will be used, and to whom the information will be available. Companies whose privacy statements meet the TRUSTe criteria can post the TRUSTe approval on their sites. When acceptance of the voluntary vetting processes of organizations such as TRUSTe are widespread, the effect is that of a standard for behavior that benefits marketers as well as consumers.

A different approach to self-regulation is illustrated by the development of technologies that enable Web users to determine whether a site's privacy policy is adequate. For example, the Platform for Privacy Preferences (**P3P**) is a software agent that is stored on the user's computer. When the user goes to a Web site using an application that has the P3P capabilities, the agent scans the site's privacy policy and provides the user with color-coded warnings that reflect different levels of privacy protection. The user can customize the agent to return warnings based on personal preferences for privacy protection. Self-regulation is expected of sites that do not wish to be identified by P3P as privacy violators.

One reason to adopt self-regulatory practices is often to forestall government regulation. In the case of privacy, companies may face a difficult task of reengineering information systems to meet data management requirements that could be imposed with legislation. For instance, companies could be required to provide **subject access.** The concept of subject access is not new; introduced to public policy with the Fair Credit Report Act (1970), subject access means that any person for whom personal information is amassed has the right to examine the information. Given the amounts of information that may have accumulated in online databases,

FIGURE 6.9 The TRUSTe Logo.

however, the challenge of figuring out how to reconfigure information systems to enable subject access is a daunting one for many companies.

Chapter Summary

Issues of public policy for the Internet tend to raise more questions than can be answered with a simple attempt to apply existing policy to the marketspace environment. The number of unanswered questions and the issues that provoke these questions suggest that the policy entity of the Internet environment will be an active force in the development of the central exchange environment for the foreseeable future.

One way to understand what issues might provoke the attention of policy makers is to consider the nature of the agencies responsible for developing and enforcing policy in the United States. To this end, we looked at the role of the Federal Trade Commission, the Food and Drug Administration, and the Federal Communications Commission in developing the policies that regulate the marketing environment.

Another means by which we can anticipate future regulatory action is by understanding the forces that guided policy development in the past, and by comparing them to forces that characterize the present environment of interest. A brief history of regulatory policy was presented to illustrate a shared and persistent emphasis on the importance of maintaining an equitable balance between a competitive environment for marketers, and a safe, yet fulfilling, environment for consumer activity. The interests of the FCC and the FTC were examined in terms of the policy issues of universal access and information use, respectively.

The process of developing policy for the marketing environment created by the Internet was described as a series of three steps: weighing the costs and benefits of regulation, determining the extent of regulation, and deciding the form of the regulation. These issues were used as the implicit basis for considering several issues for Internet-related policy. Among the issues covered were issues related to the competitive environment: taxation and liability. In addition, issues related to consumer protection were addressed, including advertising and privacy.

REVIEW SECTION

Key Terms

- laissez-faire
- universal service
- digital divide
- access issues
- capacity issues
- business activity taxes
- sales taxes
- nexus
- MP3
- product regulation
- audience regulation
- method regulation
- datastream
- cookies
- P3P
- subject access

Review Questions

1. What is the role of public policy in the Internet environment?
2. Describe the basic mandates of the FTC, FDA, and the FCC.
3. Explain the laissez-faire approach to regulating businesses.
4. Discuss the difficulties of market regulation. Specifically address the dichotomy of consumer protection and promotion of fair competition.
5. What issues did the Telecommunications Act address?
6. What is the digital divide?
7. How does the Internet influence information use?
8. How can public policy be characterized as decision making?
9. What specific problem faced by policy makers makes taxation in the Internet environment a complicated issue?
10. What are the three forms of advertising regulation?
11. How are cookies used?
12. What approach has the FTC taken with respect to privacy protection?
13. How does the TRUSTe program increase consumer confidence in online information exchanges?

Thinking Points

1. Suppose that no policy-making agencies monitored or regulated the Internet. What are some of the implications of a completely uncontrolled environment for marketers and for consumers? How might the effects of an unregulated marketspace differ from the likely effects of an unregulated marketplace?
2. The Telecommunications Act was written, in part, to attempt to reduce the digital divide. Will legislation that mandates access to the Internet be sufficient to reduce the chasm? Why, or why not?
3. What characteristics of the Internet environment may affect the way people acquire and use information?
4. Are the policy concerns raised by the Internet as a source of information different from information-related concerns in other marketing environments? If so, how are they different? What implications do the differences have for the way that marketers present information in the online environment?
5. Internet influences on information processing range from minimal to extensive. Consider the ways in which the extent of the Internet's effect on information processing might be related to the type of product (or, more generally, resource) that is being examined.
6. What characteristics do the policy concerns of taxation and liability share, with regard to the Internet?
7. What are the pros and cons for marketers that are associated with different forms of possible tax regulation? Of liability regulation?
8. What are the costs and benefits that policy makers must consider in determining whether marketing activity on the Internet should be regulated to protect consumers' privacy?

Suggested Readings

1. "Privacy, Surveillance, and Cookies," by Larry R. Leibrock. In *Electronic Marketing and the Consumer,* edited by Robert A. Peterson (Thousand Oaks, CA: Sage Publications, Inc., 1997).

2. "Interview with Christine Varney," with D. C. Denison. In *World Wide Web Journal, 2,* 3 (Summer 1997).

3. "Privacy in the Digital Economy," by Don Tapscott. In *The Digital Economy* (New York: McGraw-Hill, Inc., 1995), pp. 271–284.

4. "Universal Service and the Telecommunications Act: Myth Made Law," by Milton Mueller. *Communications of the ACM, 40,* 3 (1997), pp. 39–48.

5. "Avoiding Misuse of New Information Technologies: Legal and Societal Considerations," by Paul N. Bloom, George R. Milne, and Robert Adler. *Journal of Marketing, 58* (January 1994), pp. 98–110.

SECTION THREE

Integrating the Perspectives: The Internet as a Marketing Environment

In the first two sections, we considered characteristics of the Internet environment, and of the different perspectives of people engaged in exchange-related activities in the environment. In this section, we put the parts together, integrating the Internet environment with aspects of marketing activity, in order to understand how the nature of the Internet influences strategic marketing thinking. This section is intended to provide a general characterization of the impact of the Internet on aspects of the marketing environment, and on marketing activity within this environment. As such, it serves as the basis for more focused discussion in subsequent chapters.

In Chapter 7, we examine the nature of the Internet as an environment for marketing. We use population ecology, a biological theory developed to explain the growth of groups of organisms—like companies and industries—to describe aspects of competition and cooperation for marketing in an online environment.

In Chapter 8, we build on the theoretical basis of population ecology to consider ways in which the Internet affects the strategic marketing activities that companies undertake to obtain a competitive advantage. For example, the Internet creates opportunities for new goods and services, as well as new business models for selling them. Aspects of these models are discussed.

CHAPTER 7

The Internet's Influence on the Marketing Environment

FOCUS AND OBJECTIVES

In this chapter we examine the impact of the Internet on the goals and activities of marketing organizations. We use a theoretical perspective called population ecology to provide a basis for discussing the influence of the Internet on the marketing environment. Concepts from population ecology are used to describe competitive and cooperative behaviors. We also consider ways in which businesses structure their organizations and activities to promote effective competition in the marketing environment of the Internet.

YOUR OBJECTIVES IN STUDYING THIS CHAPTER INCLUDE THE FOLLOWING:

- Recognize the key forces that drive change in the marketing environment of the Internet.
- Understand the application of population ecology to business in the Internet environment.
- Identify the major strategies for competing in a product market.
- Identify the primary characteristics of the Internet ecology.
- Understand the Internet's potential for influencing value chain activities and market structures.

One of the most important tasks for marketing is to develop a strategic perspective to guide marketing action in a way that provides maximum benefits to the company, and that is in keeping with the strategic objectives of the entire organization. To this end, marketers must understand the nature of the environment in which the company will operate. The marketing environment creates challenges and opportunities for marketing action. This chapter is centered on the deceptively simple question, "What aspects of the Internet lead to fundamental changes in the marketing environment?" Of course, we are going to make it more complicated.

The Internet has been described as a revolution by researchers and many writers in the popular press. Typically, a revolution implies a change to the existing order: old ways are overthrown, and new ways define practice. Changes may be evident in several forms. First, we can look at the effect of the Internet on the *structure* of the marketing environment. Generally, what does the marketplace look like when the Internet plays a role? Second, we can study the effect of the Internet on the *forms* of marketing activities that can be carried out. For instance, here we might ask the questions, "What features of the Internet lead to changes in the marketing environment that enable new marketing activities?" and "How can marketers use the Internet to accomplish traditional strategic objectives in new ways?"

THE CAVEATS OF CHANGE AND CONSTRAINT

The fast pace of technological development, and of people's adoption of the technology, means that what we know and how we use the Internet to develop marketing strategy may quickly become outdated. In order to make effective use of the Internet as a marketing tool, it is important to adopt a perspective that recognizes that the marketing environment is affected—and even defined—by changes and constraints. Therefore, rather than learning specific facts, formulas, and theories based on their applications in well-defined, static situations, you must understand how the concepts work well enough to transfer them to situations that can change quickly and dramatically.

Key Forces in a Changing Marketing Environment

Recognizing changes to the market can be accomplished by understanding the forces that create change. One such force includes the advances in technology, in terms of hardware and software. In addition, peoples' reactions to technology development may also lead to dramatic changes in the marketing environment. For instance, increased ease of communication among consumers may lead to the formation of new types of referral networks and of consumer organizations related to product categories or brands. Finally, the changes to the types of interactions between marketers and consumers, made possible by the Internet, may result in regulatory policies that affect the market structure. These key forces are summarized in Figure 7.1.

In any environment characterized by rapid and dramatic changes affecting the fundamental structure and forms of activities that can be undertaken by inhabitants of the environment, it can be helpful to have a big picture to serve as a guide for organizing the issues. In the next section, we will use a basic population ecology model to characterize the environment created by the Internet and its effect on marketing activity.

A Population Ecology Approach to the Marketing Environment

Population ecology is a science developed to provide a systematic explanation of the environmental factors that determine characteristics of a population, such as its

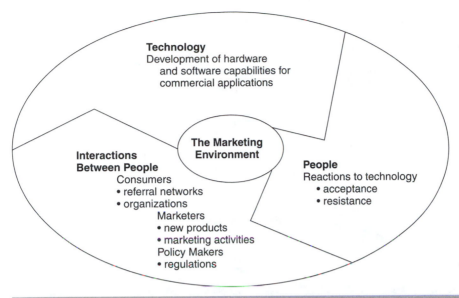

FIGURE 7.1 Key Components in an Evolving Marketing Environment.

size, distribution, and rate of growth. Although biologists use population ecology to talk about organisms, such as plants and animals, many of the concepts that describe change in organic, biological environments are readily applicable to the technological environment of marketing and the Internet.

In population ecology, **biotic potential** is the growth in the population that we would expect to observe if the environment was characterized by optimal growing conditions. Arthur Boughey, one of the earliest proponents of population ecology, provides a good description of biotic potential.[1] He notes that if a certain type of bacteria reproduced itself by dividing every 20 minutes, in one and one-half days, the entire planet would be a foot deep in bacteria. A day later, it would be over our heads.

This example makes salient two points. First, with optimal environmental conditions, a population can grow quickly, as at an exponential rate. Second, the notion of biotic potential is more of theoretical interest than actual fact—reassuring when you think about the bacteria. Most environments are not optimal for unchecked growth. Constraints to growth tend to take two forms: (1) natural circumstances, such as the availability of food, and (2) cultural conditions, such as a societally imposed limit on the number of children in a family. These constraints are jointly termed **environmental resistance.** The point at which the amount of resistance leads to a halt in growth of the population defines the **carrying capacity** of the environment for that population. Figure 7.2 depicts the relationships between growth rate, environmental resistance, and carrying capacity.

---

[1]Arthur S. Boughey, *Ecology of Populations,* New York: The Macmillan Company, 1968.

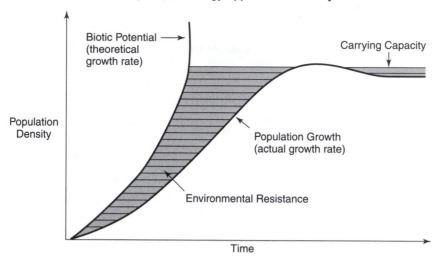

FIGURE 7.2 Population Ecology in Graphic Detail.

Population Ecology and Business

Now we are ready to apply population ecology to the environment created by the interaction of marketing and technology. The Internet constitutes a virtual ecology, in which different types of populations coexist. For example, we can think of the domains represented in the domain name system as a simplistic classification of species: commercial, educational, military, and so on. If we focus on the commercial domain, for example, different industries serve as the species populations. Each organization, or company, within the industry is analogous to the individual organism in the species population description of population ecology.

Of particular interest are the factors that sustain, encourage, or inhibit the ability of an industry or company to flourish and grow, given constraints of the Internet ecology. For example, think of the constraints that might create environmental resistance to the growth of an industry. One might be the limits that are implicitly imposed by the status of available technologies. Companies who offer sophisticated and graphics-intensive Web site hosting are affected by this constraint when the target market for their services is limited by lack of access to the type of computing equipment that enables users to experience the services as intended.

Another constraint might be the regulations imposed by policy makers on the types of activities that companies in a particular industry may conduct. For example, several tobacco companies registered Internet domains with the hope that publicizing and advertising their products would be possible on the Internet in ways that are not possible in other media, such as television. While regulatory policy for the Internet is still in its infancy, the tobacco industry has already been warned that restrictions in other media will apply to the Internet.

Digital Artifact 7.1

In the St. Louis Galleria, 170 stores are prohibited from promoting electronic commerce.

(*Source: Fort Worth Star Telegram,* **November 26, 1999, and The Internet Index, #25.**)

Types of Environmental Constraints

The constraints of technology and policy are analogous to the two types of constraints in biological settings. We can think of impediments to industry growth due to technology as **natural circumstances,** and constraints due to policy, as determined, imposed, and enforced by societal agencies, as **cultural conditions.**

In the case of natural circumstances, we can use concepts from population ecology to understand the nature of the factors that limit growth by introducing another distinction between the factors. Population growth can be limited by factors that are **density dependent** or **density independent.** Both types reflect constraints imposed by the demand on limited sets of resources. A constraint due to density dependence occurs when the number of organisms in the population affects growth. For example, an industry may be unable to continue to grow when the market for its product becomes saturated; that is, the limited pool of possible buyers is exhausted. In addition, a production-side constraint may curb industry growth when supplies needed to produce the product are unavailable. While both of these situations involve constraints due to limited resources, the first case is density dependent, and the second case is density independent; if the supplies exist for no one, then the size of the industry makes no difference to its growth.

Other examples of density independent constraints on industry growth include seasonality and the presence of cycles in consumption. Seasonality leads to often-predictable variations in the amount of consumption from a product category. Marketing researchers noted dramatic shifts in Internet consumption during the 1998 and 1999 holiday seasons. Consumers moved away from typical browsing and research use of Internet content, and toward heavier online shopping. Cycles appear to be less predictable in occurrence, but they can exert a substantial effect on the revenues of a company (e.g., in fashion, bell bottoms and fur coats have both experienced a recent resurgence in popularity).

A final set of factors that acts as constraints consists of **ethological characteristics.** These characteristics are behavioral attributes of the individual entities in the population that affect the overall size of the population. Ethological characteristics differ from the density dependent and independent constraints we have examined in that they are self-imposed, rather than being dictated by the physical environment or the supply of available resources. In addition, ethological characteristics may reflect cultural conditions (see Figure 7.3).

Because ethological characteristics often reflect the conscious decision of population members to behave in proscribed ways, these characteristics are particularly

Natural Circumstances	*Cultural Conditions*
Resource Limitations	**Ethological Characteristics**
• *Supply-side* (technological capabilities)	• *Territoriality* (niche behaviors between
—density dependent (high competition	competitors)
for necessary production materials)	—patents for intellectual property
—density independent (low availability	—product/process standards
of necessary materials, without	• *Regulatory policy* (influence of social norms)
competition)	• *Emigration* (shift to alternative product
• *Demand-side* (buyers)	focus)
—density dependent (high competition	
for consumers)	
—density independent (market is	
saturated, for all competitors)	

FIGURE 7.3 Types of Constraints to Industry Growth in the Internet Environment.

useful for describing the effects of the Internet environment on the activities of industries. We are, after all, dealing ultimately with people making decisions about the nature of their businesses. As such, many activities in the marketing and Internet ecology reflect constraints due to behavioral attributes that are closely related to aspects of strategic planning. For instance, competition may lead one industry member to develop strategies that define territories that can be defended against other companies. Patents to guard intellectual property, such as new product technologies, and the development of a de facto standard for a process or application are ways that one company can protect its ability to compete within the industry. These types of behaviors also serve as constraints on the behavior of other industry members, thus potentially limiting growth.

Competition within industries has been an important focus of marketing research. In the following section, we will take a closer look at the role of population ecology in explaining competitive behaviors that may occur in the virtual ecology.

POPULATION ECOLOGY AND COMPETITION IN MARKETS

The concepts of population ecology have been applied in marketing to provide a conceptual basis for explaining and predicting the success of competing firms as they move through the product life cycle (PLC). For example, marketing researchers Lambkin and Day have used the stages of the product life cycle—introduction, growth, maturation and decline—to develop a typology of strategies for success that integrates the company characteristics with more general characteristics of the industry.[2] This typology can be used to predict the types of companies that are likely to succeed in different stages of the PLC in the Internet environment.

In this approach, several aspects of population ecology are central. First, they consider the constraint of density dependence to be a key factor in the intensity of

---

[2]Mary Lambkin and George S. Day, "Evolutionary Processes in Competitive Markets: Beyond the Product Life Cycle." *Journal of Marketing,* 53 (July 1989), pp. 4–20.

competition; the more competitors in the market, the greater the demand on resources (e.g., consumers). Second, they incorporate the ecological idea of niches to serve as a basis for the typology of strategies. A **niche** is the combination of resources and environmental conditions, including competition, that has the ability to sustain growth of one type of population member.

Internet portals illustrate the value of niching. Portals are Web navigation hubs, such as Yahoo! and Lycos. Early portal strategies focused on being general by combining content and capabilities that would appeal to broad audiences. The strategy worked well for Yahoo! The portal increased its traffic totals by more than 50 percent in 1999. This rapid growth made it difficult for other, smaller portals to compete effectively. As a result, second-tier hubs such as Go.com and Excite@home shifted their strategies to develop competencies in specific areas. Go.com focused on entertainment and recreation, and Excite@home targeted its efforts to providing services for small business users.

The research on population ecology and competition, combined with anecdotal evidence from the Internet environment, suggests that different strategies are appropriate for different types of companies at different stages in the development of the product market. More specifically, it suggests that in new markets, characterized by low population density and weak competition, successful organizations are likely to be smaller, more specialized companies who can use their small size and focused skills to exploit a market opportunity. These types of companies are described as **specialists.** In the early days of portal development, Yahoo! focused on search and content capabilities.

For more established markets, in which more is known about the different demand for the product (that is, different market segments), and where competition is greater, companies who have expanded the specialized capabilities of the early market entrants may be most successful. Success will depend on the ability to capitalize on the experience of pioneers in the earlier niche, generating enough resources to expand to compete in the present niche. Companies with these expanded sets of capabilities are described as **generalists.** Yahoo! capitalized on its early, focused successes to develop broader capabilities, as by acquiring GeoCities and Broadcast.com.

In the later stage of the cycle, population density and competition are high. Because most of the variety of organizations that could enter the market have already done so, the amount of environmental change is relatively low. As a result, companies who tend to be successful in this type of market are those with the broad-based industry presence to be able to flexibly redirect their capabilities to exploit a particular competency or a need of a specific segment. As a result, they tend to be generalists, but with some characteristics of the early niche specialists. In the case of Internet portals, existing sites used their resources to refocus, specializing on particular market segments. New portals in market will have to be able to take on the giants, like Yahoo! and provide evidence of differentiating capabilities to pull traffic.

> *Digital Artifact 7.2*
>
> **On March 7, 2000, Arizona Democrats were the first to use the Internet to vote in a legally binding election of the Democratic presidential candidate.**
> (*Source:* **Yahoo! News, March 7, 2000.**)

Competition, Niches, and the Internet Ecology

The population ecology model of market evolution can be used to describe and explain the nature of market development when the Internet is a factor that influences the nature of the marketing environment. In a simple sense, we can look at the Internet as the source of a new product market; innovative products, and the companies that spawn them have been created to take advantage of the opportunities offered by the Internet ecology. In a more complex sense, however, we must also look at the effect of the Internet on the nature of competition in existing product markets.

Types of Product Markets

As a new product market, the Internet constitutes an embryonic niche. Early entrants into the market tend to fit the Lambkin and Day profile; smaller companies with specialized capabilities. The rapid proliferation of Internet start-up companies, and the vast amounts of venture capital that underwrite their endeavors, result from low population density and competition, and a belief that high profit potential exists in the niche. For example, eBay, the online auction company, provides a service that would not have been feasible prior to widespread adoption of the Internet as a means for communication and commerce. Another example is that of Cisco Systems, the company that produces the systems components known as routers that enable the Internet to transfer packets of information. The Internet is the reason for Cisco's existence.

For established product markets, the Internet provides an opportunity to develop a competitive niche, differentiated on the basis of technological savvy. Companies such as Amazon and eToys entered the Internet market early. They developed online competencies that earned them brand awareness, despite the fact that in both cases, the core product was not new—books for Amazon and, as the name hints, toys for eToys.

As skills and technologies develop, and as knowledge of them is shared, barriers to market entry in the Internet environment are lowered. Many long-established companies have begun to shift parts of their marketing efforts to the Internet. Some, like IBM, have begun to offer products and services specifically focused on the use of the Internet for business applications. For these companies, the Internet creates the product market. For other companies, such as Barnes and Noble, and Toys R Us, the Internet is just another outlet for selling what they have always sold. In both cases, the companies are generalists, with a broad base of resources that can be applied to take advantage of their follower status in the Internet ecology.

The entrance of established generalists changes the nature of the competitive environment (see Figure 7.4). For example, in April 1999, Toys R Us announced plans to invest $80 million in its e-commerce activities, supplanting pure-player eToys to become a dominant force in the online toy marketplace. Toys R Us sought to achieve its goal of being the market leader by 2000 by emphasizing convenience: online purchases could be returned to any Toys R Us store. The strategy was successful. During the holiday shopping season, MediaMetrix reported growth in site visits of 93 percent for eToys, compared with 277 percent for Toys R Us.

Business Ecosystems

The integration of the Internet with traditional business activities means that the types of business structures that have existed over time may evolve into forms that reflect adaptation to the new environments for commerce. Population ecologists have found that competition for resources and the structure of populations tend to be systematically related. In biological terms, this relationship is reflected by the observation that when populations can interbreed, thus sharing genes, the overall genetic variation increases. The competition leads to interaction between different populations in the environment, in order to determine the allocation of the resources. In many cases, interbreeding is a form of interaction that provides the resulting population with a resource advantage.

Similar types of interbreeding have occurred in the Internet ecology. This mingling of capabilities has led to the blurring of boundaries of the industries that

FIGURE 7.4 Strategic Activity Is Affected by Life Cycle State and Competition.

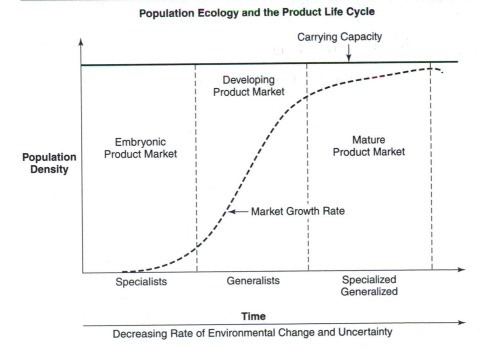

comprise the business populations of the Internet. For example, Microsoft is known primarily for its software development and sales. However, they also offer a travel service, Expedia, and an Internet browser, Internet Explorer. Although their products and services are clearly linked by the software competency, the nature of the products and services they offer crosses the boundaries of traditionally defined industries. The merger of Time-Warner and America Online (AOL) provides another example. Time-Warner, an entertainment conglomerate, is a content provider. AOL provides the service for content delivery. The interbreeding of these corporations results in a symbiotic relationship between divisions of the previously independent companies and provides them with a competitive advantage over the other population members of the two industries in which they developed. The emergence of these interbred industries has resulted in hybrid business structures, termed **business ecosystems.**

Digital Artifact 7.3

The cross-marketing alliance between AOL and Target leverages AOL's 24 million subscribers and Target's 1 billion customers a year.

(*Source:* **Yahoo! News, June 13, 2000.**)

Strategic Alliances

The concept of business ecosystems is closely related to the idea of strategic alliances. The technological and communications capabilities of the Internet have made global competition a reality for many industries. To succeed in the global economy, companies often enter **strategic alliances.** The goal of a strategic alliance is to combine complementary resources to enhance the ability of the allied companies to compete more effectively in their markets.

Strategic alliances take many forms, from formal mergers to informal partnership agreements. This approach to competition is termed **strategic network competition.** Strategic alliances differ from business ecosystems in that the companies in the strategic alliance remain independent entities, while components of the business ecosystem are subsumed under a parent company. The graphic in Figure 7.5 illustrates the array of strategic alliances that exists in the business-to-consumer realm of the Internet environment.

To this point, we have used a population ecology approach to formulate a general description of the environment for marketing that is created when the goals of marketing interact with the capabilities of the Internet made available through technology. This environment serves as a virtual ecology, complete with factors that can constrain or encourage the growth of populations, or industries, within the environment. In the following sections, we will examine in greater detail the nature of the virtual ecology, with an emphasis on describing the structure of the marketing environment, and the types of marketing activities that the environment enables.

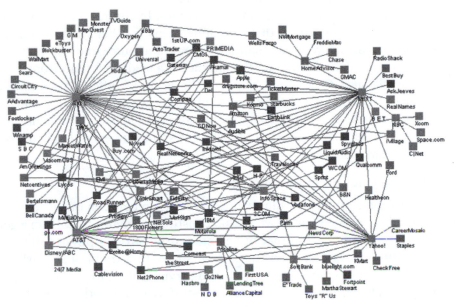

FIGURE 7.5 Strategic B2C Alliances.

We begin with a general characterization of Internet ecology, focusing on the factors that differentiate this environment from traditional marketing environments. Then we consider the types of marketing activities that can be conducted in the changing marketing environment.

CHARACTERISTICS OF THE INTERNET ECOLOGY

One of the most obvious—even defining—features of the Internet ecology is that it is virtual; that is, it exists, but not in the ways that we typically expect a concept based on physical description to exist in the physical world. Take, for example, the idea of a virtual storefront. We know that in the physical world, a storefront is a real entity with goods, salespeople, and checkout counters, in which we can touch, smell, see, hear, and, depending on the product, even taste the wares. In a virtual storefront, the physical environment shifts to a digital environment. Our use of senses to perceive the experience is currently limited to—at best—seeing and hearing product information.

The importance of the shift from a bricks-and-mortar world to a bits-and-bytes world raises issues for marketing in the Internet ecology. These issues can be understood with reference to concepts from population ecology. For example, virtualization can be characterized as one of a set of environmental characteristics. These characteristics may serve as factors that influence environmental resistance to industry growth. That is, some factors may operate as constraints on the ability of a particular industry to grow in the Internet ecology. In contrast, other factors may create opportunities for growth that cannot be found in other environments.

To illustrate the nature of the Internet ecology as a source of constraints and opportunities for populations, consider the Internet as a medium for electronic communications. While such a view oversimplifies the array of differences that sets the Internet apart from traditional marketing media, such as television, radio, and print, it underscores the novelty of the evolving marketing environment. For instance, placing the emphasis on electronic communications implies a fundamental shift in the way we describe the marketplace.

From Marketplace to Marketspace

As a means for electronically transferring information between buyers and sellers, the Internet has changed our ideas of what constitutes a marketplace. On a general level, marketing with the Internet has created a shift from a physical transaction space to an information-defined transaction space. In a traditional marketplace, buyers acquire information about goods and services, often from direct, hands-on examination of the products and through face-to-face conversations with the seller. In an Internet-created marketspace, however, the environment changes.

Environmental Constraints in the Marketspace

In the marketspace, the consumer's acquisition of product-related information is separated from the product itself; typically, a computer enables the exchange of information between the consumer and the marketer. The consumer receives information about the product and may even be able to observe a real-time use of the product to obtain a vicarious experience, but hands-on trial is not possible. In this situation, the virtual environment can be viewed as a constraint, creating environmental resistance that limits the growth of companies that rely on physical product experience. Companies whose products rely on sensory experience in modalities that cannot be offered digitally may find it difficult to persuade the consumer. Some examples include perfume manufacturers and bakeries, whose success may depend on consumers' experiential reactions to the product.

Of course, in other cases the product can be experienced on a trial basis over the Internet, as with software packages, but this opportunity is limited to products and services that are available in an appropriate digital format. For these types of companies, the Internet ecology may create opportunities for promoting and disseminating the product. In this vein, companies attempt to create virtual experiences to overcome experiential constraints in selling nondigitizable products online. Clothing retailers who use online simulations to provide consumers with the experience of "trying on" a garment are a noteworthy example.

Cultural Constraints in the Marketspace

Marketers operating within the Internet ecology may also encounter constraints that are not created simply by the nature of the environment. Remember the ethological factors that can affect the ability of a population to grow? These factors stem from the members of a population, rather than from the environment itself. An example of an ethological factor that influences growth in the Internet ecology is the set of expectations people hold about the nature of an experience, such as learning about a product in a virtual marketplace. These expectations serve as a culturally induced constraint on the interpretation of a virtual product experience. In a marketspace environment, the process of examining and evaluating a product may be influenced by the quality of the experience perceived by the consumer when interacting with the medium within which the information is acquired.

Environmental constraints and cultural constraints may join forces to influence the success of an organization in the virtual environment. For example, the quality of the experience can be compared to the effects of situational factors in a marketplace—an environmental constraint. In a traditional marketing environment, a consumer's perceptions of the situation may be affected by characteristics of the environment. Atmospherics, such as lighting, music, and temperature, have been shown to influence product evaluations. In addition, interactions with salespeople can enhance or detract from the perceived quality of a product.

In a marketspace, however, the nature of consumers' interactions with the marketing environment is different due to the unique characteristics of the environment. The environmental constraints of the virtual ecology may interact with the cultural constraints imposed by people's experience with traditional environments to affect their perceptions of the virtual product experience. Thus, while marketplaces and marketspaces may share features at a general level, it is important to understand how the situationally imposed differences may influence exchange behaviors at more specific levels.

To illustrate the idea of interaction between types of constraints, think about shopping for clothes on the Internet. We have already discussed the environmental constraint imposed by the limits of the digital environment, as well as marketers' efforts to overcome the constraint through simulated garment modeling techniques. A cultural constraint may also be in effect for online clothes shopping.

Many people like to shop with others, such as friends or family. The opinions of others serve as a gauge by which the consumer measures the benefits and reduces the uncertainty about the purchase. Shopping in an online environment, however, is often a solitary experience: a consumer, a computer, and a distant, digital Web site. As a result, the environmental factor and the cultural condition may operate together to create a barrier to online clothing purchases.

Some online clothing retailers have attempted to reduce or eliminate this barrier. One technique is to enable "buddy shopping" in which two or more people, operating from separate computers, can shop together, viewing the same item and exchanging opinions though the online medium.

The constraints of the Internet ecology illustrate the differences between a traditional marketplace and the Internet marketspace. These differences are summarized in the table in Figure 7.6.

Marketplace	Marketspace
Physical product present	Virtual product description
Face-to-face interaction	Computer-mediated interaction
	• person interactivity
	• machine interactivity
Complete sensory experience	Limited sensory experience

FIGURE 7.6 Differences Between Marketplace and Marketspace.

AN EVOLVING MARKET STRUCTURES PERSPECTIVE

We have used concepts from population ecology to describe some of the effects of the Internet ecology on the marketing environment. Now we turn our attention to the way that the environment influences the structure of marketing organizations. We continue, however, to use population ecology as a guide. The application is straightforward. Populations are structured in ways that enhance their ability to exist and to grow. The environment in which a population exists consists of factors that enhance or impede growth. Thus, the Internet environment affects the ways in which populations, or industries, will structure themselves in order to succeed.

The Internet Ecology and the Value Chain

The **value chain** is a popular term for describing the set of activities that an organization undertakes to move its products from development to the market. If you think of the process as a sequence of links, as shown in Figure 7.7, the basic idea is that each link provides an opportunity to increase the value of the offering to the end purchaser. Increased value may occur when processes can be sped up to make the product available more quickly. Value may also be added if new technologies enable the production of a higher-quality product, or a product that costs less. As a result, the way that a value chain is structured can create competitive advantage.

The environment is an important factor in the development of a value chain with a competitive advantage. It can create opportunities for change that enable a company to maximize its use of resources and to increase the value of different links.

Consider the development of a single product, from an idea to a saleable item. The increased availability and use of information communication technologies, such as those that comprise the Internet, can influence each stage in the life of the product. Input from consumers about product needs can be readily obtained, stored, tracked, analyzed, and interpreted via the Internet. Negotiations with sup-

FIGURE 7.7 Value Chains: Opportunities for Adding Value.

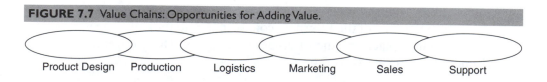

Product Design   Production   Logistics   Marketing   Sales   Support

pliers and with distributors can be conducted with greater speed and information sharing. As a result, adjacent steps in the value chain—the flow of materials and services in route to market—may be integrated and made more efficient.[3]

These changes reflect a shift from a physical value chain to a **virtual value chain,** in which information is a primary factor. The information-related activities that affect each link of the value chain include gathering, organizing, integrating, and disseminating information. Each of these activities can be conducted for separate links in the value chain, thus creating a wealth of opportunities for changing the ways that value is created. For instance, the ability to gather information via the Internet created new search engines as new products. The ability to distribute digital information as products, such as books, software, and music, via the Internet affects channel structures and logistics. The ability to disseminate information via the Internet affects promotional aspects of marketing activity, as well as sales and support processes.

Changes to the ways in which products move through the chain may be affected by fundamental changes to the functional structures of organizations. As the nature of the marketing environment changes to incorporate the opportunities of an information-defined transaction space, such as that of the Internet ecology, the ways in which companies organize their activities for getting goods and services to market change. As a result, adapting to the new, information-defined environment can lead to adaptations in the types of market structures used for all aspects of moving goods and services through the value-added chain—from manufacturing the product to marketing the product. In the next section, we will look at two types of structures.

Digital Artifact 7.4

Online shoppers will spend more than $1.9 billion in 2000 on consumables, such as health and beauty products and pet food.

(*Source:* **Nua Internet Surveys, citing ActivMedia, 2000.**)

Two Types of Market Structures

Two basic types of market structures tend to reflect the characteristics of most economic activity related to the production and distribution of products: hierarchies and markets. A hierarchical structure is illustrated by a company that uses a vertically integrated approach to the value chain. This type of structure tends to be adopted for complex products that require specific components not widely available from a pool of suppliers. In other words, the products have a complex **product**

---

[3]Even though we are taking a broad look at the effects of the Internet ecology on the structure of organizations, keep in mind the central role of marketing. Marketing knowledge is critical at every stage: from the research that indicates product need and defines the relevant set of product features, to the purchase of technologies or components for building the product, to the content of the communications to consumers about the available product.

description and high **asset specificity.** These constraints have historically tended to make it advantageous to integrate vertically, to insure the timely availability of parts and processes. In a hierarchical structure, managerial decisions control product movement through the value chain. In terms of population ecology, this structure may enhance the ability of the company or industry to survive and thrive in its environment.

In a market structure, the flow of the product through the value chain is coordinated and determined by the market forces of supply and demand. At any point in the chain, the buyer of a product component or process compares the appropriate options available from a variety of sources and selects the option that provides the optimal combination of desired benefits. A market structure is viable for products with simpler product descriptions and low asset specificity. For example, consider a large hotel with a need for a constant supply of clean towels. The laundry service needed by the hotel has low asset specificity: any service will do, provided the towels are cleaned in a timely manner. In addition, the needed service has a simple product description and its purpose can be readily communicated: use detergent, get the towels clean. As a result, the hotel can pick and choose from among a variety of service providers in a market structure to take advantage of price and performance. The ability to obtain the service in a market economy reduces the dependence of the hotel on any one laundry, thus relaxing an environmental constraint. In addition, the market economy may result in more competition for the cleaning job, potentially increasing the quality and reducing the cost of the service for the hotel.

A Shift from Hierarchies to Markets

The Internet ecology may enable industries to shift from hierarchical structures to market structures. The increasing sophistication of information technologies means that complex product descriptions can be communicated more effectively than with previous communications capabilities. For example, a company can demonstrate the nature and function of a complicated piece of machinery to a potential buyer via an online, virtual simulation—an impossible achievement with a fax machine! Even when the communication could be effectively completed face-to-face, the online environment may be cheaper and more efficient. The technology thus reduces difficulties associated with communicating information about a complex product, and the costs associated with trying to coordinate marketing activities with organizations outside the traditional, vertically integrated structure.

The technologies of the Internet ecology also influence the effect of the asset specificity constraint on industry structure. Advances in technology make it possible for companies to develop flexible production capabilities, allowing for more companies to become involved in the manufacture of highly specific product components, reducing a company's need to depend on a narrow set of suppliers. The information technologies of the Internet also make it possible to reduce the coordination costs of matching up buyers and sellers. We will look at the ways in which businesses coordinate their activities in market-type structures in greater detail in Chapter 13.

Digital Artifact 7.5

Of the 92 percent of online B2B exchanges currently conducted through direct channels, 35 percent will shift to a market structure model by 2005.

(*Source:* eMarketer, 2000, citing research by Jupiter Communications.)

Evolution of the Electronic Marketspace

We have considered how the Internet ecology may lead to a shift in the ways that industries structure their activities, from hierarchies to markets. The shifts may occur in stages, and the length of the stages may depend on the nature of the industry. Going back to ideas from population ecology, we can describe the process as one of evolution; companies will adapt to the changing nature of the environment in order to thrive, and the changes will occur over time, reflecting the dynamic, constantly changing nature of the environment.

The evolution of structures in the marketspace has been described as a three-stage process: (1) an initial, biased stage, (2) a subsequent unbiased stage, and (3) a final personalized stage. To illustrate the idea of stages, consider the development of electronic airline reservations markets. United Airlines was one of the first airlines to enable travel agents to book reservations electronically—provided the bookings were on United flights. American countered with a system that enabled agents to search all flights—of course, American's flights were at the top of any list! Subsequent regulation—largely a result of complaints by other airlines—sought to restore competition by reducing bias in the electronic markets. At this point, a true, unbiased market was achieved.

In recent years, electronic systems have become available to consumers, without having to go through a travel agent. In addition, the technologies that underlie the electronic markets have developed to a state in which personalization is possible. For instance, with Travelocity, an online travel planning and reservations service, a consumer can specify dates, desirable fare ranges, and specific airlines. These preferences can be stored, and information "pushed" to the host computer when the criteria are met.

Chapter Summary

In this chapter, we looked at the ways in which the interaction of technology and marketing creates a dynamic, new environment for marketing activity. This environment may influence the structure of marketing entities, as well as the types of marketing activities carried out by an organization.

We adopted a population ecology approach to characterize the nature of this marketing environment. Concepts associated with population ecology were used to describe the types of constraints that might be expected in the development of industries within the Internet ecology. An important aspect of the model is to characterize the nature of competition between organizations, and the role of the

Internet in creating opportunities and strategies for success in the marketing environment. We examined the impact of the Internet on the formation of strategic alliances to enhance competition. We also considered the influence of the Internet on the business activities reflected by value chains.

Using population ecology and market evolution to guide our examination, we looked at possible changes to market structures in the evolving marketplace, and we considered the characteristics of the environment that may facilitate or impede these changes. Differences between markets and hierarchies were discussed, and characteristics of industries that affect the emphasis of a market structure in the Internet environment were described.

REVIEW SECTION

Key Terms

- population ecology
- biotic potential
- environmental resistance
- carrying capacity
- natural circumstances
- cultural conditions
- density dependent

- density independent
- ethological characteristics
- niche
- specialist
- generalist
- business ecosystem
- strategic alliances

- strategic network competition
- value chain
- virtual value chain
- product description
- asset specificity

Review Questions

1. Describe the key forces that create changes in the marketing environment.
2. How is the science of population ecology relevant to the study of marketing and the Internet?
3. What two types of constraints impede industry growth?
4. Distinguish between the concepts of density dependence and density independence.
5. What role do ethological characteristics play in the Internet environment?
6. Discuss the role of specialists and generalists at different stages of the product life cycle.
7. Describe the effects of industry interbreeding in the Internet ecology.
8. How is a marketplace different from a marketspace?
9. What factors might influence the shift from a hierarchical structure to a market structure?

Thinking Points

1. What unique characteristics are available in an electronic medium?
2. Discuss the evolution of the electronic marketplace from a population ecology standpoint.

3. How do characteristics of the Internet change the way marketers can attempt to cre-ate brand equity?
4. How can we utilize a population ecology model to explain and predict the nature of competition between organizations?
5. Why might early electronic markets tend to be biased toward a specific vendor?
6. What factors encourage the evolution of markets in the Internet environment to move from being biased to being unbiased?
7. The Internet enables marketers to disaggregate the components of a product offer-ing, which creates value for consumers. Is this ability unique to the Internet?

Suggested Readings

1. *Digital Darwinism,* by Evan I. Schwartz (New York: Random House, Inc., 1999).
2. "The Internet's Impact on Competition." In *Now or Never,* by Mary Modahl (New York: HarperCollins Publishers, Inc., 2000).
3. "Evolutionary Processes in Competitive Markets," by Mary Lambkin and George S. Day. *Journal of Marketing, 53* (July, 1989), pp. 4–20.
4. "Are You Next?" edited by Jeffrey Davis. *Business 2.0* (March 1999), pp. 44–54.
5. *Ecology of Populations,* by Arthur S. Boughey (New York: The Macmillan Com-pany, Inc., 1968).

CHAPTER 8

The Internet and Marketing Planning

FOCUS AND OBJECTIVES

Strategic marketing enables companies to develop and maintain a competitive advantage in the Internet environment. This chapter is focused on describing and explaining the influence of the Internet on the need for strategic marketing and the processes for conducting it. We review types of planning, including strategic planning, strategic marketing, and marketing management. Then we focus on the role of the Internet in marketing planning to develop strategy and the marketing mix. In particular, we address business models that leverage characteristics of the Internet environment to enhance product characteristics, such as image or revenue.

YOUR OBJECTIVES IN STUDYING THIS CHAPTER INCLUDE THE FOLLOWING:

- Know the different types of planning typically undertaken by businesses.

- Understand the factors that affect the development of a competitive advantage, and how they are related to the components of marketing planning.

- Recognize characteristics of the Internet that help marketers identify opportunities and leverage resources to create a competitive advantage.

- Identify the effects of the Internet environment on the motivation, processes, and outcomes of marketing planning.

- Learn the characteristics of revenue-focused and product-focused business models for achieving strategic objectives with the Internet.

Technological advances increase the speed with which products can be developed and brought to market. These advances may also make it possible for consumers to become aware of new products, moving from trial to adoption more rapidly than before. These effects can mean that for many organizations the windows of opportunity, in which new products are envisioned, produced, and distributed, may become shorter. As a result, the importance of developing long-range and short-range plans for the way in which the organization will respond to the changing environment can be crucial for the success of the company.

The Internet can influence aspects of planning across all levels and functions of a business. Consider, for example, how the Internet has created new opportunities for products and services that have defined the focus and purpose of many companies, both small and large, and old and new. Amazon.com, an Internet retailer, entered the marketplace represented by the central exchange environment to sell books. Even though the idea of a bookstore was not new, the concept of a virtual bookstore, in which consumers can search databases of titles and reader reviews, order a book, and complete the payment part of the transaction online was novel. The opportunity for such a business did not exist until the technologies that comprise the Internet were available and accepted by a sufficient number of users to provide the online retailer with a viable target market.

In contrast, IBM, already well known and respected as a force in the international market for business machines, targeted the market for electronic business solutions. Without giving up or cannibalizing any of its existing business avenues, IBM has devoted many resources, including time, money, and personnel, to developing name recognition in the rapidly growing and developing market for electronic commerce.

The Internet can lead to an assessment and redirection of strategy, even for large, well-established companies that have no intention of marketing products online or of otherwise targeting electronic markets. For instance, a company wishing to streamline its ability to produce and distribute its products more efficiently may revamp its strategy to emphasize products that can be more feasibly developed using Internet tools. In addition, strategic changes may occur at a more focused level, targeted toward changing the way that the marketing for a particular product line is carried out. Internet facilities, such as the availability of media buying information from online sources, and competitive research from online databases, can be used to develop marketing plans for traditional, offline situations.

In this chapter we will consider the goals and processes for planning. We will focus, in particular, on the role of the Internet for strategic marketing. The importance of strategic marketing is reflected in the effects of Internet development on the resources and opportunities available to organizations, as well as on the specific activities conducted to develop and to implement marketing plans that capitalize on these opportunities.

We begin with a description of the nature and intent behind different types of planning within the organization, to set the stage for a discussion of the effects of the Internet on planning. Then we discuss the influence of the Internet on the motivation, development, and execution of planning processes that result in marketing strategy.

The Internet not only influences strategy development, but also its implementation. In the final sections of this chapter, we discuss several business models that use the Internet to achieve strategic objectives.

Digital Artifact 8.1

Californians spend more money online than consumers in any other state: $6 billion in 1999, compared with the runner-up, Texas, at $3.2 billion.

(*Source:* **CyberAtlas, citing data from International Data Corp., 2000.**)

TYPES OF PLANNING: AN OVERVIEW

Planning processes within organizations take different forms, depending on the purpose and focus of the planning effort. Three types of planning most directly related to marketing activity are strategic planning, strategic marketing, and marketing management. **Strategic planning** involves the long-term relationship of an organization to its environment (Jain, 1983), in which decisions are made about the objectives and resources of the organization. **Strategic marketing** is the component of strategic planning that is focused on determining the appropriate products and their markets for the organization. The purpose of **marketing management** is to implement the objectives of strategic planning and marketing strategy, by developing and executing plans for segmentation and the marketing mix.

Figure 8.1 illustrates the relationships between the different types of planning. For our purposes, note the central role of strategic marketing. Strategic marketing implements the broad goals of an organization, in terms of the products or services it offers. Given this objective, strategic marketing is guided by the outcomes of strategic planning, and it provides input to future strategic planning. The outcomes of strategic marketing are implemented by marketing management. In sum, strategic marketing requires knowledge of the market environment that can be used to guide higher order decisions (i.e., strategic planning), and lower-order implementation (i.e., marketing management). Let's take a brief look at the goals of each type of planning.

What Is Strategic Planning?

Strategic planning is the process by which managers develop long-range plans, implemented by shorter-range tactics, for the activities necessary to accomplish the goals of an organization. Strategic planning is important because it serves as the basis for effective decision making in many different areas of the organization. It is also the basis for decision making about a variety of different functions associated with moving the products of a company from design and production to the end consumer.

The process of strategic planning involves a within-the-organization analysis of fit between organizational resources and environmental opportunities. A strategic plan is designed to maximize the performance of a set of strategic business units. A **strategic business unit** (SBU) is the smallest unit within an organization that has responsibility and control over the determination and execution of the activities it will undertake to achieve its mission, and the resources needed to do so.

FIGURE 8.1 Marketing Relies on Different Levels and Types of Planning.

Strategic planning is intended to serve as a road map for activities designed to meet organizational objectives over an extended period of time. As information becomes available about the outcomes of completed activities, the strategic plan may be adjusted to accommodate changes to expectations and resources.

While strategic planning is intended to provide continuity of objectives and activities across and within units of the organization, the Internet may lead to shorter planning horizons. The ready availability of information with which to update expectations about market behavior, combined with the flip side—competitors are more able to learn what an organization is planning—may result in the need to adapt strategic plans with increasing frequency.

The benefits of strategic planning may become more pronounced as the Internet creates new opportunities for business products and practices in the central exchange environment. The Internet creates an opportunity to reassess strategic planning, as well as a way to develop and refine concepts and tactics associated with strategic planning. These opportunities may lead to strategic changes as dramatic as a redefinition of organizational mission or as subtle as a shift in the procedures used to share documentation within a company.

Digital Artifact 8.2

Pure-player retailers spend an average of $42 on marketing to win a new customer.
(*Source:* **ZDNet News, November 16, 1999, citing Shop.org.**)

From Strategic Planning to Marketing Planning

Strategic planning occurs at the organization level; strategic marketing takes place within a business unit. Strategic marketing translates the goals of the overall company into objectives for a specific business unit or product. Strategic marketing seeks to answer three questions: (1) Who is (are) the target market(s)? (2) What type of product will enable us to compete in this market? and (3) When is the right time to enter the market? Strategic marketing serves as an interface between macro-level, across-SBU strategic planning and micro-level, within-SBU marketing management.

The difference between strategic marketing and marketing management is reflected in the different objectives of the planning processes. Strategic marketing assesses the resources, including capabilities, of a business, in conjunction with opportunities in the environment. In essence, this process asks, "What resources do we have, and what is out there in the environment that lets us do something new that fits with organizational objectives?" The strategic marketing process concludes with the formulation of a core strategy. Planning then shifts to marketing management.

Marketing management develops marketing plans for segmentation and mix elements that implement the core strategy. While marketing strategy is focused on what can and should be done, marketing management is focused on how to do it. The key question for marketing management is, "How should we do what we want to do, given the resources we have and the targeted market(s)?"

For each type of planning, the Internet may influence the relative emphasis placed on resources and opportunities. For example, in a smaller company with a single product focus, the Internet may create an opportunity to reach new markets for the existing product. Planning activities to tap into these markets may be desirable, given the limited resources of the company to modify the product or to develop other products.

In contrast, a larger company with a diversified set of products may capitalize on the technological capabilities available through the Internet for collaborative product design and production in order to leverage existing resources for more efficient production. The enhanced resources, due to increased efficiency, may then be used to modify or develop new products.

MARKETING PLANNING IN DEPTH

Marketing planning is conducted with two chief objectives: (1) define the opportunities that exist in the environment, and (2) determine how best to leverage resources to capitalize on opportunities. Framed as questions, these objectives are "What should we do?" and "How should we do it?" The first question emphasizes the role of marketing strategy, while the second question underscores the importance of marketing management. Figure 8.2 illustrates the primary tasks for marketing planning.

FIGURE 8.2 Primary Objectives of Marketing Planning.

Defining Opportunities: What Should We Do?

A fundamental goal for marketing strategy is to develop a means by which a company can perform better than its competition. "Doing better" may translate into faster growth, greater market share, or higher profits. Each of these measures of success, however, can be related to the concept of **competitive advantage.**

As a general characterization, a company that has a competitive advantage tends to have an ability to obtain profits that are higher than average, among the pool of competition. Competitive advantage can be created in several ways. For example, having a product or process that nobody else has, and which is superior and in demand, can provide competitive advantage. In effect, a competitive advantage provides the marketer with a niche that fosters the success of the company in the environment. The factors that affect competitive advantage are presented in Figure 8.3.

Defining opportunities that can provide a competitive advantage can be complicated. Suppose that your supervisor comes up to you and tells you that your continued employment depends on your ability to develop an idea for a product—soon. Not just any product, but a product that is completely different from anything your competition presently offers. A product so new that it will meet needs that even the consumers do not know they have! And, of course, it has to be a product that your company is capable of producing. (Cheer up. If you succeed, you're set for life.)

The Internet and Opportunity

The Internet can be used to develop insights about consumers' needs and competitors' actions. In addition, marketers can use the Internet to monitor changes to conditions that might affect the viability of strategic actions (e.g., technology and policy developments).

The Internet is a source of market intelligence for defining opportunities. Marketing researchers can acquire information directly from consumers about desired product and service features, using e-mail and online survey approaches. In addition, information about consumers' preferences and attitudes can be gathered indirectly, through discussion groups and mailing lists.

Information about the competitive climate can be assessed by analyzing the product offerings and promotional material provided on the Internet by firms in

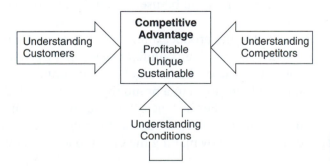

FIGURE 8.3 Factors That Affect Competitive Advantage.

product niches that are related to the product objectives of the company conducting the research. In addition, newsgroups, chat rooms, and online bulletin boards are often sources of evaluative information about the extent to which a company's approach meets consumers' needs.

Marketers can also use the Internet to assess trends and develop predictions about the nature of market conditions that can affect the efficacy of a strategy. Internet content, such as press releases, agency reports, and public and private sector databases, provides a range of ever-changing insights on the role of technology, the economy, and policy for marketing. We will examine ways to use the Internet for marketing research in far greater detail in Chapter 9.

Digital Artifact 8.3

Seventy-six percent of retail sites use sweepstakes to attract visitors.

(*Source:* ZDNet News, October 25, 1999, citing a Jupiter Communications study.)

Leveraging Resources: How Should We Do It?

Once a marketing strategy is formulated, the task of carrying out the strategy is handed to marketing management. At this level, the objective is to capitalize on characteristics of the environment that serve as resources with which to develop an effective marketing mix. The goal of mix development is to provide value to the consumer: to create a persuasive value proposition. Value can be derived from three aspects of the Internet: (1) its role as a source of content, (2) its ability to serve as a channel, and (3) its use as a form of communication.

The Internet as a Content Resource

The information-rich nature of the Internet means that it can be used as a resource in several ways. In one use, Internet content may be a product offering, when the product can be digitized (e.g., books, music). This use is closely related to the role of the Internet as a channel resource.

A second use of the Internet as a content resource is to develop and maintain information to guide product development. For instance, the data that result from marketing research can be collected, organized, and stored in internal databases that can be mined to provide insights for future product development or marketing activity. In addition, Internet technologies can be used to implement online product planning and design efforts.

As a third use, benefits related to the product offering—such as customer support and product information—can be provided online, even when the product cannot be offered in a digital form. This use of the Internet as a content resource can create **soft benefits,** or reasons for being loyal to a brand that are not related to the actual nature or function of the product. For instance, Web site content that leads a consumer through the steps of how to install and use a tax preparation software may create an advantage for the product by making the effort to learn a new package unacceptably high.

Creating content is not limited to the marketer. Consumer-created content, as enabled through online brand communities or by posting information to a product or company Web site, may create a positive consumer-marketer relationship. We will examine the role of content as a factor in strategy implementation in Chapter 10.

The Internet as a Channel Resource

To illustrate the Internet's role as a channel resource, suppose that you have a company that produces a popular software product that is widely available in retail outlets. With increasing competition, however, it has been getting harder to maintain the profit margins your software used to provide. Pressure from the competition has forced your company to cut the price of the software, but the costs of producing and getting the product to the target markets have increased. What can you do?

You might conclude that the software product could be sold and distributed entirely through the Internet. This change in practice reduces packaging costs and shipping costs. Of course, these benefits must be weighed against the loss in sales and brand recognition for packages sold in retail outlets. Management feels, however, that by increasing advertising to make consumers aware of the online availability of the software, issues of sales and brand exposure can be addressed. Thus, the change to the distribution element of the marketing mix is based on the determination of marketing management that the benefits of the Internet as a distribution outlet outweigh the costs of a diminished presence in retail outlets. Channel implications of the Internet will resurface in Chapter 11.

The Internet as a Communications Resource

The Internet can be used as a vehicle for communications between the marketer's organization and the marketplace. The multimedia, interactive nature of the Internet enables marketers to develop promotional campaigns and to provide product-related experiences in ways that differ from the forms of communications typically seen in traditional media.

The novel characteristics of the Internet as a communications medium can be used to achieve strategic objectives, such as creating awareness, or attracting attention to a brand or product. In addition, the technologies that facilitate real-time, digital interaction between a marketer and a consumer can be used to foster relationship development. These types of relationships might include a salesperson-customer exchange, or a consumer-customer service exchange.

An important aspect of marketing communications is the content of the communication. The nature of the Internet, however, makes it possible to consider the effect of the content of a communication as separate from the effect of the manner in which the content is transmitted. This distinction is explored in Chapter 12.

To this point, we have reviewed the basic characteristics of marketing planning. We have also considered how the Internet can be used to define strategic opportunities and to provide the means with which to seize these opportunities. In the next sections, we will look at the way that the Internet may influence processes for developing and implementing marketing strategy.

INTERNET EFFECTS ON STRATEGY DEVELOPMENT: PLANNING

The Internet may influence the development of marketing planning in three distinct ways. First, it may lead a business to recognize a need for new planning. Second, the Internet may influence how a business conducts its planning activities, regardless of the reason for which they originate. Third, the Internet may influence the content of a strategic plan. That is, the interactive environment may suggest changes to objectives and activities.

Internet influences on strategy development may occur at any level of planning: strategic planning, strategic marketing planning, or marketing management planning. The opportunity for these influences is depicted in Figure 8.4.

The Internet Affects Motivation for Planning

Rapid changes in technologies and Internet content present strategic challenges for marketers. For example, the rate of change to the central exchange environment of the Internet may lead to shorter windows of opportunity for introducing new products and heightened customer expectations about the rate at which new or modified products will be introduced. The strategic windows of opportunity decrease in length for three reasons. First, new technologies lead to new products, thus making old products more rapidly obsolete. Second, new technologies lead to faster communications among consumers, thus speeding adoption rates and establishing product standards. Third, new technologies lead to increased product visibility across competition, thus reducing the time needed to develop a competitive product (and the competitive advantage of a novel product). These reasons reflect the impact of conditions, consumers, and competition, respectively, on the need for marketing planning.

FIGURE 8.4 The Internet Influences Aspects of Planning.

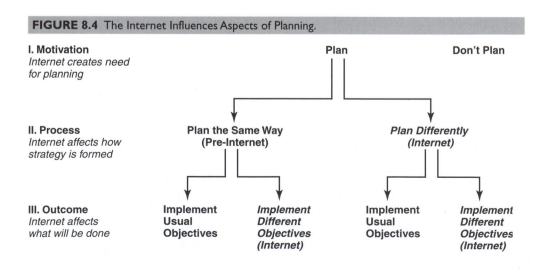

To illustrate the effect of the Internet as a motive for strategic marketing, suppose that you work for a company whose business mission is to provide music. The businesses of the organization are diverse, including concert production, instrument sales, and music recording sales. Your division is responsible for sales of recorded music. Your products, including cassettes and compact discs, have been popular since their introduction, but your research department has suggested that a new "compression technology" may make it possible to efficiently transmit music over the Internet. Although you are concerned that digital music may harm your company's sales of cassettes and compact discs, you feel that this opportunity should not be missed.

This scenario reflects strategic marketing planning motivated by environmental scanning. In this case, the environment includes the Internet and traditional formats for music recording sales. The mission of the SBU focused on music recordings may be redefined to emphasize a shift to the focus of core strategy on product type, even though the overarching mission of the larger organization is largely unchanged.

Digital Artifact 8.4

Online Americans between 8 and 24 years of age spend an estimated $164 billion per year. Of this amount, 13 percent, or $20.3 billion, is spent online.

(*Source:* **Harris Interactive, September 2000.**)

The Internet Affects Processes for Planning

As noted in Figure 8.4, the second way in which the Internet may affect planning is by influencing the manner in which planning is accomplished. That is, by changing the nature of the processes for planning.

The Internet augments resources for planning and may influence the processes for planning in two ways: (1) by facilitating communications, and (2) by serving as an information resource. For instance, strategic marketing may benefit from collaborative communications technologies available on the Internet to enable communications horizontally (within the SBU) and vertically (through organizational levels). Results of enhanced communications via the Internet may include faster planning cycles, more flexible plans, and increased cross-functional involvement in planning.

As an information resource, the Internet can be used to glean intelligence about consumers and competitors. As we have already seen, this knowledge may affect the course of strategic marketing planning by introducing new opportunities for achieving a competitive advantage in the marketplace.

The Internet Affects Outcomes of Planning

The Internet may influence the focus and structure of the strategy that results from the planning process. Characteristics of the Internet may enable marketers to carry out activities that would not be possible without the Internet, or to complete activities differently. In either case, the end result may be a shift in the objectives of strategic marketing. For instance, the Internet may serve as an opportunity for a new product, or it may make an existing product obsolete. For example, some music vendors are concerned that the ability to download music from the Internet may eliminate the markets for compact discs and cassette tapes. In addition, the Internet may provide a channel for distributing a product, or as a means of providing benefits for a market segment that was previously unreachable (e.g., international).

INTERNET EFFECTS ON STRATEGY IMPLEMENTATION: MARKETING ACTION

We have seen how the Internet can affect formulation of marketing strategy, in terms of altering the reasons for planning, the processes for planning, and the outcomes of planning. Because it can be used as a tool to help businesses implement marketing strategy, the Internet can also influence strategy execution. In this section, we will examine the role of the Internet as a means for reaching strategic objectives.

The Internet and Strategic Objectives

Think of all the products and services that are available for consumption. It is not surprising that just as many ways are used by marketers to create awareness, demand, and loyalty for these items. It would be impossible to specify every possibility, much less study them. We can simplify our task, however, by grouping strategic objectives—and the ways that marketers attempt to achieve them—into two sets. One set of objectives emphasizes a product focus, such as enhancing the image of a brand. A second set of objectives revolves around revenue, as obtained through sales or through commissions from sales.

A Product Focus: Creating Brand Equity

The shift from marketplace to marketspace has been proposed to affect the way that marketers create and communicate economic value to consumers. With the Internet as the vehicle for many marketing activities, the information provided electronically about the product takes on greater importance, and it may exert a critical influence on the success of the company.

Several core concepts of marketing may be influenced by the increased emphasis on information in a digital marketing environment, and by the separation of information and product. These concepts include the idea of brand equity. **Brand equity** can be simply defined as the value of a brand name. While defining it may be easy, however, achieving it can be far more complicated! The Internet can play an important role in developing brand equity.

Marketers attempt to create brand equity by manipulating elements of the marketing mix, such as product characteristics and distribution strategies, to differentiate their brand from competing brands. In a traditional marketplace, mix elements work together to create perceived value on the part of the consumer. The elements are viewed as dependent and inseparable—all part of a marketing program for a particular product. As a result, brand equity typically results from an aggregate-level approach to creating value in the marketplace.

In an information-defined transaction environment, however, the ability to create differentiation through traditional combinations of mix elements may be less feasible than in physical space marketing environments. Consider the following example of a car purchase in each type of environment.

Traditional marketing approaches to brand equity typically explain equity as the result of an effective combination of three elements of a transaction: content, context, and infrastructure. Content refers to the product, or to information provided about the product. Context describes the setting, or environment, in which the transaction occurs. The infrastructure is the system or facilities that enable the product to be conveyed from the marketer to the consumer. For example, in a marketplace setting, the content component of a car purchase would consist of the cars available for evaluation at a dealership. The context would be the dealership from which the car is to be purchased. The delivery of the car is facilitated by the infrastructure, which might consist of an inventory system that results in the selected car being available on-site, or an ordering system through which the car is built at the factory and then delivered to the consumer.

Now suppose that the consumer wants to purchase a car from a vendor on the Internet. The content is no longer the physically tangible car, but information about the available vehicles. The context is not the face-to-face interaction with a salesperson at the dealership, but a series of electronic, on-screen communications. The infrastructure shifts from the organizational characteristics of the dealership to the computer and communications systems that enable the transaction.

In the traditional marketplace, the components are clearly distinct. Unless all of the components are present, however, there is no product offering to be consumed. In short, value is the result of the holistic availability of all three components. More succinctly, the whole really *is* greater than the sum of its parts.

Reseachers Rayport and Sviolka note that in the Internet environment, the components can be separated so that each individual component can convey value.[1] This possibility means that marketers can attempt to create brand equity in new ways, with different combinations or implementations of components (see Figure 8.5).

For example, Amazon.com, an online vendor, is comparable in its earliest online offering, books, to other book vendors in traditional marketplaces. In contrast, however, Amazon leverages the online context to provide access to its inventory in a customized form, tailoring the information provided to customers. This creates value in the form of a new benefit for consumers. The databases of customer input and sales information also provide Amazon with the ability to obtain detailed and

---

[1]"Managing in the Marketspace," by Jeffrey F. Rayport and John J. Sviokla. *Harvard Business Review* (November–December 1999), pp. 141–150.

	Marketplace: A-1 Bookstore	*Marketspace: Amazon.com*
Content	Product offering: book at specified prices	Database of inventory and product-related information *Value opportunity: can be applied to other forms (e.g., tools and toys)*
Context	Physical location of retail outlet	Online, digital format, searchable by user preferences *Value opportunity: can be restructured to personalize presentation of product assortments*
Infrastructure	Retail capabilities: space and equipment (e.g., warehouse, shelves, employees, cash register)	Internet *Value opportunity: can be used for near real-time communication with consumers in remote locations*

FIGURE 8.5 Examples of Disaggregating Components for Differential Emphasis.

up-to-date information for inventory and distribution, thus streamlining and re-defining infrastructure.

The ability to disaggregate the components of value also enables marketers to develop brand equity by creating combinations of components in novel ways, as through developing relationships with other vendors. To illustrate, consider the success of America Online. The content is a collection of news from national newspapers, and the infrastructure is a combination of widely available communications goods and services, not owned by the company. The success of America Online is the result of the creation of a valued context that enables users to customize the information they receive online. This context is America Online's brand, and the basis for the brand equity that the company enjoys.

Customer loyalty is closely related to brand equity. Developing loyalty to a brand, product, or company in information-defined environments can be accomplished by taking advantage of the ability to separate the value components. In an Internet environment, consumers may develop loyalty to individual components, rather than to an aggregate notion of value for a particular brand, product, or vendor. For example, a company that distinguishes itself from its competition because its Internet presence provides consumers with a tailored product search or simplified ordering or a faster delivery time has capitalized on context to develop a competitive advantage that encourages loyalty.

It is important to note, however, that the aspects of the Internet that enable the development of loyalty must be managed carefully. The ready availability of information over the Internet may diminish loyalty by making comparisons across brands quick, easy, and relatively cost-free. For example, online reservation services for air travel provide consumers with information about flights and fares for several airlines. Airlines must then rely on differentiation in content, or on other aspects of the offering, to encourage loyalty. To this end, airlines can differentiate through content, such as frequent flier programs and awards. They may also differentiate through context, as with online customer service, to increase loyalty to a particular vendor.

Product-Focused Business Models: The Three I's

We can describe product-focused business models in terms of the extent to which they differentially emphasize one of three aspects of consumers' perceptions of the product—image, incentive, and improvement—as shown in Figure 8.6. The **Three I's** all contribute to brand equity. We will look at each of them in the following sections.

Image   An image-based objective emphasizes marketing activities that enhance people's perceptions of the product or brand. Companies can use the Internet to build a brand image by increasing awareness and exposure to the item. An example of a technique that can accomplish these goals is a **link exchange,** in which two companies place logos or hyperlinks to each other's Web pages on their sites. Companies may also develop more formal arrangements that foster coexistence in the marketspace. These arrangements include partnerships to co-brand products.

A goal of **co-branding** is to identify a partner whose brand, when linked with yours, has the potential for increasing customer's perceptions of your brand. For example, Lycos, a search engine, and Barnes & Noble, a bookseller, have negotiated a partnership for online presence. Lycos benefits from the long-standing reputation of Barnes & Noble in the traditional marketplace, while Barnes & Nobles gains visibility in the marketspace.

Image is also enhanced by Web site content. Content that lures users repeatedly to a site can also build brand image through exposure. In some cases, the content may be only tangentially related to the product, but the positive affect associated with the site may transfer to the brand. **Web site stickiness** describes the ability of a site's content to engage users' interest. For example, Mattel's Barbie.com site, shown in Figure 8.7, uses colorful images and interactive capabilities to provide an entertaining site visit.

FIGURE 8.6 Product-Focused Models: The Three I's.

Model Type	Image	Incentive	Improvement
Objective	Enhance consumers' perceptions of brand, product, or company	Reduce costs associated with product purchase	Create benefits in product performance or use experience
Internet Tactics	Use Web site to provide related information; create co-brands and alliances	Use Internet as channel, or to streamline processes (e.g., reduce delivery time)	Use Internet for customer support, including feedback, product customization, and product upgrades

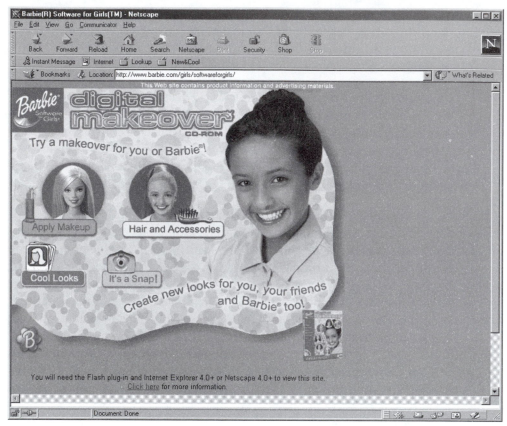

Source: BARBIE, MY DESIGN and associated trademarks are owned by and used with the permission of Mattel, Inc. © 2000, Mattel, Inc. All Rights Reserved. MY DESIGN patent pending.

FIGURE 8.7 Enhancing Product Image With Site Content.

Online brand building is important. Recent study results from Harris Interactive (2000) show that 20 percent of consumers type in the URL of a desired product, rather than searching the Web for information about the product category. The survey provides evidence for six categories of online shoppers. These categories are shown in Figure 8.8. "Brand Loyalists" know what they are looking for, and they go straight to sites where they can get it. They are the biggest spenders and report high levels of satisfaction with online shopping. In contrast, "Hunter-Gathers" are comparison shoppers. This group tends to have shoppers in their mid-thirties, married, with children. The "Hooked, Online, & Single" shoppers tend to use the Internet primarily to consume services, such as banking, investing, and entertainment. Both the Hunter-Gatherers and the Hooked segments constitute desirable markets and represent viable targets for brand building efforts. "Time-Sensitive Materialists" are another viable target for brand building. These consumers look for convenience and time savings in online shopping. Creating a strong brand that reduces search and instills loyalty addresses these objectives.

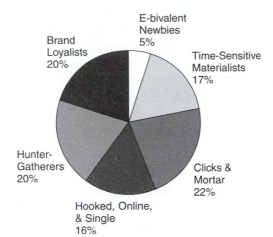

Source: Nua Internet Surveys, citing Harris Interactive, 2000.

FIGURE 8.8 Six Types of Online Shoppers.

The remaining categories exhibit fewer opportunities for online branding. Consumers in the "Clicks & Mortar" category are concerned about the security of online shopping. They tend to look for product information online, but shop in traditional outlets. The "E-bivalent Newbies" are older, less interested in online shopping, and spend the least amount of time online.

Incentive   The Internet can provide companies with ways to streamline production and distribution processes. In addition, the Internet can facilitate some forms of promotional effort, due to the ease with which content can be tailored and transmitted. These capabilities can mean that costs associated with product activities decrease. This reduced cost, when passed on to consumers, serves as an incentive to purchase the product.

Companies who wish to use an incentive-based approach can use the Internet as a resource for creating incentives in several ways. For example, a channel structure in which the Internet eliminates or reduces the number of intermediaries can lower product costs for the consumer. In addition, products for which updates or changes can be distributed digitally can also provide cost incentives to consumers. For instance, patches and upgrades to software, and revisions to published content can be handled wholly through the Internet.

Another form of incentive is represented by promotional efforts that provide free samples, trial offers, and digital coupons and rebates to encourage consumers' interactions with a product. For example, Snap, a navigation hub, promoted its portal by advertising a promise to pay $20 to consumers who made purchases through its site. Other companies have followed this approach to lure first-time online customers, including Barnes & Noble and Toys R Us.

Yet another form of incentive is illustrated by beenz.com (Figure 8.9). The company provides a system that rewards consumers with digital beenz for visiting sites, using certain ISPs and making purchases. Users collect the beenz in an online account, and can spend them at a variety of online stores that have agreed to accept

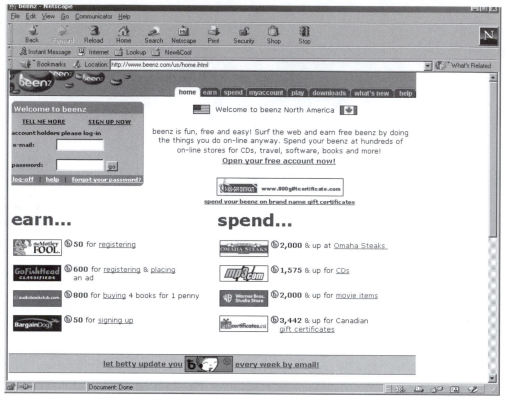

FIGURE 8.9 The beenz.com Incentive Program Rewards Consumer-Marketer Interactions.

beenz in lieu of money. Marketers can use the beenz service to attract consumers, to reward repeat shoppers, and to gather information.

Improvement   The third product-focused approach is characterized by a marketer's efforts to enhance perceptions of a product by increasing its value to consumers. The changes, or improvements, to the product offering can be implemented in a variety of ways with the Internet. As we have already noted, Web site content can serve as an added benefit of a product. Another form of improvement is customer service, both before the transaction and after. Customer service on the Internet can be as simple as posting technical manuals and tips for product use, or as technologically involved as interactive, real-time, online communication between the user and a service representative. Dell Computer e-mail support approach falls between these two extremes in terms of technological complexity and interactivity. Dell uses the Internet to allow customers to target their questions to a representative with specialized knowledge of the topic (Figure 8.10).

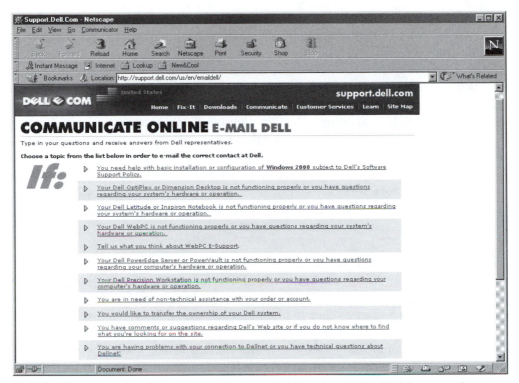

Source: Reproduced with permission of Dell Computer, Inc. Copyright © 2000. All rights reserved.

FIGURE 8.10 Using Online Customer Support to Provide Value.

These three product-focused approaches address different ways to enhance consumers' perceptions of a product experience. In some cases, one approach may address multiple objectives, such as using online customer service to reduce costs (thus creating a price incentive) and to provide an extra product benefit.

Meeting product-focused objectives with these models may sometimes result in increased costs to the marketer. For instance, creating the capability to provide on-line live help to customers can be costly. Even though the feature adds value to the product, a company may elect not to increase the price of the product. Companies must determine the amount and time frame within which the anticipated costs of implementing a product-focused model are acceptable, as well as the longer-term returns on investment.

A Revenue Focus: Show Me the Money!

Revenue-focused business models are designed to bring money into a company. The Internet enables companies to generate revenue with traditional models, and it has created the opportunity for several less traditional processes for making money. Similar to their offline counterparts, however, online revenue models follow a predictable risk-reward pattern. That is, the less predictable a source of income is, the greater the potential for reward. In addition, higher rewards tend to be accompanied by higher performance expectations. Even on the Internet, TANSTAAFL![2]

An obvious source of revenue is to sell something to someone: an exchange of one resource, such as a good, a service, or information for money. This model is popular on the Internet, as is clear from the variety of products advertised and the increasing numbers of online sales. Another familiar revenue model is to base fees on the amount of a product or service that is consumed. For example, some Internet service providers base their rates on the number of minutes a user is connected to the Internet in a fixed time span, such as a month. A third model is based on user subscription to a service, such as a news clipping service, or a business reports newsletter. In this model, the fee is usually based on a predetermined time for consumption (e.g., a one-year subscription).

The ABCs of Internet Revenue-Based Models

All of the direct, marketer-to-end-user models share one characteristic: the user is the source of revenue. Other revenue-based models, however, emphasize income from a source other than an end consumer. Many Web sites operate businesses that serve as nodes in networks that link other agents in the central exchange environment. For example, **transactions brokers,** such as Auto-by-Tel and Ticketmaster, make their money through commissions based on the sales of others companies' products. Their job is to facilitate the marketer's ability to connect with consumers.

CNET is another example of a revenue-based model that does not rely on sales to end consumers. CNET is a content site that provides news and reviews about technology products. The company began making money by charging other companies to place ads on its site. Now, the company also derives revenue from leads it provides when consumers are exposed to product information placed by a vendor on the CNET site, and then go to the vendor's site. CNET's purchase of an auction site also enables the company to get revenue from listing fees.

Variations on the theme of indirect revenue models comprise the ABCs of Internet business models. Three models that appear frequently on Web sites are associate (or affiliate), banner ad, and content sponsor models.

Affiliate Relationships   An **affiliate program,** also known as an **associate program,** operates by creating a partnership between two companies. This arrangement is a unidirectional form of linking—in contrast to a link exchange—in which the site that displays the link information can obtain revenue based on how site visitors use the link. The affiliate agrees to place information about its partner on the affiliate Web site. This information is often the logo of the partner company. The information serves to link the affiliate site to the partner company.

---

[2]There ain't no such thing as a free lunch.

Affiliates make money from the arrangement when a visitor to the site acts on the link information. In some arrangements, the affiliate earns money when the visitor uses the link to go to the partner site. In other arrangements, the affiliate only benefits when the link results in a sale of the partner's product.

Affiliate programs not only provide revenue prospects, but also have potential benefits for increasing brand image and brand equity. For the company who offers the affiliate program, benefits are obtained from increases in sales and from image enhancement due to broader exposure. For the affiliate site, being associated with the partner company can improve consumers' perceptions of the affiliate company. The presence of a well-known company, in the form of a logo, on the affiliate site may increase consumers' trust in the affiliate company, as well as enhance perceptions of the affiliate's product or service. The positive or negative impact of a company or its product on the evaluation of another entity is called a **halo effect.**

Digital Artifact 8.5

E-coupons are growing in popularity. Twenty-seven percent of Internet users have redeemed an e-coupon.

(*Source:* CyberAtlas, 2000, citing a survey by The NPD Group, Inc.)

Banner Relationships   A company may enter an agreement in which the company's site allocates space for the advertising message of another company. This message is often called a **banner.** The company who displays the banner receives revenue based on **impressions,** or how many times the banner is viewed. Alternatively, revenue can be based on the types of behaviors of a visitor to the displaying site. For example, the advertiser may pay a set amount each time that a visitor clicks through the banner to the advertiser's site. In addition, banners can be constructed so that visitors fill out registration forms within the banner, thus providing sales leads to the advertiser without leaving the displaying site. The advertiser may pay for each lead the banner generates.

A company can also generate revenue by placing an advertiser's button on a Web page. A **button** is similar to a banner, in that that goal is to expose the visitor to the advertiser's company or product. Buttons differ from banners, however, in that a button often provides less information on its initial impression, a constraint based on its generally small size. In addition, a button typically requires the visitor to push it, in order to get additional information. Buttons are popular because they are often sources of software that can be downloaded for free. Payment to the displaying site can be based on the number of downloads from a particular button. We will take a closer look at the use of banners and buttons for online advertising in Chapter 12.

Content Sponsorship Relationships   Another revenue model is based on an agreement between companies in which one company sponsors part or all of a Web site for another company. This type of agreement provides exposure for the sponsoring company, and revenue for the sponsored company. On the Internet, sponsorship is often linked to site content; that is, a company may sponsor the provision of a particular form of content on a Web site. Sponsorships are typically based on a fixed payment agreement, in which the amount of revenue is tied to a length of time in which the sponsor will be acknowledged as a sponsor on the displaying Web site.

Some companies sponsor sites as a way to increase traffic to their sites. Traffic is encouraged by creating a link to the company from the company logo on the sponsored site. Other companies sponsor content in order to increase exposure, without expectation of increasing site traffic—much like the soap operas of radio and television. These types of sponsorships are more frequent for companies with a primary offline presence.

Each of these three models operates by creating a relationship between two companies. The models differ in two ways: (1) by the behavioral commitment of the site visitor to the partner company, and (2) by the certainty or predictability of the revenues that will stem from the affiliate relationship. Figure 8.11 depicts the relationship between the nature of the commitment and the prospects for revenue. The potential for revenue is related to the amount of revenue risk that the company assumes upon entering a particular relationship.

In the affiliate relationship, the potential for revenue is highest, because the programs are often structured so that higher commissions are paid for affiliate links that result in sales, rather than just looking. When revenue is acquired through fees to place a banner ad on a site, revenue potential is typically lower than for affiliate relationships. For content sponsorship relationships, revenue potential is often lowest, reflecting the lower requirements of site visitors, in terms of exposure and purchase-related behavior in the sponsor's site.

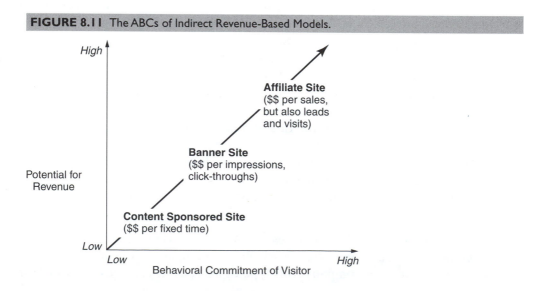

FIGURE 8.11 The ABCs of Indirect Revenue-Based Models.

Chapter Summary

Marketing strategy integrates company objectives with resources for reaching those objectives. Careful strategic development is important for creating a competitive advantage. A company's competitive advantage increases the company's prospects for long-term survival in the environment by leveraging resources of the company and the environment to capitalize on identified opportunities for growth, as through market share or profit.

In this chapter, we examined the role of the Internet on aspects of strategic marketing. We considered the way that the Internet can be used to identify possible sources of competitive advantage. For example, the Internet environment may create opportunities for new products and services, or for new ways of making existing offerings available. In addition, the Internet serves as a tool for assessing the types of opportunities that may exist. Marketing research with the Internet can provide insights into consumer needs, competitors' actions, and broader environmental conditions.

The Internet affects the planning processes used to develop strategy. We considered the implications of the Internet on three aspects of strategic planning. The Internet may motivate planning, as when it presents new opportunities for growth. The Internet may also influence the processes by which a company conducts its planning activities. For instance, the networked nature of the Internet may facilitate communications between far-flung offices and divisions of a company, thus enabling broad participation and representation in strategy development. The Internet may also influence the strategy that results from the planning process. The Internet may affect the types of objectives delimited by the planning process, as well as the nature of the activities deemed appropriate for attaining the objectives.

The Internet can also affect the implementation of a strategy. Characteristics of the Internet can be used by companies as resources to be leveraged for strategic objectives. Marketers can use the Internet as a content resource, a channel resource, and a communications resource. The relative emphasis of each characteristic depends on the types of objectives that guide the efforts of marketing management.

Business models for the Internet enable marketers to address product-related objectives and revenue-related objectives. Business models for a product focus were classified by the ability to use the Internet to (1) enhance a product's image, (2) create incentive to buy a product, and (3) improve the set of benefits associated with the product. Revenue-focused models take two forms: (1) models that reflect an exchange relationship between a marketer and a customer (e.g., a sale), and (2) models that reflect the role of the Internet in relationships between marketers as a way to influence subsequent marketer-consumer interactions (e.g., leads, exposure). In the latter group, we examined the use of affiliate programs, banner and button advertising, and content sponsorship as Internet business models.

REVIEW SECTION

Key Terms

- strategic planning
- strategic marketing
- marketing management
- strategic business unit
- competitive advantage
- soft benefits

- brand equity
- Three I's
- link exchange
- co-branding
- Web site stickiness
- transactions brokers

- affiliate programs
- associate programs
- halo effect
- banner
- impression
- button

Review Questions

1. What types of planning are used to guide marketing action?
2. Describe the differences between the goals and actions associated with each type of planning.
3. Describe the factors that can create a competitive advantage.
4. Why is a competitive advantage important for a company?
5. How might the Internet enable a company to develop a competitive advantage?
6. Describe three ways that the Internet can be used to identify strategic opportunities.
7. Describe three ways that the Internet can serve as a resource for achieving strategic objectives.
8. What are the three levels at which the Internet can influence marketing planning?
9. Identify and describe two primary classes of strategic marketing objectives.
10. How can the Internet enable marketers to disaggregate the three components of brand equity to create value?
11. What are the Three I's, and how are they related to strategic marketing?
12. In revenue-based business models, what two groups of people are the main sources of revenue?
13. Describe three types of Internet-based revenue models (hint: think ABCs).

Thinking Points

1. In what ways can the Internet influence the amount of emphasis that is placed on company resources and market opportunities for each type of marketing planning—strategic planning, strategic marketing, and marketing management?
2. How can the Internet be used to identify strategic opportunities and to leverage resource to capitalize on these opportunities?
3. The Internet has influenced the nature of competition within industries. What does this impact of the Internet suggest for the ability of any company to develop a sustainable competitive advantage?
4. Consider the motivation for, and the processes and outcomes of, marketing planning. Does the Internet affect the aspects of marketing planning in ways that differ from the same aspects of planning in traditional marketing environments?

5. How does the Internet influence the ways that marketers can create value? Does the increased ability to create value by disaggregating value components have any disadvantages?

6. Why is it necessary to have different types of business models (e.g., product-focused vs. revenue-focused) for marketing with the Internet? What types of companies or products are suited for revenue-focused models? What types are suited for product-focused models?

Suggested Readings

1. "The Virtual Countinghouse: Finance Transformed by Electronics," by Daniel P. Keegan. In *The Future of the Electronic Marketplace*, edited by Derek Leebaert (Cambridge, MA: The MIT Press, 1998), pp. 205–240.

2. "Marketing in an Information-Intensive Environment: Strategic Implications of Knowledge as an Asset," by Rashi Glazer. *Journal of Marketing, 55* (October 1991), pp. 1–19.

3. "What Makes Internet Business Models So Difficult." In *Now or Never,* by Mary Modahl (New York: HarperCollins Publishers, Inc., 2000), pp. 103–126.

4. "Commercial Scenarios for the Web: Opportunities and Challenges," by Donna L. Hoffman, Thomas P. Novak, and Patrali Chatterjee. *Journal of Computer-Mediated Communication, 1,* 3, 1995.

5. "Managing in the Marketspace," by Jeffrey F. Rayport and John J. Sviokla. *Harvard Business Review* (November–December 1999), pp. 141–150.

SECTION FOUR

Applying the Framework: Marketing Action in the Internet Environment

In this section, we focus on ways in which the Internet influences marketing action. Building on the previous section, this section illustrates the impact of the Internet as a tool for implementing strategic planning with marketing action. To this end, in Chapter 9, we examine the role of the Internet as a means of discovering marketing opportunities through marketing research. In addition, we consider the use of the Internet as a set of resources that affect marketing action. These resources are described as content, channel, and communication. The Internet enables marketers to provide information as content, to augment distribution as a channel, and to interact with consumers to facilitate communication.

In Chapters 10–12, we look at the impact of the Internet on elements of the marketing mix. In addition, we consider ways that the Internet—as content, channel, or communication—affects the actions of people in each of the four perspectives in the exchange environment.

CHAPTER 9

The Internet and Marketing Research

FOCUS AND OBJECTIVES

In this chapter, we focus on the role of the Internet as a tool for marketing research. The Internet serves as a source of information for identifying opportunities, and as a way to collect information. We review the stages in the research process, and consider the influence of the Internet on the activities associated with each stage. We also introduce a framework for classifying data and apply it to marketing research using the Internet. We discuss the implications of Internet-based marketing research in understanding consumer behavior and competitor behavior.

YOUR OBJECTIVES IN STUDYING THIS CHAPTER INCLUDE THE FOLLOWING:

- Recognize the benefits of the Internet for marketing research.
- Understand the difference between internal and external sources of data, and the role of the Internet in developing each source.
- Identify the five stages in the marketing research process, and possible influences of the Internet in each stage.
- Understand the value of the presented framework for conducting marketing research with the Internet.
- Know the classes of Intenet-based data sources and the dimensions that define them.
- Identify the risks (e.g., ethical breaches) and benefits of online marketing research.

For marketers, information is a vital component for developing marketing strategy. Information about the success and failure of previous strategies is used to guide decision making for resource allocations for a particular product. In addition, information about the products and actions of competitors is used as input for strategic marketing planning and for marketing management. Data obtained from consumers, including behavior patterns (e.g., purchase and use) and perceptions (e.g., product features and benefits), are used to develop the product positioning. Information from consumers is also used to assess market segments and to complete the market planning based on the determination of target markets.

The rapid acceptance of digital content has resulted in an increased demand for more and different types of online information. At the same time, the decreasing costs and heightened availability of standardized technology tools for digitizing and posting information have lowered the hurdles to posting information to online repositories. As a result, the information available on the Internet reflects a wide variety of interests, objectives, and budgets. For instance, information about companies and their product offerings, both online and in traditional environments, is readily available. In addition, the communication and publishing characteristics of the Internet mean that providing information is not just one-sided: consumers can also get into the act. Online news groups and chat rooms provide forums for people to express concerns about product performance, or company actions. They also enable consumers to share tips about product use and alternative products. Because of the wide array of information sources that comprise it, the Internet is a valuable asset for marketing research.

In this chapter, we will consider aspects of incorporating the Internet into methods for acquiring and analyzing data for marketing. To organize our discussion, we will examine two different ways to use the Internet to develop market intelligence: (1) as a tool for acquiring information, and (2) as a source of information. As a tool, the Internet enables marketing researchers to conduct online, interactive interviews and to develop and disseminate online surveys. As an information resource, the Internet enables marketers to access data from online sources that can be used to guide marketing strategy for online and offline marketing activities.

We will begin by looking at the role of the Internet on the process for conducting marketing research. Then we will shift our focus to the importance of the Internet as a source of research information. In this section, we will examine the types of data available to marketing researchers, and how they can be used to serve different research purposes.

THE INTERNET AND RESEARCH PERFORMANCE: THREE BENEFITS

Marketing research may be conducted for several purposes. For example, an organization may wish to assess the quality of its present strategy, to track a particular problem with a product, or to determine the profit potential of a new product. The Internet can be used to augment traditional research techniques and processes, and even to replace them. Some benefits that may be derived from using the Internet for research include the ability to gather related information across a wide array of sources; the ability to update knowledge bases rapidly; and the ability to use Internet technology to integrate the results of marketing research with decision-making processes. Figure 9.1 illustrates the different benefits of the Internet for marketing research.

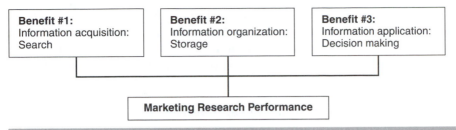

FIGURE 9.1 Internet Benefits for Marketing Research.

The Internet and Information Acquisition

The marketing research conducted by organizations is typically problem-oriented; the organization is focused on developing a strategy to leverage a limited set of resources, given a specified set of situational constraints. The problem-oriented nature of the marketing research process increases the value of the Internet as a tool for gathering market intelligence. The marketing researcher is able to conduct extensive searches through vast amounts of information, in search of specific, relevant data.

The Internet has grown rapidly in terms of the variety of information sources available. The sheer amount of information has resulted in the development of support tools for managing the information load, including search engines and intelligent agents. These tools facilitate information acquisition through matches of words and strings of words. The ability to specify the information with precision and clarity means that the information returned by a search tool will tend to have greater relevance for the problem at hand. Thus, the problem-specific focus of much marketing research is compatible with the information search capabilities available for the Internet.

The Internet and Information Organization

Markets are dynamic. For instance, technological advances enable new product development. In addition, social changes may affect the desirability of existing products. These changes mean that consumers' tastes and preferences may also change over time, and that the length of time for the change to be evident in consumption patterns can vary widely across products. The challenge for marketing researchers is to be able to provide reliable, timely information as input for marketing decision making.

The Internet makes it possible to obtain fast updates to knowledge bases for the questions related to a particular marketing problem. The availability of thousands of online databases means that marketing researchers can acquire up-to-date information. The number of databases increases the marketing researcher's ability to assess the reliability of information. Information acquired from several sources that leads to a similar conclusion reinforces the reliability of the information.

The Internet and Information Use

Once the researcher has the information that answers the research questions, the next step is to use that information for decision making. Information in marketing research can be obtained in many different ways and forms—from direct contact with respondents to automated search and retrieval from electronically managed databases. A **marketing information system,** often abbreviated as MIS, is the combination of people and procedures required to gather, organize, and integrate internal and external sources of information to meet the objectives of marketing strategy (Figure 9.2).

Internal Sources of Marketing Information

The Internet affects information use by marketing managers in two ways: (1) by enabling procedures for storing and managing internal information (e.g., a database of sales leads); and (2) by providing new forms of data on company activity.

To illustrate the second effect of the Internet, consider the information available to a company that has a Web presence. Detailed information about the performance of a Web site can be obtained with software packages that track activity in a Web site through the server that makes the site available. This software creates a log file, which serves as a record of the type of activity that occurs within a Web site. **Log files** typically contain information about the files requested from a server during a visit. A log file may also contain the times that the files were requested, or **hits,** and how long the visit lasted. In addition, the software may record the last URL, or Internet address, visited by the user, and the IP address of the user. By tracking the information stored in a log file over time, a marketer can gauge traffic to a company site, as well as which aspects of the site were most examined (i.e., through file access), and when site information was most highly in demand. In combination with other internal sources of information, a database of site traffic behavior can be useful for making decisions about the value of marketing activities that include the Internet. The following example illustrates the use of multiple sources of data.

> Your company has created a Web site to market its newest product. The site has been operational for a year, and it is time to make budget decisions that will influence the marketing mix. Your task is to determine whether the advertising budget for the previous 12 months has paid off. That is, did efforts to promote the site, both online and in traditional media, attract attention to the site?
>
> You decide that an appropriate way to measure the return on advertising dollars is to see whether a reasonable number of people have visited the Web site. Using historical data on the relationship between advertising dollars and sales, you determine that you must also get information about the sales that can be directly attributed to the Web site. With help from the Webmaster—the person responsible for maintaining the Web site—you obtain the number of site visitors per month for the past year. Then, you get the sales figures from the sales department and note the numbers, by month, of Web site sales.

FIGURE 9.2 Elements of a Marketing Information System.

Internal Sources → People and Procedures for Using Information ← External Sources

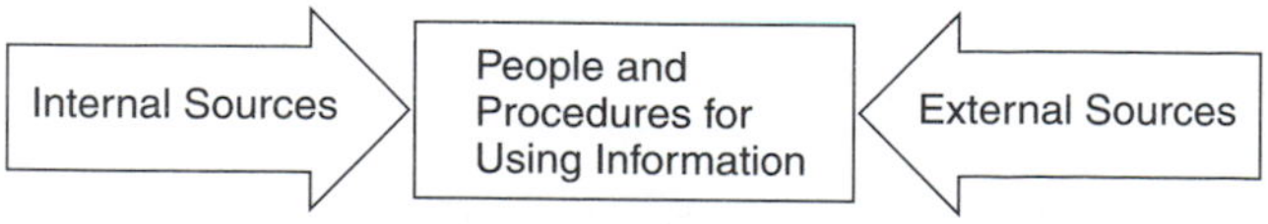

Based on your data, you determine that for every four visitors to the site, one product unit is sold. In addition, you note that visits and sales are significantly higher during the summer months (a reasonable finding for lemonade stand kits . . .). Of central importance, however, was the finding that the proportion of sales to advertising budget was nearly double that for any other form of promotion, for the same time period.

This example illustrates the use of data from two different sources. One source is the measure of customer behavior, based on his or her exposure to the Web site. The second source is the data about customer behavior that is recorded and stored in a database of information about sales that is maintained by the organization.

Because the Internet makes available a large number and variety of information sources, even the best performance of a good MIS is likely to result in an outpouring of data that might be overwhelming for a human decision maker. As a result, **decision support systems** (DSS) are often used by marketing managers to structure decisions based on the input of marketing researchers. With a DSS, the marketing manager can manipulate acquired information to draw conclusions about the likely outcomes of possible situations (e.g., if visits to our Web site increase 26 percent this year, what will our profit be, given our page view to sales ratio?).

External Sources of Marketing Information

In a marketing information system, external information sources reflect the focus of marketing research. These external sources include information about consumers, competition, and conditions that may affect the viability of marketing strategy. The Internet can be used to collect and store data that pertain to each component of marketing research. We will consider these components in more detail in the remainder of this chapter.

Integrating Internal and External Sources

The integration of types and sources of data is gaining increasing attention from companies and from developers of Internet technologies. For example, one approach is to combine databases that store back-end applications with front-end data collection. Back-end applications are the uses of technology to perform behind-the-scenes activities that are invisible to the consumer. Examples include inventory control software and distribution and logistics technologies for the Internet. Many of these applications result in databases of information about the amount of product produced, stored, and shipped.

Front-end data collection refers to the process of tracking consumer behavior with regard to a product, service, or other information provided both online and offline. This marketing research information, when considered together with the data from the back-end applications, can provide managers with information about the relative supply and demand for products, as well as the efficiency of the production and distribution processes for meeting that demand.

Sharing Information Across Organizations

Many practitioners would like to develop standard formats for tracking and registering customer behavior on the Internet, so that a wide base of information can be developed and readily shared. The Customer Profile Exchange Network (CPEX) is an example of a collection of practitioners who wish to facilitate information sharing. The members of the consortium believe that the benefits to individual organizations of the amount of information that can be obtained with standardized tracking practices will outweigh the costs of sharing what would otherwise be proprietary data.

This perspective suggests that the impact of the Internet on marketing research and decision making lies in its ability to make data available. In addition, the willingness to share information underscores the importance of the idea that the value of the information is not the information itself, but how it is used to guide marketing decision making. In other words, converting information into marketing intelligence depends not only on the quality of the initial data, but also on the quality of the analysis and interpretation applied to the data. We consider each of these requirements as stages in the marketing research process.

Digital Artifact 9.1

It is estimated that 14.5 million people gambled $651 million over the Internet in 1999, despite efforts of legislators to impose a ban on online gambling.

(*Source: Personal Computing News,* **May 21, 1999.**)

STAGES IN THE MARKETING RESEARCH PROCESS

Most marketing research involves a series of stages that include (1) defining the problem, (2) developing the research plan, (3) collecting the data, (4) analyzing the data, and (5) drawing conclusions. Each stage may be influenced by characteristics of the Internet that can facilitate or inhibit the researcher's ability to complete task components.

Problem Definition

The activities associated with marketing research begin with the specification of the research problem. For example, an organization that wishes to develop and market a new product may have a general research problem about the most desirable form of the product. This general question itself reflects a set of more specific questions. Who is the appropriate target market for the new product? What features should the product include? How different is the product from those available from competitors? Where do consumers purchase other forms of this product? Each of these questions can be addressed through marketing research. The stages are shown in Figure 9.3.

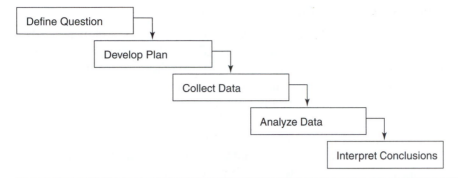

FIGURE 9.3 Stages in the Marketing Research Process.

Types of Research Information

The set of questions that creates a need for marketing research will differ from organization to organization, and over time within an organization. As a general description, however, the purpose of the research process is to provide information of three key types: **descriptive, diagnostic,** and **predictive.** For example, the question of where consumers presently purchase similar products is descriptive. If the question is re-framed to ask *why* consumers purchase at these locations, then the goal of research is to provide diagnostic information (e.g., the product is only available at that location). Finally, if the question is posed as, "How many consumers are likely to purchase from our location?" the issue becomes one of prediction.

In traditional marketing research processes, the distinction between the forms and objectives of questions for research purposes must be understood in order to interpret and use research data appropriately. The importance of appropriate use increases when the capabilities of the Internet are used to facilitate and even to automate the inclusion of research data into marketing decision making. The ready availability of information and the relative ease with which it can be incorporated into marketing decision making with Internet technologies increase the need for a clear understanding and specification of the research question. The adage, "Garbage in, garbage out," is particularly relevant for settings like the Internet, where large amounts of information can be obtained, often at low cost to the researcher. Even if collecting and incorporating data of questionable utility is relatively quick, easy, and cheap, the costs of decisions based on poor data can be high.

Data from the Internet can be used for a variety of research purposes, such as relationship development, competitive analysis, distribution network analysis and development, and target market assessment. In each of these situations, the Internet can provide marketing researchers with information and online tools to develop input for action-based decision making. For instance, information can be obtained for target market specification from comments of participants in discussion groups and e-mail lists. Direct contact with group members can be accomplished with Internet communications capabilities, enabling researchers to send questionnaires, conduct online focus groups, and complete interactive in-depth interviews.

Designing the Research Plan and Procedure

With a clear set of objectives in place, the marketing researcher is ready to develop a plan for acquiring the information that will provide answers to the research questions. In this second stage, the researcher determines the type and amount of data needed for drawing conclusions with confidence. In addition, the researcher decides *how* to obtain the data. This task entails selection of a research method and appropriate data-gathering techniques.

The data acquired by marketing researchers is often described as either primary data or secondary data. **Primary data** is information that is being collected for the first time, in order to address the problem defined by the marketing researcher. **Secondary data** is information that was collected at an earlier time, often for a different purpose. Examples of secondary information include census data and databases that are designed and constructed to provide ongoing access to stored information, which may or may not be updated.

Both types of data can be obtained with the Internet. For example, a researcher can conduct an online survey to acquire primary data about consumers' perceptions of a proposed product. In addition, the researcher might access an existing online database to develop estimates of market size for the product.

Each type of data has its advantages and its disadvantages. Primary data are desirable, and often necessary, when the research question is so new, or sufficiently specific, that you are unlikely to find any previously developed data sets that are relevant. The chief advantage of primary data is that because you designed the research to address your objectives, the data you collect are more likely to be relevant, and thus to be useful for developing insights for decision making. The downside to primary data is that it has to be collected; the research instruments (e.g., surveys and interview formats) must be developed and administered, and the data collated and recorded. These efforts can be costly in terms of labor hours and money.

Secondary data can reduce or eliminate issues of the time and money needed to prepare and administer data-gathering methods. All the available data in the world, however, will be of no use if they cannot be structured to address your research needs. The major drawback to secondary data is that often they are not sufficiently relevant to eliminate the need for primary research.

Digital Artifact 9.2

In 1999, the number of .com balloons in Macy's Thanksgiving Day parade: two. (*Source:* The Internet Index, #25.)

Gathering Data

With a research plan developed, including the type of data to be used, the next step in the marketing research process is to collect the data. The Internet provides marketing researchers with ways to gather primary and secondary data. The technologies that make up the Internet serve as tools with which the researcher can comb the Internet for information that can be combined to create the needed primary data. In addition, they enable the researcher to transmit instruments for data collection. For example, a researcher can take advantage of ubiquitous e-mail software to send a questionnaire and to receive responses electronically. In addition, Web sites can be used to gather data by providing drop-down menus or buttons that serve as responses to questions.

Searches through news groups, bulletin boards, and chat rooms can provide insights into aspects of behavior that can be used to guide strategy development. For example, a news group in which participants discuss concerns with your product can provide valuable data for the research question, "What are customers' perceptions of our product?"

Combining and Interpreting Data

With data acquired, the marketing researcher moves to the analysis and interpretation stage of the research process. Whether the data were obtained from online sources or offline sources, the Internet can be used to facilitate the combination and analysis of data. As a tool for communication, the Internet enables marketing researchers to integrate data from multiple sources. In addition, software packages enable researchers to develop statistics with online data, and to update the statistics on a continuous basis.

The variety of information sources available to marketing research may necessitate data mining. **Data mining** is the use of often-sophisticated software tools to elicit patterns and impose order on sets of information. Even though data mining can be conducted on organized databases of information, it may provide greater explanatory benefits for information that has no readily apparent structure or organization. For example, a data mining algorithm that tracks through a 12-month set of user profiles provided by visitors to a Web site may uncover the interesting finding that the majority of visitors in the summer months are over the age of 55. If this finding is in sharp contrast to the higher numbers of 20- and 30-somethings who visit the site in the other seasons, then the company may want to consider changes to its promotional tactics to appeal more directly to the apparent audience, depending on the season.

Drawing Conclusions and Delivering Insights

The final stage of the marketing research process is to formulate the report and to present the results of the project and await feedback.

Evaluating Research Results

Suppose that you have just been handed a research report on consumption patterns within target market segments for your company's Internet service product. The report notes a discrepancy between the projected consumption of the product in the target market segments and the actual consumption. The researcher concludes that the smaller-than-expected sales are due to inaccurate estimates of the target market in the previous year. How do you determine whether the conclusion is correct, and how do you protect yourself from misleading data?

The accuracy of data, particularly that related to large-scale assessment of Internet populations, has been an ongoing problem for researchers and practitioners. The importance of accurate descriptive statistics for Internet users has resulted in calls for measurement standards. In addition, companies often use data collected by a number of research firms to assess the reliability of data.

You can reduce the possibility of being misled by incorrect data in several ways. First, balance data obtained from online and offline sources. If possible, do not rely entirely on any single data source. The range and quality of data sources on the Internet can be used to determine whether the conclusions you have drawn from one set of data are supported by other data that address the same purpose. Second, assess the purpose and method of data collection, regardless of whether the data are from an online or an offline source. Understand what assumptions have been made that may affect your interpretation of the data, and why the assumptions exist. Third, update your data frequently. Many online data sources focus on particular aspects of research, such as tracking electronic commerce in a specific industry sector. By keeping up-to-date with newly posted information, you can detect trends in behaviors that may affect your research conclusions.

Communicating Research Results

Even when the preceding stages in the process are conducted in offline, traditional environments, the Internet can be used to communicate the research report and to integrate and update feedback from different functions within the organization. The communications capabilities available with the Internet can be used to shorten the time required to produce and share iterations of the research results.

Digital Artifact 9.3

Poor customer service causes 32 percent of online shoppers to abandon their shopping carts before check-out.

(*Source:* **ActivMedia, 2000.**)

THE INTERNET AS A DATA RESOURCE

As an enormous warehouse of information, widely accessed and added to by its users, the Internet is a valuable source of data for marketing research. The characteristics of the Internet, such as its rich content and rapid communications technologies, make it important to consider the types of information that marketing researchers can obtain from the Internet. In this section, we will consider the characteristics of data sources for research, and discuss several approaches by which researchers can obtain data from the Internet, and the issues associated with each approach. This discussion expands on the second stage of the research process: designing a research plan.

Clearly, you could get data from the Internet in many ways. From its online questionnaires to countless databases, the Internet is a treasure trove of potential research insight. Of course, *potential* insight will not do you any good as a marketing researcher! Knowing what data sources exist, and when to use them, however, will help.

We have already considered the distinction between primary and secondary data. For the Internet, however, it is often difficult to determine what is primary and what is secondary. For example, a set of data collected by someone else, for some other purpose, is primary data to them, and secondary data to you. Or is it? Suppose that you select data from someone else's set. Now you have created your own data set, for your own purposes. Is the data primary, or secondary? Does it matter?

We can use a framework for describing data, developed by Runkel and McGrath in the early 1970s, to better understand the differences between types of data, and the implications of these differences for appropriate research use.

A Framework for Describing Data

The Runkel and McGrath framework organizes the types of data available to a researcher by two key properties related to the situations in which the data were generated: (1) who recorded the data (data source), and (2) whether the person (or persons) who provided the data was aware that the data were being collected. Before we dive into the descriptions of these dimensions further, however, it is useful to having a working definition of what is meant by the term *data*.

In the Runkel and McGrath framework, a **datum** is based on a single behavior by a respondent. (When two or more datums get together, we call them data.) Behaviors become data when two events occur. First, the behaviors are recorded by an observer. Second, the researcher interprets the recorded behaviors, thus giving them meaning. In other words, a behavior that isn't recorded and interpreted is just a behavior, and a behavior that is recorded but not interpreted is just information. This definition means that the development of data requires four things to occur: behavior, observation, recording, and interpretation. This progression is depicted in Figure 9.4.

Sources of Data

While the observation of a behavior may tend to co-occur with its recording, the interpretation of the data can occur at a later point in time, and by a different person. In addition, the person who carries out the behavior, the respondent, may or may not be the same person who records the behavior. As a result, the

FIGURE 9.4 The Path of Events from Behavior to Data.

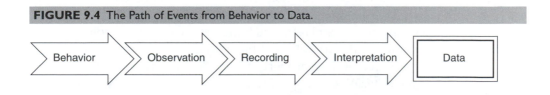

framework's property of data source has three components—the respondent, the researcher, and the recorder. The source of the data is the person who observes and records the behavior of interest.

To illustrate the concept of data source, suppose that a city council wants to obtain information about the desirability of a new public parking lot. One way to get the data is to send out a mail survey to local residents. Respondents who fill out the mail survey, essentially observing and recording their own responses, are one type of data source. Alternatively, the town could conduct a focus group. In this case, the researcher who moderates the discussion and records the behaviors serves as the data source. As a third approach, the city manager could comb through archived information about public sentiment toward similar proposals in the past. In this case, the person who recorded the responses in the past is the data source.

The data source dimension is important because it introduces the idea that the usefulness of data for a particular purpose may be affected by its source, that is, the person who recorded the information. For example, a respondent who records answers to a survey may selectively present only information that conveys a desired image, thus editing out potentially useful information for the researcher. A researcher who determines what information to record and what to ignore may also bias a data set by imposing personal ideas of what is relevant on the construction of the record. In addition, information collected in the past may be only tangentially useful for the present purpose.

Respondent Awareness

The second property of the Runkel and McGrath framework addresses the issue of whether the person, whose behavior is the basis for a data point, knew that the behavior was being observed and recorded. For the situation in which the respondent is the source of data, awareness is reflected in self-report techniques for data collection, such as surveys and questionnaires. Lack of awareness is reflected in trace measures, or situations in which behaviors are unobtrusively recorded (e.g., tracking site visits on the Internet).

The awareness issue is also relevant when the researcher observes and records the respondent's behavior. In the case of a focus group, for example, participants are usually aware that their conversation is being observed and recorded by a **visible observer.** If they are unaware that their behaviors are being recorded, the situation is described as **hidden observation.**

For the third data source, that of behaviors observed and recorded in the past, awareness is a bit trickier. In general, records of public behavior fall into the awareness category. For instance, taking a public stand on an issue, such as casting a vote in the Senate, constitutes awareness that a behavior is observed and recorded. More complex, however, is the situation in which a set of collected information is saved, without the respondent's awareness, and retrieved for use as data at a later point in time. Marketers must be aware of the ethical issues that may arise with different types of data.

As with the source of data property, respondent awareness may influence the usefulness of the data. When people are aware that their behaviors are being observed and recorded for use in research, they may become reactive, thus leading to biases or distortions in data. **Reactive effects** occur when respondents alter their behavior due to the characteristics of the situation in which they are being observed and recorded. Types of data that are acquired when the respondent is unaware that behaviors are being observed and recorded are called unobtrusive measures. These measures tend to be less prone to reactivity than data developed when the respondent is aware of the research process.

The two properties create a typology for classifying types of data. This typology is presented in Figure 9.5. In some situations, data may be classified in more than one category. For example, a user may be aware that a cookie has been placed in her browser, but unaware of the exact nature of the information that will be collected. The framework is useful as a general structure for evaluating the advantages and disadvantages of different types of data.

In the following sections, we will look at the characteristics and concerns associated with each type of data that can be obtained from the Internet. Data from Internet sources can be used to define strategic opportunities. Data can also be used to monitor the performance of strategy implementation. The information that can be acquired via the Internet can provide insights into consumer behavior and competitor behavior, regardless of the stage of the planning process. In addition, the Internet is a source of information about conditions that may affect strategic marketing.

Digital Artifact 9.4

Americans spend more time on the Web than do Europeans, averaging 11.3 hours per month, compared with 5.1 for the United Kingdom, and 4.9 for both France and Germany.

(*Source:* **CyberAtlas, citing NetValue, 2000.**)

FIGURE 9.5 Two Properties Differentiate Types of Data.

RESPONDENT AWARENESS *(Does subject know behavior is observed and recorded?)*

Source of Data (Who observes and records?)	*Respondent Aware*	*Respondent Unaware*
Respondent	Self-reports • *Online surveys* • *Tests*	Traces • *Individual's Web sites* • *IP addresses*
Researcher	Visible Observer • *Internet: Online focus groups* • *Interviews*	Hidden Observer • *Data profiling* • *Chat rooms* • *Cookies*
Recorder	Records of Public Behavior • *Newsgroup postings* • *Mailing list correspondence*	Archival Records (Secondary Records) • *E-mail correspondence*

INTERNET-BASED SOURCES OF DATA ABOUT CONSUMERS

Technological advances and their widespread adoption by many consumers make the Internet an important source of insights into consumer behavior. To simplify discussion, we can look at the data sources as a function of awareness.

The Respondent as a Data Source

Respondent Aware: Online Surveys

Surveys provide marketers with information about consumers' awareness, perceptions, attitudes, intentions, and behaviors regarding companies and their offerings. The Internet enables marketers to develop and fine-tune survey questions and formats so that pertinent information can be obtained, often at a lower cost and with a better response rate than traditional mail or phone surveys. Surveys can be conducted through e-mail or through the Web. An e-mail survey is comparable to a mail survey; both tend to have fixed, text-based question formats. Web-based surveys provide a wider range of survey design possibilities than standard text formats. One example is provided in Figure 9.6.

The multimedia, interactive nature of the Internet creates the potential for Web-based survey methods that are interesting and involving. In addition, technical capabilities of the Internet mean that surveys can use flexible formats that tailor the questions in a survey, thus reducing the probability of obtaining irrelevant information, or of tiring a respondent. For instance, a survey on a Web site can be designed so that information that clarifies a question can be acquired by clicking on a button or link in the question. This capability is helpful for respondents who need the information, without annoying respondents who do not.

Marketers who use the Internet to collect survey data must consider how issues associated with the online medium might influence the quality of the data. Three such issues are sampling, equipment, and respondent characteristics.

Sampling refers to the process by which respondents are obtained from a larger population pool. With an e-mail survey, a sample of respondents is identified and contacted. For a Web-based survey, initial contact can also be made via e-mail. Many surveys, however, rely on the user to find the site and complete the survey, an approach known as **self-selection.** This approach may lead to a **selection bias** in the data. The marketer needs to know whether the sample of survey respondents is representative of the larger population to which research conclusions will be generalized. Control over survey respondents can be implemented by requiring a respondent to use a password to access the questionnaire. In addition, marketers can obtain information about each respondent that can be used to determine the representativeness of the sample.

In primary research, the objective is to obtain the desired information from a qualified respondent; in other words, from someone whose responses are relevant to the purpose. This goal may seem obvious, but it is important to remember that people who are willing to provide data in an online format share at least two char-

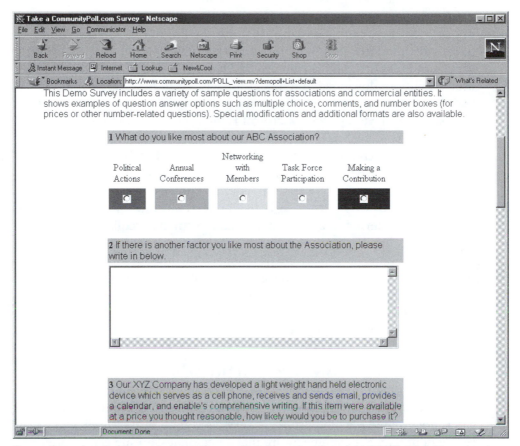

FIGURE 9.6 Online Surveys Can Provide Ease-of-Use With Attractive Graphics.

acteristics that may lead to biased responses and to a decreased ability to draw reasonable inferences from the data. First, online respondents are online. This fact may not be a problem if your research is focused on issues that can be addressed equally well by online and offline respondents (e.g., "Please indicate the likelihood that you will purchase a new vehicle in the next twelve months."). If, however, your research question addresses a behavior for which online participation prejudices the response, then your data may be worthless (e.g., "Have you ever used the Internet to acquire or provide information?").

The second caution is one common to most research. Your data should be interpreted in view of the fact that your respondents may represent only a subset of some possibly larger population. This subset may be different from the larger population in that your respondents are the people who were willing to respond to the questions. Systematic differences between respondents and nonrespondents in the same, larger population would tend to indicate the presence of a selection bias in the data.

Equipment characteristics can also influence the quality of Internet-based survey data. Surveys can be designed that use the full range of technical possibilities to provide a tailored, engaging research experience for the user. However, not all users may be able to take advantage of the experience. Capacity issues may limit a user's ability to download graphics-rich pages, or to play video and audio files. In addition, different types of computers (e.g., Macintosh and IBM) and different browsers (e.g., Netscape and Microsoft Explorer) may lead to different displays of survey pages.

Respondent characteristics, such as a user's level of familiarity with the Internet, may influence the quality of data obtained through an online survey. Marketing researchers often assess respondents' knowledge of the product or service that is the focus of a survey, to better understand the implications of the data. Because the Internet is a fairly new medium for data collection, however, marketers must also consider the possibility that the interaction between the user and the computer-mediated environment may influence the type of responses provided by the user. To reduce the likelihood of experience-based biases, researchers can directly assess respondents' levels of expertise. In addition, online surveys should be designed to minimize effects that may occur due to miscomprehension or confusion about how to move through the survey or to record responses.

Respondent Unaware: Individual Web Sites

The information that people post about themselves, and their interests, activities, and experiences, can be a useful source of data. Because the respondent's Web site is not created for the purpose of serving as data for research, and because the respondent may not even be aware that a personal Web site is interpreted as data, individual sites are categorized as respondent-generated data, but without awareness. The researcher opportunistically obtains data from whatever sites are available through targeted searches.

To illustrate the types of data that can be obtained from individuals' sites, consider that an individual may create a database that is focused on a particular interest, such as a hobby. For example, a Barbie doll aficionado might develop a site to track and post information about perceptions of beauty, as expressed by girls in different age groups, over the history of Barbie.

As an alternative illustration, suppose that your company would like to introduce a fashion doll. Your task, as marketing researcher, is to determine which profile of doll features would be most likely to appeal to girls. You can use the Internet to acquire data by searching for doll sites, and then by accumulating information about preferred dolls contained in each site. In this scenario, the data are the set of sites that contain information about perceptions of dolls.

This example illustrates the difference between a data set that is created, organized, and structured for ongoing use, and information that is gathered on an as-needed basis. If, in the latter case, the information is retained and structured so that it can be searched and used for future research purposes, then that data set becomes a database. Database development for future use is the goal of the organizations responsible for developing the CPEX standard.

Digital Artifact 9.5

Nearly half of the U.S. population will use e-mail to communicate by 2001.

(*Source: WebPromote Weekly,* **June 12, 1998.**)

The Researcher as a Data Source

Respondent Aware: Online Focus Groups

A traditional focus group consists of several people who are physically present in a room. A moderator may guide the discussion. The data from a focus group are information that the researcher determines is relevant in the group interaction, and that the researcher records for further examination.

Focus groups conducted online enable a marketer to observe and record focal behaviors that occur during the interaction of geographically dispersed respondents. The interaction may still be face-to-face, through the use of cameras.

Online focus groups can be conducted using software that enables a researcher to form a discussion group (e.g., NetMeeting). Respondents type responses into a text box, and then send the comments to a group board. The board provides an ongoing record of the conversation that each respondent can review by scrolling backward and forward.

A primary advantage of the online focus group is the ability to integrate the beliefs, experiences, and opinions of respondents who are not in the same location. This ability may enable a marketer to gauge reactions to a product or concept in greater depth and with more generalizability than with a traditional focus group. In addition, the online technique is often more economical than a traditional focus group.

A primary disadvantage of online focus groups is the loss of some contextual richness that is available through physical presence. For instance, tone of voice and body language convey information that influence people's interactions. As a result, the text-based communication that serves as the record of the group interaction may provide the researcher with impoverished information in two ways. First, nonverbal information may be less able to be tracked and interpreted. Second, the absence of nonverbal information as cues for participant interaction may affect what people say and how they say it, thus introducing a possible bias into the data.

Respondent Unaware: Cookies and Data Profiling

A researcher can create data from several different Internet sources. One source of data is obtained through cookies. A **cookie** is a text file that contains a unique user identifier. When the user visits a Web site, the site's server may place a cookie in the user's browser. As the user goes from page to page in the site, the identifying information in the cookie can be sent back to the server. In this way, the server can track the movement of the user through the Web site.

More interesting, however, is the situation in which a company can acquire information about a user's across-site behavior. For instance, a company that operates as an ad server, like DoubleClick, has subscribers who pay to have the company serve their advertising. When the user visits a site with an agreement to display ads from the ad server's subscribers, the ad server places a cookie in the user's browser. When the user moves to another banner or site that also subscribes to the ad server, the ad server is able to review the cookie information and update its database about the user's preferences. This information can be used to target advertising to the user. Even when the advertising is targeted, the user remains anonymous.

The value of cookie information to a marketer increases when the information about site visits can be combined with information that identifies the user to the company. The combination of this demographic information with behavior information is called **data profiling.** Data profiling is possible when databases of user information can be linked to the Internet search habits of a specific user. These types of databases exist in several forms. For example, the type of information needed to identify a user is available when the user makes a purchase from a Web site, or when the user completes a registration form. All a marketer has to have is the identifying information, and a way to match up that information to the database of Internet search activity, stored by the unique user identifiers on cookies. With the match-up completed, the marketer has detailed information about the user and about his or her preferences, based on past Internet behavior.

The ability to identify users by name, and to combine identities with behaviors has ethical implications for marketers. Consumer groups have argued that data profiling violates consumers' privacy, and that adequate notification to consumers about the profiling activities is necessary, but not widely practiced.

One issue for marketers in the use of cookie data is that the cookie is associated with a browser—not with an individual user. As a result, the tracked information comes from anyone who used that browser. A related issue with trace data is that even when the cookie is mapped to a single user, the user's behavior may not reflect personal preferences. For instance, suppose that you search a site for vitamin supplements for the geriatric set as a favor for your grandmother. The marketer who interprets the information from the related cookie may target ads to you for a variety of products for the elderly.

The Recorder (in the Past) as a Data Source

Respondent Aware: Online Newsgroups and Mailing Lists

Marketers can use newsgroup postings and mailing lists to ascertain users' reactions to companies and to brands and products. Because the content of the newsgroup is public, and because users are aware that their communications will be made public, this potential source of information falls under the respondent aware heading. Because the records of behavior (i.e., the postings) can be interpreted as data for a particular research purpose other than the original reason for the recorded correspondence, newsgroups and mailing lists fall into the recorder category of data sources.

Newsgroups   Newsgroups are collections of people with Internet access who wish to exchange information about various topics. Each newsgroup has a specific topical focus, and the postings of messages to the newsgroup tend to revolve around the central subject matter. The newgroups are often called "Usenet" newsgroups, short for user network. Newsgroups are organized in hierarchies, which serve as a way to organize and transmit related information between different news servers. The nine primary hierarchies and their content focus are given in Figure 9.7.

Newsgroups may often be a form of online word-of-mouth, in which communications between users about products and services provide the users with the benefits that characterize offline word-of-mouth. These benefits include two-way communication, increased credibility of the information source, and vicarious experience. The interactive nature of the Internet is particularly conducive to the exchange of information. It is important to note that while offline word-of-mouth may often take a sequential form, in which Person A speaks to Person B, who then speaks with Person C, the Internet may expose several people to the exchange of information simultaneously. As a result, the transmission of information between individuals about a product or service, regardless of its accuracy, may occur more rapidly online than offline.

Users must access newsgroup information from the appropriate site. This selective exposure to the information in the newsgroup has benefits for marketers who use the newsgroup content as a source of market information. First, participation in the newsgroup indicates involvement with the topic and serves as a gauge for importance of product-related issues addressed in newsgroup postings.

Second, the effort to join and participate in the discussion may be related to the credibility of a user. Similar to word-of-mouth in offline environments, newsgroup participants often communicate experiences and opinions, in the absence of any incentive to do so that would increase skepticism by other users (e.g., payment for a favorable product testimonial).

FIGURE 9.7 Primary Usenet Newsgroup Classifications.

Hierarchy	Content
alt	Discussions about a wide range of issues and topics not typically contained in the remaining hierarchies
comp	Discussions of computers, and technology-related issues
humanities	Topics pertaining to the arts and humanities
misc	Topics that do not clearly belong in any other hierarchy
news	Discussion of issues regarding newsgroups
rec	Discussion of recreational opportunities and activities, including hobbies
sci	Issues related to the study of science
soc	Discussion of cultural and social issues
talk	Anything and everything that does not clearly fit in one of the preceding groups

Third, the discussions in a newsgroup are organized by subtopics, or threads. Following a particular thread can provide a marketer with an efficient way to obtain detailed information about the perceptions of the discussion focus, whether it is a product, a vendor, a service, or other aspect of the product offering. This ability to be easily selective may mean that marketing researchers can obtain detailed, longitudinal information about the perceptions and beliefs of newsgroup participants on a particular topic. In some cases, the information from a newsgroup discussion may be used instead of conducting and analyzing a focus group discussion.

Finally, newsgroups participants, with their demonstrated interest in a particular product, may represent viable target markets. The likes and dislikes reflected in message postings can be used by marketers to design effective communications for the target market, while the newsgroup itself presents a forum in which the marketing communication can be made available to interested participants.

Internet Mailing Lists   Online mailing lists are classified by the same reasoning as newsgroups—behaviors recorded with the user's awareness, but not for a specified purpose of research. A mailing list is a collection of online users who have chosen to belong to an e-mail-based information exchange. Mailing lists can be announcement or broadcast lists, in which subscribers merely receive mail, but do not send e-mail to the list, or they can be discussion lists. Discussion lists enable subscribers to engage in communications with other list subscribers. Discussion lists may be moderated, in which case one person receives all messages for the list and determines whether they should be sent on to all subscribers, or unmoderated, where all messages are transmitted to all subscribers.

Mailing lists differ from newsgroups in three ways that influence the nature of their usefulness for marketing research. First, a user must sign up to participate in a mailing list, but not for a newsgroup. For the researcher, a user's willingness to sign up may indicate a stronger commitment to the topic addressed in the list than to a similar topic in a newsgroup.

Second, mailing lists are automatically delivered to subscribers' e-mail addresses, while users must actively seek out newsgroup discussion content. For the researcher, this requirement may indicate greater interest in the topic on the part of users who frequently access the newsgroup, compared to users who access it infrequently. Passive receipt of mailing list information may mean that the user is more likely to be exposed to the message content than if it had to be actively sought, but it may also mean that the message content is simply ignored.

The third characteristic difference with implications for marketing research is the nature of the content organization. Mailing lists are linear in structure, with content arranged in a simple, chronological fashion. This characteristic differs from newsgroups, in which discussions are threaded by topic. The chronological, linear structure may increase the difficulty of obtaining relevant information for the researcher's purpose.

Respondent Unaware: E-mail and Databases

E-mail   As noted in Chapter 6, regulation to protect the privacy of Internet-based communications in the private sector is sparse. For instance, employers can monitor the e-mail correspondence of employees. In addition to the absence of regulatory policy on the privacy of e-mail, technology also creates situations in which information recorded at one point in time may turn up as data at another point. As e-mail travels over the networks of the Internet, it may pass through many servers, which are visible to anyone who is willing and able to take a look at the content. As with data profiling, e-mail as a data source has ethical implications due to the user's lack of awareness of the unintended use of information, combined with the expectation that the information is confidential.

Archival Records: Databases on the Internet   Databases on the Internet are an important source of data for research that can be conducted with information recorded in the past. A **database** is a collection of information related to a particular purpose, and that can typically be organized for efficient search. The collection of databases contained on the Internet can be loosely classified into three categories: government, not-for-profit, and commercial (Figure 9.8).

Government-provided databases contain information gathered and structured by federal agencies. For example, census data—useful for understanding general societal trends, such as age, occupation, and income—is made available on the Internet by the Census Bureau of the U.S. Department of Commerce. In addition, the Central Intelligence Agency and the Environmental Protection Agency provide online access to compiled data. These types of sources can be used for macroanalysis of trends and conditions that may affect marketing strategy.

Not-for-profit organizations also provide access to online databases. These databases offer many different forms of information, including statistics, archives of research papers, descriptions of organizational objectives and agendas, and personnel. Many organizations are international in scope, such as the World Health Organization; their information can be used to develop insights into economic,

FIGURE 9.8 The Internet as a Database of Databases.

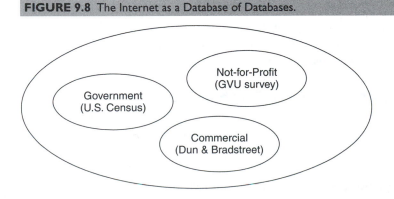

technological, and societal characteristics that may facilitate the formulation of comparative market performance projections for domestic and international strategy. A second source of not-for-profit data is made available by academic institutions. For example, the GVU Survey of Internet-related activities is published by researchers in the Graphics, Visualization, and Usability Center at Georgia Tech. This survey, conducted nearly every year since 1994, provides demographic information about people who use the Internet.

Commercial databases are a source of potential insight about competitors' actions. We consider commercial databases and other data sources for competitor research in the next section.

INTERNET-BASED SOURCES OF DATA ABOUT COMPETITION

The sources of data in the framework can also be applied to organize information from the Internet for competitor analysis. In general, given the nature of competition and the importance of protecting proprietary information, most of the data are constructed without the awareness of the competing company.

The three data sources are as follows: (1) the company, who is the respondent; (2) the researcher, who is the party conducting the research; and (3) the secondary data sources, such as databases or other publicly available information recorded at an earlier time.

The Company as a Respondent Data Source

Two forms of information can be obtained from the company as the respondent. Data can be derived from information posted by a company in its Web sites, such as company objectives, product initiatives, and customer outreach activities. In addition, information can be acquired about a particular product or service. For instance, e-mail can be used to request product information. In the case of Web sites, the information can provide a general overview of the company, while for requested information, the returned data may be more specific to a product. In both cases, however, the respondent is the source of the data, because the company conducts, observes, and records the behavior that will comprise the data. As with consumer-side analysis of self-reported behaviors, the researcher must recognize that the information being recorded and transmitted may be subject to distortions, whether intended or not, by the company who provides the information.

The Marketing Researcher as a Data Source

When a marketing researcher collects information about competitors' actions and records it for analysis, the researcher is the data source. Benchmarking studies and link analysis of competitors' sites are examples of situations in which the researcher is the data source.

In a **benchmarking** study, the marketing researcher identifies a set of characteristics or goals that the company would like to achieve. The definition of the set may be based on what competitors are presently doing, and how well they are doing it. Alternatively, the set may be based on a behavior that would be new to the industry segment, but observable in other companies' activities. In either case, the researcher tracks and records the focal behavior of the other companies, as well as the actions of the researcher's company. The data from the benchmarking process is used to guide the company's effort and direction in achieving its goals.

Benchmarking may take the form of establishing standards that must be reached, hurdles that must be surpassed, or pitfalls that must be avoided. The information used to define the company performance objectives may be obtained from a content analysis of the Web sites and Internet-based communications (e.g., newsgroup postings, press information) of the companies who serve as the focus of the benchmarking study. Because the information to be used for benchmarking is determined and recorded by the marketing researcher, the researcher is the data source.

Reverse linking can provide information about the performance of a competitor. **Reverse linking** is the process used to develop a data set about the nature of the Web links between a competing company and other companies. A researcher can use Internet search engines (e.g., Hotbot) to generate a list of links to a specified URL, or Internet address. Analysis of the types of organizations uncovered by this search can be used to develop insights about a competitor's target markets, as well as the nature of partnership arrangements.

Previously Recorded Information as a Data Source

Competitive analysis can be conducted using data from sources of observed and recorded information in the past. Two such sources include databases and press-related information on the Internet.

Databases   Several different types of databases can be used to research the competition. These types include databases compiled through public sector initiatives, and databases compiled through private sector initiatives. For instance, patents filed by competitors can be examined using the Community of Science patents database, while information about a competitor's industry rating can be obtained from the Dow Jones online database of company profiles.

Although databases provided by government and not-for-profit organizations tend to be available at no cost, the same is not always true for databases with a commercial focus. Some of the largest online databases are created by companies that conduct detailed research on businesses within a range of industries (e.g., Dun & Bradstreet). These research firms provide the results of their research to interested buyers.

In contrast, other databases reflect a focus within a particular industry. Many such databases are available at no cost (e.g., Trade Show Central). For example, a database might contain information provided by a group of companies who specialize in a single product type. The purpose of the database is twofold. First, the database enables people with a need for the product to search for and find vendors.

Second, the database can be used as a way to generate revenue through advertising on the database site. This advertising opportunity may be particularly desirable because anyone who uses the database has already implicitly provided the information of interest for the database focus—a good opportunity to gain brand awareness for a company that markets an item related to the database focus.

Press-Related Information   Several sites on the Internet provide services that search for and deliver news items about companies and their products. For example, eWatch provides companies with a clipping service, for a fee, that scans the Internet in search of targeted material that can be delivered, or **pushed,** to a subscriber of the service. Although some services are fee-based, others provide rudimentary search-and-deliver capabilities as a feature of the Web site (e.g., Yahoo!).

CAUTIONS FOR INTERNET-BASED RESEARCH

The Internet can provide marketing researchers with information, but ultimately the judgment of whether the information has value for decision making is up to the human decision makers in the process. The nature of the Internet raises several issues that influence the use of its information in marketing research. These issues include the relevance of information and the role of time constraints.

Information Relevance in Marketing Research

In an online environment, the manager has access to the information resources that comprise the Internet. The ready availability of information may enable a researcher to search for and acquire information needed for decision making more efficiently online than in a traditional offline context. The information that may be obtained through standard search facilities on the Internet (e.g., search engines) may, paradoxically, provide the manager with too much information and not enough information at the same time. Search tools may return results of search matches in the thousands, but provide no guarantee that the results will supply a set of sources with informational utility (i.e., high quality, relevant information) for the marketing researcher's purpose.

Concerns with information quality are also raised by the freedom with which information can be published on the Internet. The Internet is largely unregulated in terms of the content that can be published. In addition, publishing software has decreased in cost and complexity to a point where it is readily available and usable. These characteristics combine to create an information environment that varies widely in terms of quality, credibility, and depth.

One way to manage concerns associated with online information is to combine online and offline aspects of marketing research. Insights obtained from environmental scanning that leverages the array of information on the Internet can be used to guide the acquisition and interpretation of additional, detailed data from offline expert sources.

Time Constraints on Information Use

The online environment may also introduce time constraints into decision making that are not experienced in the traditional, offline decision processes. One time constraint reflects an increase in productivity expectations. As the availability of information and communications resources spreads, demands on performance may escalate. These demands can result in heightened expectations of the marketing researcher.

Another type of time constraint is introduced when the rate at which information is published on the Internet increases the rate at which information becomes obsolete. The ease with which information can be posted and transmitted in online environments effectively shortens the life cycle of many types of information. Time constraints on information use can be managed by decreasing the cost needed to acquire the information. Internet support tools such as search engines can efficiently examine many information sources and return lists of sites that match the search keywords.

Linking the issues of relevance and time constraint, however, is the fact that search engines differ in the way that they search available information. For example, some engines examine information stored in a category-based organization (e.g., Yahoo!), while other engines complete across-category, across-Internet searches with little prior structure (e.g., Altavista). The nature of the search process influences the quality of the search result. To illustrate, suppose that you must conduct a competitive analysis for a new product. If the product is sufficiently new that it has not yet been indexed in category-based systems, you are unlikely to acquire any information for your purpose with a category-based search engine. Marketing researchers must tailor the means for data collection not only to the purpose for the research, but also in conjunction with the technological capabilities and characteristics of the Internet.

Market Research for Hire

Commercial market research firms with Internet expertise provide a valuable service to many companies with an interest in the marketing environment of the Internet. The decision to have an outside firm do research, rather than conduct it within the company, may be based on several reasons. For instance, the complexity of the data available from the Internet, combined with the fast pace of commercial activity online, has led many companies to rely on external sources for data collection, analysis, and interpretation. Another reason for outsourcing marketing research is to protect consumers. Auto-by-Tel, for example, felt that asking customers to provide information about their purchases might be considered intrusive. To avoid the potential backlash from irritating their consumers, the company hired an outside firm to conduct, analyze, and interpret its existing records (wsj.com, 1998).

Different research companies use different methods to gather their information. The issues we have covered in this chapter apply to anyone who conducts market research. As a result, it is important to understand the methods that guide the research practices of any company hired to complete a research project, and the implications of the methods for the value of the data.

Chapter Summary

In this chapter, we examined the role of the Internet as a source of opportunity for a marketing information system. A marketing information system consists of internal and external information sources. Internal sources include databases of information about company operations and activities. The Internet can be used to acquire, track, store, and communicate internal information. A source of internal information for marketers who use the Internet for marketing activity is the database of site activity that is stored in a log file.

External information sources are the focus of marketing research. The Internet can be used to acquire, store, and communicate the results of research on consumers, competitors, and market conditions. The results of internal and external information acquisition can be integrated using Internet technologies to provide input for marketing strategy and implementation.

We considered the impact of the Internet on the marketing research process. The marketing research process consists of five stages: defining the problem, developing the research plan, collecting the data, analyzing the data, and presenting the results. We saw that each stage in the process may be influenced by Internet characteristics that facilitate or inhibit progress through the stage.

As a tool for conducting research, the Internet makes available a variety of data sources. A framework was used to describe the types of data sources, and to indicate the advantages and disadvantages of each type. Two properties were used to classify data types: (1) the source of the data, and (2) respondent awareness of the research. Sources of data are defined in terms of the person who observes and records the behavior of research interest—the respondent, the researcher, or a recorder in the past.

The framework was applied to marketing research that uses the Internet to provide insights into consumer behavior and competitor behavior. Forms of data collection for each objective were discussed.

REVIEW SECTION

Key Terms

- marketing information system
- log files
- hits
- decision support systems

- front-end data collection
- descriptive
- diagnostic
- predictive
- primary data

- secondary data
- data mining
- datum
- visible observer
- hidden observation

- reactive effects
- sampling
- self-selection
- selection bias

- cookie
- data profiling
- database

- benchmarking
- reverse linking
- pushed

Review Questions

1. What are three benefits of using the Internet for marketing research?
2. How can marketing researchers assess the reliability of information gathered on the Internet?
3. Briefly describe the elements that comprise a marketing information system.
4. What information may be provided by a DSS (decision support system)?
5. What is the overall purpose of the marketing research process?
6. Distinguish between primary and secondary data.
7. How can a marketing researcher reduce the possibility of being misled by incorrect data?
8. According to the Runkel and McGrath framework, what four things must occur to facilitate the development of data?
9. Why is it important to know the exact source of data?
10. Explain the problem of selection bias.
11. What is an advantage of data profiling? What is a disadvantage?
12. What are the benefits of using newsgroup content as a source of market information?
13. Where may marketing researchers gather information about their company's competitors?

Thinking Points

1. The Internet is often described as an information-rich environment. Does the amount of information that can be obtained from the Internet increase or decrease the importance of marketing research designed to provide actionable intelligence to marketers? In other words, is the Internet likely to affect the value of marketing research?
2. How does the open nature of the Internet affect the type of information available to marketers? What complications or issues are raised by the use of the Internet as a source of market information?
3. One goal of some practitioners (e.g., CPEX) is to facilitate the sharing of information collected from consumers. What impact might such widespread access to common data have on the need to conduct marketing research, and the methods for conducting marketing research?
4. What are the advantages and disadvantages of
   a. the Internet as a tool for conducting research?
   b. the Internet as a source of information for research?
5. Issues of sampling and subject/respondent consent are common in many forms of marketing research. What aspects of marketing research using the Internet make these concerns particularly salient? How might a marketer address these concerns?

6. What is the value of differentiating between different types of data using the properties of the Runkel and McGrath framework (i.e., data source and respondent awareness)?

7. What Internet-based data collection situations can be accommodated by the framework that would not exist in traditional environments for gathering data?

Suggested Readings

1. "Online Experiments: Ethically Fair or Foul?" by Beth Azar. *APA Monitor on Psychology, 31* (April 2000), pp. 50–65.

2. "Internet and Interactive Voice Response Surveys," in *Mail and Internet Surveys: The Tailored Design Method,* 2d ed., by Don A. Dillman (New York: John Wiley & Sons, Inc., 2000), pp. 352–412.

3. "Planning to Gather Evidence: Techniques for Observing and Recording Behavior," in *Research on Human Behavior: A Systematic Guide to Method,* by Philip Runkel and Joseph E. McGrath (New York: Holt, Rhinehart & Winston, 1972), pp. 173–193.

4. "Interactive Marketing: Exploiting the Age of Addressability," by Robert C. Blattberg and John Deighton. *Sloan Management Review* (Fall 1991), pp. 5–14.

5. "Information Technology, Marketing Practice, and Consumer Privacy: Ethical Issues," by Ellen R. Foxman and Paula Kilcoyne. *Journal of Public Policy & Marketing, 12,* 1 (Spring 1993), pp. 106–119.

CHAPTER 10

The Internet as a Content Resource

FOCUS AND OBJECTIVES

In this chapter, we focus on the role of the Internet as a content resource for achieving marketing objectives. Topics include the sources of content for use by marketers, as well as the different types of content that are made available through the technology and marketer relationship. Different purposes for online content with respect to elements of the marketing mix are discussed. Content-related issues are considered for each of the perspectives in the exchange framework.

YOUR OBJECTIVES IN STUDYING THIS CHAPTER INCLUDE THE FOLLOWING:

- Recognize the role of content as a resource for marketers.

- Know the different sources of online content and their pros and cons.

- Understand the differences between different forms of content that are enabled by technology.

- Understand ways in which online content affects mix decisions.

- Develop familiarity with issues for each perspective that are raised by online content.

Make airline reservations for vacation, enter a sweepstakes, look up medical information, buy a birthday gift, scan the news headlines, play a game, buy some stock, check your bank account—all in one session at your computer. These activities only scratch the surface of what the Internet enables people to do online. Although the activities are different, they are connected by a common thread: content. Each of these activities is possible because of the information that can be obtained from the Internet. The technology that makes it possible to transmit digital information between computers is a necessary component of the Internet. The information that is transmitted, however, is the lifeblood of the network.

The importance of content is evident in two observations. One is the rate at which the *amount* of information is increasing. Another is the rate at which *access* to the information is increasing. The Global Internet Project, an organization that tracks Internet growth and adoption, estimates that the amount of information on the Internet doubles every year. The size of this accomplishment is reflected in the estimated addition of 300,000 new pages to the Web, weekly. Of course, not all of the content that is created will survive. For a variety of reasons, Web sites often disappear. The International Data Corporation estimated that 25 to 30 percent of commercial Web sites would fail in their efforts in 1997. This statistic underscores the need to understand the role of content as a resource for marketing.

Understanding the role of content for marketing requires us to answer three questions. First, what are the sources of content? We will examine the influence of consumers and other groups of people on the creation of Internet content by and for marketers. Second, what types of content can be created? The answer to this question emphasizes the importance of technology as a factor in content creation. Third, how does content affect marketing action? To begin to answer this question, we must look at the implications of content for elements of the marketing mix. Content can be a product, as well as a way to develop a product and to promote a product. In addition, content can be used to create a virtual place, or a context for marketing activity. Finally, content may affect pricing, as when price comparisons are readily available to consumers.

SOURCES OF CONTENT: PEOPLE AS PUBLISHERS

Content can come from sources internal to a company, or from sources external to a company. Examples of internal, company-generated content include product information and promotional material. External sources of content may be consumers, competitors, or publicity. A company may decide to use only one type of source, or a combination of sources, depending on the objectives for the content. A summary of content sources is provided in Figure 10.1.

Internal Sources of Content

Internal sources of content can address several purposes. For instance, a company may develop content in order to make product information accessible online. Web sites that provide product specifications, or that describe applications for a product, reflect a product information focus. Company-created content may also be used to promote a product. Web sites can be used to create a brand image, and to provide incentive to purchase (e.g., with online coupons and rebates). In addition, a com-

FIGURE 10.1 Sources of Site Content.

Company	Customer	Competitor	Other
• Product information	• Testimonials	• Site links for comparisons	• Press (e.g., reviews, articles)
• Promotional information	• Articles	• Product information	• Links to databases
• Databases	• Product reviews		• Link lists (e.g., partners, related sites)
• Articles	• Content submission (e.g., photos)		
	• Chat rooms		
	• Bulletin boards		

pany can create content that will be displayed on an external Web site, as through an ad server that places the company's banner ad on a set of subscriber sites.

Another reason for a company to create content is to enhance the benefits of a product experience for its customers. For example, companies can provide answers to common questions about product usage and performance. These sets of frequently asked questions, or FAQs, can decrease demand on human customer service resources. Content can also consist of product manuals and online descriptions of product installation and troubleshooting processes.

When interactive customer service is necessary, content can be developed to serve as the interface between the consumer and the company's customer service representatives. For instance, a company can use software designed to assess the general nature of a question or problem, and to direct the user to the most appropriate source of help. This form of filtering creates efficiencies for the consumer and for the company.

We will consider the use of company-created content in greater detail when we examine the implications of content for the marketing mix.

External Sources of Content

A company can integrate information from external sources with content developed within the company, to meet marketing objectives. External sources take a variety of forms. Each form offers unique opportunities and challenges for a marketer.

Customer-Created Content

Content can be developed with input from customers. Solicited input, as in the form of testimonials or product reviews, has advantages for the marketer. These advantages include the ability to provide additional content to site visitors, as well as the potential to use the customer input as a form of word-of-mouth. Consumer recommendations of a product may tend to decrease skepticism about stated product benefits, because they come from a source with lesser vested interest in the sale and adoption of a product than a salesperson.

Customer submissions are another form of customer-created content available to marketers of a digitally transmitted product. For example, online magazines and other digital forms of information can, as products, make use of customer submissions. One such Web site exists as a forum for displaying tattoos as art. Magazine readers provide the photographs that are organized into galleries of tattoo types (e.g., symbols, concepts). To keep visitors returning to the site, photo submissions are organized as contests. Pictures of tattoos that are deemed superior on specific criteria are the winners, and they are displayed on the home page of the magazine. These forms of solicited input enable the marketer to exercise control over which material will be presented as content.

Other forms of customer-created content provide lesser levels of content control. For example, online bulletin boards and chat rooms serve as forums in which consumers can discuss product experiences and make suggestions to other participants. These features serve to draw visitors to the site, and they encourage repeat visits, which provide opportunities for a marketer to provide new products and new information about existing products. In addition, they operate as a more traditional form of word-of-mouth, in which communication is two-way, between consumers.

A potential downside to online word-of-mouth as an established source of site content is its unpredictability. Long dry spells in which postings to the forum diminish may devalue the content and decrease site traffic. More problematic, however, is the potential for negative information about the company's product or service to be published as customer-created content. Because the marketer only controls the availability of the forum, and not the content, constant oversight is needed to insure timely remediation of concerns or complaints that are voiced in the online context.

Competitor-Created Content

The Internet facilitates comparisons of products and services across sites. Marketers with a competitive advantage related to a specific product can create links to competitors' sites to make salient a product advantage. In addition, product information provided on competitors' sites can be used to develop internal content that draws comparisons between competing products.

The effects of Web-provided information are substantial. Research conducted by Yankelovich Partners (2000) indicates that 93 percent of online consumers researched a product online. Eighty-eight percent felt that it was important to have all the necessary information in one place, thus underscoring the importance of content completeness.

Other External Sources of Content

Publicly available information can be used as an external source of content. Links to related sites provide content that can augment the central focus of a marketer's site. These links may provide background about a product, or they may facilitate desirable comparisons between a company's product and competitors' products. The Web site in Figure 10.2 illustrates the use of links to provide background about the product, a private school, and to indicate affiliation with related organizations.

Links can also serve as product benefits, when the set of links enhances the value of a product or brand to the consumer. For instance, a company that sells camping equipment may provide links to other companies that sell related, non-competing products, to travel companies and tour guides, and to sites of national parks and campgrounds.

Companies use lists of links to indicate partnership agreements. These lists not only serve as information resources for visitors, but they may also influence visitors' perceptions of the company or product. A visitor's attitude toward a brand may be improved when the product is evaluated against a backdrop of well-known, reputable companies with whom the selling company has partnership agreements. When such a halo effect occurs, the positive affect associated with another company or its product is transferred to the evaluation of the present product.

These opportunities for the use of externally obtained content can be related to the objectives of marketing strategy with a product focus: image, improvement, and incentive—the Three I's (see Figure 10.3). For instance, links can promote

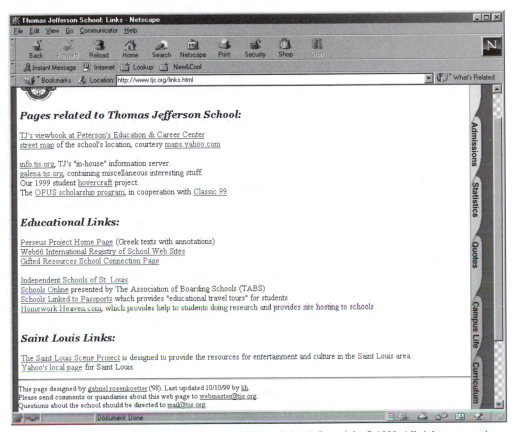

FIGURE 10.2 Links Create Interest and Explain the Product.

FIGURE 10.3 External Sources of Content and the Three I's.

Model	Sample Link Type	Desired Effect
Image	Prestigious partners	Halo effect; recategorization of product as higher level or quality
Incentive	Competitors who are inferior on a key feature	Highlight product dominance on one or more features
	Public sites/databases (e.g., health-related)	Underscore product function or need
Improvement	Sites with related products	Position product as central; simplify acquisition of other, complementary products
	Sites with product use-related information (e.g., camping sites)	Stimulate product involvement; increase perceived benefits

image through association with other companies or organizations with a desired reputation. Comparisons with competing brands through links to their sites can demonstrate price and other attribute advantages, thus creating incentives for consumers. Links to sites with related products and information that enhances the value of the company's product can serve an improvement objective.

TYPES OF CONTENT: THE ROLE OF TECHNOLOGY

The sources of content for marketing use are often similar to the information sources encountered in traditional, offline marketing environments. For instance, in each type of environment, consumer-to-consumer communications can provide information as word-of-mouth. In the marketspace, however, the ways in which the sources are implemented to create different types of content vary markedly from offline instances. In this section, we will look at the role of technology as the means by which content is made available for consumption on the Internet.

The enabling role of technology for creating different types of content reflects the importance of telepresence. Recall from Chapter 5 that telepresence is the user's perception of being present in the computer-mediated environment. In theoretical terms, telepresence is due to vividness and interactivity. In technical terms, vividness, or sensory richness, is provided by different uses of media, such as audio and video technologies. Interactivity is created by technology that enables the user to change the form, or representation, of the computer-mediated environment. Telepresence is the result of the effective combination of technology with user behavior to integrate multimedia capabilities with interactive capabilities. (See, for example, Figure 10.4.)

Different levels of multimedia capability and interactivity characterize the types of content that are possible in the Internet environment. The desired level of complexity in content type is a function of the marketer's objectives for the content, as well as the technical capabilities of the company or the content creator, and the anticipated behaviors and computing capacity of the end user (see Figure 10.5). The marketer must decide which combinations of content types will best communicate the goals of the company in regard to the marketing effort.

Multimedia Types of Content

The Internet differs from traditional media for providing information because it enables the integration of text, audio, and video in flexible formats that can be, to some extent, controlled by the user. Three types of multimedia technologies illustrate the range of possibilities for providing content: downloadable audio/video, streaming audio/video, and three-dimensional animation.

Downloadable Audio/Video

Audio and video content can be stored as files that can be requested by a user from a company site. In a **downloadable file,** content is transferred from the server that houses the site's files to the user's computer. Once downloaded, the file is

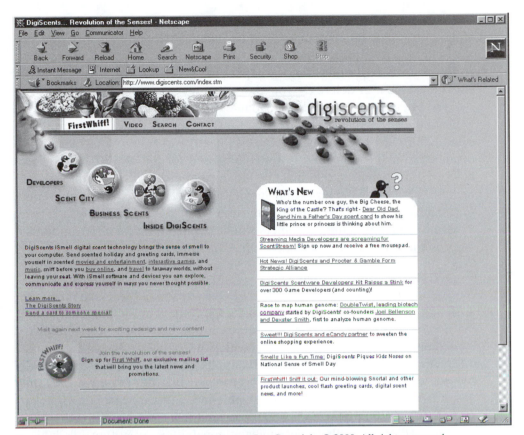

FIGURE 10.4 The Ability to Transmit Odors May Enhance Telepresence.

stored in its entirety on the user's computer and is available to be played. Examples of downloadable files include a television commercial that is available on a Web site, or clips from an audio recording or a televised speech. Downloadable files can be used to provide product exposure (e.g., with a movie or music), or to create links

FIGURE 10.5 Factors That Influence Content Complexity.

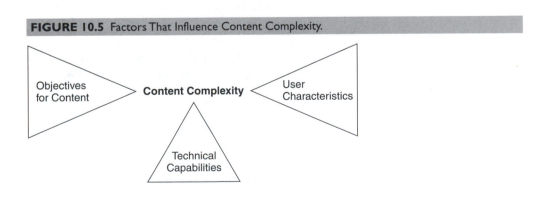

between the different media used in a promotional campaign. The ability to provide audio and video content can be used to enhance the vividness of a site's content. Another benefit of the downloadable format is that it can be retrieved and replayed by the user whenever revisiting the experience is desired: once downloaded, the file exists until the user deletes it from the computer's memory.

The disadvantages of a downloadable file are the time needed to download the file, and the space that files can require for storage on the user's computer. For instance, with a 28.8 Kbps modem, it can take nearly two hours to download a 60-second commercial in a format that is not compressed for the downloading process. The amount of information that must be digitized in order to create the file—and that makes the long downloading time inevitable—means that the file will require a lot of room for storage. In a world where Internet time is a fact of life, it is reasonable to assume that not many consumers will be willing to invest large amounts of time and computer memory to download an advertising message!

Streaming Audio/Video

An alternative to a downloadable file is a **streaming file.** As the name suggests, a streaming file provides the user with the file content at the time that the file is being accessed. Streaming content offers real-time playback; no content is downloaded and stored, so users experience no wait to receive the file and no demand on their computer storage capacity. Examples of streaming content include Internet radio and live broadcasts of concert footage. In order to play a streaming file, a user must often download a plug-in. A **plug-in** is software that interprets the information in a streaming file and communicates it in a recognizable form to the user's computer. Plug-ins with basic playback capabilities are often available free of charge to users (e.g., RealPlayer).

Three-Dimensional Animation

Much like Saturday morning cartoons, 3-D animation on the Internet provides visual interest and vividness to otherwise static content. Software packages (e.g., Shockwave and Flash) provide marketers with the tools to create content with action. Similar to streaming files, animated files may require an appropriate plug-in to enable execution of the file.

Animated images are related to the concept of virtual reality. A goal of virtual reality is to create a computer-based environment that provides the user with sense of being in the computer-created environment, or telepresence. Programs to create virtual reality environments, such as VRML (virtual reality mark-up language), operate by translating geometric elements of objects into a series of mathematical equations that can be represented digitally.

Virtual reality environments are a hybrid of multimedia and interactive capabilities. These environments are often created with **virtual reality photography.** This technology creates an environment by connecting several photographs of an object (e.g., a car) or a scene (e.g., a store) to produce a panoramic image. The user can use a mouse to examine different parts of the image as if he were moving around in the actual environment. Because the user can navigate a virtual reality scenario, and because the context changes as the user exerts control over the environment, the situation exhibits interactivity.

Types of Interactive Content

In addition to the user actions that affect content with virtual reality applications, marketers can incorporate interactive content into a Web site with contests, games, and customer service. The role of interactivity differs across applications to the extent the behaviors of a site visitor affect the marketing actions of the company. For instance, interactivity can be used to accumulate information about customer needs and preferences, as with an online survey that uses a respondent's answers to structure subsequent parts of the questionnaire. This application reflects a role of interactivity as a way to develop and refine marketing action. In contrast, interactivity in the form of a game may promote user involvement with the site, brand, or company, but the visitor's actions are not tracked and used as data for marketing decision making. A continuum of the role of interactivity is presented in Figure 10.6.

Online Games

Online games can be used to increase visitor involvement with a Web site. Companies can use games as interactive content to keep visitors in a site longer, thus potentially increasing exposure to the company's brands, or to advertising and promotional material offered on the site. In addition, companies can use games as an incentive to visitors to return to a Web site, as by changing the nature of the game (e.g., playing options, difficulty level). To participate in an online game, a visitor may be required to provide registration information. This information can provide the marketer with simple data about site visitors.

Online Contests

Marketers can use online contests not only as sources of customer leads, but also as a source of content. As with online games, participation in a contest may require the participant to provide registration information. (It is hard to acknowledge a winner if you cannot identify the contestant.) In addition to serving as a source of user information, contests can be developed that require the user to

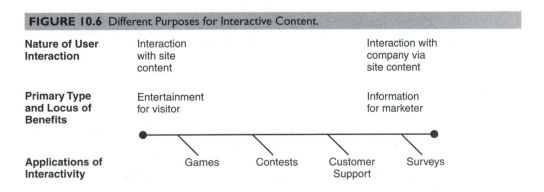

FIGURE 10.6 Different Purposes for Interactive Content.

Nature of User Interaction	Interaction with site content			Interaction with company via site content
Primary Type and Locus of Benefits	Entertainment for visitor			Information for marketer
Applications of Interactivity	Games	Contests	Customer Support	Surveys

provide information that can be placed on the site as content. For example, an online publisher of a camera magazine might run a digital photography contest in which winners' photographs are displayed.

Online Customer Support

Online games are served to the user as interactive content, and online contests can result in the interactive creation of content. Even farther along the continuum of interactive purposes is customer support. Interactive applications to create content to facilitate communication between company and customer include moderated discussion groups and mailing lists, as well as more private forms of communication, such as real-time live help.

Online Research

Web site content can provide marketers with information for developing and implementing aspects of marketing strategy. Insights can be obtained from customer support activities, such as online discussion groups and bulletin boards, as well as from interaction with individual users. Online contests can also provide information. For example, Budweiser uses its Web site to foster brand image. One aspect of the site is a quiz that lets visitors assess whether they are "beer meisters." The user completes a quiz that is immediately scored. In addition to providing entertainment and information to the user, the results of this type of quiz, if tracked and analyzed, constitute a set of data about consumers' knowledge of the product and the product category.

Interactive surveys in which users are aware of the data collection serve as content that provides the company with user feedback. This feedback can be directed toward a company, a product, or even the Web site. Data collection as content may also have an incidental benefit; unhappy customers who are able to complain directly to a company may be less likely to complain to other consumers.

> *Digital Artifact 10.1*
>
> **In 1999, the average number of characters in a domain name was 11.**
>
> (*Source:* **Network Solutions and The Internet Index, #27.**)

PURPOSES OF CONTENT: IMPLICATIONS FOR THE MARKETING MIX

Marketers can use content to carry out aspects of marketing management related to each element of the marketing mix. As a result, online content is often developed for widely varying purposes. For example, a marketer can provide an online game with a goal of keeping visitors returning to a particular site. On its site to promote the *Toy Story* movie and merchandising, Disney changes characteristics of its game on a weekly basis, thus encouraging sustained interest and visits.

In this section, we will consider the way that the Internet as a content resource can influence each of the four Ps, as well as sample issues that may stem from this influence.

Content and Product

As a content resource, the Internet influences decisions about product strategy. For example, the Internet can influence a company's product strategy by creating an opportunity for new types of products and services. Consider the role of Internet service providers, or ISPs, such as Compuserve and America Online. An important benefit of these services is to make Internet content accessible to users. Without an Internet, who needs an ISP? In addition, content can be used to provide information about a product, and even as a tool for developing a product.

Using Internet Content as a Product

The Internet can influence product strategy by changing the nature of the need for a product. This situation occurs when the technologies pioneered through the Internet make existing products that fulfill a similar need less desirable. For example, consumers can have music on demand by purchasing a compact disc, a cassette, a record, or even an eight-track tape. With the advent of Internet technologies such as MP3, a format that enables people to download a huge variety of recorded music, the benefits of previous formats pale dramatically.

The types of companies and products reflected in the ISP and MP3 examples exist because of the abilities inherent in the Internet to create digital products—products that only exist in a digital, electronic environment, and because of the presence of such an environment. Obviously, not all products are suitable for a digital medium. In addition, even when a product is a viable candidate for digitization, marketers must decide whether the Internet environment presents advantages for developing and selling products in a digital form. The digital form may complement or replace existing product forms.

Decisions about whether a digital product form is desirable should take into account consumers and competitors in developing a product strategy. For instance, books are a product that can be readily digitized. Suppose that a bookseller determines that production costs will be substantially reduced if books are sold in a downloadable form from the Internet. Eliminating the hardcopy production component of the business makes sense only if the bookseller correctly understands the nature of the target market. Do consumers in the target market have Internet access? Are these consumers likely to adapt their buying behaviors to adopt the online form of the product?

If the market is identifiable, accessible, and sufficient, the decision to switch product forms may be guided by competitors' actions. For example, EMI International, a recording company that produces and markets records and compact discs, recognized that the availability of music over the Internet created a challenge for EMI's ability to be successful selling recorded music in traditional formats. In this case, the challenge came not from competitors in the traditional marketplace (e.g., other recording companies), but from competitors in the marketspace. The company was faced with the need to work proactively to create a product strategy capable of providing long-term opportunities for surviving and thriving, given the increasing popularity of online sources of music. As a result, EMI partnered with LiquidAudio, a provider of software and services for digital music formats, to explore opportunities for developing an online product presence.

Using Content to Provide Product Information

From the early days of brochureware, the use of the Internet as a way to provide information about products and services has changed dramatically. Marketers can use the technological characteristics of the Internet to provide information in ways that augment forms of communication available in traditional media. For example, a catalog that arrives in your mailbox contains a specific set of product descriptions. All, some, or none of them may be of interest to you. With the Internet, however, a marketer can maintain a database of product information, but provide to customers only those descriptions that match stated needs or interests. As a result, the content can be customized to provide a better match between the customer's needs and the company's offerings.

Marketers can use the Internet as a content resource to provide product descriptions, to suggest product applications, and to facilitate product use. As an illustration of the latter benefit of the Internet, a marketer might create a Web site that contains technical manuals that can be downloaded on demand for different products. In addition, the site could contain step-by-step installation instructions, and even tips for troubleshooting.

Content from the Internet affects offline shopping. A study by Jupiter Communications (2000) describes **Web-impacted spending,** which combines the revenue from online purchases with offline purchases influenced by Internet-based information to provide a quantitative estimate of the Internet's influence. In 2000, Web-impacted spending was estimated at $235 billion, with projected growth to $831 billion in 2005.

Using Content to Create a Product

Internet content can be used as a tool for product development. Using the Internet as a content resource may influence the activities related to each phase of a three-stage framework for product development: planning, design, and implementation.

In the planning stage, multiple information sources are used to determine desired product characteristics. These sources might include the anticipated market and its needs, as well as input from the production and marketing personnel in the organization. As a content resource, the Internet can be used to conduct market research about customers' needs, and to investigate competitors' products and actions.

In the design stage, the inputs from the planning stage are used to guide the development of a product, from a set of desired characteristics to a coherent product concept. Digital content can be used to develop product plans and to create product simulations that can be shared and revised despite geographical differences. Digital design packages such as CATIA (computer-aided three-dimensional interactive application), through IBM, enable teams of engineers and planners to work simultaneously to develop product prototypes. This development serves as a map for the implementation stage, in which the product moves from a concept to reality.

To implement a concept, Internet content in the form of product component databases and relationship histories between suppliers and producers expedites the process of manufacturing a product.

Digital Artifact 10.2

Successful sites that provide sex-related content have profit margins of 30 percent to 40 percent.

(*Source: The New York Times 2000 Almanac.*)

Content and Price

The ready availability of information on the Internet makes it easier for consumers to acquire price information about products and services. This **price transparency** has advantages and disadvantages for marketers. For instance, when a marketer has a competitive price, it is advantageous to have that information easily accessible to consumers. Suppose, however, that the price is substantially higher than that of the competition. Even if product characteristics, such as extra features or performance capabilities, cause or merit the higher price, customers shopping on the Internet may tend to focus on the price.

The focus on price may result from consumers' ability to use shopping agents on the Internet to gather and create spontaneously generated content about sets of products. A **shopping agent** is an application that, when provided with specific information, serves as the basis for a search through Internet content. For instance, a user could look for digital cameras made by a particular company, and within a set price range (e.g., Kodak cameras between $500 and $1,000).

Shopping agents often create brand/attribute matrixes that display available specifications for a designated set of products. A brand/attribute matrix may contain information about a set of different brands with comparable features, or a display of the different locations and purchase characteristics associated with a single brand. In the latter instance, the location, or storefront, becomes the brand. An example of this type of display is shown in Figure 10.7. Typically, price information is listed from cheapest to most expensive, in a set. As noted, a marketer with a low price can benefit from the exposure provided by shopping agents.

For a marketer, one difficulty with shopping agents is that they result in a presentation of content that the marketer does not control. Of course, similar situations exist in traditional media, too. For instance, product reviews and ratings in *Consumer Reports* provide the consumer with an across-brand comparison benefit

Kodak DC215 Zoom Millenium Edition

Merchant	Price	State	Shipping	In Stock
Buy.com	$273.95	CA	5.95	No
eCost.com	$274.99	CA	FREE	No
Camera Sound	$275.00	PA	see site	call
Egghead.com	$288.99	WA	FREE	Limited
BuyDig.com	$293.00	NJ	19.95+	Yes

FIGURE 10.7 A Sample Merchant-Based Brand/Attribute Display.

similar to the shopping agent function. With the Internet, however, the ease with which informational content can be posted and altered increases the importance of frequently monitoring competitors' price-related actions. In addition, the flexible nature of the brand/attribute displays means that a marketer must consider the likely specifications for a user-initiated search, and how the results of different searches might depict the product, relative to the competition.

Content and Place

Two ways in which the Internet as a content resource affects decisions about the place component of the mix are (1) by serving as a source of information about consumption locations, and (2) by creating contexts for consumption, or virtual places.

Whether the product is digital or physical, a marketer can use Internet content to guide customers to purchase opportunities. For instance, e-mail marketing is content created to directly market to a delimited set of targets. Alternatively, a Web site might contain a list of locations from which a product is available, perhaps divided into geographic regions.

The Internet can also act as a place. One goal for developers of virtual reality is to create contexts that provide realistic simulations of physical environments. This technology can be used to create shopping malls and stores. A consumer can navigate through a store, looking at items on racks and shelves. Some programs enable the user to use a computer mouse and cursor to "pick up" an item from a shelf, turning it around and over to examine the product from different angles. Real estate companies have used the Internet to guide prospective buyers through homes, and museums use the virtual modeling technology to provide tours to distant visitors. These examples illustrate situations in which the role of the Internet as a content resource is closely related to its role as a channel resource. We will consider this interaction in detail in Chapter 11.

To create a more vivid perception of experience, some programs that create virtual places allow the user to enter the environment with a virtual persona. These personae, called **avatars,** act as the digital representation of a person in the virtual environment. For instance, suppose that you wanted to go shopping in an online store that welcomes avatars. You could send your virtual representative to the store, to meet with the store's sales representative, perhaps another avatar. In spite of the science fiction nature of the scenario, the technology can help marketers create a more involving and realistic experience for consumers.

On a simpler level, the format and appearance of a Web site can create a context that influences user perceptions and behavior. Researchers have demonstrated that the choice of a background for product information can alter the importance a visitor places on a particular product attribute. For example, vague images of coins on a description of a car result in increased weight placed on price by consumers who examine the description. Pictures of clouds on a background of sofa profiles increase the importance of comfort as a product attribute. The effects of these subtle changes to context illustrate the potential importance of content elements as factors that resemble more traditional effects of place as a context for product evaluation (e.g., atmospherics).

Digital Artifact 10.3

Fifty percent of online orders during the holiday season were from women.

(*Source:* **Bizrate, and The Internet Index, #26.**)

Content and Promotion

The Internet has received attention as a means for promoting goods and services. It is a channel of communication with potential for reaching a global audience. In addition, the technologies that comprise the Internet make it possible for marketers to create promotional content in forms capable of addressing a wide range of promotional objectives. We will look at the use of content for the three objectives of image, improvement, and incentive. The vehicles used to deliver the content to users, such as banners, buttons, and mailing lists, receive additional attention in Chapter 12.

Using Content to Enhance Image

Image-based business models use content to influence consumers' perceptions of a brand or a company. With this approach, the marketer's goal is to provide content that adds value for the customer without functionally changing the experience of product use. For instance, companies have developed Web site content designed to create exposure to a brand or a company, even when the site does not enable product purchase. For example, Procter and Gamble's Crest site contains an interactive brushing demonstration that is applicable for any brand of toothpaste. The interest and involvement experienced by a user who visits the site and tries out the demonstration, however, may increase the favorability of an attitude toward the Crest product. Similar efforts and objectives are evident in the Web site activities of Mattel. Mattel's Barbie site lets visitors play with make-up to change the appearance of a doll.

Using Content to Create Incentive

Incentive to purchase a particular product can be created with promotional content that demonstrates the advantages, as in time efficiency or cost reduction, of the marketer's product over other competing products. For instance, content can facilitate product trial, making it easier for consumers to determine whether a product is appropriate for their individual needs. Examples of companies who use content for product trial are research firms, such as Nua Online and Dun and Bradstreet. These companies make available sample reports, and they routinely provide free research results that indicate the focus and scope of their services. Free online trials create time efficiency by reducing search and evaluation costs, as well as financial risk.

Internet content can be used to reduce the costs associated with product production, and with creating and maintaining the relationship formed by the product transaction between marketer and consumer. These savings can be passed on to consumers in the form of lower prices, without narrowing the producer's profit margin. As we saw in Chapter 8, an important benefit of the Internet is the ability to provide consumers with customer support, any time. For the marketer, providing self-help content that a customer can search through and use on demand may not only enhance marketer-customer interactions, but it may also be less costly to manage the relationship through the Internet than through phone, mail, or in-person customer service interactions.

Incentives that reduce risk and lower price offer indirect savings to the consumer. Many marketers have used the Internet to take a more direct approach, as by simply giving consumers money to reward them for making purchases through their Web sites. For example, Barnes and Noble sought to increase holiday traffic through its Web site in 1999 by giving first-time buyers $20. Other merchants have provided rebates, free shipping and returns, and gift certificates to induce purchases and repeat purchases.

Some online retailers use electronic coupons to spur purchasing. E-coupon Web sites such as Coolsavings.com and Valupage.com provide consumers with collections of vendors' coupons that can be printed and redeemed. The results of a June 2000 study by The NPD Group, Inc. indicate that e-coupons for products typically associated with online sales, such as toys (87 percent) and books (83 percent), were redeemed online more frequently than e-coupons for products in other categories. E-coupon redemption in offline stores was highest for fast foods (96 percent) and groceries (94 percent).

As the screen in Figure 10.8 illustrates, marketers can use coupons as content on individual company Web sites to create purchase incentive.

Using Content for Product Improvement
Promotional content that provides the user with extra product-related benefits accomplishes an improvement objective. Using promotional content to augment product benefits often blurs the distinction between product and promotion. For example, Crest's site enables visitors to sign up for free dental check-up reminders. The reminder is delivered via e-mail to the user, and provides an opportunity for the marketer to remind the user about Crest. Even though the reminder does not affect the performance of the toothpaste, it may become encoded in memory as one of a set of associations between the brand name and product benefits.

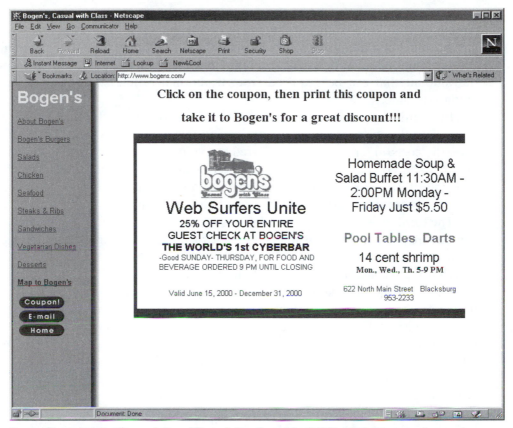

FIGURE 10.8 Creating Online Incentive for Offline Consumption.

CAUTIONS FOR CONTENT

The extent to which the Internet as a content resource can be used effectively in different aspects of the marketing mix depends on the interaction of people and technology. People create content and interpret content, and technology enables the representation of that content. The interaction between people and technology can raise issues about the nature of content, and how it affects the behaviors of people. In using the Internet as a content resource, marketers must be aware of the possible issues that may impede the effectiveness of a marketing action. We can look at these issues from the different perspectives that influence marketing in the Internet environment.

Consumer Issues

Marketing inputs as Internet content differ from marketing inputs in traditional consumption environments. Some of the characteristics that differentiate the content environments include the amount of readily available content, the cost to search the content, and who controls the format of the content (i.e., marketer or user).

Each of these three differences may affect the ways that consumers use Internet content, and the extent to which their behaviors differ from what might occur in traditional marketing information contexts (e.g., television, radio). For example, the sheer amount of information from the Internet as a single source often exceeds the amount that can be acquired from traditional offline sources in the same amount of time.

In addition, the costs of searching for information with the Internet may be lower than the costs associated with information acquisition in other venues. Consider the costs, in terms of time, incurred by typing a request for car specifications on a car site, compared with those incurred by driving to an equal number of car dealerships. The ease with which information can be obtained may lead consumers to gather more information than they would in other environments.

The third difference in content focuses on control. Many traditional sources of content are presented to consumers (e.g., television ads), who are passive recipients of the information and its format. With Internet content, however, users can actively search for and construct displays of desired marketing content.

Research on information processing provides a basis for understanding and predicting how consumers might use content as the basis for making product-related decisions. This knowledge provides a basis for helping marketers develop effective presentations of content. For example, we know that people tend to trade off effort to process information against anticipated decision accuracy or quality. This result can be extended to include information search and evaluation. That is, more effort to search for information may lead to less effort invested in understanding the information to make product judgments. In addition, given the user's ability to actively structure some types of Internet content (remember interactivity?), more effort to structure content may be followed by less effort to process information to make a decision. Marketers should provide content in a form and amount that does not overload or confuse consumers.

Other insights from information-processing and decision-making research suggest that people often use heuristics to process information. For example, if all brands but one in a comparison format provide information about a feature, users will tend to eliminate the incomplete brand from consideration. An alternative behavior is to infer a value for the brand that tends to be lower than the values for other brands. Either outcome does not work to the brand's advantage. These findings suggest that marketers must be aware not only of how the content they provide will appear to consumers, but also how the type of information in a site compares with that of the competition, in terms of completeness.

Digital Artifact 10.4

China permits foreign ownership of no more than 50 percent for Chinese Internet content or service providers.

(*Source: The Wall Street Journal,* **January 26, 2000, and The Internet Index, #26.**)

Marketer Issues

What Is the Content? Goods or Services

The nature of the Internet raises several issues for conceptions of content-derived products as goods or services. For example, consider the traditional manner of defining a product. In the marketing literature, **products** are often described as bundles of benefits that satisfy particular needs of a consuming populace, whether individuals or organizations, for which the populace is willing to give up something of value in exchange. Both goods and services are products.

The Internet influences the range of possibilities for bundles of benefits, by making new goods possible, and by enabling changes to existing benefit bundles. Of course, services can also provide bundles of benefits to consumers. Because service marketing can require the development of a strategy that is markedly different from a marketing strategy for goods, it is important to understand what is actually being conveyed, and whether the benefits of the offering are perceived as characteristic of a good or of a service.

The Internet may affect our ability to differentiate goods from services using accepted characterizations of their differences. For instance, goods are sometimes differentiated from services by tangibility: goods are generally tangible, services are intangible. The Internet is an environment characterized by intangible, digitized information. Given the nature of the medium, goods that can be conveyed by the technologies that enable the medium are definitionally intangible, thus blurring one possible way of discriminating goods from services.

Services have also been differentiated from products by the nature of their consumption. Goods and their benefits, whether tangible, like an ice cream cone, or intangible, like software code, can be purchased and consumed at another place or time. (Although, with ice cream, it is generally best to consume sooner, rather than later.) In traditional venues, services are consumed at the time of production, like a maid service, a car wash, or a hair cut. Another way of characterizing the difference is that the benefits of any marketing offering are not obtained until consumption for either a product or a service. However, for a service, the benefits are not even available until the offering is consumed. Under this approach, goods have some created, existing, untapped potential for need satisfaction that services do not possess. Services have the benefit potential only when the service is enacted, or performed.

With the Internet, concepts of time and place differ from traditional exchange environments. Internet services, such as PointCast for topical news, provide benefits in the form of digitized results of actions designed to provide desired benefits. The ability to digitize the end result of the service means the result can be stored and the benefits of its existence can be consumed at a later time. This capability means that the outcome of the production actions can be viewed as a good. In short, the difference between Internet-based goods and Internet-based services is blurred by the technological capability to digitize and store the results of the activities that create the offering.

To determine whether an offering should be marketed as a good or a service, it is necessary for the marketer to recognize how visible the benefits of a technology are to the end user. For instance, the Internet has created many opportunities for products that enable users to perform Internet-related activities, such as sending and receiving e-mail and searching online databases. In many cases, however, the consumers of the informational benefits of these activities may be unaware of the underlying hardware or software products that make receiving the benefits of the activities possible. Instead, they may simply focus on the entity that makes available the benefits. Depending on the marketer's goals, making salient either the benefits or the underlying technology product may shift the user's perception, evaluation, and adoption of an offering from one vendor to another.

In general, the nature of the Internet as an environment of intangible, digitized information may suggest an increasing importance and emphasis on the role of service marketing issues and tactics in the development of marketing strategy. In addition, traditional approaches to product strategy, in which goods are often described and promoted on the basis of tangible features, may be largely replaced by marketing efforts that emphasize the relatively more tangible benefits of Internet-related products, rather than the intangible products themselves.

The Internet and Product Innovation

A frequently encountered term with respect to the Internet is *innovation*. The Internet has itself been described as an innovation with respect to communication. In addition, the Internet has been characterized as a set of technologies that has resulted in the development of innovative products that capitalize on the technological capabilities of the Internet. In many instances, these products are digital content. Developing effective marketing strategy for a digital product may depend on the extent to which the product will be perceived as innovative. It is necessary to separate the Internet as an innovative environment for marketing from Internet content as products that may (or may not) be innovative.

Defining Innovation   Several different definitions of innovation have been proposed and defended by researchers, including firm-oriented, product-oriented, and market-oriented perspectives. A firm-oriented perspective describes as innovative a product that is new to the producing organization. A product-oriented perspective characterizes a product's newness in terms of the extent to which it differs from existing products. Note that neither of these two perspectives takes into account the impact of the product on the people who will use it. In contrast, a market-oriented perspective focuses directly on the impact of the product on the target market. That is, will the product change the way that the market carries out activities related to the purpose of the product? If so, how dramatic a change will be observed?

Because we have defined products as a function of the effect they have on the market—that is, the benefits that can be obtained through consumption—it makes sense to employ a parallel definition of innovation. For our purposes, then, **innovation** is determined and defined by the impact of a product on the user's behavior.

Products that exert a greater influence on patterns of behavior are more innovative than products that exert less influence on patterns of behavior.

The impact of an innovation can be further classified by the nature of the product's impact on behavior. If the consumption of a product affects whether a behavior is carried out, the product is described as a **discontinuous innovation.** In other words, the product creates a break in the behavior pattern, hence the discontinuity. If, however, the product still enables the user to carry out the same behavior, but affects the way that the behavior occurs, the product is classified as a **continuous innovation.** An ISP is an example of a discontinuous innovation, because it requires a fundamental change to the way people communicate and obtain information. In contrast, MP3 is an example of a continuous innovation; people do not need to dramatically change their music listening patterns to consume the product.

An important point to remember is that it is possible for a product to be new, but not to be particularly innovative. This distinction is important because it may affect the way people adopt the product, as a function of its similarity in appearance, usage, performance, or benefits to existing products. In addition, it is possible for a product to be similar in application to an existing product (e.g., online newspapers), but to completely change the manner in which the application-related behavior is carried out (e.g., online newspapers from around the world, focused with push technology to provide specific, topical information). Recognition of these differences should guide the development of marketing strategy.

Policy Issues

Two issues illustrate the role of the policy perspective in content provision. One issue is the source of online content, an issue that introduces concerns of copyright. Another issue is the nature of online content; that is, what content is allowable?

Copyright Concerns: The Source of Content

The rapid growth of information on the Internet, and particularly on the World Wide Web, raises concerns about how to protect intellectual property. The importance of protecting intellectual property has increased with the development of technologies that make it easier to copy and distribute protected works.

The importance of protecting people's creative efforts has a history in the United States almost as long as the history of the country. In the U.S. Constitution, Congress was given the power to secure ". . . for limited times to authors and inventors the exclusive rights to their respective writings and discoveries" (Art. 1, Sec. 8). Congress passed the first copyright law in 1790.

The advent of computer technologies led to the need to refine and expand the classification of works that would be considered protected by law. The National Information Infrastructure (NII) Copyright Protection Act of 1995 updated existing copyright laws to encompass the digital transmission of a work. This legislation simply means that the creator of a copyrighted work has the right to authorize or forbid the distribution of a piece of work, even through the Internet.

A key concern with copyright protection on the Internet is how to enforce the legislation that protects the creator of a work. The ease with which information can be adapted, or even copied, into a Web site, coupled with the ease of altering the site should the violation be detected, presents a challenge for policy makers.

From a marketer's perspective, however, understanding the restrictions of copyright protection, as well as the intent behind the legislation, can reduce the potential for inadvertent violations of the law. In general, content that is created with original, creative material from someone else, and which is to be used within a commercial context, can only be reproduced and made available to an audience with the consent of the original author.

In the case of Web sites that provide computer software as part of their content, explicit contracts with the software developer may transfer the copyright or provide a license to use or sell the material. In addition, software for which distribution is not restricted, such as **freeware** or **shareware,** should be clearly noted as such to potential users.

The Nature of Content

As a means of disseminating information, the Internet has an unparalleled reach. Of concern to policy makers is the type of information that can be transmitted. In creating or reusing content from another source, marketers must be careful not to violate legislation that exists to protect two sets of people: (1) Internet users who should not be exposed to certain types of material (e.g., children and pornography, or anyone and child pornography); and (2) people who might be unjustly harmed by negative material provided as Internet content.

The policy focus that protects both sets of people is freedom of expression. In the United States, policy makers attempt to strike a balance between protecting people's ability to express themselves, and protecting those who might be placed at risk by unfettered expression. Laws that place limits on freedom of expression have been developed prior to the advent of the Internet, and this legislation extends to Internet content.

Three areas of content restriction are addressed by specific legislation. One is the restriction on content designed to provoke or incite unlawful behaviors. For instance, a Web site that provided plans for building a bomb, and information about how to distract authoritarian attention at a high school in order to facilitate bomb placement would likely be deemed in violation of the law.

A second limit to freedom of expression that restricts Internet content is defamation. Defamatory content consists of remarks that might harm the reputation of another person. For instance, a person who posts on a Web site the comment that a competitor's hamburgers are "chock full of *e. coli*" might risk a defamation lawsuit. Given the large number of people with access to the Internet, the potential for harming someone's reputation is great, and cases are decided on the likelihood of harm, rather than on the actual harm done. It is important to remember, however, that remarks that are true are not considered defamatory.

A third type of content restricted by existing legislation is material that is indecent or obscene. The determination of what constitutes obscenity is made on a state-by-state basis, and the local community has served as the standard for applying the law. Because a company will be governed by the law of the state in which the material is received, marketers of obscene or indecent material must be aware of the laws that guide legal action in each state to which the content might be transmitted.

Digital Artifact 10.5

In 1999, Congress reallocated $5.5 million of the SEC budget to investigate financial fraud on the Internet.

(*Source: U.S. News & World Report,* **November 15, 1999.**)

Technology Issues

A major technology issue for marketers in using the Internet as a content resource is bandwidth. Limits to bandwidth and demands on bandwidth affect the speed with which content can be transmitted and received. In general, backbone providers attempt to make available sufficient bandwidth to meet demand, but supply is limited. This constraint applies to all who wish to use the Internet to transfer content.

A more specific bandwidth concern is what is often called the last-mile problem. The **last-mile problem** is a capacity issue. It refers to constraints on the lines that transfer digital information from a service provider into the user's computer. Both the general and the specific bandwidth constraints suggest that marketers should exercise caution when deciding what forms of content to use.

Efforts to reduce the demand on bandwidth can create additional issues for marketers who attempt to make their content widely available on a frequently changing basis. The reasons for the additional issues are **proxy servers** and **caching functions.** A proxy server works as an intermediary between a user and the Internet. The proxy server takes the request for Web content (e.g., a particular page or file) from the user. To the user, the proxy server is invisible. The proxy server simply transfers the requested content from the Internet to the user's computer.

In the interest of reducing demand on bandwidth, however, some organizations coordinate the actions of a proxy server with a cache server. For instance, if a Web page is in high demand by the users within an organization, the page may be stored after an earlier retrieval into a cache—sort of like an electronic filing system. Then, when the user requests the Web file, the proxy server gets it from the cache, without contacting the Internet. Suppose that you are a marketer who has a policy of updating your Web site prices daily, in order to match your competition. If your file has been stored in a cache, users who request the file may only receive an outdated version.

Caching also creates problems for promotional content in the forms of banners and buttons. Companies that operate as ad servers may be less able to distribute advertising content to interested users, and less able to track the number of impressions for a banner. A banner that is cached with a heavily demanded file may receive high exposure among users associated with the proxy server, but the ad server will not be able to track exposure. In contrast, a banner on a site that is not being requested by a proxy server because a cached version is available will receive less exposure than it should.

Several programming options can help overcome the issues associated with proxy servers and caching. Marketers must be aware of the potential for a problem, and knowledgeable about the appropriate means for handling the different types of file concerns.

Chapter Summary

The Internet serves as a content resource for marketers. The rapidly increasing rate of content production on the Internet underscores the importance of understanding the role of content as a resource. In this chapter we considered the different sources of content that can be used by marketers in Internet-related marketing activities. The sources were classified as internal sources and external sources. Internal sources reflect content developed by the company, while external sources include content provided by customers, press, and publicly available information.

Technology makes it possible to represent information as Internet content. We reviewed different types of content that reflect the integration of the two dimensions of telepresence: vividness and interactivity. The ability to integrate different forms of media, such as print, audio, and video with Internet technologies enables marketers to create multimedia presentations of content. In addition to multimedia characteristics, some types of content also enable the user to interact with the digital environment. Different types of interactive content serve different purposes for marketers, ranging from increasing the entertainment value of a Web site to a user, to providing marketers with data to use in marketing decision making.

As a content resource, the Internet has the potential to affect strategy regarding each element of the marketing mix. For instance, the ability to create digital products may influence product strategy. In addition, the availability of product information as content and content-creating tools, such as shopping agents, can affect pricing strategy by making price comparisons between competing brands transparent. Content can also be used to create a context, or a virtual representation of place, that can affect product and brand evaluations. For promotion, content can be used to create brand image, to provide an incentive for a consumer to carry out a desired product-related behavior, and to provide the consumer with added value in the form of benefits related to product consumption.

In addition to its benefits as a content resource, the Internet raises several issues for marketers. These issues reflect an interaction of people and technology, and can be organized by each of the four main perspectives on marketing and the Internet: consumers, marketers, public policy, and technology. Marketers must recognize limits to consumers' information processing capabilities and be able to respond to the heuristics and biases that different forms of content may engender. In addition, marketers must understand the implications of the Internet as a content resource for defining offerings as products or services, and as innovative or not. These determinations may affect the appropriateness of a selected marketing strategy.

Policy and technology also come into play in terms of content-related issues. Policy makers determine the level and nature of regulation about the protection of the sources of content, in the form of copyright. They must also deal with issues related to the nature of content, such as whether the content violates legislation that limits freedom of expression. Technology works to overcome constraints on the form and reception of content dictated by capacity limits. In some cases, however, the technological solutions, such as proxy servers and caches, create additional problems for marketers. Marketers must look across issues and perspectives to create, implement, and manage marketing programs.

REVIEW SECTION

Key Terms

- downloadable file
- streaming file
- plug-in
- virtual reality photography
- Web-impacted spending
- price transparency

- shopping agent
- avatars
- products
- innovation
- discontinuous innovation
- continuous innovation

- freeware
- shareware
- last-mile problem
- proxy servers
- caching functions

Review Questions

1. Name three people-based sources of Internet content.
2. Describe how technology-enabled interactivity in the marketspace changes content.
3. What benefits do links provide in terms of satisfying strategic objectives?
4. How can content facilitate telepresence?
5. What is the difference between a downloadable file and a streaming file?
6. How can online games or contests benefit marketers?
7. What are the possible advantages and disadvantages of price transparency to a marketer?
8. How might the Internet affect a company's product strategy? Pricing strategy? Place strategy? Promotion strategy?
9. Is the Internet itself a continuous or discontinuous innovation? Why?
10. What challenges face public policy makers with respect to Internet content?
11. What problems do proxy servers and caching functions create for marketers? What benefits do they provide?

Thinking Points

1. Content can take on different roles: as a product, to develop a product, and to promote a product. How does the flexibility of content as an Internet resource affect how we think about the marketing mix in the Internet environment?
2. What are the costs and benefits that a marketer might encounter when using content from internal sources (i.e., company), compared with external sources (e.g., customers)?
3. What characteristics of the Internet environment affect marketers' ability to create content to encourage telepresence in ways that differ from traditional media?
4. Marketers place great value on creating sites that can attract and hold consumers' attention. How is telepresence related to this objective?
5. Is telepresence always beneficial? Consider situations in which complete immersion in the computer-mediated environment by consumers may have undesirable results for marketers and for consumers.
6. How does being able to use the Internet to develop products affect market competition?
7. Is the Internet an innovation? If so, why is it? What type of innovation is it? Does its classification as an innovation depend on its intended use?

Suggested Readings

1. "The Ascent of Content," by Edward D. Horowitz. In *The Future of the Electronic Marketplace* (Cambridge, MA: The MIT Press, 1998), pp. 91–114.
2. "In Virtual Fashion," by Stephen Gray. *IEEE Spectrum* (February 1998), pp. 18–25.
3. "Less Than Zero Margins," by Brian E. Taptich. *Red Herring, 64* (March 1999), pp. 46–53.
4. "Made to Odor," by Jeffrey Davis. *Business 2.0* (December 1999), pp. 216–228.
5. "Giveaways—They Pay Off on the Web," by Richard Shim. *ZDNet News* (June 12, 2000).

CHAPTER 11

The Internet as a Channel Resource

FOCUS AND OBJECTIVES

This chapter addresses the role of the Internet as a channel resource for marketers. Differences in channel structure, function, and management are considered for on-line and offline distribution approaches, using a relationship perspective. The impact of the Internet is considered on the dyadic interactions between channel members, and characteristics of Internet intermediaries are discussed. Implications of the Internet as a channel resource for marketing mix development are considered.

YOUR OBJECTIVES IN STUDYING THIS CHAPTER INCLUDE THE FOLLOWING:

- Know the basic forms of channel structures.

- Recognize the relationship aspects of channel structure and performance.

- Understand the possible influences of the Internet on channel structure and performance.

- Understand the ways in which the Internet as a channel resource can affect mix element decisions.

- Be familiar with the issues raised by the Internet as a channel resource for each of the four perspectives on the Internet environment.

The number of businesses that use the Internet as a way to distribute products and information to consumers is growing at a rapid pace. Increases in the .com domain dramatically outstrip increases in any of the other domains. The variety of goods and services that can be purchased through the Internet covers the gamut of possibility—from the prosaic to the bizarre. Despite the differences in company and product types, each business has faced the need to make decisions about the role of the Internet for distributing its products.

As a channel resource, the Internet has the potential to affect all aspects of distribution. For example, the Internet can be used as a channel itself, directly linking the manufacturer to the consumer. In this situation, many activities that are conducted by channel members in traditional channels can be eliminated. For example, a magazine that can be delivered digitally eliminates the need for distributors to stock the newsstands and magazine racks.

A second use of the Internet as a channel resource is as one component of a channel, rather than as the entire channel. Amazon.com uses the Internet as a retail outlet: a virtual bookstore. The company relies on offline channel members, such as wholesalers, to carry out traditional functions. The physical products—originally just books, but now a wide variety of product categories—are still stored in warehouses until shipped to consumers. The Internet eliminates the need for a bricks-and-mortar retail location.

The Internet can also influence distribution strategy by serving as a tool for channel planning and implementation. In addition to using the Internet as a channel for distributing its product to consumers, Dell Computer leverages information technologies of the Internet to move information and customer orders from its Internet site to the appropriate suppliers. Dell uses the Internet to let customers design the configuration of their computers. The company communicates with its suppliers, often using Internet capabilities, to put together the computer system. This approach enables the company to achieve cost savings on warehouse needs and to manage inventory efficiently. Dell's actions illustrate one way to use the Internet to simplify and streamline channel structure and function. Retail outlets are not necessary for Dell, and customers get customized computers quickly.

The transfer of a product from a producer to the customer is often a complex process that may involve several intermediaries who serve different functions in the distribution process. The nature of the relationships that exist between each pair of agents in the distribution process can differ greatly, depending on the product type and on the distribution objectives. The Internet can influence the relationships that exist between members of the distribution channel.

The Internet can facilitate the formation of new relationships, as between a manufacturer and a customer or a retailer and a customer. In addition, the Internet can alter the nature of an existing relationship. For example, FedEx uses the Internet to provide customers with a way to track the delivery progress of shipped packages. Although the distribution of the product—in this case, a service—occurs through standard, offline means, the Internet affects customer and company activities, as well as perceptions of the interaction. For instance, a customer can check the status of a package at any time. From the company's perspective, automated online tracking reduces demand on customer service personnel. In this use of the Internet as a channel resource for relationship management, the Internet's communications capabilities affect the relationship between the service provider and its customers.

Each of these examples illustrates opportunities to use the Internet as a component of channel strategy. As with most opportunities, however, the Internet also presents unique challenges that must be managed in order to obtain the desired benefits for distribution strategy. For instance, concerns of channel members about their relevance in distribution processes influenced by the Internet may result in a resistance to change. In addition, a shift from making products available to consumers through a traditional retailer to making them directly available through the Internet may lead to consumer confusion. These issues, among others, suggest that successful integration of the Internet into distribution strategy can be best accomplished by considering not only the benefits of doing so, but also the possible pitfalls.

In this chapter, we will examine the impact of the Internet on channel planning, organization, and performance. Our primary objectives are to assess the effect of the Internet as a channel resource on channel characteristics, and to consider the influence of the Internet as a channel resource on components of the marketing mix. We will also consider several issues that channel applications of the Internet raise for the different perspectives on the Internet environment—marketer, consumer, policy maker, and technology developer.

Digital Artifact 11.1

Information technology creates stress for professors. Of 34,000 professors surveyed by UCLA researchers, 67 percent said that keeping up with technology is stressful. Computer-related stress outranked teaching (62 percent) and publishing (50 percent).

(*Source:* **Nua Online, citing Associated Press, August 31, 1999.**)

CHANNELS OF DISTRIBUTION: A BRIEF PRIMER

A channel of distribution is defined by the set of organizations involved in the processes for transfering ownership from a producer to customers. Distribution channels exist to match customers with products. Most manufacturers produce a small range of products that they need to distribute to a wide range of customers. In contrast, most customers would like to obtain small quantities of many different products. Intermediaries facilitate the spread of the product, thus matching up manufacturers and consumers.

The organization of a distribution channel, in terms of the specific types of channel members, is based on the idea that different channel members have different competencies that facilitate product distribution. For example, channel members enable a channel manager to exploit efficiencies and develop economies of scale. Each member provides a skill or skills that are necessary. As a result, the channel members depend on each other to create an efficient distribution system from manufacturer to consumer.

Who Distributes? Types of Channel Members

A channel member is an organization that is involved in the **negotiatory functions** associated with moving a product from producer to end user. Negotiatory functions include the actions of buying, selling, and transferring title to goods and services. For the majority of product categories, the four main channel members are (1) the manufacturer, who produces the product; (2) the wholesaler, who buys goods for

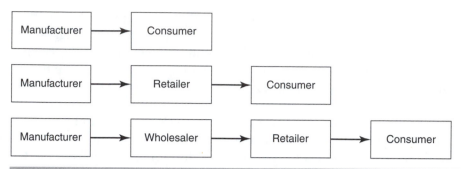

FIGURE 11.1 Basic Forms of Channel Structures.

resale; (3) the retailer, who buys goods to sell to the end user; and (4) the consumer, who buys goods for personal or household use. The different combinations of these members reflect different **channel structures.** Figure 11.1 illustrates several types of channel structures.

Of course, distribution strategy is also necessary in the business-to-business market. These channels of distribution often differ from the members and the structure of channels in the business-to-consumer market. We will examine the implications of the Internet as a channel resource for the business-to-business market in Chapter 13.

Channel members who perform negotiatory functions are active exchange agents in the distribution process, taking ownership of the product and selling it to another channel participant. Other organizations conduct activities that facilitate the exchange process, but they do not become involved in the negotiation and transaction activities that affect product ownership (e.g., transportation companies and advertising agencies). Still other organizations may function to facilitate the transfer of ownership, as by brokering transactions and representing the interests of the active exchange agents. These types of organizations comprise the **ancillary structure** of a channel (see Figure 11.2). Despite the different functions that they service, all the organizations share a common goal: to facilitate the exchanges that result in the transfer of ownership from the producer to the consumer.

FIGURE 11.2 Channels With Ancillary Participants.

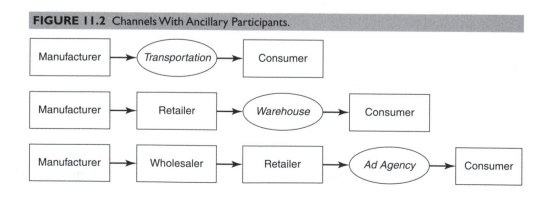

What Is Distributed? Types of Flows

At a basic level, channels exist to distribute goods and services. The process by which products are available to channel members at the appropriate times is known as **logistics management.** Logistics activities are reflected in the movement of products from a manufacturer to a wholesaler, and then to a retailer and an end consumer.

In order to facilitate the flow of products, flows of information, money, negotiation, and promotion are also necessary. These flows, in conjunction with **product flow,** comprise **channel strategy.** Manufacturers rely on information about consumer needs and competitor actions to determine the optimal form and amount of a product. This information often comes from channel members who have closer contact with sources of demand than does the manufacturer. For instance, a wholesaler in frequent and ongoing contact with retailers has access to information about the quantity of product requested. Retailers in contact with the end consumers often have information about the liked and disliked features of products. As a result, information flow is central to product distribution strategies.

Negotiation flow is the mutual exchanges between channel members that determine the conditions of product ownership at different points in the distribution channel. For instance, a manufacturer and a wholesaler negotiate to reach an agreement about how much money the manufacturer will receive in order to transfer the title of ownership for an amount of product to the wholesaler. The **money flow** reflects the agreement reached in the negotiation flow about the terms of payment for ownership: how much money will be paid, and when. The **promotion flow** creates awareness of the product and incentive to take ownership of the product by different members in the channel.

Channels as Relationships

The interactions between channel members can be viewed as **dyadic relationships.** A dyadic relationship refers to the communications and activities that take place between a pair of entities, such as channel members. Some examples of dyadic relationships in a channel include manufacturer-retailer dyads, wholesaler-retailer dyads, and manufacturer-consumer dyads.

Power in Relationships

The concept of dyadic relationships is important for channel strategy because characteristics of each member in a dyad influence the ability of the dyad to meet its responsibilities. For example, dyad members can differ in terms of the amount of power or influence that each member exerts in the relationship, and the nature of the power. Power can be exercised—if possessed—by any channel member.

Researchers have delimited five main sources of power: reward, coercive, legitimate, expert, and referent. Each type is relevant for understanding the relationships that may exist between channel members. A hallmark of power is that it relies heavily on perception; that is, a channel member will alter a given behavior to the extent of the power the other party in the relationship is perceived to hold.

Reward power exists in a relationship when one member acts in a way that conforms to the desires of the other member in order to obtain some set of benefits or reward. In channel relationships, the reward tends to take the form of financial gains. A manufacturer who has a reputation for market success will be better able to use reward power to influence channel member behavior than a manufacturer with weak market performance.

Coercive power is the flip side of reward power. Coercive power reflects the perception that the other member of the relationship can impose some cost for behavioral nonconformity. For instance, a retailer can refuse to sell a wholesaler's products.

Legitimate power reflects the belief that one party has the authority to direct the behavior of the other party in the relationship. In channels, this type of power is seen in contractual relationships, in which one channel member has formally agreed to complete certain activities in a predetermined manner. For example, in a franchise operation, the franchisor has legitimate power over the franchisee. The contractual agreement typically specifies how the franchisor will exercise power if contractually agreed conditions are not met.

Expert power exists when one party in a relationship perceives that the other party has skills or knowledge that make conforming to influence attempts more likely to result in benefits for both parties. Retailers who accept the advice and assistance of manufacturers in displaying and promoting products tend to do so when they perceive that the knowledge possessed by manufacturers has provided beneficial results for conforming behaviors in the past, or for other retailers.

When channel members perceive their goals to be similar to the goals of another channel member, the other member may have **referent power.** Referent power is the ability of one party to serve as a referent, or a point of comparison, that influences another's behavior. Although it is possible for a negative referent to exist (e.g., "I really don't want to do what they did. Look where it got *them*!"), most occurrences of referent power in channels reflect influence attempts based on perceived, desirable similarity in goals.

Relationship Development and Influence Tactics

An important goal of channel strategy is to develop, grow, and maintain the relationships that facilitate distribution. Different tactics and processes for influencing relationships may be needed at each of these different stages. For instance, the benefits of exercising different power bases may vary by relationship stage. In addition, different stages and power bases in relationships may indicate different uses of negotiation, as indicated in Figure 11.3. For example, it may be desirable to give up a benefit (i.e., foregoing a reward) early in a channel relationship to get it established. In contrast, increasing the salience of shared goals may be more effective to maintain an established relationship (i.e., referent power).

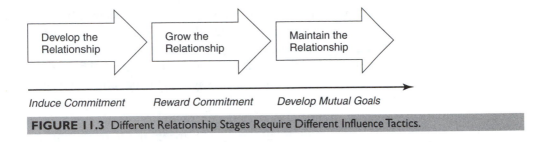

Grow the Relationship

Maintain the Relationship

Induce Commitment   *Reward Commitment*   *Develop Mutual Goals*

FIGURE 11.3 Different Relationship Stages Require Different Influence Tactics.

THE INTERNET'S IMPACT ON ASPECTS OF CHANNEL STRATEGY

As a channel resource, the Internet can influence the effectiveness of channel strategy, often described as channel efficiency. **Channel efficiency** is achieved when the combination of efforts undertaken to distribute a product optimizes possible output. Marketers must understand the nature of the Internet's influence on different aspects of channel strategy in order to maximize channel efficiency. Each of the basic concepts of channel strategy—flows, intermediary functions, and relationships— may be influenced by the Internet as a channel resource.

Establishing Distribution Objectives: Distribution Flows

The role of the Internet as a channel resource should be guided by the determination of the role of the distribution strategy, in general, for achieving strategic marketing objectives. For instance, how important is distribution relative to other components of the mix? How much emphasis will distribution receive in terms of company resources? Will the Internet change the relative importance of distribution? A key factor in establishing the weight to be placed on distribution is the extent to which it can be used to create competitive advantage.

Next, the marketer must evaluate the costs and benefits of integrating the Internet into distribution strategy. At this point, the questions focus on the impact of the Internet as a way to increase channel efficiency. For instance, the Internet can be used as a tool for managing existing channels to increase flows of information and negotiation. An alternative role for the Internet is as a channel for distribution, or as one part of a channel of distribution.

One issue in determining the role of the Internet as a channel resource is the nature of the product. This issue is related to product flow. Internet technologies have made rapid and remarkable advances in the past few years, but they are still not capable of digitizing and transmitting a soft drink! Products that can be conveyed in a digital format, such as books, software, and music are all viable candidates for an entirely Internet-based distribution channel. Other products, with some amount of physical attributes, can still benefit from the Internet, but the channel members complete functions that are ancillary to the actual conveyance of the product between channel members.

Although the Internet's inability to transfer a physical product may be a limitation, the ability to facilitate many other functions, including all aspects of completing a transaction that do not entail physical exchange of product, make the Internet a viable channel for many goods and services. The issue is to be able to determine how and to what extent the Internet can be leveraged in such a way that the benefits outweigh the implementation costs.

Possible uses of the Internet cover a wide range: from managing a traditional strategy with Internet capabilities, all the way to dropping the traditional distribution channel in favor of a direct, online channel. The benefits and costs of using the Internet as a channel resource at any level may depend on the nature of channel members, and the relationships between these members, in the actual and potential channels.

Digital Artifact 11.2

Slow sites cause 37 percent of shoppers to permanently stop using a site, or to find an alternative.

(*Source:* **ZDNet News, September 21, 1999, citing Jupiter Communications.**)

The Internet and Channel Structure

Once the marketer has decided the Internet should be integrated into channel strategy, the next set of decisions revolves around the appropriate channel structure. In situations for which the Internet will facilitate performance of offline channel activities, the channel structure may not need to change. For instance, the Internet can be used to complete negotiations, automate order processing, and coordinate product transfer—all for the existing set of channel members. In this situation, one effect of the Internet may be to improve the relationships that exist between channel members.

If channel objectives cannot be met with existing members, then a marketer must consider changing the channel structure. Two situations illustrate the reasons change may be necessary. First, suppose that a manufacturer has decided that Internet capabilities for information transfer can be leveraged to increase channel efficiency. The only way to achieve the desired channel performance is for all members to adopt and effectively use a new, Internet-based tracking system. If one or more members are either unwilling or unable to make the shift, however, the system falls apart. A new structure is necessary.

A second situation that indicates a need for channel restructuring occurs when the Internet makes it possible for a channel member to carry out activities that were previously carried out by another channel member, or when a set of activities that were once necessary are no longer needed. One example would be when a manufacturer decides to create an online channel to market directly to consumers. The latter situation occurs when the Internet can be used to coordinate customer orders with supplier inventory, to ship directly from the supplier. In the first situation, the traditional retailer becomes obsolete. In the second situation, the traditional distributor arrangements lose their value. These various levels of investment are shown in Figure 11.4.

In the following sections we will consider four channel strategies that involve differential emphasis on the Internet as a channel resource: direct channel strategy, indirect channel strategy, hybrid channel strategy, and multichannel strategy. We will also look at several issues associated with each of these different types of channel structures.

The Internet as a Direct Channel

One possible channel structure is a **direct channel** in which the manufacturer sells online directly to consumers. No intermediaries are used. This type of structure is used in the offline world by companies such as L.L. Bean and Avon. In the online world, examples of direct channels include sales of computers by Dell, and of software by Egghead.com.

In each case, the company has decided that the benefits of marketing directly to the end consumer outweigh the benefits that could be provided by intermediaries. Shifting from a traditional retail setting to an online setting may reduce costs associated with the need to maintain a physical location (e.g., rent and utilities), as well as costs associated with the need to maintain a physical inventory (e.g., warehouses and personnel). Inventory advantages can be obtained by maintaining a **virtual inventory** that spans several suppliers and distributors. Product manufacturing and shipping can be coordinated electronically, without the need to maintain a central warehouse. On the retail side, the Internet enables online retailers to virtually aggregate a large assortment of products that might not be possible in a physical location. This **virtual aggregation** can provide customers with the ability to pick and choose products that best meet their needs.

The Internet as an Indirect Channel

An **indirect channel** includes intermediaries. Many traditional channel structures take an indirect form, by including wholesalers or retailers. Online examples of indirect channels consist of companies that rely on other, online channel members to create assortments of goods from a number of manufacturers, and to manage

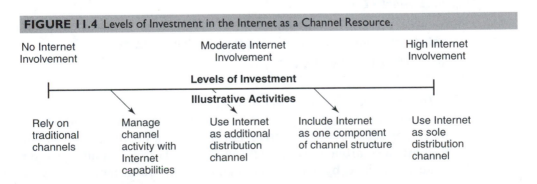

FIGURE 11.4 Levels of Investment in the Internet as a Channel Resource.

No Internet Involvement	Moderate Internet Involvement	High Internet Involvement

Levels of Investment

Illustrative Activities

| Rely on traditional channels | Manage channel activity with Internet capabilities | Use Internet as additional distribution channel | Include Internet as one component of channel structure | Use Internet as sole distribution channel |

interactions with consumers. Indirect channels that are entirely online are a rare animal, because unless the product can be moved, aggregated, sorted, and shipped digitally, some functions will necessarily be conducted by offline members.

Amazon.com is an example of a company with an indirect distribution channel. The books that you buy online through Amazon originate with one of several book publishers. Wholesalers buy books from the publishers. Amazon collects orders from consumers with its Internet retail site, and then sends the collected orders for books owned by a particular wholesaler to be processed. The wholesaler fills the order and ships it to Amazon's warehouse. At the warehouse, the wholesale order is broken down into shipments to individual consumers. Offline channel members conduct the publishing and wholesaling activities, while Amazon conducts the retail effort online.

The Internet as a Hybrid Channel

Hybrid channels exist when more than one channel member participates in the transaction with the consumer. For example, technology products that combine hardware with software, produced by separate companies, to provide an integrated product in a single transaction for a consumer are the result of hybrid channels. Hybrid channels are definitionally indirect channels.

Many information technology goods and services use hybrid channels. The hybrid channels are necessary to integrate the application that will be used by the end consumer with the infrastructure, such as computing capability, needed to make the application work. Because hybrid channels require the coordinated activity of multiple channel members in the transaction phase with the consumer, they are often more complex and difficult to manage than direct or indirect channel structures.

Hybrid channels for goods and services that leverage the Internet are often managed through strategic alliances. For example, AOL's alliance with Target means that AOL subscribers will be able to purchase Target products through the AOL Web site. In this situation, the "product" is really the capability, or service, that the partners provide—being able to purchase Target products through AOL. To make this hybrid channel operate effectively, both AOL and Target must coordinate their activities to bring consumers to the transaction stage.

Digital Artifact 11.3

Eighty-three percent of companies with e-commerce interests plan to use extranets to communicate with suppliers and other partners.

(*Source:* **CNNfn, October 12, 1998.**)

The Internet and Multichannel Strategy

With a **multichannel strategy,** more than one type of distribution channel is used to achieve distribution objectives. For instance, a manufacturer may sell directly to consumers through a catalog, through a set of offline retailers, and through a Web site maintained by a different organization. Multichannel strategies are common in traditional marketplaces. Sears & Roebuck Company used catalogs and storefronts for many years to increase product availability and convenience for consumers. Companies such as The Gap, J. Crew, and L.L. Bean exemplify multi-channel strategies in which two direct strategies are used, combining the benefits of different types of infrastructure for developing relationships with consumers.

Each type of channel structure may provide marketers with unique sets of advantages and disadvantages. For example, for a company with a physical product, a traditional channel member who can use the Internet to complete sorting tasks, and also take physical possession of the product to create product assortments, may be more efficient than a channel member with only an online presence. The online channel member must introduce an additional organization to complete the sorting function. Companies with offline retail experience and facilities are also often better equipped to manage product returns. Online retailers must develop the back-end applications and infrastructure needed to manage the reversed channel flow of returns.

The introduction of online channel members to a channel structure may alter the length and complexity of the structure. Changes to structure are important because they affect the performance of the channel; that is, the level of channel efficiency that can be obtained. This effect may occur due to the reduction or addition of channel participants, and because of the motivation of channel members. As a result, marketers have to be aware of the effect that structural changes to a channel might have on psychological and sociological factors that affect channel member performance. We will look at the issues raised for marketers by channel structure changes in the following section.

Internet Issues for Channel Structure

As a channel resource, the Internet may affect the complexity of channel structures. If the Internet facilitates the ability of a channel member to do the work of another channel member, then the opportunity exists to eliminate the newly redundant member. In contrast, the decision to shift some portion of distribution activity to the Internet may create the need for a channel member who manages functions that are conducted online. The first situation reflects disintermediation, while the second situation reflects reintermediation.

Disintermediation

The ability to use the Internet to perform aspects of all the channel functions—barring transfer of a physical product—creates the possibility that fewer channel participants will be needed to effect distribution strategy. The process of reducing distribution reliance on intermediaries is termed **disintermediation.** The potential for disintermediation is significant because it suggests that the services of many wholesalers and retailers will no longer be necessary. For instance, if a manufacturer can use the Internet to provide information about its products and their direct acquisition to a large enough number of consumers, intermediaries are not needed.

Reintermediation

Even though the potential for disintermediation does exist, it is not equally likely for all channels. In fact, for many businesses, managing distribution using the Internet has resulted in increasing the number of channel participants. This phenomenon has been labeled **reintermediation.** For physical products, the Internet may often lead to the inclusion of an additional channel participant to handle the virtual representation of the product. In the case of Amazon, the inclusion of book wholesalers is an example of reintermediation.

Infomediaries: New Intermediaries

Using the Internet as a channel element may require the services of an online agent or a broker to develop and negotiate the transfer agreement between the producer and the consumer. As a result, it is likely that the increasing integration of the Internet into distribution strategy will be matched by an increase in the participation of Internet-based organizations that operate as **cybermediaries,** or **infomediaries.** These organizations may develop solely for the purpose of operating as online channel members, designed to effectively meet channel needs in the marketspace.

The development of infomediaries as participants in channel activities underscores two ways in which the Internet changes the way we think about channel strategy. First, the infomediaries do not take ownership of the product being distributed. Strictly speaking, they are not channel members, but part of the ancillary structure. They do, however, exert an influence on channel complexity, meaning that the term *disintermediation* should be used with caution. A change in channel structure may eliminate traditional channel members, thus exhibiting disintermediation. At the same time, however, the change may lead to the inclusion of infomediaries through reintermediation. As a result, the disintermediation and reintermediation are not truly mutually exclusive results.

The nature of the activities performed by the Internet-based intermediaries reflects the second change to the way we think about channel strategy. In traditional views of distribution strategy, the primary function of channel members is to move the product—by taking ownership—from the manufacturer to the consumer. Infomediaries can facilitate product movement, but they do not tend to have contact with the actual product. Instead, they provide a service. The increasing prevalence of Internet infomediaries suggests that the service functions of Internet-based intermediaries will occupy a central position in the formulation of channel strategy. In business-to-consumer markets, these services take three main forms: information brokers, transaction brokers, and marketplace concentrators.

Information Brokers   The role of an **information broker** is to provide consumers with information about the price and availability of products. Information brokers do not enable consumers to complete transactions through their Web sites. Instead, consumers must go to vendors' sites to consummate exchanges. An example of an Internet information broker is CNET. The company provides product descriptions and reviews for a wide range of technology products, as well as links to vendor sites, but it does not provide any products of its own.

Transaction Brokers   In contrast to information brokers, **Internet transaction brokers (ITBs)** exist to facilitate buying and selling. Transaction brokers create links between buyers and sellers, thus serving a function similar to the traditional retailer, but without incurring the risks of product ownership. Sites such as CarsDirect, Carpoint, and Auto-by-Tel are examples of transaction brokers on the Internet. In each case, the Internet is used to match a consumer to a dealer, thus creating the potential for a direct relationship between the buyer and the seller.

Marketplace Concentrators   **Marketplace concentrators** are Internet intermediaries that aggregate information about the products available from a variety of vendors in one location. Consumers can complete a purchase through the site, or go to the site of the specific vendor. For example, Travelocity.com enables consumers to search for airfares and complete ticket purchases online. The service includes a range of different airlines. Consumers can use the site just to gather information, and then they can effect the actual transaction through the airline or through a travel agent. Alternatively, the transaction can be completed through the Travelocity site. Other examples of marketplace concentrators are online shopping malls, and services such as online ticket sales for events and online stock trading. In general, marketplace concentrators do not result in the formation of a direct relationship between the buyer and seller. A comparison of these intermediary services is given in Figure 11.5.

Channel Management: Internet Effects on Channel Member Relationships

We have seen that the Internet makes it possible for marketers to develop new types of channel structures. One factor that guides the determination of which structure to use is the nature of the relationships within the structure. As noted earlier, a channel is a set of dyadic relationships. The overall success of a channel is related to the way in which each relationship contributes to channel efficiency. The Internet may influence the nature of more than one channel member's participation in a channel at a time. In addition, the relationship between any pair of channel members who take and transfer ownership of the product can be viewed as a

FIGURE 11.5 Types and Examples of Infomediaries on the Internet.

Information Brokers	*Transaction Brokers*	*Marketplace Concentrators*
Provide Information	*Facilitate Exchange*	*Aggregate Opportunities*
♦ CNET	♦ CarsDirect.com	♦ Buy.com
	♦ Carpoint.com	♦ eBay.com
		♦ Travelocity.com
		♦ Ticketmaster

unique central exchange environment; the channel members make use of technology to facilitate exchange. These characteristics mean that marketers must be aware of the interplay between each dyad in the channel, and the effects of that interplay on overall channel performance.

Power and Channel Structure With the Internet

One factor that can affect the viability of a channel strategy that leverages the Internet is power. A business that opts to use the Internet as a component of a channel strategy will be more successful in altering the channel organization if it is in a position to influence the behavior of other channel members. For example, a manufacturer with reward or coercive power based on market success can induce its retailer partners to develop an online presence more effectively than a weak manufacturer can.

In contrast, a powerful retailer can influence the ability of its manufacturers to set up direct distribution channels online. This influence may occur due to expert power, when the retailer is able to demonstrate potential pitfalls with the online plan. Alternatively, other forms of power can be employed to influence channel member behaviors. For instance, in 1999, Home Depot, a large retailer of do-it-yourself home products, sent a letter to its suppliers. The letter was an attempt to exert coercive power to dissuade the suppliers from using the Internet as a direct channel for marketing their wares to consumers. Suppliers were warned that Home Depot would view any online marketing efforts as competition, and that Home Depot would be disinclined to carry the products of competitors in their stores.[1]

The Internet and Channel Conflict

A concern with the use of the Internet as a channel resource is the potential for creating channel conflict. **Channel conflict** occurs when a channel member's perceptions of roles, responsibilities, and accomplishments are not consistent with the perceptions of these facets of behavior by other channel members. For instance, the Internet introduces the potential for conflict when it enables a channel member to carry out tasks that were previously the responsibility of another channel member. For example, a manufacturer who sets up an Internet site to sell products may antagonize members of its existing channel, such as wholesalers and retailers. The online site may be perceived as a threat to the financial well-being of the traditional intermediaries.

Such a situation occurred when Levi Strauss attempted to control all of its online sales of made-to-fit jeans, excluding long-time retail partners, such as J.C. Penney's, from the effort. The online site was not successful. A primary reason for the failure was the inability to appeal to the targeted teen market, due in part to Web site characteristics that required more bandwidth than possessed by the targeted market. Levi's concluded that the tasks of product fulfillment and customer support were better left to those with more experience. In the meantime, however,

---

[1]Reported in Forbes.com, April 17, 2000.

retailers in the channel shifted their marketing focus to private-label brands, thus creating additional sales losses for Levi's. After a year of attempting to make the online operation a success, Levi Strauss gave up. The company handed the online operations to their retailers.

Concerns about potential channel conflict have kept several large manufacturers from using the Internet to sell directly to consumers, among them Rubbermaid, Maytag, and Black and Decker. The Gartner Group, a research and analysis firm, estimates that 90 percent of manufacturers avoid direct sales through the Internet due to concerns about channel conflict with their traditional distributors.

The issue of how to reduce the potential for Internet-derived channel conflict is centered on the concern with how to manage disintermediation. One strategy is for channel members to develop alternative capabilities or characteristics that provide value to the channel. Leveraged cooperation is one approach for managing potential conflict and disintermediation. **Leveraged cooperation** occurs when channel members create partnerships to provide a new, online source of value to channel members. For example, one online information broker for the airline industry, SABRE, encouraged travel agents to develop content sites that described their individual offerings. The resulting network of agent-developed content provides benefits for all channel members: richer content for the broker, additional visibility for the airlines, exposure for the travel agents, and greater selection for consumers.

Channel Management and Performance

Different types and structures of channels provide different levels of outcome benefits. The outcomes of a channel structure can be described in terms of channel performance. The determination of whether a channel has performed as effectively as expected is based on the match between the objectives established for a particular distribution strategy and the results of measures developed to reflect the extent to which the desired outcomes were achieved.

Different channel strategy objectives necessitate different measures of outcomes. An objective of increasing distribution coverage suggests the use of different measures of channel performance than would be suitable for an objective of reducing the time to move a product from producer to consumer. This distinction may seem quite obvious. (After all, not many people would suggest using a ruler to determine the temperature outdoors.)

More complicated, but equally important, however, is the determination of how the Internet influences channel performance, and how to measure the performance. For example, the relationship between a technology agent and a wholesaler may include rapid transmission of information about the types and amounts of products that need to be transferred to retailers. The technology agent may provide a means by which the wholesaler can accumulate information about product distribution needs from a number of producers. These products can then be combined into product assortments that are desired in different forms and quantities by various retailers. The use of the Internet to transmit the product information provides channel benefits by speeding the flow of information, and potentially reducing the logistical difficulties of product inventory storage. In addition, the Internet increases the wholesaler's ability to create product assortments, thus enabling the wholesaler to supply a wider number and variety of retailers. This benefit increases both distribution coverage and the product sales for the producer.

The effect of the Internet on channel performance can be gauged with several measures. These measures include the amount of time savings, product sales, and distribution reach. At a general level, the types of measures used to assess channel performance may be similar to those used in more traditional channels. At a more specific level, however, the way information is obtained may be different. For instance, much of the information can be obtained through the Internet. Online retailers can track site traffic and compare it with sales. Wholesalers can track inventory, demand, and rate of product flow.

> *Digital Artifact 11.4*
>
> **Twenty-nine percent of online consumers shop on the Internet because it is more fun than traditional outlets.**
>
> (*Source:* **CyberAtlas, citing Ernst & Young, 1999.**)

MIX IMPLICATIONS OF THE INTERNET AS CHANNEL RESOURCE

What does having the Internet as a channel resource mean for elements of the marketing mix? In this section we will consider ways in which the Internet can influence marketing decisions about product, price, place, and promotion.

Effects on Product Strategy

As a channel resource, the Internet affects decisions about the type of product to produce, given distribution capabilities. Changes to the way that a product can be delivered to an end user create opportunities to change the form of an existing product, and even create opportunities for entirely new products. As described in Chapter 10, EMI, a recording company, was concerned that with the increasing popularity of digitally formatted music, its traditional profit base of compact disc and cassette sales was at risk. EMI concluded that the popularity of digitally formatted music, as evidenced through consumer demand, necessitated a change in product strategy for the company. EMI teamed up with LiquidAudio, a company that specializes in delivering digital music, to develop new product options.

EMI's decision to consider alternative product forms illustrates the effect that the Internet can exert as a channel. In this example, EMI's actions also illustrate the role of power in channel relationships. Demand for digital music by consumers, a position often supported by the artists (e.g., singers and songwriters), resulted in diminished sales by retailers, and reduced benefits for all channel members, except the consumers. Evidence of the benefits of acquiring music directly from the Internet, rather than through record companies, is provided by the growth in traffic to sites that provide or enable access to MP3 files, an alternative to the digital format supported by LiquidAudio (see Figure 11.6).

The Internet creates product opportunities even for companies whose core business is not threatened. For example, major newspapers and magazines have developed online content as product, an action only made possible by the existence of the Internet as a channel resource. The publishers use the Internet in conjunction with offline publishing activities, increasing brand exposure and recognition, and familiarity with the editorial style of the publication.

For retailers who use the Internet as a storefront, the Internet may affect product strategy by increasing the assortment of products that can be displayed. As we saw earlier, virtual aggregation enables a retailer to relax constraints on inventory that are imposed in a physical space.

The Internet can also affect product strategy decisions about product line depth and product mix width. **Product line depth** is the number of items in a particular product line. **Product mix width** refers to the number of product lines offered by a company. Companies attempt to maximize sales by matching the depth of a product line to target markets of viable size and accessibility. Expanding product mix width can reduce company risk by increasing sales and profits.

With the Internet as a distribution channel, companies can tailor line depth and mix width decisions to capitalize on Internet channel capabilities. For instance, the global reach of the Internet may create opportunities for new products in a line, if new market segments can be identified and served with the Internet. In addition, the ease with which storefronts can be constructed and altered on the Internet, compared to their brick-and-mortar counterparts, suggests that different lines in a product mix can be marketed in specially designed Web showcases. The ability to separate the display of product lines enables marketers to tailor presentations to different target markets, and it reduces the potential for confusing consumers.

FIGURE 11.6 MP3 Site Traffic Indicates Propularity of the Direct Channel.

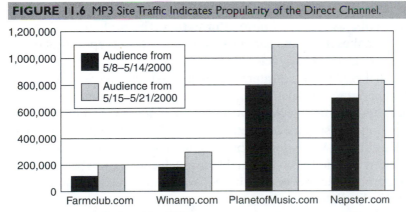

Source: Nielson/NetRatings, May 2000.

Effects on Price Strategy

Internet effects on price can occur through two different avenues of the Internet as a channel resource. One avenue is channel performance. In general, if the use of the Internet increases channel efficiency, then a company will realize cost savings. In a competitive marketplace, the increased cost savings may be passed on to consumers in the form of price reductions. Several companies with a strong Internet presence credit their substantial cost savings to use of the Internet as a channel resource. For instance Cisco Systems, the manufacturer of network components that make the Internet a reality, estimates that the ability to use the Internet as a distribution channel saves the company $130 million per year.

A second way that the Internet affects prices as a channel resource reflects the nature of the channel, and of who has power within the channel relationships. Consider the notion of supply and demand. When supply is high, prices tend to be lower. When supply is low, prices tend to be higher. In online markets, these principles apply. For instance, in an online auction for a one-of-a-kind item, increased demand results in an increased price. In this situation, the balance of power is tilted in favor of the seller. Because the Internet serves as a channel with potential for global reach, one effect of online auctions as a channel for goods may be that prices tend to be higher than they would be if the audience, or source of demand, were more restricted.

An alternative effect of an Internet channel on price is evident with companies who use the Internet to coordinate product volume and price. For example, several Web sites enable consumers to express purchase interest in products (e.g., Buy.com, Mercata.com). As the number of people interested in buying a particular item increases, the price decreases. In this situation, the buyers, collectively, exercise power.

Effects on Place Strategy

As more and more products become available through online channels, consumers have the opportunity to examine and compare products, and the price and promotional material associated with the products. This situation approximates what economists describe as a state of **pure information.** The problem with pure information is that it makes it difficult for marketers to create perceptions of differences between product offerings to develop a competitive advantage.

One potential benefit of the Internet as a channel resource is as a way for marketers to differentiate a product offering from that of the competition. For online channels, marketers can use the Web site and the manner of distribution through the Internet to leverage consumers' perceptions of the site as place. As a virtual location for product distribution, Web sites can be structured to create consumer experiences that are perceived as benefits not attainable through competitors' distribution practices. For this purpose, the uses of the Internet as a content resource and as a channel resource are closely related.

Effects on Promotion Strategy

As a channel resource, the Internet may affect promotion strategy at different points in the channel structure. For example, marketers may alter the emphasis on the promotion element of the marketing mix to persuade channel members to adopt Internet-related channel activities. In this situation, promotion is a means to obtain a desired channel strategy structure. It is important to note that promotion strategy must be developed for each dyad in the channel structure, and that the nature of the promotion strategy should be tailored to reflect the type of relationship (e.g., who has power, and what type). Promotion strategy should also be based on the stage of relationship development. For instance, a manufacturer might provide promotional deals to wholesalers and retailers early in a relationship, in order to motivate channel member performance.

CAUTIONS FOR USING THE INTERNET AS A CHANNEL RESOURCE

The Internet creates opportunities for marketers to redesign channel structures and to develop new avenues for distributing products to customers. At the same time, the Internet also serves as a source of challenges for each of the key perspectives in the exchange environment. Marketers must anticipate and understand the source and effect of these challenges on channel strategy.

Marketer Issues

For any marketer who plans to use the Internet as a channel for selling to customers, an important issue is that of how to initiate contacts with consumers, and how to develop those contacts into ongoing relationships. A key function of an intermediary in a channel is to link sellers, such as manufacturers, with buyers, such as retailers and consumers. The advantage to companies of an intermediary, in terms of reducing contacts, is shown in Figure 11.7.

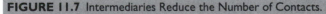

FIGURE 11.7 Intermediaries Reduce the Number of Contacts.

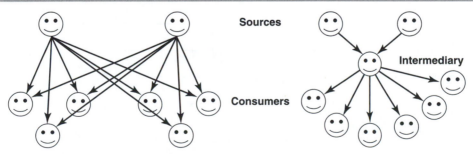

contacts = # sources (2) × # consumers (6) = 12   # contacts = # sources (2) + # consumers (6) = 8

Without the intermediary, the total number of different contacts between companies (e.g., manufacturers) and consumers is equal to the number of companies times the number of consumers. In this example, the total number is 12. With an intermediary to manage the manufacturer-consumer contacts, only 8 contacts are needed: 2 from the manufacturers to the intermediary, and 6 from the intermediary to the consumers. From the perspective of each company, the benefits are even greater. Instead of managing 6 contacts, the companies only manage 1 contact—with the intermediary.

Suppose that a company decides to shift from a channel structure in which intermediaries, such as retailers, undertook the responsibility for customer contact to a direct, online channel. Because the retailer has been the source of contact for consumers with the product, the retailer may have information about customer preferences pertaining to product form and use. The manufacturer must develop this knowledge base. In addition, the original intermediary, such as wholesaler, may have a database of existing customers and qualified prospects. If the manufacturer disintermediates the wholesaler, then the manufacturer must work to construct a targeted set of customers.

The costs of acquiring customers are not insignificant. The Boston Consulting Group surveyed 100 e-commerce companies and found that they spent, on average, 40 percent of revenues on marketing costs. This amount is substantially higher than the 14.2 percent typically spent by department stores, and the 7.2 percent averaged by specialty stores. The chart in Figure 11.8 shows estimated customer acquisition costs for a range of companies that market through an online channel. We can see that some types of online services have much higher acquistion costs than others.

Using the Internet as a channel creates other challenges for marketers. For instance, for physical products sold via the Internet, the marketer must still manage the logistics of distribution. In traditional channels, some distribution functions can be carried out economically by combining sets of products or amassing substantial

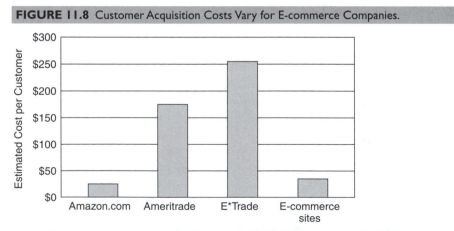

FIGURE 11.8 Customer Acquisition Costs Vary for E-commerce Companies.

Source: Based on data from *Fortune* (February 1, 1999), Fool.com (May 26, 1999), and Computer World (October 12, 1998).

orders for a single product, and then shipping them at one time, as to a retailer. With a direct, Internet channel, order fulfillment may be necessary in a more piecemeal fashion, which may increase shipping and handling costs to the company. In addition, the absence of expertise early in the process of developing relationships with customers may lead to frustration on both sides and a decline in brand loyalty.

Consumer Issues

A major issue for consumers who purchase through Internet is that of trust. Trust takes different forms. For instance, creating a storefront on the Internet is fairly simple, compared to creating a bricks-and-mortar counterpart. As a result, many small businesses have developed, often touting exotic, unique wares. For a consumer who finds one of these "stores," however, it may be difficult to evaluate the quality of the company and its product. In traditional marketplaces, consumers use heuristics such as company reputation, store location, and atmospherics to determine whether a company's claims about its products should be trusted. With new, online businesses, these heuristics are less useful.

Even when the company is well known, with a long and reputable history offline prior to developing an online channel, the issue of trust is still central for consumers. Many people are concerned with the security of providing personal information or financial information through the Internet. Companies must use policies and procedures that not only ensure the security of information, but that can also be clearly communicated to consumers.

Policy Issues

The Internet can serve as a channel for distributing many different types of goods and services. Some of them may be illegal. Policy makers are concerned with consumers' ability to obtain products that have the potential to do harm. For instance, the Internet can be used to convey information about where and how to negotiate a transaction of weapons and services for violent intent.

Even when product distribution is not intended to result in harm, the potential for the misuse of products obtained through Internet channels does exist. For example, online drugstores enable consumers to effectively write their own prescriptions. On some sites, diagnosis of a medical condition can be made using an interactive questionnaire. On other sites, doctors answer questions and make suggestions. In some cases, consumers can order medication directly from the site. Of concern to policy makers is the potential for misuse or abuse of drugs that are not prescribed for a particular person by a qualified doctor or nurse.

Technology Issues

The ability to use the Internet as a channel resource underscores the importance of technology. As more companies develop an Internet channel presence, or use the Internet as a means for managing channels, the need for enhanced technologies will continue to grow.

Early forms of electronically aided coordination between channel members used electronic data interchange (EDI) technologies. The present-day version of EDI leverages the network infrastructure of the Internet to form extranets that can enable information, negotiation, and money flows. Many extranets are developed as public networks. A **public network** consists of two or more company intranets, or internal networks, that are connected by the Internet. One concern with public networks is that information is only protected when it is within the companies' intranets, and not when it moves across the Internet. A company can form a virtual private network that relies on passing information over the Internet through **encrypted tunnels** to keep data secure.

Despite the advances in technology, extranets still present disadvantages to marketers. First, the price of security is computing power. Keeping data safe means a need for powerful computers, at each part of the network. A related issue is that substantial effort and financial investment is required to develop the extranet. Thus, companies must be confident that the channel structure and the relationships within the structure are worth the investment.

Digital Artifact 11.5

A 13-year-old boy placed \$3.1 million in bids on eBay before the company realized that they were dealing with a "deadbeat bidder."

(*Source:* **CNNfn, April 29, 1999.**)

Chapter Summary

In this chapter, we examined the role of the Internet as a channel resource. We began with a review of channel issues, including channel members, distribution flows, and the role of relationships. Subsequent sections of the chapter addressed the impact of the Internet as a channel resource on characteristics of channel strategy; on components of the marketing mix; and on the different perspectives in the marketing environment of the Internet.

The Internet can influence channel strategy with varying degrees of invasiveness. For instance, the Internet may be used as a tool for managing an existing channel structure. Alternatively, it might serve as a medium for an online channel member, in conjunction with other offline members. In its most extreme form of impact, the Internet might be used as the sole alternative to a traditional offline structure. Given the newness of the Internet as a channel resource and the costs associated with developing efficient channel structures, it is likely that many companies will adopt a multichannel strategy in which the Internet is merely one aspect of an overall channel strategy.

Regardless of the form of the distribution channel, the Internet may influence the types of relationships that exist between dyads, or pairs of channel members. We considered the effects of different types of power bases in relationships, and the likely effect of different relationships on the willingness to accept Internet-related channel structures. The effect of the Internet on relationships was also considered in terms of reducing channel length through disintermediation, and of extending channel length through reintermediation.

Reintermediation is often characterized by the introduction of new intermediaries to an Internet-based distribution channel, often known as infomediaries. We considered several types of infomediaries and their effects on channel relationships. One possible effect of change to channel structure is channel conflict. Attempts to avoid or reduce channel conflict may take the form of creating new roles and responsibilities for channel members.

As a channel resource, the Internet affects mix decisions. For example, the Internet may increase the desirability of new forms of products, or new products. The nature of the Internet as a channel for distributing goods and services may increase marketers' ability to successfully lengthen product lines and widen product mixes. Different types of channels for product purchase may influence pricing strategy. The difference in the Internet's influence on price may reflect different amounts of power between buyers and sellers. This power, in turn, may stem from increased access to products on the Internet.

As an outlet for goods and services, the Internet can affect the importance of place in the marketing mix. Reduced ability to create a competitive advantage with product, price, and promotion may increase the importance of place. Promotion strategy is affected by the need to tailor promotion to the different relationships in the channel structure, and by the need to build relationships in new channel structures that involve the Internet.

Each of the four key perspectives in the Internet environment is affected by the role of the Internet as a channel resource. Marketers must deal with issues of contact management, consumers with issues of security, policy makers with the distribution of harmful products, and technology developers with the need to provide hardware and software solutions that can keep up with the demands of increasingly sophisticated channel strategy.

REVIEW SECTION

Key Terms

- negotiatory functions
- channel structures
- ancillary structure
- logistics management
- product flow
- channel strategy
- information flow
- negotiation flow
- money flow
- promotion flow
- dyadic relationships
- reward power
- coercive power
- legitimate power
- expert power
- referent power
- channel efficiency
- direct channel

- virtual inventory
- virtual aggregation
- indirect channel
- hybrid channel
- multichannel strategy
- disintermediation
- reintermediation

- cybermediaries
- infomediaries
- information broker
- Internet transaction brokers (ITB)
- marketplace concentrators

- channel conflict
- leveraged cooperation
- product line depth
- product mix width
- pure information
- public networks
- encrypted tunnels

Review Questions

1. Name two ways the Internet may be used as a channel resource.
2. What is the main goal of a channel of distribution?
3. What is the role of ancillary channel structure?
4. What types of flows exist in a distribution channel?
5. Explain the concept of a dyadic relationship.
6. Why is power an important consideration in channel relationships?
7. How does the Internet influence channel efficiency?
8. How can marketers determine the appropriate channel structures for their businesses?
9. What different types of channel strategies can be implemented by organizations?
10. Describe how disintermediation and reintermediation are inextricably linked.
11. How may channel conflict arise when using the Internet as a channel resource?
12. What are the effects of using the Internet as a channel resource on product strategy? Price strategy? Place strategy? Promotion strategy?
13. What issues do consumers and marketers face when using the Internet as a channel resource?

Thinking Points

1. Channel participants operate in dyadic relationships, and different forms of power are used to influence partners. In the Internet environment, are any types of power likely to be disproportionately influential? Which ones, when, and why?
2. Different influence tactics may be more or less effective at different stages of relationships. How might Internet time be expected to affect the selection and efficacy of influence tactics?
3. What issues might a marketer encounter in deciding to
   a. move from a traditional to a virtual channel?
   b. to create a hybrid channel?
   c. to use the Internet as an additional channel?
4. How might the level of investment in the Internet as a channel resource be influenced by the nature of the product? The company? The industry?
5. Are infomediaries intermediaries? Why, or why not?
6. Relate the concepts of disintermediation and reintermediation to the concepts of power and conflict in channels.

7. What tradeoffs does a company make when using an intermediary to reduce the number of contacts with consumers? How does the Internet potentially influence the desirability of the tradeoffs?

Suggested Readings

1. "Coping with Internet Channel Conflict," in *Now or Never,* by Mary Modahl (New York: HarperCollins Publishers, Inc., 2000), pp. 169–186.
2. "Electronic Marketing: The Dell Computer Experience," by Kenneth Hill. In *Electronic Marketing and the Consumer,* edited by Robert A. Peterson (Thousand Oaks, CA: Sage Publications, Inc., 1997), pp. 89–100.
3. "501 Blues," by Cindy Waxter. *Business 2.0* (January 2000).
4. "Intermediaries and Cybermediaries: A Continuing Role for Mediating Players in the Electronic Marketplace," by Mitra Barun Sarkar, Brian Butler, and Charles Steinfield. *Journal of Computer-Mediated Communication, 1,* 3, 1995.
5. "Disabling the System," by Karl Taro Greenfeld. *Time Digital* (September 6, 1999), pp. 26–31.

CHAPTER 12

The Internet as a Communications Resource

FOCUS AND OBJECTIVES

Chapters 10 and 11 focused on the dual roles of the Internet as a source of information and as a channel for delivering content. This chapter is focused on the role of the Internet as a vehicle for communicating content, through the channel infrastructure of the network. We consider the nature of communication, and the impact of the Internet on the interactions between marketers, consumers, and content that are the basis for communication. Different forms of communication enabled by the Internet are discussed, as are the impacts of these forms on mix elements. Issues raised by the role of the Internet as a communications resource are considered for each of the four perspectives.

YOUR OBJECTIVES IN STUDYING THIS CHAPTER INCLUDE THE FOLLOWING:

- Know the basic components of a model for communication.
- Understand the different forms of interactivity in the computer-mediated environment of the Internet.
- Recognize the implications of interactivity for communication, including personalized content.
- Know the difference between personalization and customization.
- Understand the implications of the Internet as a communication resource for mix element decisions.

Imagine that you are sitting in front of your television, watching your favorite Sunday evening program. As the program goes to a commercial break, you pick up the remote control to mute the volume. Before you hit the button, the spokesperson looks you in the eye and says, "I know that last time you looked at cars, you were looking for a hatchback, but that you liked the Honda better than ours. I think that this time, we have something that's right up your alley. Check out our new model, the Miasma!"

A bit surprised by the spokeperson's knowledge of your preferences, you think aloud while reaching for the remote you have dropped, "Yeah, right. Me and two million other people just like me. What are the odds that I can get that car for under $280 a month?" Before you can hit the mute button, the spokesperson comments, "Actually, with our $1,500 rebate, you could buy the Miasma right now for only $275 a month. Did you know a dealership is only 15 minutes from your house?"

Sounds unlikely, right? Perhaps, with television. With the Internet, however, personal and interactive communications *are* possible. With the Internet, marketers can communicate with many consumers at once, or focus on just one person. This flexibility reflects a fundamental difference between the Internet and traditional forms for communicating promotional material to target markets. In addition, with the Internet, consumers can exercise flexibility in the use of marketing information. They can pick and choose the format of information they would like, such as text-only or text plus graphics, and they can determine how much information they would like to acquire about a particular topic. A third key difference stems from the interactivity enabled by the Internet technology: consumers and marketers have available to them a variety of ways in which they can communicate—from the in-your-face tactics of banner ads to virtual, real-time exchanges of information.

The influence of these differences on marketing strategy can be seen in the shift in how a product purchase opportunity is viewed from a traditional marketing perspective and from an Internet perspective. A popular view of the role of the marketing mix elements is that product, price, and place issues must be addressed to create an opportunity to buy a product. In contrast, promotion is needed primarily to communicate the existence and desirability of the opportunity. With the integration of the Internet into marketing activity, the role of promotion, as a form of communication, becomes a central one. In fact, some researchers have argued that with the Internet, "the medium is the message!"

This shift in the relative emphasis placed on mix elements underscores the importance of the Internet as an information-rich marketing environment. The Internet blurs the borders of mix elements that have tended to be treated as separate components. For instance, the ability to offer products that can be digitized and transmitted via electronic channels, such as music, videos, software, and books, means that strategic issues related to product, place, and promotion can be combined to achieve marketing objectives. The central role of information in this process suggests that marketers will need to understand and use the Internet to develop effective communications campaigns.

In this chapter, we will examine aspects of Internet communication as they relate to the development, implementation, and tracking of marketing communications. We begin with a discussion of the characteristics, such as interactivity, that differentiate the Internet from other forms of marketing communication. With a general description of the communications environment in place, we then look at the implications of interactivity for marketing communication. Next, we consider the effect of the Internet as a resource for communication on elements of the marketing mix. We also consider several of the issues that Internet-based communications raise for each of our four perspectives.

Digital Artifact 12.1

Dot-com companies spent an estimated $3.1 billion on advertising in 1999.
(*Source: The Wall Street Journal*, April 24, 2000, and The Internet Index, #27.)

THE INTERNET AS A RESOURCE FOR COMMUNICATION

The Internet provides marketers with a context that can be used to deliver content in a variety of ways to consumers. This capability highlights the distinction between the information in marketing communication and the vehicle used to deliver the information; that is, content differs from communication. In addition, the context in which information is communicated on the Internet can be described independently of the infrastructure that transmits the information. In other words, the basic network structure and function of the Internet remains the same, whether the information is transmitted to consumers as banner advertising or as e-mail.

As a communications resource, the Internet enables several types of vehicles to serve as contexts for information to be transmitted, including banner ads, e-mail, and promotions. The versatility of the Internet as a context for communications means that marketers can integrate different forms of marketing communications, such as advertising, public relations, and promotions, into a strategy that combines online and offline tactics to meet strategic promotional objectives.

Characterizing Communication

A basic model for communication consists of a source, a message, and a receiver. The **source,** such as the marketer, creates the message, determining what information it should contain, the format of that information, and the vehicle in which it will be delivered. This set of actions is a process termed **encoding.** On the other end of the communication, the **receiver,** typically the consumer, attends to, perceives, and interprets the message. This process is known as **decoding.**

The two processes are closely linked; how a message is encoded will affect how it is decoded. For instance, researchers have found that the **modality** of the message affects its decoding. Modality refers to the form of the information, and it is often related to the medium in which the information is delivered (Figure 12.1). For ex-

FIGURE 12.1 A Simple Model of Communication.

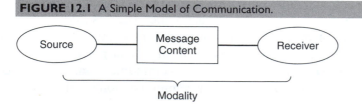

ample, modalities include textual formats (e.g., print media), aural formats (e.g., radio), and visual or audio/visual formats (e.g., television). Different formats influence attention, comprehension, and recall. For instance, audio/visual formats tend to increase attention, presumably because of their sensory richness. In contrast, textual formats tend to increase comprehension and recall; consumers exposed to print messages exhibit more accurate knowledge of presented information, and they can retrieve more information from memory than consumers exposed to messages in other modalities.

Marketing communications can refer to the message and its form, or to the process by which messages are passed between sources and receivers. For example, we can describe a television ad or a piece of direct mail as a marketing communication. Describing marketing communication as a thing emphasizes the role of content, a topic addressed in Chapter 10. In contrast, we can think of marketing communication as a process of sharing information between a source and a receiver. Viewed as a process, marketing communication emphasizes the benefits of interaction.

An important feature of the Internet is its ability to facilitate interaction between users. In the following section, we will examine how the interactivity possible with the Internet affects processes of marketing communication.

Interactivity and Marketing Communication

The Internet acts as a medium for communication, as do television, radio, newspaper ads, and other traditional types of marketing communications. Despite the similarity in purpose, the Internet differs in two main ways from traditional media for marketing communication. First, the Internet enables interactive communication between a source and a receiver. Second, the Internet makes it possible for consumers to exercise some control over the format of the communication. These two characteristics both reflect interactivity. In the first instance, the receiver interacts with the source. This interaction reflects the role of the Internet as a channel for information exchange. In the second instance, the receiver interacts with the content. This interaction underscores the importance of the Internet's role as a source of information. In both situations, the interactions occur within the computer-mediated environment (see Figure 12.2).

THE COMPUTER-MEDIATED ENVIRONMENT

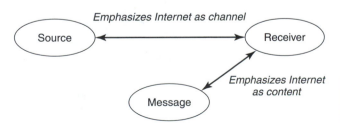

FIGURE 12.2 Types of Interactivity in a Computer-Mediated Environment.

Source and Receiver Interactivity

From its inception, the Internet was designed to foster communication. The technological advances that linked computers to transfer information at near real-time speeds allowed researchers to share facilities, data, and research results more rapidly and economically than they could prior to the advent of the digital network. People could interact, working collaboratively for common goals and unrestricted by geography.

The benefits of the Internet as an interactive medium affect its use as a resource for marketing communications. In particular, text-based forms of communication, such as e-mail and newsgroups, can be used to deliver information about products to consumers, and to gather product-related information from consumers. In addition, the Web, with its graphics capabilities, creates opportunities for presenting promotional information in novel ways.

One dimension that can be used to understand the opportunities for communication with the Internet is the size of the targeted audience: from one massive, undifferentiated segment to segments of one person each.

The Internet as Broadcast Communication   Television, radio, and print media are typically used as **broadcast** forms of communication. Marketers develop a message, and they deliver the message to large numbers of consumers, a process known as one-to-many communication as shown in Figure 12.3. Broadcast communications are useful because they enable marketers to provide information to large audiences.

Traditional forms of broadcast communications have several limitations, however. For instance, with television and radio, the message may miss its target if consumers in the desired audience are otherwise occupied. As a result, marketers spend a great deal of money to place messages in programs and time slots where the likelihood of exposure is high (e.g., Super Bowl ads). The exposure problem is reduced for print media, because the window of opportunity for exposure is longer. Newspapers may sit around for a day, and magazines for a month, or more. Of course, the tradeoff between television or radio and print media is that the former media can be delivered to a passive audience, while print media tend to require a little more effort on the receiver's part.

FIGURE 12.3 Traditional Media Emphasize One-to-Many Communications.

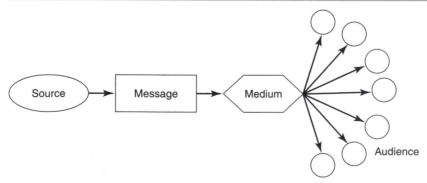

With the Internet, marketers can broadcast information in forms similar to those of television and radio. For example, Victoria's Secret, a lingerie company, previewed its line in an Internet fashion show. Although demand for access to the online preview overwhelmed the company's server—a problem that does not exist for television technology—the presentation of the message was similar to televised fashion events.

The Internet and Narrowcast Communication   In addition to broadcast communications, the Internet enables narrowcast communications, and even pointcast communications. **Narrowcast communication** refers to messages that can be selectively provided to a target audience that is typically smaller than a target audience for a broadcast message. For instance, qualified prospects can be invited to visit a site to preview a product. In addition to limiting awareness, marketers can also limit access by providing passwords to invited visitors.

Narrowcast communication is not unique to the Internet environment. Specialized television channels, such as those available through cable and satellite services, are a form of narrowcasting. What is different about narrowcasting with the Internet is that the marketer must take a more active role to initiate the communication process than in television narrowcast situations.

The Internet and Pointcast Communication   **Pointcast communications** are a form of one-to-one interaction. In contrast to broadcast, pointcast communication emphasizes the provision of a message to a single receiver. This capability can overcome limits to communication effectiveness that may occur in a more impersonal medium, such as radio or television.

Pointcast communications take many forms. The one-to-one nature of the communication may be as simple as sending a largely standardized message to a set of receivers, changing only the name of the receiver in the message. This approach to pointcast communication is reflected in some types of direct mail. In contrast, one-to-one communication may take the form of highly individualized messages, tailored to meet the receiver's needs, habits, and preferences, and personalized to emphasize the uniqueness of the communication and the individual.

A marketer's ability to provide individualized messages is often a result of interaction with a consumer. A consumer can provide information about specific needs to guide the marketing communication. Alternatively, information obtained simply as a result of the consumer's interaction with the marketer via the Internet can provide information that can be used to structure a marketing message. For example, a domain name can provide occupational information, and information stored in cookies can provide insights into product interests.

Digital Artifact 12.2

Of consumers who reported instances of online auction fraud in 1999, the average amount lost was $293. Auction fraud constituted 68 percent of reported Internet fraud.

(*Source:* **National Consumers League Internet Fraud Watch, 2000.**)

Source and Content Interactivity

In the last section, we considered communication as interaction between a receiver and a source. Now, we shift to the interaction that occurs between the receiver and the content. With the Internet, marketers can combine print, audio, and video modalities. For instance, a message can be created in which persuasive elements are presented with text and graphics, much like a magazine ad. In addition, moving images can be presented using animation technologies, and sound can be integrated into the presentation of the message, similar to television.

In contrast to traditional media, the user can influence the combination of modalities, and hence the form of the message. The ultimate form of the message may be influenced by user preferences for content and for modality, and by constraints on the user's computing capacity. The user is an active participant in the construction of the communication, rather than a passive recipient of a preset presentation of information. Consider the difference in activity needed to obtain product information from a Web site, compared with watching an ad on television. The receiver's ability to influence the representation of content reflects interactivity between the receiver and the content.

Differences in the extent to which the receiver controls exposure to a message and the form of the message are related to the idea of push versus pull forms of information delivery. Broadcast communications are typically push communications. **Push communications** originate with the marketing organization, and they are delivered to a relatively passive audience. **Pull communications** are initiated by the receiver, and hence require higher levels of activity.

For Internet communications, all forms of communication—from broadcast to pointcast—may be pushed to the receiver. Unlike traditional broadcast media, however, the Internet also enables pull communications. When a receiver interacts with content to structure the form of the information, the selectivity that creates the message reflects a pull approach rather than a push approach to communication. Information acquired from a Web page by a receiver reflects pull, while information obtained from an e-mail sent to a receiver reflects push. Other pointcast forms of pushed information are also provided by software that tailors content, based on specifications provided by the receiver or by the source (e.g., customized content of an online news service).

Implications of Interactivity for Content

We have seen that interaction between the user, or receiver, with the source and with the content can be used to change the nature of the content that is communicated. Marketers can use the Internet to provide content, such as products and information, that matches the idiosyncratic needs of consumers. That is, the nature of the product in the exchange relationship is different for each consumer. The process of using the Internet to create such an individualized offering is termed **personalization** (Figure 12.4).

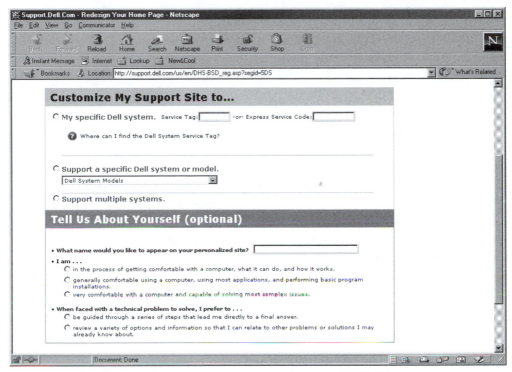

Source: Reproduced with permission of Dell Computer, Inc. Copyright © 2000. All rights reserved.

FIGURE 12.4 Consumers Create Personalized Support Sites at Dell.com.

The idea that underlies personalization is that of uniqueness; the outcome of personalization is an entity in a form that has higher value to the user than it would to anyone else. Personalization exists outside the Internet. Monograms on towels and shirts, and names on plaques and certificates illustrate the concept of personalization. Who else would place as high a value on a Mickey Mouse cap, replete with ears, as the child whose name is embroidered across the front?

The difference between push and pull forms of communication is related to personalization. Receiver specifications about the form of content to be delivered reflect pull. In contrast, a communications source can use information about user preferences, as from cookies or from registration information, to develop personalized communications for individual users. This approach is a push form of communication. Recognizing the difference in pull and push forms, even when the end goal of personalization is the same, is important for marketers. In general, pulled information may be a closer match to the receiver's needs and expectations than pushed information that has been developed based on inferences about user preferences. We will consider possible ramifications of unsolicited, pushed information as an issue for public policy later in this chapter. Figure 12.5 contains an example of pushed, personalized communication.

Subject: Oil Change Reminder: Chevrolet S10 Blazer
Date: Tue, 18 Apr 2000 16:55:55 -0700
From: Carpoint Notifier notifier@microsoft.com
To: ecoupey@vt.edu
Tuesday, April 18, 2000
Dear ecoupey@vt.edu,

According to your Personal Auto Page on MSN CarPoint, your 1994 Chevrolet S10 Blazer is due for its 63,000-mile oil change very soon.

Visit your Personal Auto Page now for money-saving details by clicking the following link or by entering it in your Web browser's address line.
http://ownership.carpoint.msn.com/ownership/home.asp?veh=1105787&m=4#o

---

Your Personal Auto Page is a free, personalized service that helps you manage and reduce the cost of auto ownership. Visit your Personal Auto Page at any time to see:

YOUR CAR'S CURRENT BLUE BOOK VALUE

YOUR NEXT SCHEDULED SERVICE OF $100 OR MORE

YOUR CAR'S RECALL HISTORY

SEASONAL ADVICE ARTICLES

Advertisement: Jiffy Lube International is the nation's largest fast lube service franchise, with more than 2,000 centers in 49 states. Click the link below for special offers from Jiffy Lube.
http://ownership.carpoint.msn.com/ownership/qlube.asp

Source: Personal correspondence with MSN CarPoint.

FIGURE 12.5 Push Communications Can Be Delivered Via E-mail.

MARKETING MIX IMPLICATIONS OF THE INTERNET AS A COMMUNICATIONS RESOURCE

Communication is central to the existence of an exchange relationship. Required, of course, are resources for which exchange is desirable and a means of effecting the exchange, such as a channel. Communication is necessary, however, to determine the availability of an item for exchange, and the extent to which it meets needs. As a means for communication between agents in exchange relationships, the Internet influences all aspects of the marketing mix.

Communication and Product Development

By the beginning of the twentieth century, the development of technologies that spurred the Industrial Revolution had resulted in the mass production of goods for consumption. Cottage industries and one-of-a-kind production gave way to the efficiency and quality consistency of assembly line production in large factories. Advances in communications technology, and the diffusion of radio, telephone, and television, created mass markets for standardized products.

By the end of the twentieth century, technological advances had once again changed the face of production and influenced the nature of consumer demand.

Leveraging the communications capabilities of the Internet, marketers can meet the demand of mass markets through mass customization. **Mass customization** is the ability to provide a product that is differentiated from other forms of the same product produced by the same company. The Internet enables marketers to assess consumers' needs for particular features of a product, and to develop product forms that reflect these needs.

Mass customization with the Internet is aided by two factors: (1) receiver-content interactivity, and (2) product modularization. Receiver-content interactivity enables a marketer to develop online menus of product features from which a consumer can specify a product configuration. This capability automates the product design process. Product modularization is necessary to create menus of product features. **Modularization** is the ability to separate a product into sets of features that can be flexibly rearranged to create different product forms.

Customization and Personalization

Customization is not the same as personalization. A customized offering may be developed for an individual consumer, but the demand for the customized form of the product is not necessarily unique to that consumer. For instance, a custom-built Rolls-Royce may be produced for a customer, but it *is* possible that other people might have a similar level of interest in owning the identical vehicle.

Another distinguishing characteristic of customization is the nature of the process used to create the customized product. In many instances, a customized product is the result of a consumer's selection of desired product features and their configuration from a bounded set. This set of possibilities is made available to other possible customers, and it is expected that multiple, identical versions of the product will be produced.

Customization and personalization can be described as relative locations on a continuum of uniqueness. As is illustrated in Figure 12.6, mass production anchors one end of the continuum: a single product form is produced for everyone in the market. Personalization is at the other end of the continuum; a personalized product is matched to a single customer.

FIGURE 12.6 Products Described as a Function of Feature-to-User Uniqueness.

Mass Production	Customization	Personalization
One product form, *n* users		*n* customers, *n* product forms
Low source-receiver interactivity	*Characteristic Interactivity* →	High source-receiver interactivity
Develop feature profile for target market, Optimize feature set interactivity	*Characteristic Process* → Develop sets of features and feature levels	Develop features and levels based on individually measured preferences

Interactivity and Processes of Customization

At a fundamental level, customizing a product depends on communication; marketers have to know what consumers want. The exchange of information via the Internet facilitates customization. This exchange can differ in terms of the nature of the interaction between the marketer and the consumer, that is, whether the interaction is a direct communication between source and receiver, or an indirect one, between the receiver and the site content. For instance, customization may result from a direct interaction with a consumer about the desired form of a product. Visitors to the Dell Computer site are active participants in the process of designing the configuration of their computers (see the screen in Figure 12.7). This situation reflects source-receiver interactivity used for **collaborative customization,** because the source, Dell, participates in the creation of the final product.

In contrast, a product can be customized based on the consumer's interaction with Web site content without active participation by the source at any point in the creation of the end product. This interaction can take two forms. In one form, the consumer selects content options to specify the customization. For example, users can select subsets of preferred channels from the set of options provided by

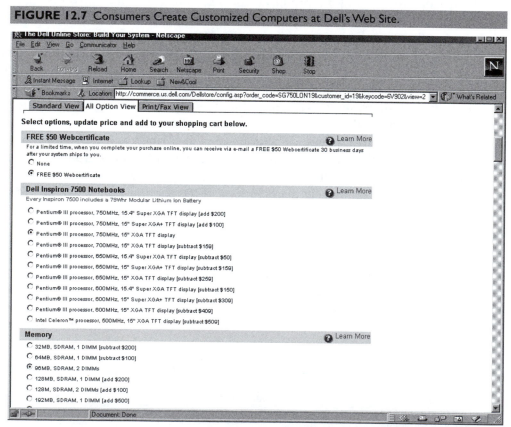

FIGURE 12.7 Consumers Create Customized Computers at Dell's Web Site.

RealPlayer to meet individual interests. This pull form of indirect communication results in **adaptive customization.** In a second form of interaction, customization is based on information provided by the consumer, as through a cookie, but without any direct communication between marketer and consumer—and without awareness on the part of the consumer. The result of this process is called **transparent customization.** For example, an online news service might track a user's previous site behavior to selectively push information that matches categories or topics previously viewed.[1]

Interactivity and Forms of Customization

Interactivity can result in different forms of customization. These forms are described with two dimensions: (1) the extent of product change, and (2) consumer awareness of the change.

For the first dimension, product customization can be as simple as a cosmetic change to the way a product is represented. For instance, a marketer can collect user information by asking site visitors to register. Communication back to the user can then be customized by including the user's name on an otherwise standard offering. After registering with Travelocity's online reservation service, users are greeted with a personal welcome, even though the basic form of the product, as online content, is undifferentiated. This process reflects cosmetic customization. Alternatively, customization can be as complex as a change to the nature and function of attributes that constitute the product. On Mattel's Web site for Barbie, users can create customized dolls, choosing from a specified set of appearance options (see, for example, Figure 12.8).

The second dimension that characterizes customization is the extent to which the consumer is aware of the customization. For example, ad servers target ads to users based on information gathered from the users' past site behaviors. This is a form of passive communication that results from receiver-content interactivity. Active collaboration based on source-receiver interactivity can result in a dramatic reconfiguration of the base, or standard, product. When the nature and configuration of product features are developed solely on the basis of a consumer's preferences, and are not limited by the set of features and possible levels, the product is personalized.

Communication and Price Strategy

A range of possible pricing models exists for the Internet marketspace. One option is to follow a fixed price model, in which a product targeted to a specific market has one price for all buyers in that market. This model is useful for products and services with little differentiation and low price elasticity. For product categories in which prices are variable, the Internet facilitates price transparency. Price transparency may increase consumers' price sensitivity. As a result, a fixed price model may become less desirable for many products.

---

[1] These forms of customization are based on a typology developed by James H. Gilmore and B. Joseph Pine II, in "The Four Faces of Mass Customization," *Harvard Business Review,* January-February 1997, pp. 91–101.

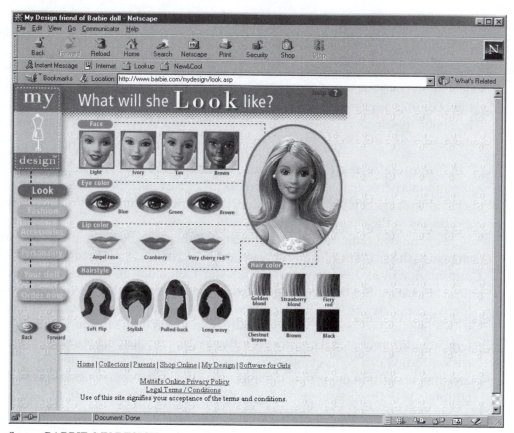

Source: BARBIE, MY DESIGN and associated trademarks are owned by and used with the permission of Mattel, Inc. © 2000 Mattel, Inc. All Rights Reserved. MY DESIGN patent pending.

FIGURE 12.8 Customization to Change the Nature of Product Attributes.

As a communication resource, the Internet can be used to implement alternative pricing models. The interaction between buyers and sellers creates an opportunity for real-time, or dynamic pricing. **Dynamic pricing** reflects variations in prices due to supply and demand.

Dynamic pricing models are often implemented online with infomediaries. For example, online auctions are a form of dynamic pricing that reflects forces of supply and demand. Online auctions rely on Internet-based communication between buyers and sellers to set prices. In general, auctions tend to be effective for products that depreciate rapidly, or that have a finite expiration date. These products have a limited window of sales opportunity; marketers have to get rid of them, and consumers have to want them. Otherwise, consumers could simply wait for a bargain. Auctions also tend to be more effective for unique items than for readily acquired commodities, and in fragmented markets. A **fragmented market** is a market in which product availability and characteristics are difficult to compare across a range of options.

Another form of dynamic pricing is practiced by intermediary companies that establish price. For example, Priceline collects customer requests and schedule constraints for airline reservations. Then they attempt to buy the ticket from an airline, for a set amount (e.g., $10) less than the amount stated by the consumer. If an airline accepts Priceline's offer, Priceline buys the ticket and resells it to the consumer. By communicating schedule and price preferences to Priceline, customers often get tickets at lower prices than through traditional channels. For the airline, the benefits include the ability to sell more tickets, while maintaining their usual retail pricing structures. Because Priceline acts as the intermediary and negotiates directly with a set of airlines whose anonymity is protected, the airlines avoid alienating customers who purchase tickets directly from the airline at higher prices than ticketholders who purchase cheaper tickets through Priceline. The method for pricing used by Priceline is called **buyer-driven commerce.**

Mercata.com employs a different form of buyer-driven commerce. The company uses group buying to obtain manufacturer discounts. A product is offered for a limited time, at a starting price. When a specified number of consumers agree to purchase the product at the offered price, the price drops. The process continues until the time limit expires. All consumers receive the product for the most recent, lowest price.

Digital Artifact 12.3

Approximate number of stock options received by William Shatner for priceline.com advertising, as reported in *USA Today*, December 28, 1999: 100,000.

(*Source:* **The Internet Index, #26.**)

Communication and Distribution Strategy

Communication enabled by the interactive nature of the Internet provides marketers with new options for deciding where to market their products. As we saw in Chapter 11, the Internet can be used as a point of distribution. Whether a virtual store is the best strategy for a company may depend on the company's understanding of its product, and how to use the Internet to communicate product benefits to potential consumers.

Options for using the Internet to communicate product benefits run a gamut from Web sites that provide comprehensive communications about all aspects of the product and its consumption to simple banner advertising. Three approaches illustrate the decisions a marketer must make: destination sites, micro-sites, and Internet promotion strategy.

Destination sites are appropriate for situations in which aspects of marketing communication and product transaction can be conducted more efficiently online than offline. Creating an effective destination site entails the use of Internet-based communications to provide an engaging and entertaining experience that guides the user through all aspects of the buying decision, including post-purchase and repeat visits.

Micro-sites are collections of information about a company's brands that are hosted by content sites or networks. In essence, a micro-site is a small virtual store that depends on traffic to its host site for product exposure. Micro-sites enable the marketer to communicate detailed, focused information to consumers, without the expense of maintaining a destination site. In addition, micro-sites can capitalize on the visibility of the host site. Micro-sites tend to be effective for products characterized by higher degrees of consideration and lower efficiency of online channels (e.g., home appliances, furniture).

If neither a destination site nor a micro-site is appropriate, a third option is to use the communications capabilities of the Internet to implement cost-effective aspects of a promotion strategy. For instance, a company can choose to use interactive banners to build brand awareness, sponsor product-related content to enhance brand image, or build a corporate site to foster public relations. We will consider these possibilities in greater detail as aspects of promotion.

Communication and Promotion Strategy

Many forms of marketing communications for the Internet that tend to come quickly to mind are those that mirror promotion activities in traditional media, like advertising on television and in magazines. These forms have tended to appear on the Web, given the existence of graphics support and communications standards. It is important to remember, however, that other forms of communication, such as direct mailing to targeted lists of Internet users, can also be effective methods of promoting a product or service online. In this section we will consider applications of the Internet as a communications resource for promotion strategy that includes advertising, sales promotions, publicity, and personal selling.

Advertising as Marketing Communication

Internet advertising is big business. In its annual advertising revenue report for 1999, the **Internet Advertising Bureau (IAB)** reported that revenues for online ads topped $4.62 billion dollars—an increase of 141 percent in just one year. The IAB is an association of businesses and individuals interested in developing research and standards for online advertising.

The results of research on advertising effectiveness commissioned by the IAB provide insight into the rapid growth in online-generated revenue. Survey results collected from nearly 17,000 respondents in mid-1997 indicated that online advertising increased brand awareness, improved brand perceptions, and increased sales potential after only one exposure. The results of a study by Forrester Research suggested that users were migrating from television to the Internet, thus increasing the potential for advertising exposure. Seventy-eight percent of respondents stated that they gave up television time to access the Internet. Given these statistics, marketers should understand the promotional options available through the online medium.

The Internet makes possible two main types of advertising: text-based and multimedia-based. **Text-based advertising** can be conducted throughout the Internet, but **multimedia advertising** is constrained to the Web, which facilitates transmission of graphics and other media forms (e.g., animation, streaming audio and video).

The Internet and Text-Based Advertising   Text-based forms of advertising are often used by marketers with an advertising goal of eliciting a direct response. **Direct response** refers to the goal of getting a consumer to carry out a behavior that is related to an end goal of product purchase. For example, requesting further information after receiving an e-mail notification of a product, or actually purchasing the product are forms of direct responses. E-mail advertising can be conducted by buying or renting distribution lists of e-mail addresses. As with traditional forms of direct mail, lists vary in expense and quality.

E-mail works. A Bizrate (2000) survey found that television ads accounted for only 6 percent of online purchases, while commercial e-mail accounted for 13 percent. In another study, NFO Interactive (2000) surveyed 1,000 users and found that 89 percent believe that e-mail is a good way to get product information. To avoid commercial e-mail overload, however, consumers prefer to receive permission-based e-mail. **Permission-based,** or **opt-in e-mail,** allows consumers to decide whether they wish to receive additional e-mail from a particular company. Fifty-eight percent of respondents said they had learned about a product through permission-based e-mail.

The Web and Multimedia Advertising: Banners, Buttons, and Beyond   The World Wide Web has facilitated the development of several forms of multimedia advertising. Most popular among these forms are banner ads and buttons. Other forms of advertising are increasing in frequency, including daughter windows and interstitials, or online commercials.

Banner ads are the most popular form of Web advertising. They can be used for a variety of goals, from simply exposing the viewer to the product or company name to providing an interactive experience with the product. The chart in Figure 12.9

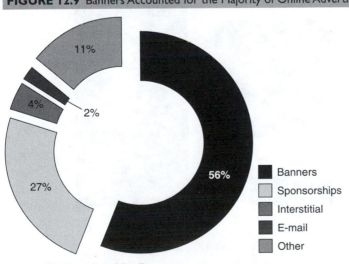

FIGURE 12.9 Banners Accounted for the Majority of Online Advertising in 1999.

11%

4%

2%

27%

56%

■ Banners
□ Sponsorships
■ Interstitial
■ E-mail
■ Other

Source: Internet Advertising Bureau

provides the relative use of different advertising types in 1999, as reported by the Internet Advertising Bureau.

As with traditional media, the success of banner advertising depends heavily on the extent to which the environment in which the ad is placed will be viewed, as well as on the ad content. Reflecting this reality, many advertisers have tended to place their banner ads on a relatively small number of Web sites.

Banners come in different shapes and sizes. To facilitate comparisons of advertising rates and performance measures, the IAB, together with the **Coalition for Advertising Supported Information and Entertainment (CASIE)**, developed a set of standard sizes for banner ads. These sizes are described in Figure 12.10.

FIGURE 12.10 Standard Sizes for Banners and Buttons, Proposed by the IAB.

IAB/CASIE Advertising Banner Sizes

468 × 60 Pixels (Full Banner)

392 × 72 Pixels (Full Banner with Vertical Navigation Bar)

234 × 60 Pixels (Half Banner)

120 × 90 Pixels
(Button 1)

125 × 125 Pixels
(Square Button)

120 × 60 Pixels
(Button 2)

88 × 31 Pixels
(Micro Button)

120 × 240 Pixels
(Vertical Banner)

Source: Reproduced with permission of the Internet Advertising Bureau.

Early banner ads were simple in design and performance, intended to increase brand awareness and to get users to click through to the vendor's site. Newer generations of banner ads incorporate animation to capture attention. Many banners also make use of interactive technology to provide pull-down menus within a banner. Some banners allow the user to complete a transaction solely within the banner. These banners reduce frustration caused when a user clicks through a banner and then cannot return to the site that hosted the banner.

Daughter ads and interstitials are newer versions of online advertising. **Daughter windows** are small windows that appear in the corner of a screen view. Their existence depends on the presence of the larger, parent window. The main window spawns the daughter window. For instance, when opening a browser, a daughter window may appear to inform the user about a new version of the browser software that is available.

Interstitials are virtual clones of television ads. They can be programmed to appear in the time that elapses while a file is loading. Interstitials have benefits and drawbacks. Because of their full-screen size and sophisticated multimedia presentation, they are attention-getting. These same characteristics, of course, may irritate users for whom computing capacity limits the speed needed to execute the high bandwidth advertising. In addition, interstitials cannot be ignored in favor of other parts of the screen view, because they *are* the view. As a result, they may be perceived as an unwelcome intrusion into a medium over which the user typically exercises viewing control.

Animation can be used to attract and hold attention in banners, daughter windows, and interstitials. Another use of animation is to create figures that can move around a screen view. These ads, called **Shoshkeles,** are produced by a company that imbues the mobile advertisers with the ability to speak, thus making them attention-getting. In addition, Shoshkeles do not disappear as a screen is scrolled, as do banner ads.

Understanding Online Advertising Costs   Online advertising costs vary with the size and position of the banner or button, and with the quality of the site. Sites that can provide greater exposure and sites that can provide highly targeted audiences tend to command high prices, as with traditional media. Pricing models for online advertising also vary. The models reflect assumptions about the effectiveness of the form of advertising. Some of the more common models include pricing by cost-per-thousand exposures, cost per click-through, and flat-fee pricing.

A **cost-per-thousand exposures (CPM)** model is based on assumptions about the ability of a banner to achieve brand awareness and brand-building through exposure. This approach resembles ad pricing in traditional media. In a **cost per click-through** model, the publisher is responsible for viewer response. Because revenue is based on behavior (i.e., clicking through to the vendor's site), click-through models may reflect higher levels of viewer involvement. The click-through model differs from traditional ad models that separate the ad content responsibility from the ad

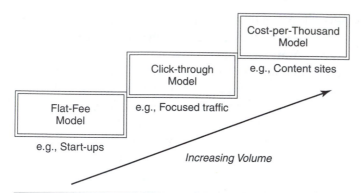

FIGURE 12.11 Pricing Models Reflect Performance Assumptions.

availability responsibility. Of course, the ultimate measure of click-through activity is the transaction.

Flat-fee pricing models are typically used in two opposite situations. They are popular for sites that have no history of visitor activity on which to base pricing: often for new sites or content. The other situation in which flat fees are popular is for highly desirable sites, such as search engines with high traffic, although they offer no visitor traffic guarantees. The general trend for using the various pricing models is presented in Figure 12.11.

Expectations about advertising performance often lead marketers to develop hybrid strategies that integrate two or more forms of online advertising. As you can see from the percentages in Figure 12.12, performance-based advertising, such as click-through ads, accounts for a relatively low portion of advertising revenue. Two related concerns with click-through advertising are (1) its low impact on brand enhancement, and (2) the difficulty in assessing the value of a click-through. In the earlier-cited study commissioned by the IAB, banner exposure accounted for 96 percent of brand enhancement, compared with only 4 percent enhancement attributed to click-through. Click-through was originally envisioned as an online

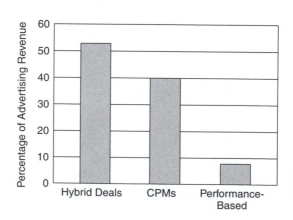

Source: Internet Advertising Bureau

FIGURE 12.12 Relative Popularity of Online Advertising Strategies.

analog to the direct mail response of opening a letter. Marketers, however, are less interested in the behavior of opening an envelope or clicking on a banner than they are with whether the behavior resulted in a sale. As a result, click-through rates tend to be an incomplete measure of advertising effectiveness.

One way to assess the value of an online advertising strategy is to calculate the expected return on advertising investment. When compared with the actual return, the resulting difference provides information about whether advertising goals were met. A formula for calculating return on investment is

# of impressions purchased ✕ average click-through rate ✕ average customer turnover (visitors to customers) ✕ average net profit/sale = expected return

For example, suppose that you purchase 100,000 impressions, and you make an average profit on your digital widget of $2. With statistical averages of 4 percent for click-through and 5 percent customer turnover, your formula is now

$$100,000 \times .04 \times .05 \times \$2 = \$400$$

This result means that the online advertising is responsible for $400 in new sales. To evaluate the merits of your approach, you would need to compare the cost of the campaign with the $400 result. For example, if you paid $30 for each 1,000 impressions, your cost was $3,000. Unless you have reason to believe that turnover or click-through rates will improve over time, it seems like an unwise investment! If you can get one of every two visitors to purchase, the return increases to $4,000.

Online Sales Promotions

Sales promotions are short-term incentives to induce purchase. Sales promotions on the Internet share similarities with sales promotions in traditional marketing media, both in the types of promotions that can be implemented, and in the manner in which they can be implemented. For example, coupons and rebates, as well as games and sweepstakes, are used by online merchants for the same purposes as they are used by offline merchants: to create interest and enthusiasm for a product, and to promote product trial. The promotion serves as an incentive to carry out a specific activity related to the marketer's objective in offering the promotion. For example, a consumer who completes an online survey about her perceptions and attitude toward a brand is entered in a sweepstake where the winning player receives the brand free. The marketer receives information about the consumer's evaluation of product features and creates product trial through the sweepstakes prize giveaway. All aspects of the promotion, including prize delivery if the product can be digitized, can be administered through the Internet.

The short-run effects of promotion activity can be interpreted in terms of their effect on behavior. That is, people participate in promotions to receive the relatively immediate benefits of the participation, such as the coupon, the excitement of competing in a contest, or the chance of winning the prize in a sweepstake. Marketers can use online promotion tactics to influence the early stages of a relationship. That is, a promotion, such as an online contest or a coupon, can create interaction between a consumer and a marketer.

The challenge for an Internet-based promotion resembles that for a traditional promotion—to make the consumer aware of the link between the promotion and the product, in order to create long-term effects of the promotion. One tactic for online marketers is to combine different forms of marketing communications to increase brand exposure and to build brand recognition. For example, marketers can encourage viewer interaction by drawing users to ads with incentives, thus combining sales promotions and advertising. This combined approach has a dual goal of capturing attention and generating interaction (e.g., content traded for viewing ads, money for surveys, etc.).

Public Relations and Publicity

One goal of promotion is to create positive public relations. **Public relations** reflect corporate image, or the way a company represents its objectives and characteristics to internal and external stakeholders. Public relations are important for organizations with a primary online presence, due to market concerns with the intangibility and viability of digital products and their benefits.

Publicity is a form of promotion used to influence public relations. Publicity refers to information about the products or services produced by the organization, but that does not typically come directly from the organization. Good public relations are linked to publicity; a company with a favorable corporate image is more likely to garner positive publicity than a company with poor public relations.

The Internet can be used to carry out traditional approaches to publicity, such as sending product release information to editors, writers, and publishers via the Internet. Marketers can use the Internet to facilitate the processes for publicity. For instance, the Internet can be used to create a database of publicity targets, and to distribute information through discussion groups and mailing lists. In addition to a push approach to publicity, the Internet provides a means to provide publicity-related information on demand. This form of pull communication can result from the direct interaction of inquiring media with the company, or from the indirect interaction with a company's Web site content. Promotional events can also generate publicity (e.g., online concerts and charity auctions).

The opportunity for content-receiver interactivity with the Internet reflects a technology-enabled form of public relations that is unique to the medium. The ability to provide searchable content for publicity purposes may enable marketers to bypass traditional public relations intermediaries. Content can be frequently updated and organized to address different public relations interests. For example, a site might include pages for community relations, new product releases, and previous publicity. This type of content structure can shift the emphasis on promotional activity for public relations from an active approach to a passive approach on the part of the company.

Personal Selling

Advertising, promotion, and publicity can all be effectively implemented in electronic environments. Personal selling is more difficult. The essence of a personal selling interaction is the personal contact, typically embodied in the set of cues exchanged in a face-to-face communication. Even though the Internet enables real-time interactivity between active agents in the exchange, it does so through the computer-mediated environment, or CME. The presence of the electronic mediator that makes the exchange environment possible is the same reason that the personal exchange encounter is not possible. At a fundamental level, computer mediation means that the exchange environment is definitionally impersonal.

Definitionally impersonal does not, however, completely preclude the possibility to use the Internet for selling efforts that emulate face-to-face encounters. Technological capabilities make it possible for consumers to interact with digital representations of sales people. That is, you can see them, hear them, and talk with them, just as if they were in the same room. Of course, other sensory experiences are limited by the digital medium, including touch, taste, and smell. These limitations seem less a drawback for sales encounters, however, than for product encounters. Smelling and tasting salespeople would seem to account for an infinitesimally small percentage of face-to-face sales encounter activity!

While the Internet does not enable full implementation of personal selling online, it does, however, serve as a useful tool for facilitating personal selling offline. For example, a salesperson can use the Internet to amass a database of contact information in order to generate lists of prospects that are characterized by desired qualifications (e.g., past histories of purchase characteristics). In addition, decision support tools that operate via the Internet can be used for personal selling by scripting sequences of activities that, if carried out in a proscribed manner, increase the likelihood of a sale. To augment information provided in a face-to-face encounter, content-laden Web sites can be used to present product descriptions or usage information. These and other uses of the Internet's communication capabilities can augment the credibility of a salesperson in a personal sales exchange.

Digital Artifact 12.4

Approximately 7.3 billion commercial e-mail messages are sent each day in the United States.

(*Source:* **The Internet Index, #25, citing eMarketer.**)

ISSUES FOR PERSPECTIVES IN THE MARKETSPACE

Communication and interactivity are inextricably linked. With the Internet, however, the way in which interactivity enables communication can create unique challenges for each of the four key perspectives. To make effective use of the Internet as a communications resource, marketers must be able to recognize and understand the situations in which these issues may arise.

Marketers and Marketing Communication

Communications may influence what people think and feel, as well as what they do. Marketers must develop ways to track and evaluate these different influences of online communications. For instance, a banner ad may increase brand awareness, even though people who see the ad do not click through to the vendor's site. In contrast, a button that provides downloadable software, such as the plug-in necessary to view a file, may result in a behavior (i.e., download the product), but without an effect on brand awareness (e.g., improve attitude toward the brand).

These examples illustrate the need for performance measures for online communications that reflect the different objectives and outcomes of the communication effort. Measures of online activity can be obtained from information that is automatically tracked and recorded by software programs. This information can be consumer-centric, such as data obtained from a cookie file, or server-centric, as with log files of site activity. To assess psychological dimensions of communication effects, however, marketers may need to design and implement primary research programs that require active, aware communication between the marketer and the consumer/respondent.

Consumers and Marketing Communication

With the Internet, and more specifically, the World Wide Web, marketers can combine the modalities of television, print, and radio into a single presentation of video, text, and sound. This combination of modalities may influence consumers' information search, choice, and memory. For example, if consumers are typically exposed to advertisements in a print media (e.g., some prescription drugs), then use of an interactive medium that combines video and print components may cause retroactive interference for cognitive processes that involve memory. **Retroactive interference** occurs when newly presented information reduces a consumer's ability to retrieve previously stored information. The potential for interference increases when the new information is similar on some dimensions (e.g., the brand information), but is dissimilar on others (e.g., the modality). Interference may reduce the quality of consumers' decisions about—and memory for—the information contained in the advertisement.

On the Internet, consumers can exercise greater amounts of control over the variety and amount of marketing communications that they view. The "pull" nature of the environment also means that consumers can determine, in varying degrees, the form and content of the communication. For instance, consumers can specify desired characteristics of a product as the basis for information that will be included in the constructed display (e.g., products under a cutoff price). In addition, consumers can acquire information about products and services from multiple sources and restructure the information to facilitate decision making. Each of these differences may affect how much and what type of information consumers acquire, the strategies with which they integrate the information to make a choice, and the amount and structure of information they can store in memory for subsequent purchases.

Policy Makers and Marketing Communication

Two characteristics of the Internet as a communications resource raise issues for policy marketers. One characteristic is the active pull nature of information use. Another is the global reach of the Internet as a communications medium.

User Control and Spam

As we have seen, marketing communications on the Internet are characterized by greater amounts of user control than are communications on traditional media. One outgrowth of this characteristic is a resistance to unwanted information that is "pushed" to the consumer. As an indirect influence on the central exchange environment, policy makers react to concerns voiced by consumers about perceived infringements on Internet usability.

Policy makers determine what types of marketing communications are permissible on the Internet. For instance, should e-mail, which can be considered a point-cast form of communication, be subject to the restrictions that govern regular mail, or should it be considered more similar to faxes? It is illegal to send unsolicited marketing communications to fax machines, under the Telephone Consumer Protection Act of 1991. The legislation was enacted because the recipient incurs a cost to receive a fax (i.e., paper, ink, and fax machine time). Unsolicited marketing mailings are not illegal via the postal service, however. Junk mail is a nuisance—not a crime.

Whether e-mail is found to be more similar to fax or postal mail will affect many online marketers. The practice of sending large amounts of unsolicited e-mails is known as **spamming.** Spam is a common occurrence. Similar to the complaints of fax-based junk mail recipients, spam recipients claim that spam uses up computer processing capacity and wastes human time. The annoyance expressed by spam recipients is often due to the low relevance of the unsolicited e-mail to the user.

Lack of relevance reflects an additional concern: that of how the e-mail addresses are collected. In many cases, e-mail lists are harvested from newsgroups and bulletin boards by programs designed to scavenge the Internet and record e-mail addresses. These automated scavengers sift through sites and return e-mail information, often with few restrictions on source content. As a result, the correlation between user needs and interests and spam based on the use of mailing lists created with harvested addresses is unsurprisingly low. Marketers should evaluate the ability of a mailing list to provide qualified, relevant leads. They should also be aware of the negative effects on brand image that may result from a spam-based introduction.

Digital Artifact 12.5

Thirty-two percent of consumers delete commercial e-mails before they read them.
(*Source:* **CyberAtlas, citing Forrester Research, 2000.**)

Local Legislation and Global Reach

A variety of techniques can be used to persuade consumers of the advantages of purchasing a product. These commercial offers can be communicated via the Internet to a global set of targeted users. The potential for global reach of online promotional offers is a concern for policy makers, particularly when national restrictions on the form of commercial offers differ. For instance, contests are often used to provoke consumer interest in a product. In the United States, legislation prohibits contests that take the form of a lottery. In other countries, however, legislation is less restrictive.

One issue for policy makers is that of how to protect consumers from exposure to the potentially negative effects of a commercial offer that is communicated from a source in a less restricted location. A second issue is that of how to prevent advertisers from shifting bases for developing offers and promotion attempts from a more restrictive locale to a less restrictive locale.

Technology Developers and Marketing Communication

The desirability of products often depends on their ability to be meaningfully differentiated from other related products. Personalization is one way to effect meaningful differentiation on an individual level. Effective approaches to personalization can be effort-intensive. For instance, personalization requires an often detailed and complex understanding of a consumer's preferences and values. The nature and scope of knowledge that must be elicited, stored, and incorporated into personalized product design and production presents a challenge for technology developers.

Technological approaches exist to facilitate some forms of product customization. For example, **rule-based systems** are used to track user behavior and present products and information that best match inferences based on behavior patterns. Another approach to online customization is to involve the consumer more directly in the customization process by allowing the consumer to specify preferred features, a process of **customer-assisted customization.**

Each of these methods has drawbacks. Because they operate on relatively rudimentary bases of information, rule-based systems may result in incorrect inferences about preferences for product form. Consumer-assisted approaches may fall short of effective differentiation when the set of customization options does not reflect the range or specificity of consumer preferences. Moving from customization to true personalization will require technology to advance to a point at which processes for assessing individual consumer needs and preferences can be measured, interpreted, implemented, and stored for efficient product development and delivery.

Chapter Summary

In Chapters 10 and 11, we considered the Internet as a content resource and as a channel resource. In this chapter, we looked at ways that marketers can piggyback on content and channel capabilities, building on different types of interactivity to facilitate marketing communication.

To set the stage for an examination of Internet interactivity as communication, we reviewed a basic model of communication. This model included a source who encodes a message and embeds it within a modality (e.g., textual, graphical) and a vehicle (e.g., ad, press release), and transmits it via a medium (e.g., television, Internet) to a receiver, who decodes the message.

Using this basic communication model, we considered characteristics of the Internet that differentiate it from traditional media for delivering content, including many-to-many communications, real-time interactivity, and user control over the content and form (e.g., modality and organization) of the message. These characteristics underscore the need for marketers to recognize the importance of the interactions that may occur between the processes used to encode a communication, and the processes used to decode a communication.

Within the computer-mediated environment, we considered two different processes of interactivity. First, we looked at the interaction between the source and the receiver. Types of source-receiver interactivity were characterized on a dimension that reflects the size of the target audience: from broadcast to pointcast. Second, we examined the influence of receiver-content interactivity on push and pull forms of communication.

The Internet's ability to facilitate interactive communications enables marketers to tailor product forms to meet consumers' needs. We considered the role of interactivity for product personalization and customization. Personalization results from the unique match of consumer needs to feature configuration. In contrast, customization matches needs to feature configuration, but the configuration is based on a constrained set of options, and assumptions about uniqueness are relaxed.

Interactive communications influence all aspects of the marketing mix. Opportunities for customization and personalization affect product strategy. Dynamic pricing strategies result from the widespread interaction between buyers and sellers. Decisions about the Internet as a distribution channel are affected by the nature of anticipated information exchanges. Finally, the Internet's communication capabilities influence the costs and benefits associated with different forms of promotional strategy. For instance, banner ads, the most popular form of online advertising, exert a stronger influence on brand-related perceptions than on purchase-related behaviors. Online sales promotions and public relations can be used to establish a consumer-product relationship.

Challenges for integrating the Internet into marketing activity as a communications resource were considered for each of the four main perspectives on marketing in an Internet environment. For marketers, these challenges include measuring communication effectiveness and integrating online and offline forms of marketing communications. Consumers must manage issues associated with the effects of the online medium for communication on decoding processes. Global reach and the ready availability of an audience who can be reached with unsolicited marketing communications create headaches for marketers. As the group largely responsible for creating the environment that facilitates interactive communications, technology developers must grapple with the ever-present need to develop technology that advances present capabilities. A key concern is the desire for applications capable of remembering users' previously expressed preferences for customization and predicting future preferences.

REVIEW SECTION

Key Terms

- source
- encoding
- receiver
- decoding
- modality
- broadcast
- narrowcast communications
- pointcast communications
- push communications
- pull communications
- personalization
- mass customization
- modularization
- collaborative customization

- adaptive customization
- transparent customization
- dynamic pricing
- fragmented market
- buyer-driven commerce
- destination sites
- micro-sites
- Internet Advertising Bureau (IAB)
- text-based advertising
- multimedia advertising
- direct response
- opt-in/permission e-mail
- Coalition for Advertising Supported Information

and Entertainment (CASIE)
- daughter windows
- interstitials
- Shoshkeles
- cost-per-thousand exposures (CPM)
- cost per click-through
- flat-fee pricing
- public relations
- publicity
- retroactive interference
- spamming
- rule-based systems
- customer-assisted customization

Review Questions

1. In what two main ways does the Internet differ from traditional media for marketing communication?
2. What benefits are provided by narrowcasting?
3. Distinguish between customization and personalization.
4. How is the Internet characterized by both "push" and "pull" communications?
5. What types of pricing strategies address supply and demand issues in the marketspace?
6. What is the key focus for the IAB (Internet Advertising Bureau)?
7. What performance assumptions are implicit in each of the advertising pricing models discussed in this chapter?

8. Discuss the merits and demerits of click-through advertising.
9. If you purchase 50,000 impressions, assume 6 percent customer turnover, carefully estimate click-through at 3 percent, and make an average profit of $4 per sale, what is your expected return on investment?
10. What form of promotion is used to influence public relations?
11. Why is retroactive interference a big concern for marketers who use the Internet as the context within which to transmit marketing communications?
12. What are two technological opportunities available to assist marketers with product customization?

Thinking Points

1. What characteristics of the Internet as a communications resource differentiate it from traditional means of communication?
2. A simple communications model includes a source, a message, and a receiver. In general, how a message is encoded affects how it is decoded, and characteristics of the source and the receiver affect the encoding and decoding processes. How might the Internet affect the importance of the interaction that may exist between the source and the receiver?
3. What benefits do the two different types of interactivity with a computer-mediated environment provide marketers?
4. The Internet can facilitate personalization for promotions, such as targeted ads, and for products. Relate the types of personalization (i.e., promotion or product) to push versus pull forms of delivery.
5. Personalization can be accomplished in a variety of ways. What types of personalization are most likely to be associated with higher perceived value by consumers?
6. Why is the concept of modularization critical to the ability to mass customize products?
7. It has been argued that the Internet has increased buyer power, relative to seller power. How is the Internet as a communications resource related to this power shift?

Suggested Readings

1. "Conversations with Practitioners," in *Advertising and the World Wide Web,* edited by David W. Schumann (Mahwah, NJ: Lawrence Erlbaum Associates, Publishers, 1999), pp. 287–300.
2. "Offering Custom Products on the Internet," in *Understanding Electronic Commerce,* by David Kosiur (Redmond, WA: Microsoft Press, 1997), pp. 117–132.
3. "The Impact of Interactive Communication on Advertising and Marketing," by Edward Forrest, Lance Kinney, and Michael Chamberlain. In *Cybermarketing: Your Interactive Marketing Consultant,* edited by Regina Brady, Edward Forrest, and Richard Mizerki (Chicago: NTC Business Books, 1997), pp. 79–92.
4. "Whither the Banner," interview by Kim Cross. *Business 2.0* (December 1999), pp. 137–144.
5. "eBay vs. Amazon.com," by Robert D. Hof and Linda Himelstein. *BusinessWeek* (May 31, 1999), pp. 128–140.

SECTION FIVE

Extending the Framework over Time: Exchange Relationships in the Internet Environment

The impact of the Internet environment on exchange relationships has been emphasized throughout this book. Different types of relationships exist in the marketing environment, and the Internet affects many of them. In this final section, we focus on relationships in greater detail. In Chapter 13, we examine the Internet's influence on business-to-business exchange. Of particular interest is the way in which the Internet creates opportunities for new markets that facilitate exchanges of goods and services.

Relationships change over time and as a function of many factors. While earlier chapters in this book address issues related to starting business relationships, marketers must understand how to develop and maintain relationships. In Chapter 14, we look at issues that affect ongoing relational exchanges, such as satisfaction, trust, and commitment. We consider factors that foster or inhibit relationship development in the business-to-consumer and business-to-business markets.

CHAPTER 13

Business-to-Business Exchanges and the Internet

FOCUS AND OBJECTIVES

This chapter is focused on business-to-business (B2B) exchange. Business-to-business marketing entails the formation of relationships that differ in predictable ways from the relationships that describe business-to-consumer marketing. These differences are discussed with respect to the influence of the Internet as a resource for content, channel, and communication. The impact of the Internet on strategies for B2B marketing and on the structure of the processes for B2B exchanges is examined. Electronic hubs are described as a new form of intermediary in the exchange process.

YOUR OBJECTIVES IN STUDYING THIS CHAPTER INCLUDE THE FOLLOWING:

- Identify the key differences between business-to-business and business-to-consumer exchange processes.
- Know the main types of customers for B2B exchange and the characteristics usually associated with B2B exchange processes.
- Understand the influence of the Internet in different stages of B2B exchange processes.
- Develop familiarity with the role and types of online market makers as intermediaries for B2B exchange.

Imagine that you have been asked by your boss to locate a piece of equipment that is used to manufacture the core product for your company. The equipment is highly specialized and expensive. Only a few companies have the capability to produce the machinery, and it is important that the company you choose as the supplier will provide the highest level of quality, both in product and in follow-up service. Your task is complicated by the need to get the equipment by next week; otherwise, production will fall behind schedule, and relationships with distributors will deteriorate. Perhaps more importantly, you will be fired.

This scenario illustrates several factors that distinguish business-to-business marketing from business-to-consumer marketing. For example, although consumers are often faced with the need to find a particular product in a limited amount of time, in the business marketplace, this situation tends to be a consistent characteristic of purchase decisions. In addition, the types of products sought are often asset-specific. As a result, they are available from a narrower set of providers than are many types of consumer products. Another distinguishing characteristic is cost; many business-related purchases are for products that are expensive, or they are for bulk acquisitions that involve large expenditures. The need to maintain favorable channel relationships is also more pronounced in the business-to-business marketplace than in many business-to-consumer markets, because the purchase process may be repeated more frequently.

The Internet can be used to carry out a range of business-to-business activities. Many of the influences of the Internet on exchange relationships that we have considered in earlier chapters are relevant for exchanges in the business-to-business environment. For instance, the activities that reflect a business-to-business relationship involve the bidirectional exchange of resources. In the business-to-business marketplace, these exchanges may include transfers of information, money, services, and goods. In addition, the role of the Internet as a set of resources that can facilitate exchange is applicable to the business-to-business environment. For example, as a content resource, the Internet enables businesses to provide information about the goods and services that they provide. As a channel resource, the Internet can be used to transfer purchased goods and services. As a communications resource, the Internet facilitates negotiations between businesses that may affect the price, quantity, and form of the products that are purchased.

Because the nature of business-to-business exchanges is substantially different, in many cases, from business-to-consumer exchanges, the influence of the Internet on marketing aspects of business-to-business exchange is also different. In this chapter, we will consider the nature of the Internet's influence on business-to-business exchanges. We begin with a description of key characteristics of business-to-business exchanges, including a discussion of contrasts with business-to-consumer exchanges. We then consider the impact of the Internet on business-to-business marketing by looking at demographic characteristics of industrial marketing with the Internet. Insight into the possible effects of the Internet on business-to-business marketing is also obtained by considering the types of business-to-business activities that are influenced by the Internet, as well as the participants and the processes involved in these activities.

Digital Artifact 13.1

More than half of the online budget of a typical small business (fewer than 100 employees) is targeted for purchases of office supplies and computers.

(*Source:* **Nua Internet Surveys, citing Cyber Dialogue, 2000.**)

DIFFERENCES BETWEEN BUSINESS-TO-BUSINESS AND BUSINESS-TO-CONSUMER EXCHANGES

Although the goal of completing a transaction is common to business-to-business exchanges and business-to-consumer (B2C) exchanges, many other aspects of exchange activity are different. These differences include the type of customer, the nature of product demand, and the processes associated with business-to-business exchanges.

Difference in the Targeted Customer

A focal distinction between business-to-business and business-to-consumer exchanges is the purpose for product purchase. In business-to-consumer exchanges, consumers typically buy products for personal or household consumption. For marketers, these exchanges emphasize the importance of consumers' perceptions of personal consumption. In contrast, business-to-business exchanges involve consumption necessary for the production of good and services or for the sale of goods and services.

The difference in *why* the exchange occurs is related to the difference in *who* is involved in the exchange. For example, business-to-business exchanges occur when manufacturers sell products to distributors, who in turn sell the products to retailers. In addition, business-to-business exchanges occur when parts suppliers sell product components to product manufacturers. Another business-to-business exchange is characterized by sales of products and services that do not become part of the product sold to consumers but are necessary for the company to be able to create the product. For example, a company may purchase computers to manage its internal functions to efficiently produce a product. These examples illustrate different types of business-to-business transactions.

Difference in the Nature of Demand

Many business-to-business exchanges are conducted to facilitate the manufacture and distribution of products to consumers. The demand for industrial products is termed **derived demand,** because it occurs as the result of the demand for the consumer product. Derived demand tends to be characterized by sharper increases and decreases in demand than consumer demand, given the difficulties in developing accurate forecasts of consumer demand. As a result, manufacturers tend to overestimate inventory needs when consumer demand increases, and they tend to overestimate the need to reduce the inventory when consumer demand decreases.

The nature of demand for industrial products also differs from consumer products in the number of buyers who will be interested in a product. Because industrial products are often asset-specific and may be built to meet a narrow set of needs, the market for any given industrial product tends to be smaller than for many consumer products. B2B exchanges also differ from B2C exchanges in the variability of purchase volume. B2C purchases are for personal consumption, so many purchases occur in volumes of one. After all, how many rubber gasket seals for a clothes dryer door does a single consumer need? In contrast, the gasket manufacturer may supply tens of thousands of gaskets to an appliance manufacturer and additional thousands to several different appliance repair companies.

Differences in Exchange-Related Processes

B2B exchanges also differ from B2C exchanges in terms of the processes that buyers and sellers use to complete the transaction. The greater cost and complexity of many business purchases means that procurement processes are often conducted with formalized buying procedures and may be conducted by **purchasing agents** or **purchasing managers** who have professional expertise in making buying decisions. These agents may conduct negotiations with the sellers that are more extensive and complex than buyer-seller negotiations in B2C markets. In addition, the need for asset-specific industrial products means that B2B exchanges are often characterized by more direct interaction between the seller and the buyer, which may be conducted to obtain higher levels of product customization. Figure 13.1 summarizes the differences typically present between B2B and B2C exchanges.

Another characteristic difference between the B2B and the B2C markets is the volume of sales. Sales volume in the B2B market is higher than in the B2C market, even though the total number of customers is lower. The volume difference makes sense, however, if you consider that several industrial purchases may be necessary to create the product that results in a single sale to a consumer. The volume difference is also observed in the marketing environment of the Internet. In the next section, we will examine the demographics of online B2B exchanges.

FIGURE 13.1 B2B and B2C Exchanges Are Different.

Business-to-Consumer Exchanges	*Business-to-Business Exchanges*
Target Customer	*Target Customer*
◆ Consumer	◆ Business consumer
—Personal use	—Reseller
—Household use	—Industrial market
Nature of Demand	*Nature of Demand*
◆ Consumer-driven	◆ Derived, based on consumer demand
Exchange Processes	*Exchange Processes*
◆ Informal	◆ Formal
—Fewer constraints on purchases	—More constraints on purchases
—Fewer decision makers	—More decision makers
◆ Indirect producer-consumer link	◆ More direct producer-consumer contact
◆ Simple negotiation	◆ Complex negotiations

DESCRIBING ONLINE BUSINESS-TO-BUSINESS ACTIVITY

The Internet has received much attention as a marketplace for consumer goods. Behind the scenes, however, the business-to-business markets that have developed have quickly outpaced the amount of revenue associated with business-to-consumer activity on the Internet. We can describe online B2B marketing with the market demographics and with the types of activities facilitated by characteristics of the Internet environment.

Online B2B Demographics

Although estimates of the potential amount of B2B revenues vary widely, they all consistently reflect the prediction that online B2B revenues will increase disproportionately, relative to B2C revenues, in the coming years. The table in Figure 13.2 contains conservative forecasts of growth in each sector. The table in Figure 13.3 compares the projected rates of online B2B growth in the United States and worldwide.

The sheer size and relative weights of these numbers indicate the critical role of the Internet for business-to-business marketing. In the next section, we will look at several aspects of business-to-business exchanges to consider the implications of the Internet for business-to-business marketing.

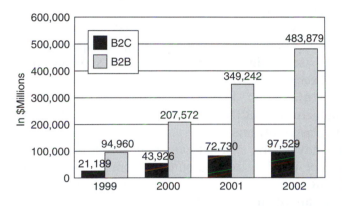

Source: Giga Information Group

FIGURE 13.2 Conservative Projections of Online Commerce Revenues.

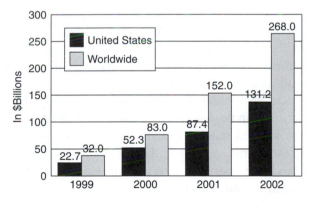

Source: eMarketer

FIGURE 13.3 A Comparison of U.S. and Worldwide B2B Forecasts.

THE INTERNET AND COMPONENTS OF BUSINESS-TO-BUSINESS EXCHANGE

In this section, we examine the Internet's influence on three aspects of business-to-business marketing: (1) purposes of exchange, (2) processes for exchange, and (3) participants in the exchange.

Purposes of B2B Exchanges

We can divide the business-to-business marketplace into three main categories. These categories are defined by the motivation of the buyers and the sellers for conducting the exchange. The categories include the following customers:

1. Buyers who serve as intermediaries to resell products to consumers
2. Buyers who incorporate a product into the manufacture of their own product
3. Buyers who use a product to facilitate business operations

Who Are B2B Customers?

First, a business-to-business exchange may involve selling to an organization that then sells the product to the end consumer. In this market, wholesalers and retailers act as **resellers** who add value to the product through marketing activity. As we saw in Chapter 11, the Internet affects the nature of exchange relationships within the reseller segment with its ability to serve as a channel resource.

Second, an exchange may involve selling to an organization that uses the product to manufacture its own product. For example, an **original equipment manufacturer (OEM)** may purchase product components from a supplier to assemble another product. This exchange is motivated by the purpose of adding value through manufacturing. In addition, a company may procure products that are needed to enable manufacturing but that do not become part of the end product (e.g., machine parts of an assembly line).

Third, an exchange may involve selling to an organization that uses the product to operate. For instance, purchases of computer equipment, office supplies, and janitorial services are often needed to facilitate the normal operations of a business. These types of sales are often referred to as **MROs,** for maintenance, repair, and operating.

The second and third categories that emphasize manufacturing and operations are often classified under the label of industrial marketing. The types of processes that may be carried out under this general label, however, are also found in markets for which governments and institutions are the target customers.

The division of business customers into the second and third categories of manufacturing and operations can be described as two different forms of markets: vertical and horizontal. A **vertical market** is a market that emphasizes products and services necessary to the manufacturing and sales of products in a specific industry. Vertical markets tend to be narrow in focus. For example, a vertical market in the lumber industry might include business-to-business marketing of products for logging and sawmill functions. In contrast, **horizontal markets** are focused on providing products and services to fulfill functional needs that may exist across a variety of industries. For example, a horizontal market for transportation services might include trucking services capable of moving loads of lumber from a sawmill to lumberyards, as well as steel from mills to factories and bolts of cloth from factories to stores.

B2B Buyers and Sellers on the Internet

To better understand what types of B2B exchanges are being conducted online, we can look at the U.S. forecasts for 2002, by market segment. Of the $131.2 billion that eStats, a company that tracks Internet-related statistics, projects for B2B exchange (see Figure 13.3), more than one-half will involve wholesale and retail exchanges ($65.6 billion). This projection emphasizes the importance of resellers as B2B customers, as well as the impact of the Internet on B2B activity in this market segment.

We can also look at the statistics to understand the implications of the Internet for business customers in the industrial market. Nearly one-third of the projected total will involve exchanges related to manufacturing ($40.6 billion). The remaining revenues reflect exchanges related to the procurement of services ($18.4 billion) and utilities ($6.6 billion). These numbers indicate the need to understand how the Internet can be used to conduct exchanges in vertical and horizontal markets.

B2B Exchange Processes

B2B exchanges, just like B2C exchanges, involve buyers and sellers. As we saw earlier, however, the nature of the exchanges between buyers and sellers is different. The exchange process differences, such as higher costs and greater product complexity and asset-specificity, increase the importance of choosing the right seller. In B2B exchanges likely to occur repeatedly, establishing an efficient and effective buyer-seller relationship is an important goal of the buying, or **procurement,** process.

Stages in the Procurement Process

The exchange process for procurement consists of three main stages: information gathering, transaction negotiation, and settlement (Figure 13.4). In the **information gathering stage,** the buyer decides what type of product is needed and develops information about possible sources for the product. In the **transaction negotiation stage,** communication with potential sellers establishes terms for the exchange, including product configuration, price, quantity, and delivery. In the **settlement stage,** the transfer of the product is completed.

Types of B2B Exchanges and Procurement Stages

Depending on the newness of the procurement situation, different emphasis may be placed on each of the three stages. Three types of B2B exchanges often illustrate the history of the relationship between a seller and buyer: new buy, modified rebuy, and straight rebuy. These situations range from an entirely new purchase

FIGURE 13.4 Stages in a General Procurement Process.

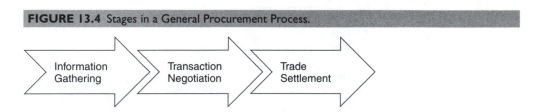

Information Gathering → Transaction Negotiation → Trade Settlement

situation in which no relationship exists to a routinized purchase decision based on a long-term relationship with a seller. In a **new buy** situation, information gathering is disproportionately important. In a **modified rebuy,** attention is often directed to negotiation that alters some aspect of the previous arrangement. In a **straight rebuy,** a preexisting agreement to effect an exchange is enacted with no changes to terms of the transaction. The table in Figure 13.5 reflects the amounts of activity that are typically conducted in each stage of the procurement process, as a function of the type of exchange relationship. The shaded boxes reflect heightened activity.

Internet Effects on B2B Exchange Stages

The Internet affects what business marketers can do to conduct B2B exchanges, depending on the type of exchange relationship to be conducted. Marketers can leverage the Internet's ability to serve as a resource for content, channel, and communication to effect B2B exchange activity as a function of the stage of the procurement process. More simply put, different capabilities afforded by the Internet are emphasized at different stages of the buying process.

The Internet and New Buys   For example, a new buy situation tends to be characterized by the absence of an ongoing seller-buyer relationship. In the new buy situation, the buyer must complete all stages of the procurement process. Information must be sought about possible vendors, and negotiations must be effectively concluded before the product is transferred to the buyer. In this situation, the Internet can be used as a source of information for sellers and buyers, enabling buyers to accomplish information gathering tasks. In the information gathering stage, the Internet exerts its strongest effect as a content resource. Business buyers can request information from sellers through e-mail. In addition, information can also be acquired from sellers' Web sites. Banners with links to sellers' sites also provide information.

The Internet and Modified Rebuys   In a modified rebuy exchange, the Internet is primarily effective as a communication resource. It facilitates negotations that enable buyers and sellers to alter various aspects of an existing exchange agreement.

FIGURE 13.5 Stage-Related Activity Changes as Relationships Develop.

TYPE OF RELATIONAL EXCHANGE

Procurement Process Stage	New Buy	Modified Rebuy	Straight Rebuy
Information Gathering	▓▓▓		
Transaction Negotiation	▓▓▓	▓▓▓	
Trade Settlement	▓▓▓	▓▓▓	▓▓▓

For instance, two-way interactivity provides buyers and sellers with the ability to conduct a near real-time negotiation to change the form of an ordered product part, as well as its amount, and the timing and destination of its delivery. In this role, the Internet enables the buyer and the seller to customize a product order and to personalize aspects of the exchange process.

An important aspect of the interaction capabilities of the Internet for modified rebuys, however, is the need for the seller to understand the expectations of the buyer and to incorporate recognition of them into the processes for reaching customized product agreements. A modified rebuy represents a middle-ground position in relationship development. Business customers may tend to expect that sellers will incorporate previous experience with them into present and future attempts to solidify business relationships. When used effectively, technological characteristics of the Internet can enable sellers to record and track buyer information, as through server-based data (e.g., log files) and through user-based data (e.g., cookies). This ability to retain information about buyer preferences and past behaviors can reduce the transaction costs associated with the new buy situation. It can also increase switching costs when the effort to provide the seller with company-specific requirements is not negligible.

The interactive, immediate nature of the Internet-enabled relationship places a new requirement on sellers to not only recognize the import of previous interactions on a current interaction, but to be able to integrate and develop the implications of the interaction rapidly. In this respect, Internet-based exchanges resemble personal selling in the business marketplace.

In addition to the communications that are conducted between the buyer and the seller, communications that affect the specifications for the exchange can take place via the Internet within the company. For instance, private internal networks, or intranets, can be used to obtain information about needed product characteristics, as well as cost constraints and purchase approval.

Digital Artifact 13.2

B2B sites need help. None of 30 sites assessed by Forrester Research met criteria set of acceptable value, reliability, and ease of use.

(*Source:* **Nua Internet Surveys, citing Forrester Research.**)

The Internet and Straight Rebuys   For an exchange that is a straight rebuy, the Internet functions as a channel resource. Because the exchange does not need to be negotiated, and because all necessary information is already available to both parties, the primary benefit of the Internet is as a conduit for transmission. This transmission may take the form of the request to complete an automated exchange, or to effect the delivery of the actual product, or both.

Prior to the Internet, companies often used privately established networks for electronic data interchange (EDI). EDI makes it possible for organizations to efficiently conduct standardized business exchanges, such as straight rebuys. EDI does, however, have several significant drawbacks. These networks are often expensive to establish, and their complexity requires trained users. In addition, EDI networks tend to limit users to the transfer of a small number of properly formatted documents.

The Internet enables business buyers and sellers to overcome several obstacles associated with the use of EDI to process business exchanges. Because the Internet is an open network, companies can use its infrastructure to develop private intranets and extranets that allow users to transfer documents in a wide variety of formats. Because a selling organization can receive exchange-related documents in a variety of formats, buying organizations can transmit purchase orders that fit their organizational requirements, thus facilitating movement toward repetitive, straight rebuy situations by decreasing implementation costs (see Figure 13.6).

Buying Needs and Types of Exchanges

One dimension that affects whether a buying situation is new, modified, or routinized is the type of need that exists for the product. The need for some products and services may be highly predictable, while the need for other types is more variable. For example, a car manufacturer can reliably predict that as long as production continues, tires will be needed. In contrast, the need for an employment service to handle the task of finding a replacement for a line manager who was just hired away by the competition reflects a less predictable business exchange. In general, business exchange activities that are frequently repeated—and on a predictable timetable—often result in **systematic sourcing.** Exchange-related activities due to less predictable needs are typically met with **spot sourcing.**

Systematic sourcing is often associated with straight rebuy relationships, in which product needs are clear and predictable. Spot sourcing reflects buying behavior in which need is less predictable, and which tends to result in more oppor-

---

FIGURE 13.6 Internet Resources Provide a Variety of Benefits for B2B Exchanges.

THE INTERNET AS RESOURCE TYPE

Type of Relational Exchange	Content	Communication	Channel
New Buy	Buyer: facilitates acquisition of product information Seller: facilitates lead generation		
Modified Rebuy		Buyer: facilitates negotiation Seller: facilitates pricing	
Straight Rebuy			Buyer: facilitates automated ordering Seller: facilitates scheduling and delivery

tunistic purchasing behavior. A buying agent may examine several potential vendors and engage in negotiations each time the product or service need arises, thus creating situations that more closely resemble new buys than established relationships.

Digital Artifact 13.3

B2B online exchanges are predicted to increase from $336 billion in 2000 to more than $6 trillion in 2005, a twenty-fold growth.

(*Source:* **eMarketer, citing Jupiter Communications, 2000.**)

B2B Exchange Participants

B2B exchanges take one of two forms: direct or indirect. A **direct exchange** involves communication between the buyer and the seller, with no intermediaries. In contrast, an **indirect exchange** introduces intermediaries that facilitate the transfer of products from the seller to the buyer. Indirect exchanges are often conducted through online markets, or electronic hubs. The chart in Figure 13.7 illustrates the difference in projected growth rates of indirect exchanges through e-hubs, compared with other forms of B2B exchange.

Direct B2B Exchange and the Internet

One challenge for participants in many types of B2B exchanges is finding exchange partners. The difficulty in identifying exchange partners exists for buyers and for sellers. From a buyer's perspective, multiple sellers may exist, but characteristics of the buyer's situation—such as budget and time constraints, and high levels of asset specificity—may narrow the range of products and vendors that are acceptable. From a seller's perspective in a B2B environment, identifying promising sales leads and developing suitable agreements can be difficult in an environment characterized by smaller target markets and greater awareness of competitors than in many B2C markets.

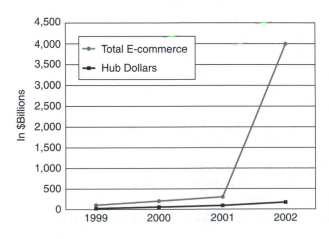

Source: eMarketer

FIGURE 13.7 Alternative Forms of B2B Exchanges Will Outstrip E-hubs.

The Internet can be used by buyers to find sellers, and vice versa. Buyers can use Internet search engines to hunt for specific products and industries. In addition, B2B directories exist that facilitate buyer search by aggregating sellers by product or service, and by industry.

Sellers' Web sites also serve to initiate direct contact. Sellers can provide content about product offerings and customization flexibility. Sellers can also use banner ads on external sites to generate leads. Whether attached to a company's Web site or to a banner, **Web response forms (WRFs)** can be used to enable potential buyers to express interest in a particular product. A Web response form is an online form used by buyers to request product information, and by sellers to qualify sales prospects. A buyer who visits a seller's Web site might leave behind information in a server's log file about in-site information acquisition, and the URL from which he or she entered the site. With a Web response form, however, the seller can obtain more detailed information about the motives behind the buyer's Web site visit (i.e., lead qualification), as well as a way to initiate subsequent contact with the buyer. Benefits for buyers include the ability to receive information tailored to needs and experience, as well as rapid fulfillment. A WRF can be used within a seller's Web site or through a link placed in a banner ad on an external Web site. Many business sites use automated outbound e-mail response applications to provide quick responses to buyer inquiries initiated with WRFs.

E-mail capabilities on the Internet can be used to influence the information gathering stage of the buying process in several ways. We have noted the fulfillment capabilities of the Internet as a way to respond to inbound e-mail and WRF requests for information. In addition, business marketers can send unsolicited mailings to targeted businesses, in the hope that the pushed information is relevant. Other uses of e-mail to create direct exchanges between sellers and buyers include distribution of press releases and newsletters to potential customers. Interactive surveys can provide contact with prospects and generate interest in an existing product or in the development of a new product. Sellers can also use e-mail to manage discussion groups on industry-related issues. Buyer participation in online discussion forums can provide information for both buyers and sellers that can influence the exchange process.

Many uses of the Internet by sellers who seek to establish a direct exchange with buyers are similar to traditional forms of direct marketing. For instance, sellers can use outbound e-mail to develop pointcast messages to recipients. As with traditional mail-based lead generation approaches, the seller incurs costs associated with list acquisition. In general, however, direct marketing on the Internet reduces costs because printing and mailing expenses are eliminated. Figure 13.8 contains a sample of B2B activities that can be used by a business marketer to incorporate the Internet into direct exchange efforts.

Indirect B2B Exchange and the Internet

Indirect exchanges involve the introduction of an intermediary into the buying process conducted between a buyer and a seller. In the B2B environment, these intermediaries often function to create links between buyers and sellers, thus pro-

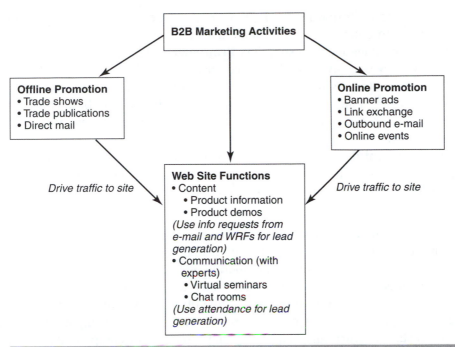

FIGURE 13.8 Business Marketers Integrate Multiple Activities to Initiate Direct Exchanges.

viding an alternative means of contact to a direct exchange. The intermediaries operate by creating collections of buyers and collections of sellers through organized systems that allow information sharing between buyers and sellers. Some organized markets establish standards that affect the way that exchanges are conducted, including information gathering, transaction negotiation, and trade settlement. Firms that impose structure across the range of activities in the exchange process are called **market-making firms.**

An important benefit of organized markets is that they can reduce transaction costs associated with each stage of the exchange process. For example, a market-making firm that aggregates collections of information about the wares of different vendors in a sector of industry can drastically reduce the effort needed by a buyer to search for product information. In addition, organized markets can affect costs of negotiating. Different types of firms impose different structures and procedures for reaching agreements on factors such as price. These established procedures can reduce transaction costs by decreasing confusion about the types of agreements that are possible. In the settlement stage, policies that reflect norms and codes of conduct can reduce difficulties with enforcing exchange contracts.

Types of Online Markets   Three primary forms of online markets have been identified by eMarketer analysts: consortia-led exchanges, proprietary exchanges, and third-party exchanges. **Consortia-led exchanges** are collections of companies who share ownership, often in conjunction with a technology partner who creates the online exchange forum. For example, General Motors, Ford, and Chrysler joined with Covisint to create a consortia-led exchange to facilitate B2B exchanges between the companies and their suppliers. **Proprietary exchanges** are privately owned and managed by one—typically large—company (e.g., Wal-Mart's RetailLink). The goal of a proprietary exchange is to increase revenues by creating more efficient exchanges between members of the company's supply chain. In both consortia-led exchanges and proprietary markets, the owners participate in the buying and selling activities of the markets.

In contrast, **third-party exchanges** function as intermediaries who are not trading partners. In the following section, we will look at the characteristics of third-party hubs as online intermediaries for B2B exchange.

Third-Party Hubs as Online Intermediaries   The Internet is the host environment for several new forms of market-making intermediaries. These intermediaries are electronic hubs that operate within vertical or horizontal B2B markets to mediate transactions between buyers and sellers. Some hubs are focused on particular sections of industry, while other hubs emphasize the provision of services or functions that extend across industries. For example, in a vertical hub for restaurant furniture, suppliers for products and components associated with restaurant furniture production, maintenance, and repair might offer their wares. In contrast, in a horizontal hub, a buyer might find vendors who specialize in processes that can be used in a range of industries. For instance, a company that repairs torn vinyl upholstery might sell its services in a horizontal hub to buyers in the restaurant industry, the airline industry, and the professional-waiting-room industry.

With its networked structure and relatively inexpensive access, the Internet is a fertile medium for third-party hubs. The ability to communicate product and price information in near real-time between buyers and sellers enables exchange participants to update inventory availability and to react to price fluctuations. This capability enables exchange participants to better manage derived demand. In addition, markets on the Internet decouple product flows from information flows; an exchange agreement can be reached without the physical presence of the product. This characteristic provides logistics benefits and increases the geographic scope of the market.

Despite the advantages they can provide, market-making intermediaries on the Internet also present disadvantages. Among the disadvantages are the increased transaction risks that arise when a buyer must rely on the computer-mediated environment to obtain an accurate understanding of the product offering. In addition, the newness of many online markets means that buyers and sellers may enter exchange agreements with little information about the performance history of either partner in satisfying terms of the agreement. These disadvantages act as barriers to adoption by B2B buyers and sellers.

Digital Artifact 13.4

Electronic markets, or e-hubs, will account for between 45 percent and 74 percent of supply chain activity by 2004.

(*Source:* **eMarketer, citing Forrester Research, 2000.**)

First-Mover Advantage for Online Intermediaries   The disadvantages associated with online intermediaries underscore the importance of a **first-mover advantage,** or benefits that can be attributed to an early presence in a market. Being early in the market for buyers and sellers increases the likelihood that an online intermediary will be able to develop a large enough base of potential buyers and sellers to create market liquidity. **Market liquidity** refers to the presence of sufficient numbers of buyers and sellers in a marketplace to enable good matches between buyers and sellers. The number of participants required to achieve market liquidity is described as **critical mass.**

The size of the participant base reduces risks for buyers and sellers in several ways. First, risks associated with the ability to locate a buyer or a seller decrease as market size increases. Second, increased numbers of transactions provide more information (e.g., via word-of-mouth) about participants. Third, increased market size is often accompanied by the development of formal standards and mechanisms for participation and performance. These requirements protect participants in the exchange process.

Online Intermediaries as Value-Adders   Online B2B intermediaries play different roles in the exchange processes between businesses. We can describe these roles in terms of two different ways that the intermediaries provide value to the buyers and sellers in the exchange process: aggregation and matching. When the objective of the intermediary is **aggregation,** value is achieved by creating collections of buyers and sellers. When the objective is **matching,** value is achieved by facilitating exchanges between buyers and sellers.

In an aggregation model, value is measured in numbers of sellers and their products, and of buyers. Intermediaries who add value through aggregation often adopt a **catalog approach,** in which the wares of a large number of vendors, in either a vertical or a horizontal market, are accumulated and made available to a collection of buyers. Aggregation models are characterized by prenegotiated prices and a large variety of specialized products (i.e., noncommodity).

A second type of value added by online B2B intermediaries is through matching; the intermediary provides a mechanism through which buyers and sellers can negotiate prices to effect an exchange. An important aspect of matching is the need for liquidity. Because liquidity depends on an adequate numbers of buyers and sellers, matching models benefit from aggregation.

Matching is accomplished with auctions and bid-ask exchanges. In **auctions,** pricing is **buyer-driven** when buyers' bids for a product build on previous buyers' bids. This B2B model is analogous to standard bidding with eBay, an online auction in the B2C marketplace. Pricing is **seller-driven** when the seller sets an initial price and lowers the price until a buyer accepts the price. A **Dutch auction** is an example of seller-driven auction pricing. The Dutch auction model was developed in the flower market in Holland as a means for tulip growers to establish selling prices for their harvests.

Bid-ask exchanges are based on real-time matching of bid and asking prices. For example, a vendor of bandwidth can "ask" a certain price for unused inventory. If the asked price matches a buyer's bid price, the exchange is transacted (for example, see Figure 13.9). Exchange models are most effective for commodity-type products that are traded in large volumes, and for which demand—and hence, price—tends to fluctuate.

Classifying Intermediary B2B Hubs Several of the characteristics used to describe B2B exchange activity can be used to classify different types of B2B hubs as business models. Such classification is useful because it helps marketers to determine the type of hub that is most appropriate for conducting a particular business exchange.

A taxonomy of B2B hubs suggested by Sawhney and Kaplan integrates *what* businesses buy (i.e., manufacturing or operating), with *how* businesses buy (i.e., sys-

FIGURE 13.9 FreeMarkets Uses an Auction Mechanism to Match Purchasing Agents with Suppliers.

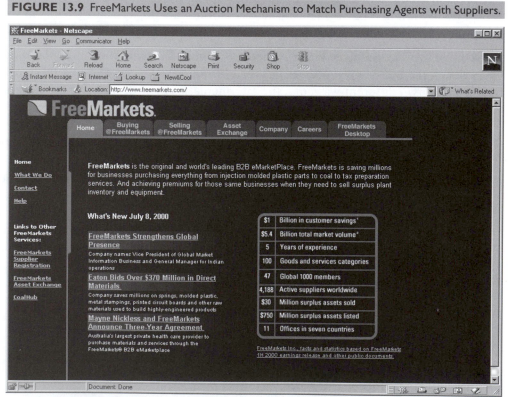

tematic or spot sourcing).[1] As a general rule, systematic sourcing is associated with aggregation models and static pricing. Spot sourcing, given the higher volatility in demand, is associated with hubs that use a matching mechanism to enable dynamic pricing. The integration of what and how businesses buy results in four different types of B2B intermediaries, each of which provides different benefits to participating buyers and sellers. The four types of hubs are (1) MRO hubs, (2) catalog hubs, (3) yield managers, and (4) exchanges.

MRO hubs focus on business processes that provide necessary functions across a variety of industries. Because the functions are needed on an ongoing basis, they reflect systematic sourcing in a horizontal market. In contrast, **yield managers** take a spot sourcing focus to provide operating inputs that have less predictable demand, such as employment services.

Online hubs that provide manufacturing products adopt a vertical focus. **Catalog hubs** aggregate products within an industry and are characterized by prenegotiated prices and systematic sourcing. **Exchanges** emphasize commodity-type products that are purchased on a spot basis. The characteristics that differentiate the online intermediary hubs are illustrated in Figure 13.10.

Kaplan and Sawhney note that online B2B hubs can be neutral or biased. A **neutral hub** does not favor buyers or sellers. Neutral hubs are most effective in cases of **bilateral fragmentation.** Bilateral fragmentation refers to the presence of high differentiation of participants on each side of the exchange process. Neutral hubs require participation of both buyers and sellers to provide value, whether the market uses an aggregation mechanism or a matching mechanism. With an aggregation mechanism, a neutral hub increases the value it adds by providing a wider range of opportunities to buyers and sellers. With a matching mechanism, a neutral hub increases its value by improving the quality of matches between buyers and sellers.

Biased hubs focus on providing benefits for buyers or for sellers—but not both. Biased hubs tend to be most effective for **unilateral fragmentation.** Unilateral

FIGURE 13.10 Online Intermediaries Classified by Business Activities.

		How Businesses Buy	
		Spot Sourcing	Manufacturing Inputs
What Businesses Buy	Operating Supplies	Yield Managers	MROs
	Manufacturing Supplies	Exchanges	Catalogs

Source: Adapted from Kaplan and Sawhney, 1999

---

[1]"B2B E-Commerce Hubs: Towards a Taxonomy of Business Models," by Steven Kaplan and Mohanbir Sawhney. Working paper, University of Chicago, Graduate School of Business, December 1999.

fragmentation refers to situations in which only one side of the market exhibits low concentration. Biased hubs operate in favor of the fragmented side of the market. For instance, characteristics of the Internet make it possible for a hub to aggregate buyer demand from a collection of highly fragmented buyers. The aggregator can negotiate more effectively with a collection of concentrated sellers than if the buyers negotiated independently. This situation is termed **reverse aggregation,** in contrast to more traditional markets, in which an aggregator combines services offered by resellers to increase selling power, a process of **forward aggregation.**

The presence of online B2B intermediaries presents business marketers with new outlets for buying and selling products. In addition, the novel characteristics of some online intermediaries, such as reverse aggregators, mean that buyers and sellers must adapt their B2B exchange processes to effectively leverage aspects of these biased markets. Shifts in the processes for conducting B2B exchanges may also affect the nature of relationships that develop between participants in the exchanges. We will consider the impact of the Internet on aspects of relationship development in detail in Chapter 14.

Digital Artifact 13.5

In April 2000, analysts reported the existence of more than 620 online exchanges, or hubs. This number is predicted to increase to 4,200 by 2003.

(*Source:* **eMarketer, citing Keenan Vision, 2000.**)

Chapter Summary

The impact of the Internet on marketing activity is evident in the business-to-business environment. Businesses have relied on technologies that enable the electronic exchange of data and of dollars in B2B transactions for several decades. The impact of Internet-related computing technologies, however, has extended far beyond these early electronic commerce applications to include a wide range of business marketing activities. The ability of organizations to conduct B2B activities online has resulted in projections of e-commerce revenues for business-to-business in excess of $1.3 trillion by 2003.

Applications for business marketing continue to develop, often resulting in new uses of the Internet. For example, the development of industry-niched, vertical market portals on the Internet not only creates a new business opportunity for the portal developer who provides a hub that connects buyers and sellers, but it also provides the participating vendors with a new forum for selling their products.

In this chapter, we examined the role of the Internet for aspects of business-to-business marketing. We began by describing the differences between B2C and B2B marketing activity. These differences included the types of customers, the nature of product demand, and the processes for conducting exchange activities. Rapid increases in the development of B2B Internet applications—as indicated by a comparison of B2C and B2B revenues—illustrated the importance of online marketing between businesses.

The Internet's role in B2B marketing was considered in terms of three aspects of business exchanges: exchange purposes, exchange processes, and exchange participants. The Internet exerts a strong influence on purposes for B2B exchanges. We noted that more than half of the B2B online revenues by 2002 are projected to stem from reseller activity. In addition, the industrial market, comprised of manufacturing and operating activities, are expected to account for approximately one-third and one-fifth of online B2B exchanges, respectively, by 2002.

We also examined the effect on the Internet in stages of the procurement process. These stages include information gathering, transaction negotiation, and trade settlement. The Internet affects the amount of buyer activity conducted in each stage, depending on whether the exchange is a new buy, a modified rebuy, or a straight rebuy. For new buys, the Internet provides benefits as a content resource for obtaining information in the early stage of the procurement process. For modified rebuys, the Internet exerts influence as a communications resource for facilitating negotiation and customization. In straight rebuy situations, the Internet is an effective channel for automating processes for product orders, invoices, and logistics.

The Internet affects the nature and function of participants in direct and indirect B2B processes. A key problem for buyers and sellers in direct exchanges is the need to identify appropriate exchange partners. The Internet has introduced new intermediaries for indirect exchange that seek to address the difficulties of direct online B2B exchanges. These intermediaries were described as electronic hubs: organized markets that create value through aggregation and matching mechanisms. The appropriate selection of online intermediaries for B2B exchanges was considered in terms of exchange characteristics, such as the type of purchase and the predictability of product need.

REVIEW SECTION

Key Terms

- derived demand
- purchasing agents
- purchasing managers
- resellers
- original equipment manufacturer (OEM)
- MROs
- vertical market
- horizontal market
- procurement
- information gathering stage
- transaction negotiation stage
- settlement stage
- new buy
- modified rebuy
- straight rebuy
- systematic sourcing
- spot sourcing
- direct exchange
- indirect exchange
- Web response forms (WRFs)
- market-making firms
- consortia-led exchanges
- proprietary exchanges
- third-party exchanges
- first-mover advantage
- market liquidity
- critical mass
- aggregation
- matching
- catalog approach
- auction
- buyer-driven

- seller-driven
- Dutch auction
- bid-ask exchanges
- MRO hubs

- yield managers
- catalog hubs
- exchanges
- neutral hub

- bilateral fragmentation
- unilateral fragmentation
- reverse aggregation
- forward aggregation

Review Questions

1. Describe three differences between B2B and B2C exchanges.
2. Explain why B2B markets account for a disproportionate amount of online revenue.
3. What three aspects of business exchanges does the Internet influence?
4. What is the difference between a vertical market and a horizontal market?
5. On what stage of the procurement process is a procurement officer who is conducting a modified rebuy most likely focused?
6. In a new buy situation, how may buyers take advantage of the Internet? In a modified rebuy exchange?
7. What are some of the drawbacks of electronic data interchange? How does the Internet address these EDI drawbacks?
8. How may e-mail capabilities on the Internet influence direct B2B exchange?
9. Describe some of the advantages and disadvantages associated with market-making intermediaries, which may be experienced by buyers and sellers.
10. In what two ways can intermediaries provide value to buyers and sellers in the exchange process?
11. Discuss the different types of B2B hubs in terms of what and how businesses buy.

Thinking Points

1. What characteristics of the Internet might account for the disproportionate adoption of the Internet as a market for B2B exchanges relative to B2C exchanges?
2. What characteristics of B2B exchanges may account for the disproportionate adoption of the Internet as a market for B2B exchanges relative to B2C exchanges?
3. How might the capabilities of the Internet serve to smooth the spikes in derived demand that result from overly optimistic and pessimistic forecasts of consumer consumption?
4. In which type of market, vertical or horizontal, is the formation of a personalized relationship that exists between the producer and the buyer more likely to be a central factor in the development of the relationship? Why?
5. In which type of market, vertical or horizontal, is the formation of a personalized relationship that exists between the producer (or the buyer) and the Internet-based market-maker more likely to be a central factor in the development of the relationship? Why?
6. Consider the role of the Internet as a content resource, a channel resource, and a communications resource. Are these resources likely to be differently emphasized in different types of B2B exchanges (i.e., new buy, modified rebuy, straight rebuy)?

7. What characteristics of the Internet have contributed to the rapid growth—in number and in popularity—of online markets that serve as intermediaries for B2B exchanges?
8. What are the implications of reverse aggregation for the development of market intermediaries?

Suggested Readings

1. *Business-to-Business Internet Marketing,* by Barry Silverstein (Gulf Breeze, FL: Maximum Press, 1998).
2. "Impacts of the Electronic Marketplace on Transaction Cost and Market Structure," by Ho Geun Lee and Theodore H. Clark. *International Journal of Electronic Commerce, 1,* 1, pp. 127–149.
3. "Let's Get Vertical," by Mohanbir Sawhney and Steven Kaplan. *Business 2.0* (September 1999), pp. 85–92.
4. "The Impact of Interorganizational Networks on Buyer-Seller Relationships," by Charles Steinfield, Robert Kraut, and Alice Plummer. *Journal of Computer-Mediated Communication, 1,* 3.

CHAPTER 14

Fostering Relational Exchange With the Internet

FOCUS AND OBJECTIVES

This chapter addresses the role of the Internet as a force that influences marketers' ability to develop and maintain exchange relationships. The growing importance of developing ongoing relational exchanges is described, and a framework for thinking about relational exchange is discussed. We use this theoretical basis to consider ways that value is created in B2C and B2B exchanges. In B2C exchanges, we consider ways in which the Internet affects relational development by influencing satisfaction, trust, and commitment. In B2B exchanges, we examine the Internet's influence on different classes of B2B relationships.

YOUR OBJECTIVES IN STUDYING THIS CHAPTER INCLUDE THE FOLLOWING:

- Understand the difference between initiating relational exchange, and developing and maintaining the exchange.

- Recognize key shifts in marketing activity that illustrate the increasing importance of ongoing relational exchange.

- Understand which types of exchanges provide benefits from ongoing interaction and how the Internet affects the creation of these benefits.

- Identify primary determinants of perceived value in B2C relationships and the Internet-related factors that influence them.

- Identify major classes of B2B relationships, the dimensions that define them, and the Internet characteristics that influence them.

Throughout this book we have demonstrated the importance of the relationships that exist in the Internet environment. In Chapter 1, we considered the interaction between marketing and technology as a backdrop for the study of marketing and the Internet. In Chapter 2, we developed a framework based on the exchange relationships between participants in the Internet environment. The activities of these participants were discussed in Chapters 3 through 6 as relationships formed to meet the exchange needs of marketers, consumers, technology developers, and policy makers.

In Chapters 7 and 8, we extended our view to examine the effect of the Internet on the nature of competition—among companies and among consumers—for resources in the environment. We looked at ways in which the Internet influences strategic marketing, including defining objectives and leveraging resources. Using the Internet to identify relationships that meet strategic objectives was addressed in Chapter 9. In Chapters 10 through 13, we learned how marketers can leverage the content, channel, and communication resources of the Internet to initiate relational exchanges. Business-to-business relational exchanges were the focus of Chapter 13.

The importance of relationships to marketing is evident when you consider the many types of relationships that can exist between a company and its customers. These relationships not only include links to the end consumer, but to all the participants in the value chain. For instance, a company might have ongoing relationships with a set of suppliers, some value-added resellers, and a collection of retailers.

The Internet, with its ability to transmit information and to store data, can affect the ways that companies manage relationships with other participants in value chain activities. The importance of exchanges that occur—other than sales transactions—is evident in the influence of policy makers and technology developers on the exchanges between marketers and consumers at many links in the value chain.

Beyond affecting the beginning of relationships, the Internet can influence the ways that marketers conduct activities that foster valued relationships and terminate ineffective relationships. In this chapter, we shift our focus to consider the Internet as a factor that affects marketers' efforts to build ongoing interactions. Earlier chapters emphasized the role of the Internet as a factor that facilitates or inhibits the beginning of exchange relationships. Now we will consider the Internet as a means for developing and maintaining relational exchange.

We begin with a review of the history that illustrates the growing importance of relationship-oriented marketing. Then we adopt a theoretical perspective on relational exchange to describe the nature of exchanges, including the ways that relationships add value for partners, and how value is measured. We build on this theoretical base to examine the role of the Internet as a factor that influences marketers' ability to foster relational exchanges in business-to-consumer and in business-to-business markets.

Digital Artifact 14.1

Developing relationships is important. Research results indicate that a consumer must shop at an online store four times before the store profits from the customer.

(*Source:* **Nua Internet Surveys, citing Mainspring, 2000.**)

THE INCREASING IMPORTANCE OF RELATIONSHIPS

Marketers are interested in relationships for a straightforward reason: building relationships with customers can improve profits. Researchers have estimated that the cost of making a sale to a new customer is six to nine times as expensive as making a sale to a repeat customer. This expense makes sense if we adopt a social exchange perspective in which researchers describe relationships as marriages. Courting is expensive: The getting-to-know-you-and-trying-to-impress-you phase of a new relationship often involves significant transaction costs for the suitor. Even if the object of affection is sufficiently enlightened to split the cost, the overall expense does not decrease.

Developing an ongoing relationship not only reduces monetary costs, it also provides a marketer with less uncertainty about exchange-related outcomes, more time to pursue other relationships (here, the marriage analogy weakens . . .), and greater satisfaction on the part of the other partner. This latter benefit illustrates the concept that relationships provide value for both partners. Satisfaction results from the improved knowledge of preferences and needs that guides the exchange. For a marketer, customer satisfaction increases the likelihood of getting referrals through positive word-of-mouth.

Because it can be used to gather and store information about customer needs, and to facilitate interaction with customers, the Internet is expected to affect the importance that marketers place on developing relationships, as well as the methods they use to do so. Strategies that are focused on developing unique, sustained relationships with individual customers are described as **1:1 marketing.**[1] Because it has the capability to facilitate personalized, customized interaction between marketers and consumers, the Internet is an important factor in 1:1 marketing activity.

As an area of academic study, relationship marketing is relatively young. Although companies have formed partnerships for mutual benefit for hundreds of years, the formal study of relationships for marketing activity did not receive widespread attention until the 1980s. The increased attention to the role of relationships in marketing practice can be attributed to changes in the way that we view marketing exchange.

Shifts in Perspectives on Exchange

The importance of relationships for marketing is evident in four fundamental shifts in the ways that marketing researchers and practitioners address marketing exchange. These shifts are (1) from a product focus to a person focus; (2) from a competition focus to a cooperation focus; (3) from a discrete, company-based focus to a networked focus; and (4) from a transactional focus to a relational exchange focus.

---

[1]Read as "one-to-one marketing."

From Products to People

In both business-to-consumer and business-to-business markets, increasing attention is being paid to the importance of the customer, as with 1:1 marketing strategies. Advances in communications technologies have facilitated interactions between buyers and sellers. Buyers can communicate preferences and dissatisfaction rapidly and directly, and sellers can target products and promotions to specific audiences. These two capabilities reflect accountability and addressability. **Accountability** refers to the burden placed on sellers to meet the buyers' expectations. **Addressability** refers to the ability of marketers to identify and target individual consumers, as with pointcast technologies. In addition, advances in product development technologies have made it possible to modularize the construction of many products. As we saw in Chapter 12, this modularization enables mass customization, thus making it possible for companies to respond to customers' needs more effectively. One effect of the increasing ability to mass customize products is a parallel increase in buyers' expectations of seller accountability.

From Competition to Cooperation

Economists have long attempted to understand and explain marketplace behavior with models of competition. Competition means that companies treat each other as adversaries in their quests to meet their own goals. Recent efforts to describe markets, however, have been focused on cooperation. Cooperation exists when a subset of companies operates jointly, maximizing each company's core competencies for a mutual goal. A brief explanation of each perspective is useful for understanding why a shift from competition to cooperative has occurred, and what the shift means for the Internet and relationship marketing.

Researchers in economics and in marketing have developed theories of competition and explanations of firm behavior. For example, theorists describe competition as horizontal or hierarchical in nature. In horizontal competition, businesses compete with other businesses at the same level of the industry. In contrast, in hierarchical competition, businesses integrate vertically to develop portfolios of strengths that augment their ability to compete against other businesses that are also busy integrating vertically. Vertical integration creates the opportunity for a company to engage in a series of partnerships that provide benefits by reducing uncertainty about the ability to acquire needed materials and services.

Cooperation can help companies compete. Managing competition through cooperation is reflected by the growth of strategic alliances. Recall that strategic alliances are partnerships between independent companies that might otherwise be in competition with each other. An alliance can provide each partner with needed capabilities, but without the headaches of ownership that often occur with vertical integration. A company may form multiple strategic alliances. These alliances reflect a hybrid response to competition when the alliances leverage aspects of horizontal and vertical competition to create networks of relationships that provide the network with a competitive advantage through cooperation.

From Stand-Alone to Networked

The shifts in focus we have just considered are each related to technological advances that increase the ways in which people can interact. These technological developments, and their adoption by businesses and by consumers, alter the nature of competition and increase the importance of cooperation. For instance, consumers can use the Internet to compare competing products and to order customized products. Because the increased transparency of product offerings may affect marketers' ability to develop and sustain a competitive advantage in the product offering, marketers compete for customers, often working to develop long-term relationships that add value for the customer, independent of the product offering. The interactive capabilities of the Internet provide a means by which marketers can tailor marketing activities to develop a one-to-one relationship with consumers.

From Transactions to Relationships

The three shifts just discussed suggest the importance of the fourth shift from a focus on single transactions to a focus on ongoing interactions. (These four shifts are summarized in Figure 14.1.) Prior to the emergence of relationship marketing, marketing researchers and practitioners emphasized the importance of understanding and implementing practices that promoted a company's ability to consummate transactions, such as making a sale. This orientation is often described as a functional approach to interactions between agents in the marketplace.

A relational exchange perspective provides a better description of the types of exchanges that take place daily between organizations in the marketing environment than does a transaction-focused approach. As we saw in the first section of this book, transactions are merely the end result of an exchange process. We also saw that exchange processes are not limited to products and money; businesses engage in exchange processes that transfer many different resources. Relational exchange takes into account the different types and methods of resource exchange that receive little attention in transaction-focused descriptions of marketing activity.

During the 1980s marketing researchers introduced ideas from several different academic areas to marketing. For example, social exchange theory was borrowed from social psychology to describe the relationships characterized by

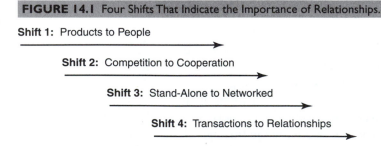

FIGURE 14.1 Four Shifts That Indicate the Importance of Relationships.

Shift 1: Products to People

Shift 2: Competition to Cooperation

Shift 3: Stand-Alone to Networked

Shift 4: Transactions to Relationships

different levels of power, dependence, and uncertainty. In addition, transactions cost analysis was adapted from its economics base to explain patterns of relational interactions between participants in business exchanges.

Despite different approaches to the study of relationships and their impact on marketing practice, a shared characteristic is that relationships provide value to partners in ways that are less readily attained without the interaction. Three primary sources of value in relationships are (1) decreased costs to carry out desired transactions, (2) decreased uncertainties about the outcomes that will result from a transaction, and (3) decreased opportunism, or the reduced likelihood that a partner will carry out environmental scanning to search for better opportunities.

A CONTINUUM OF RELATIONAL EXCHANGE

Exchange relationships can be described as a continuum. Relationships that take a transaction-oriented focus are at one end, while relationships that emphasize ongoing interaction between the partners are at the other extreme. This continuum is depicted in Figure 14.2.

The location of a relationship on the continuum depends on the extent to which the partners adopt a collaborative orientation toward the exchange. A **collaborative orientation** exists when an interaction between two parties indicates cooperative actions undertaken for mutual benefit. A collaborative orientation in a relationship suggests that both partners will be willing to make changes to accomplish relational goals and that each party anticipates future interactions.

The focus on collaborative orientation underscores the idea that the actual transaction is often not the most useful descriptor of a relationship. Many different types of exchanges occur from the time of the initial contact between the active agents until the final transaction of money and product. The number and nature of the exchanges may differ depending on the exchange agents and their objectives. For instance, in a B2C relationship, the exchange may involve a one-time purchase with limited interaction and relationship development. In contrast, in a B2B setting, the exchange process may be more complex and it may be repeated.

For many types of exchanges, the process by which the transaction is reached can be critically important. For instance, in a business-to-business exchange, characterized by high costs and high levels of asset specificity, the give-and-take nature of the exchange between the businesses may be an important determinant of the relationship, even though transactions may be infrequent.

FIGURE 14.2 Relationships Described as a Continuum of Exchange Processes.

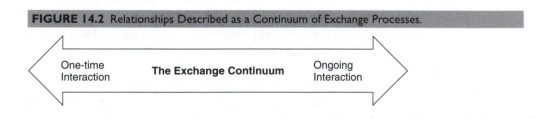

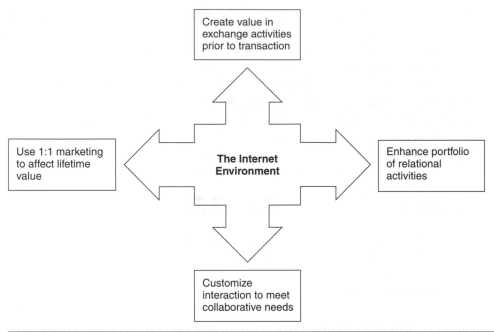

FIGURE 14.3 The Internet and Relational Exchange.

Digital Artifact 14.2

The average repeat customer at an online store spends 67 percent more in the third year of visiting the site than when shopping there in the first six months.

(*Source:* Nua Internet Surveys, citing Mainspring, 2000.)

Implications of the Continuum for Marketing and the Internet

Applying the relational exchange continuum to marketing and the Internet environment raises several issues for marketers. As we have already noted, the continuum suggests that all forms of exchange can affect the perceived value of a relationship. As a result, opportunities for creating value are not limited to the final transaction. For both partners in an exchange, value can be created through the transfer of all forms of resources, and not just products and money. For instance, the communication of product maintenance information and product updates from a marketer to a consumer via the Internet can enhance the value of the interaction between a marketer and a consumer. The consumer receives useful information, and the marketer benefits through the reduced costs of using the Internet to transfer the information. This implication illustrates the shift from a stand-alone to a networked perspective on exchange.

A second implication of the continuum is that the opportunities to add value to an exchange process increase as the interaction shifts from transactional to relational. An increase in the number of exchange-related activities and the extended duration of these activities provides both partners with multiple occasions and ways in which to provide and experience benefits of the interaction based on recognition of each other's abilities, interests, and needs. With the Internet, marketers and their customers can interact in near real-time to create exchange processes that are mutually advantageous. For example, consumers can acquire desired information about product features and performance, and marketers can obtain knowledge of consumer preferences, even in the absence of a transaction. This implication reflects the shift from a product focus to a people focus.

Another implication of the continuum is that different types of relational exchanges may have different benefits for the partners in the exchange (see Figure 14.3). We described the location of a relationship on the continuum in terms of the extent to which the interaction reflected a collaborative orientation. Although the Internet has received a lot of attention for its ability to promote the development of relationships, not all transactions require the same investment in the formation and maintenance of a one-to-one interaction. In addition, consumers may differ in the importance they place on developing an ongoing relationship with a marketer for a particular product. The difference in types of relational exchanges reflected by the continuum is related to the shift from competition to cooperation.

Movement along the continuum from transactions to relationships also suggests changes in the ways that marketers measure the value of exchange. An emphasis on transactions means that value is measured in market share, or how many consumers in a targeted market buy a product. With a relational, or 1:1 focus, the emphasis shifts to share-of-consumer, or how loyal the consumer is to a particular company or product. This shift is assessed by considering the life-time value of a customer. **Life-time value (LTV)** is the total amount of profits, discounted over time, that will result from sales to a customer.

LTV provides a summary measure, in dollars, of relationship value. In the next section, we will look at different characteristics of relationships that can also be used to assess relationship value.

Assessing the Value of Relational Exchange

Researchers often describe relational exchange with behavioral and psychological characteristics. Behavioral characteristics are the observable outcomes of interaction. In contrast, psychological characteristics are the unobservable measures that reflect the partner's perceptions of a relationship.

Behavioral Characteristics of Relational Exchange

With behavioral characteristics, we can describe a relationship in terms of the number of times that the partners have completed transactions, the frequency with which the partners interact, and the types of activities that each partner has carried out in order to facilitate the interaction. For example, in a business-to-consumer relationship, the seller might create a database to keep track of a customer's preferences.

In a business-to-business relationship, a buyer might adjust a requested delivery schedule to accommodate the production capabilities of a valued supplier.

Psychological Characteristics of Relational Exchange

Three psychological descriptors of relationships are satisfaction, trust, and commitment. Research results suggest that these measures are related to perceptions of relationship value. **Satisfaction** is defined as the overall evaluation of the experiences related to the purchase and consumption of a product over time.[2] **Trust** is exhibited as willingness to rely on an exchange partner, based on perceptions of the partner's reliability and integrity.[3] **Commitment** is defined as a lasting desire to maintain a valued relationship.[4]

Satisfaction, trust, and commitment often affect the link between components of a consumer's attitude toward a product or a company and future intentions toward consuming a product from the company. Researchers have demonstrated that these mediating effects of satisfaction, trust, and commitment are influenced by the collaborative orientation of the partner in the relational exchange. In general, satisfaction is more closely related to intentions to conduct future exchanges when the collaborative orientation is weak. When the collaborative orientation is strong, trust and commitment become more influential than satisfaction.

We can use behavioral and psychological characteristics of relationships, in conjunction with the concepts from the relational exchange continuum, to consider ways in which the ability to foster relational development might differ in B2C and B2B exchanges.

Differences Between B2C and B2B Relationships

Similar to B2C interactions, B2B interactions have a superordinate goal of effecting a transaction. As we saw in Chapter 13, however, the exchange processes exhibit several key differences. First, business-to-business transactions may be subject to greater time constraints than most marketer-consumer transactions. Business customers may have a specific task that can be accomplished in a desired time frame only with the purchase of a particular product. In addition, they may have a clear sense of product need based on multiple past purchase experiences.

The higher incidence of repeat purchases illustrates a second difference between the two types of exchange relationships: the likelihood of developing an ongoing exchange relationship may often be greater for business-to-business situations than for business-to-consumer situations. As a result, B2B interactions may tend to be more relational than B2C relationships, which may tend to emphasize a transactional approach to exchange.

The process of effecting a business-to-business transaction may often be more complex than the process for completing a business-to-consumer transaction. More steps may be needed to obtain approval for a transaction, to assess the quality of

---

[2]Based on Anderson, Fornell, and Lehmann (1994).
[3]Based on Moorman, Deshpande, and Zaltman (1993) and Morgan and Hunt (1994).
[4]Based on Moorman, Deshpande, and Zaltman (1993).

the transaction, and to document the execution of the transaction. The increased complexity of B2B exchanges may also mean the inclusion of more people in the decision-making process. These characteristics—increased activities and participants—suggest that the impact of the Internet on the development of relational exchange is best examined using psychological indicators of value for B2C exchanges, but behavioral indicators of value for B2B exchanges.

In the next two sections, we will use the concepts of the relational exchange continuum, sources of value, and ways to assess value to consider ways that the Internet can be used to foster relational exchange in B2C and B2B interactions.

BUILDING BUSINESS-TO-CONSUMER RELATIONSHIPS WITH THE INTERNET

In this section, we will consider the effect of the Internet on relational exchange between marketers and consumers. We will examine ways in which the Internet facilitates or inhibits the value created by the interaction between exchange partners. To illustrate the effect of the Internet on value creation, we consider the decision process that initiates the exchange in three stages: prepurchase, purchase, and post-purchase (see Figure 14.4). Although the Internet can, in many ways, help or harm value creation, for the sake of clarity, we focus on one value source in each decision stage: satisfaction for prepurchase processes, trust for purchase processes, and commitment for post-purchase processes.

Prepurchase: Search and Satisfaction

Researchers who study consumer decision making have found that satisfaction with a decision is related to perceptions of confidence in the processes for making the decision. As we learned in Chapter 3, processes for making a decision include the ways information is acquired, the amount of information obtained, and the strategy used to evaluate the information.

As a content and communication resource, the Internet provides consumers with a great deal of information and the opportunity to ask marketers for even

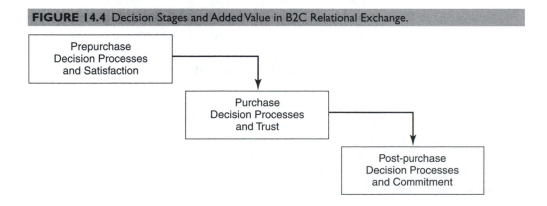

FIGURE 14.4 Decision Stages and Added Value in B2C Relational Exchange.

more. From a marketer's perspective, the task is to determine how to facilitate a customer's search and evaluation processes. In an online environment, search costs may be reduced by the ease with which the online environment can be used to obtain information from different vendors. A side effect of reduced search cost may be a significant increase in the numbers of sources returned by a general search. As a result, the consumer may encounter increased evaluation costs. These evaluation costs may be higher than those experienced in offline situations, given the amount of information. In addition, vendors may provide information in different forms, increasing the complexity of integrating the acquired information for evaluation.

Characteristics of Software Agents for Search and Evaluation

Marketers can use Internet-based **software agents** to aid consumers with information search and evaluation. These agents can range from simplistic programs that take only a few keystrokes to complete a search task, all the way to sophisticated tools that seem to have minds of their own. Software agents can be described with three key characteristics: (1) **agency,** or the extent to which they can operate independently of the user; (2) **intelligence,** or the extent to which the agent's actions reflect an ability to build a knowledge base; and (3) **mobility,** the extent to which the agent can travel the Internet from computer to computer.

Agency means that the software tool has the ability to work autonomously, without the user's presence. Software agents can reduce search costs because they serve as a stand-in for the user, by representing the user's interests in a search task. For example, a software agent can be sent to complete a search for prices available on the Internet for a particular model of car. The consumer specifies the type of car, and the price criterion, and the agent conducts the search.

Intelligence refers to the agent's ability to incorporate knowledge of the consumer's preferences in its actions. In addition, intelligence is related to the amount of learning that an agent exhibits. Some simple forms of agents operate on sets of specified rules (e.g., search online dealers for a Ford Taurus; find the ten cheapest offers). Other agents can learn consumer's preferences, and then carry out search actions that match this knowledge with knowledge of other users' preferences. These agents are called **collaborative filtering agents** or **recommender systems.** For instance, Firefly, an agent used by Amazon.com, can keep track of what a customer orders, look for other customers who purchased the same book, see what else they purchased, and then make a recommendation back to the customer.

The ability to conduct effective searches depends on the mobility of the agent (Figure 14.5). Some software agents are designed to run on a single computer, either the customer/client or the marketer/server. In contrast, other agents can roam from computer to computer, gathering information and interacting with other agents. Although increased mobility has advantages in terms of a wider base for collecting information, it comes with costs due to potential security hazards.

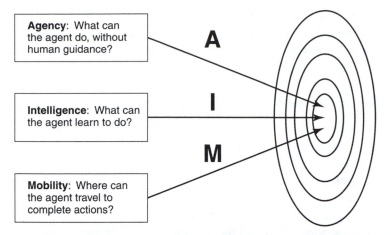

FIGURE 14.5 Characteristics of Software Agents.

Types of Software Agents

The effects of agents on marketing can be seen by looking at three types of software agents: search engines, intelligent agents, and scripting agents. Search engines facilitate information acquisition, while intelligent agents and scripting agents can influence search and evaluation.

Search Engines   Search engines are simple software agents that operate based on opportunistic discoveries of keyword matches. Search engines such as those available at Yahoo! or AltaVista reduce the costs of information search. It would be impossible for a consumer to visit or find every relevant site on the Internet using a manual process.

Although they can reduce search costs, current search engines (as well as those available in the near future) also present substantial challenges to consumers. Even well-refined searches often result in an unmanageable number of hits. A large list of hits may result in information overload and create time pressure for the consumer. To help manage this complexity, most search engines order the hits in a ranking scheme. Of course, most consumers do not know and cannot control the criteria for determining the relative rankings. In addition, search engines only index a fraction of the Internet, a fact that can create uncertainty about whether all the appropriate information is available.

Intelligent Agents   An intelligent agent is a software tool that can act as a proxy for the user in the online environment. An agent can carry out tasks such as actively gathering information based on its interpretation of the user's interests, bidding in an online auction according to the user's preferences, and completing online transactions. Search engines and intelligent agents can both provide the user with decision information. In contrast to a search engine, which only provides information from one indexing process, an intelligent agent can conduct a search with several engines, and then filter the search results to provide the user with only the hits that appear frequently. A search engine leaves the user with the task of visiting the sites, evaluating the information available, and then making a decision based on visiting all of the sites. The intelligent agent can visit many sites, extract the relevant information, compare information between sites, select the best alternative, and effect the transaction for the decision maker, all in accord with its interpretation of the user's interests.

Task Scripting   A different form of decision support is provided by the ability to automate complex sequences of tasks. Scripting software facilitates decision making by augmenting, rather than by replacing, human information processing ability. A **scripting agent** allows a user to group a sequence of operations together as a single executable task for repeated execution. For instance, a consumer could use a scripting agent to automate a search for auctions of 1962 Chatty Cathy dolls. The script could be programmed to find the auctions and initiate user bidding, stopping when an auction is won or a price limit is reached.

Demand and Decision Agents

Each of the three types of software agents can be used by marketers and by consumers. The purpose for which they are used, however, may be quite different. We can classify an agent as either a demand or a decision agent, depending on who is using it. Agents that operate in the seller's interest are **demand agents.** Demand agents can present information about products and services to search engines and in response to user requests for information. Agents that operate on behalf of the customer are **decision agents.**

The extent to which these agents foster relational exchange may be determined by the ability of the agents to interact with each other. For instance, a demand agent that can acquire and store data about the type of information requested by several decision agents can enable a marketer to update inventory, tailor product lines and products, and design targeted communications to consumers.

From the marketer's perspective, an intelligent agent that conducts search and evaluation activities for the consumer may increase brand loyalty at the expense of company loyalty. Wide searches for the best deals can increase the likelihood of opportunistic behavior on the consumer's part, undercutting the value of the relationship for one or both partners.

Digital Artifact 14.3

The most popular term searched for with Lycos in 1999: Pokemon.

(*Source:* **Lycos 50, and The Internet Index, #26.**)

Purchase: Transactions and Trust

In Chapter 2, we characterized the marketing process as a series of exchanges between active agents. These exchange activities can be viewed as subgoals to a larger goal of making a transaction—actually trading the good or service for money or for some other item of acceptable value. The Internet provides marketers and consumers with new ways to effect transactions, including new forms of payment and of product delivery. Consumers' perceptions of the risk involved with these methods and their level of trust in the marketer's ability to deliver the good are key factors in their decision to complete a transaction. As a result, it is necessary to know how different characteristics of a transaction situation are related to the issues that will influence the behavior of any partner in a transaction.

Transferring Payment on the Internet

Transactions can be described in terms of the expectations people have about the general characteristics of payment systems, and of the benefits of these systems. In addition, transactions can be described by the specific methods for exchanging a product or service for money. General characteristics of a payment system include authentication, confidentiality, and integrity.

Authentication   **Authentication** simply means that each party in a transaction is able to verify that the other party is who he or she claims to be. Even though this concept may seem simple, it can often be difficult to put into practice. Consider a face-to-face transaction, such as buying jeans in a mall store. You can verify the vendor's authenticity by dint of being in the store. The vendor can verify your authenticity by requesting some form of identification, typically your driver's license. Now consider an Internet purchase. Neither party can verify the other's authenticity in the same manner. Of course, this situation occurs in many transactions. For example, when we place orders over the phone, neither party is able to verify identity.

Advances in technology development are improving options for authentication. Some methods of authentication that are presently available include biometrics, smart cards, and digital certificates. As the name hints, **biometrics** authenticate user identity by matching a biological indicator, such as a fingerprint, a voiceprint, or even a retinal scan, to a previously stored image. **Smart cards** contain computer chips that store personal and unique identifying information. As with biometrics, authentication is based on matching; when scanned by a card reader, the information on the smart card must match stored information on the computer. Digital certificates take smart cards a step farther. A **digital certificate** is an encrypted file, protected by a password. The file contains information for user identification, much like a smart card. The encrypted file information is verified by a **certificate authority,** who creates the digital certificate.

Confidentiality   The second requirement of a payment system is **confidentiality.** Purchasers expect that the financial information they provide to a marketer will be made available only to people who have an appropriate need to know the information. For instance, your credit card number may be taken from an Internet order form and transmitted to the institution that manages your card, in order to receive payment.

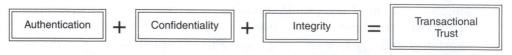

FIGURE 14.6 Trust in Transactions: Goals for Payment Systems.

Integrity   The third expectation of a payment system is **integrity.** The buyer expects that the features of the transaction will be implemented as agreed; that is, the buyer will receive the product ordered, and the seller will charge the quoted or listed price, unless specific exceptions have been discussed and accepted. Suppose you place an order, using your credit card, for a pair of Tough-hide jeans, and the selling price is $26.99 with tax and shipping included. You expect to receive not only the Tough-hide jeans, but also a credit card statement that reflects a charge of $26.99, rather than a different amount.

In contrast to authentication and confidentiality, for which there are technical ways to fulfill customers' expectations, integrity is based on consumers' perceptions. For offline companies who develop an online presence, a favorable prior reputation and history may reduce consumer concerns with online shopping. For new companies, however, marketers must manage the signals that their transactions capabilities send to consumers to create a basis for trust through integrity. Figure 14.6 illustrates the connection of the expectations in a payment system.

In an Internet-based transaction, the extent to which the buyer believes that the general expectations are met may depend on characteristics of the selling entity. Among these characteristics are company reputation, brand image, and company longevity. In addition, a buyer's past experiences with the company may also serve to reduce perceptions of risk about the transaction, despite a brief company history or an unknown reputation.

Trust and Transactions

Expectations of authentication, confidentiality, and integrity underscore the importance of being able to assure consumers in the Internet exchange environment of privacy and security. Being able to protect access to information during its transmission is a necessary precursor to insuring privacy. If it is possible for someone to gain access to financial or personal data, either while it is being transmitted through the Internet or after it is stored in an online database, then privacy has been compromised by weaknesses in security.

Privacy and security are related to trust. The development of trust in the exchange environment is important to exchange partners because it may increase the likelihood of completing a transaction. In addition, trust may enhance the buyer's satisfaction with the transaction, which may influence positive relationship development in situations with a brief history of relational exchange, or for consumers with low collaborative orientations.

When little is known about an online vendor, consumers often use seals of approval as heuristics for assessing trustworthiness. The AICPA/CICA's WebTrust service assesses Web sites to ensure that they meet established standards for protecting transactions and information. When a site passes the examination by a trained CPA, it receives a WebTrust seal. When clicked, the seal (shown in Figure 14.7) provides consumers with access to the examination report. Other organizations that provide related services include TRUSTe and BBBOnline.

Security and privacy issues must be addressed in order to create trust in the seller's ability to protect the information transmitted by the buyer. Trust, however, is not limited to the ability of the marketer to meet buyers' expectations about aspects of the final transactions of money for goods. Building trust by creating interactions that demonstrate reliability and integrity can add value to a relationship at any point in the exchange process. The content, channel, and communication capabilities of the Internet provide marketers with ways to create, manage, and monitor consumers' beliefs and expectations about product and company performance.

Post-Purchase: Complaints and Commitment

Recall that commitment is based on the belief that a partner's actions demonstrate reliability and integrity. These beliefs are often based on the match between expectations and actual experience. When a consumer's expectations are matched or exceeded by post-purchase experience, satisfaction and trust may lead to further interaction with the seller. When expectations are not met, future interaction becomes less likely. (This notion works in the other direction, too. For instance, marketers are often reluctant to accept a personal check from a customer who has written one or more checks on an inadequate bank balance in the past.)

Source: Reproduced with permission of AICPA/CICA.[5] Copyright © 2000. All rights reserved.

FIGURE 14.7 Seals of Approval Encourage Trust for New Shoppers.

---

[5]The CPA WebTrust seal of assurance is a graphical representation intended to indicate a Web site's compliance with the WebTrust Principles and Criteria and is produced herein for illustrative purposes only.

Internet Resources and Post-Purchase Interaction

The Internet creates opportunities and challenges for managing relationships with consumers after the transaction. As we have already noted, customers with high lifetime value to a company are an important reason for managing post-purchase processes. As a content resource, the Internet can be used to provide general product information, such as usage tips, that add value for consumers. Marketers can also provide information targeted to particular customers. For instance, a recall notice on a specific model of a product can be addressed only to customers with that model, thus influencing perceived integrity and reliability by using the Internet as a channel resource. As a communication resource, the Internet serves as a **response device,** or a means for obtaining feedback about the product experience from the consumer.

Suppose that the feedback is not positive; a consumer has a complaint. Effective complaint management is important for fostering relational exchange. Researchers have shown that complaint handling is related to trust and commitment. Poor complaint management harms trust and commitment, particularly in newly developed relationships. Even a long and positive prior history with a company cannot overcome poor complaint management. A positive history of relational exchange reduces the effects of poor complaint management on commitment, but it is not enough to keep the consumer's trust undiminished.

The need to manage consumer dissatisfaction increases when we consider that consumers can voice their dissatisfaction to other consumers. The power of word-of-mouth means that factors that diminish satisfaction, trust, and commitment are not limited in their impact to consumers with direct negative experience. This concern is magnified in the online environment, in which dissatisfied consumers can create Web sites to provide forums for airing concerns and outrage. This possibility underscores the importance of the need to understand and manage complaints effectively, using the Internet.

Using Justice Theory and the Internet for Complaint Management

We can describe complaint management and consider the effect of the Internet as a tool for complaint management with justice theory. **Justice theory** provides a framework that integrates complaint management processes with the psychological measures of relational exchange. In a nutshell, justice is related to the appropriateness of decisions. If we think of complaint management as a process, we can see that several different decisions are made, based on the interaction between the consumer and the marketer. For instance, decisions are made about the processes for handling the complaint, the outcomes of the complaint process, and the nature of the interpersonal interactions. Justice theory considers these decisions as the dimensions of procedural justice, distributive justice, and interactional justice, respectively. Consumers evaluate the perceived justice associated with each type of decision to evaluate the quality of complaint handling. Figure 14.8 depicts these aspects of justice theory.

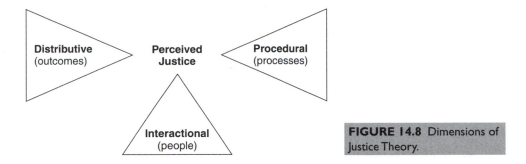

FIGURE 14.8 Dimensions of Justice Theory.

Procedural Justice and the Internet   Four aspects influence consumers' perceptions of **procedural justice:** (1) the ease with which a complaint can be made; (2) the flexibility of the complaint procedure; (3) the extent to which the consumer has control over the processes that result in an outcome; and (4) the efficiency of the complaint process, measured by convenience and speed.

For companies with an established offline presence, the Internet can provide an additional venue for placing a complaint, thus decreasing costs of traveling to a physical location, of waiting on hold by phone, or of writing and posting a letter, and increasing consumers' perceptions of control. Online customer service facilities that provide immediate confirmation of a compliant, as by automated e-mail, can also increase perceptions of efficiency. An appropriate infrastructure for accepting and responding to online complaints is critical, however, given the potential of the medium for decreasing interpersonal communications. For instance, an automated e-mail response that is not followed by timely and personalized action may be more harmful to consumers' perceptions of a company and its product than the absence of the online complaint capability. This result may occur when an automated, impersonal response effectively creates unmet expectations that the problem will be addressed. In this situation, a marketer is now faced with a consumer with two grievances: the initial complaint and a procedural complaint.

Distributive Justice and the Internet   **Distributive justice** is based on perceptions of outcome appropriateness. The basis for gauging whether an outcome was just may differ from situation to situation, and from consumer to consumer. For instance, for one consumer, simply being able to voice a complaint may suffice, while another consumer may require an apology, and yet another consumer may require an apology and compensation.

The type of outcome demanded often depends on the basis for dissatisfaction, or the reason for which expectations are believed to be unmet. Three bases for assessing distributive justice are (1) **distributive needs** (Did I get what I wanted/needed?); (2) **distributive equity** (Did I get what I deserved?); and (3) **distributive equality** (Did I get what other people got?).

Managing complaints based on needs requires marketers to understand the extent to which the actual experience deviated from expectations. We can think of this deviation in terms of costs. A dissatisfied consumer incurs costs not only from the consumption experience, but also from the complaint process. Building on the idea of using the Internet to increase the procedural efficiency to complain, we can see that the Internet can be used to reduce complaint costs, thus reducing the need-based sources of dissatisfaction for distributive justice.

Equity issues underscore the importance of prior experience for effective complaint management; knowing what you deserve implies a comparison to a similar previous experience. The Internet can be used to store customer profiles and purchase histories, as with cookies and online databases. Customer relationship management (CRM) software provides marketers with the means to collect and store data online about the customers' interactions with a company, a process known as **data warehousing.** By integrating and analyzing the stored data, through a process known as **data mining,** marketers can better match targeted offers to customer needs and expectations. Effective use of online consumer data can decrease the possibility for dissatisfaction based on a then-and-now mismatch in experience.

1:1 marketing with the Internet affects the equality basis for consumers' perceptions of distributive justice. Customized and personalized offerings that are delivered individually via the Internet can make it difficult for consumers to assess deviation from expectation based on others' experiences.

Suppose you go to a single price store in your local strip mall, where everything is $8. You pick out a shirt, and you go to the cashier. After waiting through a long line in which every one of the 16 people in front of you pays $8 plus tax for each item (remember, physical presence means sales taxes), you finally reach the counter. The cashier tells you that you owe $11 plus tax. Clearly, something is not fair; you saw what everyone else paid, and you know the store's pricing policy. If, however, you purchase the shirt from a Web site, on which prices fluctuate based on supply and demand, or on some other algorithm, the basis for comparison is more difficult.

The Internet also provides consumers with a forum for airing experiences that can serve as a basis for comparison. A consumer who has just negotiated a terrific deal on a product may post that experience and the tactics used on a bulletin board to other people with a similar interest. This situation creates new opportunities for comparison and perceived distributive injustice. The development of clear and defensible procedures for creating product offers can reduce the potential for postpurchase dissatisfaction, due to the outcome of the product experience and the complaint experience.

Interactional Justice and the Internet   **Interactional justice** is based on people's perceptions of the communication that occurred between the person complaining and the company representative. Even when a customer believes that procedures and outcomes were appropriate, a perception that the interpersonal communication was inappropriate can damage the quality of the complaint process. Bases for deciding whether the interaction was fair include politeness, effort, concern, and honesty.

With its lack of face-to-face communication, the Internet can be a difficult environment for positively influencing consumers' perceptions of interactions. For instance, we may often rely on signals such as body language and verbal intonation as nonverbal cues for politeness and concern. The Internet is better suited for communications that emphasize the content of the message, such as the description of the complaint process or possible outcomes, rather than its packaging.

For complaint situations in which an appropriate remedy is available and the processes for determining the outcome are clear-cut, interactional justice may be less important than distributive and procedural justice. When the processes and outcomes for a complaint situation are more ambiguous, however, the nature of the communication increases in importance. In these situations, a marketer can use the Internet to demonstrate effort and honesty. For instance, a timely response that provides a detailed, personalized understanding of the complaint connotes effort. A match between stated procedures and actions throughout the complaint management process conveys honesty.

Satisfaction, trust, and commitment are important factors for fostering B2C and B2B exchanges. As we saw earlier, however, the unique characteristics of B2B exchanges mean that we can use not only the psychological determinants of relationships, but also a set of behavioral aspects of relationships to consider ways to create value in ongoing B2B interactions.

Digital Artifact 14.4

Online shoppers often get no satisfaction. More than 50 percent of consumers who contact customer support do so for post-sales help. More than half of the questions by these consumers about returns and deliveries are not settled within 24 hours.

(*Source:* CyberAtlas, citing Greenfield Online, 2000.)

BUILDING BUSINESS-TO-BUSINESS RELATIONSHIPS WITH THE INTERNET

The Internet can provide value to both partners in a B2B exchange. In many instances, the ability to exchange information through Internet channels can speed up the transaction process, by making necessary information available to all involved parties simultaneously. In addition, the Internet may simplify the exchange process by eliminating the need for multiple forms of documentation and of means for storing transaction-related documentation. For instance, templates for ordering, for tracking inventory and distribution, and for invoicing customers can all be stored and maintained in a single digital electronic database. Similarly, histories of customer interactions can be readily stored and retrieved to streamline future use. Each of these features can increase the value of interaction for the exchange partners. We will look at the behavioral characteristics that define B2B exchanges, and at the ways in which the Internet can influence the development of these exchanges in the following sections.

Classifying B2B Relationships

As we have seen, many different types of relationships can exist to facilitate exchange. These relationships are formed to meet organizational goals and to address environmental challenges that can create uncertainty and dependence. In this section we will examine a framework for understanding B2B relationships. This framework, created by Cannon and Perreault, integrates market characteristics and situational factors with dimensions that describe behaviors in relational exchanges to develop a classification of B2B relationships.[6] We can use this framework to consider the implications of the Internet for fostering B2B relational exchanges.

Environmental Effects on Relationships

Business relationships are formed to manage challenges posed by aspects of the business environment. In the B2B environment, these challenges can stem from supply market characteristics or from situational characteristics. **Supply market characteristics** include the availability of alternative sources for products or product components and the **supply market dynamism,** or variability of change in supply sources. Availability and dynamism are broad market forces. In contrast, **situational characteristics** reflect the perspective of a single buyer in the market. Situational characteristics include supply complexity and supply importance. **Supply complexity** is the extent to which a buyer's needs are specific and complicated. **Supply importance** refers to the centrality of the supply to the buyer's objectives.

Dimensions of B2B Relationships

The types of relationships that companies may form to address environmental challenges are described with relationship connectors. **Relationship connectors** are "dimensions that reflect the behaviors and expectations of behavior in a particular buyer-seller relationship."[7] Relationship connectors are operational or structural. Operational connectors affect the processes for exchange, while structural connectors affect the forms of exchange. Operational connectors are (1) information exchange, (2) cooperative norms, and (3) operational linkages. Structural connectors are (1) legal bonds, and (2) adaptation by the buyer or the seller. Brief descriptions of these connectors are provided in Figure 14.9.

Relationship connectors describe the extent to which the partners in a B2B exchange are "connected." Self-reports of connector importance in a particular relationship are used to classify the relationship as more or less connected, relative to other forms of relationships.

---

[6]Joseph P. Cannon and William D. Perreault, Jr. "Buyer-Seller Relationships in Business Markets," *Journal of Marketing Research, 36* (1999), pp. 439–460.
[7]*Ibid,* p. 442.

Type	Description	Example
Information Exchange	Open communication of mutually useful information	Share product design specifications with suppliers
Cooperative Norms	Joint efforts to achieve shared and individual goals	Develop affiliate program (e.g., Amazon.com)
Operational Linkages	Merged routines and systems that facilitate organizational activities of both partners	Build extranets to include suppliers and distributors
Legal Bonds	Contractual agreements to specify responsibilities and activities of each partner	Formalize strategic alliances (e.g., AOL and Target ally to co-brand Target products and promote them via AOL)
Seller Adaptation	Alteration of process or product by seller to meet buyer needs	Change product design to meet user specifications (e.g., customizable CRM software)
Buyer Adaptation	Alteration of process or requirements by buyer to meet seller needs	Change company data-entry processes to make use of CRM software

FIGURE 14.9 Relationship Connectors Reflect Behavior and Expectations.

A Classification of B2B Relationships

Relationships can be classified into types that reflect different levels of each of the relationship connectors. Cannon and Perreault describe eight relationships with nicknames that capture the nature of the exchange. These relationships—from least connected to most connected—are (1) basic buying and selling, (2) bare bones, (3) contractual, (4) custom supply, (5) cooperative systems, (6) collaborative, (7) mutually adaptive, and (8) customer is king. The role of the relationship connectors in each type of relationship is provided in Figure 14.10.

The types of relationships are related to market and situational characteristics. For instance, when the market supply is not variable, and when supply alternatives are readily available, exchange needs can be met with basic buying and selling, bare bones, and contractual relationships. Cooperative systems, characterized by operational links, also facilitate exchange, as by adding value through customized logistics systems.

In contrast, when the market supply is dynamic, and when supply alternatives are limited, more closely connected relationships provide business buyers with ways to manage the difficulties of procurement. These relationships, such as the mutually adaptive and the customer is king interactions, emphasize operational *and* structural connectors. The links between market and situational characteristics and relationship types are depicted in Figure 14.11.

Internet Implications for B2B Relational Exchange

We can use the framework developed by Cannon and Perreault to assess the effect of the Internet on B2B relationships. By extending the market and situational characteristics to encompass the Internet, we can consider ways that B2B relationships

	Information Exchange	Cooperative Norms	Operational Linkages	Legal Bonds	Seller Adaptation	Buyer Adaptation
Basic Buying and Selling	High	High	Low	Low	Low	Low
Bare Bones	Low	Low	Moderate	Low	Moderate	Low
Contractual Transaction	Low	Low	Moderate	High	Moderate	Low
Custom Supply	Moderate	Moderate	Moderate	Moderate	High	Moderate
Cooperative Situations	Moderate	High	High	Low	Moderate	Low
Collaborative	High	High	Moderate	Moderate	Moderate	Moderate
Mutually Adaptive	High	Moderate	High	Low	High	High
Customer Is King	High	High	High	High	High	Low

FIGURE 14.10 Relationship Profiles Based on Relationship Connectors.

Geometric Representation of Rotated Discriminant Function Solution for Relationship Types

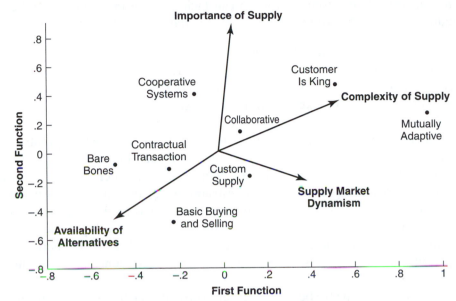

Source: Reprinted with permission from the *Journal of Marketing Research,* published by the American Marketing Association, Joseph P. Cannon and William D. Perreault, Jr., Vol. 36, November 1999, p. 453.

FIGURE 14.11 Relationships Enable Partners to Manage Environmental Challenges.

may be influenced as business partners react to the environment. In addition, we can use the classification of relationships to understand how business can operate proactively, leveraging the resources of the Internet to create relationships that optimize business goals for both partners.

Reactive Relational Exchange

The Internet can alter the impact of supply market and situational influences on B2B exchanges by changing the costs and benefits associated with different types of relationships. For instance, in considering supply market effects, the global communication capability of the Internet increases buyers' ability to locate alternative sources of supply. Such an effect decreases the need to foster relationships based on reducing supply uncertainty. In addition, the ability to communicate in near real-time can influence variability in supply sources. In some cases, communication can increase the unpredictability of supply, as when electronic hubs conceal the identity of participants and the amount of available supply. This outcome would indicate a need to solidify a relationship to reduce uncertainty. In other cases, increased communication can enhance buyers' ability to gauge supply availability and price, thus decreasing the need to depend on a sole supplier.

For situational characteristics, the ability to communicate needs and to interact to clarify those needs via the Internet can influence supply complexity. For instance, being able to send digital descriptions of parts, including verbal and graphic specifications, to potential suppliers may result in interactions that simplify the product. Alternatively, digital communication can facilitate the location of suppliers with qualifications that make them better able to adapt to fill the buyer's needs.

Proactive Relational Exchange

As an environment for B2B exchange, the Internet can affect the value of different relationships for its participants. As a set of resources for relational exchange, however, the Internet makes it possible for businesses to operate proactively, using the Internet to encourage forms of relationship connectors that create ongoing interactions. For example, interactivity via the Internet can foster operational connections that increase structural connections. Through increased ease of informational exchange, buyers can learn of constraints on seller abilities, and adjust planned activities to reflect those constraints (e.g., pick an alternative delivery schedule, find a different supplier). In this instance, increased information exchange increases buyer adaptation, which perpetuates the relationship. Sellers can tailor products and product offers, customizing and personalizing them to better meet the needs of individual buyers, potentially increasing dependence and switching costs for the buyer.

The Internet can also be used to develop operational linkages. For instance, outside intranets and extranets provide infrastructures to facilitate B2B exchanges. In addition, the ability to share information through online databases can streamline processes and solidify interactions. For example, a supplier can create a shared database facility that monitors a buyer's inventory and makes the information available to the supplier. When the inventory is low, an automated rebuy is initiated. Benefits to the buyer include reduced costs to monitor inventory and reduced costs to negotiate with alternative suppliers. A potential downside to the arrangement for the buyer is the lost opportunity to identify better deals.

Cautions for B2B Relational Exchange

As we have seen, the Internet creates challenges and opportunities for B2B relationships. It is important to recognize that businesses often form several relationships, that these relationships may take different forms, and the assortment of relationships must be strategically managed so that the complete set of relationships achieves the marketers' objectives. As a result, the impact of the Internet on any relationship in the set can affect the entire set in terms of relational performance.

One effect of the Internet is to create the possibility for new relationships. In Chapter 13, we learned about the growth of electronic hubs as online market intermediaries. These hubs influence market supply characteristics. E-hubs can shift the partnership arrangement from between a seller and a buyer to the market maker and the buyer. In this situation, marketers must recognize the potential for decreased commitment to the producer and increased commitment to the intermediary.

RELATIONAL EXCHANGE: BEYOND MARKETING

The behavioral characteristics that can be used to describe B2B relational exchange with the Internet often entail changes to business practices that extend beyond the marketing function. For example, creating operational linkages to foster a B2B relationship may necessitate the introduction of new business structures and processes, such as those described in Chapter 4, to integrate the operations of people in several functional areas of a business.

Internet software applications that emphasize customer relationship management (CRM) and enterprise relationship management (ERM) provide businesses with the ability to create operational linkages using intranets and extranets, which connect the activities of previously separate spheres of influence. The growing popularity and effect of these integrative business applications emphasize the importance of marketing activity for effective implementation of strategies for electronic commerce.

Digital Artifact 14.5

Effective customer relationship management is related to return on sales, accounting for 50 percent of the variation in profits in surveyed communications and chemicals companies.

(*Source:* **Marketing, March 9, 2000, citing Anderson Consulting.**)

Chapter Summary

In previous chapters, we focused on the formation of relationships between participants in the Internet exchange environment. In this chapter, we examined the impact of the Internet for developing and maintaining relational exchange. Relational exchange was described as an ongoing interaction between partners that provides value for each partner.

The Internet has been touted as a force that will enable the development of relationships between buyers and sellers, and that will increase the value of relational exchange to each partner. This increased emphasis on relationship development was described as the outgrowth of four changes to the way that marketers view exchange-related behaviors. These shifts were (1) from products to people, (2) from competition to cooperation, (3) from stand-alone to networked, and (4) from transactions to relationships.

We considered the effect of these shifts on relationship development with a continuum of relational exchange, anchored by a transactional orientation at one end and a relational orientation at the other end. This continuum suggests that the Internet can affect the value of relational exchange by (1) enabling different resource exchanges, (2) creating new opportunities for interaction in exchange processes, and (3) emphasizing the need to understand the collaborative orientation of both partners in an exchange.

Building on the idea of added value through relational exchange, we next examined the measurement of value in relationships. We looked at behavioral characteristics (e.g., number of transactions, types of interaction activities) and psychological characteristics (i.e., satisfaction, trust, commitment). Differences between B2C relationships and B2B relationships suggest that psychological dimensions better reflect value in B2C relationships, while behavioral dimensions better reflect value in B2B relationships.

Tactics for the strategic development of B2C and B2B relationships were discussed in separate sections. To illustrate how marketers can create relational value in B2C exchanges, we considered the role of the Internet at each stage of the decision process, focusing on satisfaction through information search, trust through transactional security, and commitment through effective complaint management.

For B2B exchanges, we adopted a framework that uses environmental characteristics and behavioral characteristics to create a classification of relationship types. This framework served as the basis for assessing the impact of the Internet on the types of B2B relationships that occur. We also applied the framework concept of relationship connectors, such as operational linkages and information exchange, to consider strategies for fostering B2B relationships. The effect on business structures of the increased connectedness via the Internet was addressed with a general discussion of the relation between marketing and electronic commerce.

REVIEW SECTION

Key Terms

- 1:1 marketing
- accountability
- addressability
- collaborative orientation
- life-time value (LTV)
- satisfaction
- trust
- commitment
- software agents
- agency
- intelligence
- mobility
- collaborative filtering agent

- recommender system
- scripting agent
- demand agent
- decision agent
- authentication
- biometrics
- smart cards
- digital certificate
- certificate authority
- confidentiality
- integrity
- response device
- justice theory
- procedural justice

- distributive justice
- distributive needs
- distributive equity
- distributive equality
- data warehousing
- data mining
- interactional justice
- supply market characteristics
- supply market dynamism
- situational characteristics
- supply complexity
- supply importance
- relationship connectors

Review Questions

1. What are the primary objectives of 1:1 marketing?
2. Describe the four fundamental shifts in perspectives on relational exchange.

3. Compare and contrast cooperation and competition.
4. Describe the continuum of exchange processes.
5. How do marketers assess the value of a relational exchange? Consumers?
6. Discuss the importance of satisfaction, trust, and commitment at different stages of the purchasing process.
7. Review the differences between B2C and B2B exchange relationships.
8. What three characteristics define software agents?
9. Discuss the advantages and disadvantages of different types of software agents.
10. What three characteristics are essential to a successful payment system?
11. How do payment systems in the marketspace differ from those in the marketplace? How are they similar?
12. Explain the ideas behind justice theory and the different dimensions of justice.
13. What functions are provided by CRM software? How are these activities conducted?
14. What are operational connectors in B2B exchanges? Structural connectors?
15. What are the benefits of proactive relational exchange as opposed to reactive relational exchange?

Thinking Points

1. Consider the types of relationships that can exist between consumers, marketers, policy makers, and technology developers. What are some implications of different stages of relationship development—of any two perspectives—for marketing? That is, how might an early stage relationship between, for example, consumers and policy makers in the Internet environment affect marketing activity differently than a more developed relationship with a longer history of interaction?

2. How does the Internet contribute to an increasing emphasis on cooperation between businesses as a way to compete? What characteristics of the Internet facilitate cooperation? What characteristics facilitate competition?

3. The concept of collaborative orientation suggests that people differ in their perceptions of the desirability of developing relationships. Different products may also affect the desirability of a relational orientation. Does the Internet change the benefits of relational exchange for consumers? For marketers?

4. When difficulty in finding and comparing products is reduced by Internet features, consumer loyalty may shift from companies/retailers to specific brands. How can marketers use the Internet to build relationships with consumers that create loyalty to the vendor, rather than to the brand?

5. Building on the previous question, what does the potential shift in loyalty focus (i.e., from vendor to brand) imply for the structure of businesses on the Internet? That is, what type of business model would you recommend?

6. Why are behavioral measures of relational exchange more appropriate for a B2B exchange than psychological measures? What characteristics of the setting (i.e., B2B versus B2C) influence the measurement of satisfaction, trust, and commitment in each type of exchange?

7. In B2C relational exchange, how can the Internet be used to create satisfaction, trust, and commitment in each of the decision stages (i.e., prepurchase, purchase, and post-purchase)?

8. In B2B relational exchange, which combinations of behavioral characteristics most clearly reflect the importance of satisfaction to exchange partners? Which combinations reflect a stronger importance of trust? Of commitment?

Suggested Readings

1. "Enhancing Customer Relationships with the Internet," in *Business-to-Business Internet Marketing,* by Barry Silverstein (Gulf Breeze, FL: Maximum Press, 1998), pp. 294–324.

2. *The One-to-One Future: Building Relationships One Customer at a Time,* by Don Peppers and Martha Rodgers (New York: Doubleday, 1993).

3. "Paying Up: Payment Systems for Digital Commerce," by Stephen D. Crocker and Russell B. Stevenson Jr. In *The Future of the Electronic Marketplace,* edited by Derek Leebaert (Cambridge, MA: The MIT Press, 1998), pp. 303–334.

4. "Building Consumer Trust Online," by Donna L. Hoffman, Thomas P. Novak, and Marcos Peralta. *Communications of the ACM, 42,* 4 (April 1999), pp. 80–85.

5. "Agents That Reduce Workload and Information Overload," by Pattie Maes. *Communications of the ACM, 37,* 7 (July 1994), pp. 31–40.

Bibliography

Abrams, Marc, ed., *World Wide Web: Beyond the Basics*, Upper Saddle River, NJ: Prentice-Hall, Inc., 1998.

Achrol, Ravi S., "Evolution of the Marketing Organization: New Forms for Turbulent Environments," *Journal of Marketing, 55* (October 1991), 77–93.

Alba, Joseph et al., "Interactive Home Shopping: Consumer, Retailer, and Manufacturer Incentives to Participate in Electronic Marketplaces," *Journal of Marketing, 61* (July 1997), 38–53.

Anderson, Paul F., "Marketing, Strategic Planning, and the Theory of the Firm," *Journal of Marketing, 46* (Spring 1982), 15–26.

Anderson, Eugene W., Claes Fornell, and Donald R. Lehmann, "Customer Satisfaction, Market Share, and Profitability: Findings from Sweden," *Journal of Marketing, 58* (July 1994), pp. 53–66.

"AOL, Target in Marketing Alliance," *Yahoo News, Reuters* (June 2000).

Azar, Beth, "Online Experiments: Ethically Fair or Foul?" *Monitor on Psychology, 31*, no. 4 (April 2000), 50–52.

Bakos, J. Yannis, "A Strategic Analysis of Electronic Marketplaces," *MIS Quarterly* (September 1991), 295–310.

Benjamin, Robert, and Rolf Wigand, "Electronic Markets and Virtual Value Chains on the Information Superhighway," *Sloan Management Review* (Winter 1995), 62–72.

Bettman, James R., and Pradeep Kakkar, "Effects of Information Presentation Format on Consumer Information Acquisition Strategies," *Journal of Consumer Research, 3* (March 1977), 233–239.

Bezjian-Avery, Alexa, Bobby Calder, and Dawn Iacobucci, "New Media Interactive Advertising vs. Traditional Advertising," *Journal of Advertising Research* (July–August 1998), 23–32.

Biocca, Frank, "Communication Within Virtual Reality: Creating a Space for Research," *Journal of Communication, 42*, no. 4 (Autumn 1992), 5–22.

Blattberg, Robert, and John Deighton, "Interactive Marketing: Exploiting the Age of Addressability," *Sloan Management Review* (Fall 1991), 5–14.

Bloom, Paul N., George R. Milne, and Robert Adler, "Avoiding Misuse of New Information Technologies: Legal and Societal Considerations," *Journal of Marketing, 58* (January 1994), 98–110.

Canter, David, Rod Rivers, and Graham Storrs, "Characterizing User Navigation Through Complex Data Structures," *Behaviors and Information Technology, 4*, no. 2 (1985), 93–102.

Cataudella, Joe, Ben Sawyer, and Dave Greely, *Creating Stores on the Web*, Berkeley, CA: Peachpit Press, 1998.

Chase, Larry, *Essential Business Tactics for the Net*, New York: John Wiley & Sons, Inc., 1998.

Cook, Don Lloyd, and Eloise Coupey, "Consumer Behavior and Unresolved Regulatory Issues in Electronic Marketing," *Journal of Business Research, 41* (1998), 231–238.

Comer, Douglas E., *Computer Networks and Internets*, Upper Saddle River, NJ: Prentice-Hall, Inc., 1997.

Coupey, Eloise, "Restructuring: Constructive Processing of Information Displays in Consumer Choice," *Journal of Consumer Research, 21* (June 1994), 83–99.

Davis, Jeffrey, ed., "B2B Boom," *Business 2.0* (September 1999), 84–124.

Davis, Jeffrey, ed., "The New eCommerce Engine: How It Works," *Business 2.0* (February 2000), 112–140.

Dennis, Alan R., Susan T. Kinney, and Yu-Ting Caisy Hung, "Gender Differences in the Effects of Media Richness," *Small Group Research, 30*, no. 4 (August 1999), 405–437.

Dillman, Don A., *Mail and Internet Surveys: The Tailored Design Method*, 2d ed., New York: John Wiley & Sons, Inc., 2000.

Dillman, Don A., and Donald M. Beck, "Information Technologies and Rural Development in the 1990s," *The Journal of State Government* (1991), 29–38.

Do, Orlantha et al., "Intelligent Agents and The Internet: Effects on Electronic Commerce and Marketing," *http://bold.coba.unr.edu/odie/paper.html*, 6 pages.

Duncan, Tom, and Sandra E. Moriarty, "A Communication-Based Marketing Model for Managing Relationships," *Journal of Marketing, 62*, no. 2 (April 1998), 1–13.

EBUSINESS, "501 Blues," *Business2.0* (January 2000), powered by Hire.com.

Foxall, Gordon R., and John R. Fawn, "An Evolutionary Model of Technological Innovation as a Strategic Management Process," *Technovation, 12*, no. 3 (April 1992), 191–202.

Foxman, Ellen R., and Paula Kilcoyne, "Information Technology, Marketing Practice, and Consumer Privacy: Ethical Issues," *Journal of Public Policy & Marketing, 12*, no. 1 (Spring 1993), 106–119.

Garbarino, Ellen, and Mark S. Johnson, "The Different Roles of Satisfaction, Trust, and Commitment in Customer Relationships," *Journal of Marketing, 63*, no. 2 (April 1999), 70–87.

Gardner, Donald G., Richard L. Dukes, and Richard Discenza, "Computer Use, Self-Confidence, and Attitudes: A Causal Analysis," *Computers in Human Behavior, 9* (1993), 427–440.

Gebauer, Judith, and Heike Schad, "Building an Internet-Based Workflow System—The Case of Lawrence Livermore National Laboratories' Zephyr Project," Fisher Center Working Paper 98-WP-1030 (April 1998).

Ghose, Sanjoy, and Wenyu Dou, "Interactive Functions and Their Impacts on the Appeal of Internet Presence Sites," *Journal of Advertising Research* (March–April 1998), 29–43.

Glazer, Rashi, "Marketing in an Information-Intensive Environment: Strategic Implications of Knowledge as an Asset," *Journal of Marketing*, 55 (October 1991), 1–19.

Glazer, Rashi, and Allen M. Weiss, "Marketing in Turbulent Environments: Decision Processes and the Time-Sensitivity of Information," *Journal of Marketing Research, XXX* (November 1993), 509–521.

Gray, Stephen, "In Virtual Fashion," *IEEE Spectrum* (February 1998), 18–25.

Grayson, Kent, and Tim Ambler, "The Dark Side of Long-Term Relationships in Marketing Services," *Journal of Marketing Research, 36*, no. 1 (February 1999), 132–141.

Gulati, Ranjay, and Jason Garino, "Get the Right Mix of Bricks and Clicks," *Harvard Business Review, 78*, no. 3 (May–June 2000), 107–114.

Ha, Louisa, and E. Lincoln James, "Interactivity Reexamined: A Baseline Analysis of Early Business Web Sites," *Journal of Broadcasting & Electronic Media, 42*, no. 4 (Fall 1998), 457–474.

Hafner, Katie, and Matthew Lyon, *Where Wizards Stay Up Late: The Origins of the Internet*, New York: Simon & Schuster, Inc., 1996.

Hahn, Robert W., and John A. Hird, "The Costs and Benefits of Regulation: Review and Synthesis," *Yale Journal on Regulation* (1991), 233–277.

Hammond, Kathy, Gil McWilliam, and Andrea Narholz Diaz, "Fun and Work on the Web: Differences in Attitudes Between Novices and Experienced Users," *Advances in Consumer Research, 25* (1998), 372–378.

Hance, Olivier, *Business and Law on the Internet*, New York: McGraw-Hill, 1996.

Hannon, Neal J., *The Business of the Internet*, Cambridge, MA: International Thomson Publishing, Course Technology, 1998.

Hanson, Ward, *Principles of Internet Marketing*, Cincinnati, OH: South-Western College Publishing, 2000.

Hauser, John R., Glen L. Urban, and Bruce D. Weinberg, "How Consumers Allocate Their Time When Searching for Information," *Journal of Marketing Research, XXX* (November 1993), 452–466.

Hesse, Bradford W., Carol M. Werner, and Irwin Altman, "Temporal Aspects of Computer-Mediated Communication," *Computers in Human Behavior, 4* (1988), 147–165.

Hirschman, Elizabeth, "People as Products: Analysis of a Complex Marketing Exchange," *Journal of Marketing, 51* (January 1987), 98–108.

Hoffman, Donna L., and Thomas P. Novak, *Marketing in Hypermedia Computer-Mediated Environments: Conceptual Foundations*, Working Paper No. 1 (Revised July 11, 1995), Project 2000: Research Program on Marketing in Computer-Mediated Environments.

Hoffman, Donna L., William D. Kalsbeek, and Thomas P. Novak, "Internet and Web Use in the United States: Baselines for Commercial Development," Project 2000 Working Paper (draft date: July 10, 1996).

Hollingshead, Andrea B., Joseph E. McGrath, and Kathleen M. O'Connor, "Group Task Performance and Communication Technology: A Longitudinal Study of Computer-Mediated Versus Face-to-Face Work Groups," *Small Group Research, 24*, no. 3 (August 1993), 307–333.

Hunt, Shelby D., and Robert M. Morgan, "Relationship Marketing in the Era of Network Competition," *Marketing Management, 3*, no. 1 (1994), 18–29.

Jain, Subhash C., "The Evolution of Strategic Marketing," *Journal of Business Research, 11* (December 1983), 409–425.

Kaplan, Steven, and Mohanbir Sawhney, "B2B E-Commerce Hubs: Toward a Taxonomy of Business Models," (December 1999), Working Paper.

Klein, Lisa R., "Evaluating the Potential of Interactive Media Through a New Lens: Search Versus Experience Goods," *Journal of Business Research, 41* (1998), 195–203.

Kleinmuntz, Don N., and David A. Schkade, *Cognitive Processes and Information Displays in Computer-Supported Decision Making: Implications for Research*, Faculty Working Paper No. 90-1625 (February 1990).

Korthauer, Ralph D., and Richard J. Koubek, "An Empirical Evaluation of Knowledge, Cognitive Style, and Structure upon the Performance of a Hypertext Task," *International Journal of Human-Computer Interaction, 6*, no. 4 (1994), 373–390.

Kosiur, David, *Understanding Electronic Commerce: How Online Commerce Can Grow Your Business*, Redmond, WA: Microsoft Press, 1997.

Kraut, Robert et al., "Social Impact of the Internet: What Does It Mean?" *Communications of the ACM, 41*, no. 12 (1998), 21–22.

Lamb, Charles W., Joseph F. Hair, Jr., and Carl McDaniel, *Principles of Marketing*, Cincinnati, OH: South-Western Publishing Co., 1992.

Lambkin, Mary, and George S. Day, "Evolutionary Processes in Competitive Markets: Beyond the Product Life Cycle, *Journal of Marketing, 53* (July 1989), 4–20.

Lea, Martin, and Russell Spears, "Computer-Mediated Communication, De-individuation and Group Decision-Making," *International Journal Management—Machine Studies, 34* (1991), 283–301.

Lee, Ho Geun, and Theodore H. Clark, "Impacts of the Electronic Marketplace on Transaction Cost and Market Structure," *International Journal of Electronic Commerce, 1*, no. 1 (Fall 1996), 127–149.

Lee, Ho Geun, and Theodore H. Clark, "Market Process Reengineering Through Electronic Market Systems: Opportunities and Challenges," *Journal of Management Information Systems, 13*, no. 3 (Winter 1996–97), 113–136.

Malone, Thomas W., Joanne Yates, and Robert I. Benjamin, "Electronic Markets and Electronic Hierarchies," *Communications of the ACM, 30*, no. 6 (June 1987), 484–497.

Mazis, Michael B. et al., "A Framework for Evaluating Consumer Information Regulation," *Journal of Marketing, 45* (Winter 1981), 11–21.

Mehta, Raj, and Eugene Sivadas, "Direct Marketing on the Internet: An Empirical Assessment of Consumer Attitudes," *Journal of Direct Marketing, 9*, no. 3 (Summer 1995), 21–32.

Molinsky, Andrew L., "Sanding Down the Edges: Paradoxical Impediments to Organizational Change," *The Journal of Applied Behavioral Science, 35*, no. 1 (March 1999), 8–24.

Moorman, Christine, Rohit Deshpande, and Gerald Zaltman, "Factors Affecting Trust in Market Relationships," *Journal of Marketing, 57* (January 1993), pp. 81–101.

Morgan, Robert M., and Shelby D. Hunt, "The Commitment-Trust Theory of Relationship Marketing," *Journal of Marketing, 58* (July 1994), 20–38.

Novak, Thomas P., and Donna L. Hoffman, "Bridging the Digital Divide: The Impact of Race on Computer Access and Internet Use," Project 2000 Working Paper. This working paper is a longer version of the article, "Bridging the Racial Divide on the Internet," *Science* (April 17, 1998).

Nowak, Glen J., and Joseph Phelps, "Direct Marketing and the Use of Individual-Level Consumer Information: Determining How and When 'Privacy' Matters," *Journal of Direct Marketing, 9*, no. 3 (Summer 1995), 46–60.

Pine, B. Joseph, II, and James H. Gilmore, "The Four Faces of Mass Customization," *Harvard Business Review* (January–February 1997).

Pitter, Keiko et al., *Every Student's Guide to the Internet*, San Francisco, CA: The McGraw-Hill Companies, Inc., 1995.

Porter, David, ed., *Internet Culture*, New York: Routledge Inc., 1997.

Rayport, Jeffrey, and John J. Sviokla, "Managing in the Marketspace," *Harvard Business Review* (November–December 1994), 141–150.

Resnick, Paul, and Hal R. Varian, "Recommender Systems," *Communications of the ACM, 40*, no. 3 (1997), 56–58.

Rheingold, Howard, *The Virtual Community: Homesteading on the Electronic Frontier*, Reading, MA: Addison-Wesley Pub., 1993.

Rohner, Kurt, *Marketing in the Cyber Age: The What, The Why, and The How*, Chichester, England: John Wiley & Sons, Ltd., 1998.

Rosenblum, Bert, *Marketing Channels: A Management View*, 6th ed., Fort Worth, TX: The Dryden Press, 1999.

Runkel, Philip, and Joseph E. McGrath, "Planning to Gather Evidence: Techniques for Observing and Recording Behavior," pp. 173–193. In *Research in Human Behavior: A Systematic Guide to Method*, New York: Holt, Rhinehard & Winston, 1972.

Sager, Ira et al., "Cyber Crime," *BusinessWeek* (February 21, 2000), 36–42.

Sarkar, Mitra Barun, Brian Butler, and Charles Steinfield, "Intermediaries and Cybermediaries: A Continuing Role for Mediating Players in the Electronic Marketplace," *Journal of Computer-Mediated Communication, 1*, no. 3 (1995).

Schibsted, Evantheia, "Are You Next? 20 Industries That Must Change," *Business 2.0* (March 1999), 44–52.

Schkade, David A., and Kleinmuntz, Don N., "Information Displays and Choice Processes: Differential Effects of Organization, Form, and Sequence," *Organization Behavior and Human Decision Processes*, in press.

Schlosser, Ann E., and Alana Canfer, "Interactivity in Commercial Web Sites: Implications for Web Site Effectiveness," Working Paper, University of Illinois.

Schmidt, Jeffrey B., and Richard A. Spring, "A Proposed Model of External Consumer Information Search," *Journal of the Academy of Marketing Science, 24*, no. 3 (1996), 246–256.

Schnaars, Steven P., *Marketing Strategy: A Customer-Driven Approach*, New York: Macmillan, Inc., 1991.

Schumann, David W., and Esther Thorson, eds., *Advertising and the World Wide Web*, Mahwah, NJ: Lawrence Erlbaum Associates, Publishers,1999.

Shim, Richard, "Giveaways—They Pay Off on the Web," *Yahoo News*, from PC Data Online (June 2000).

Slivovitz, Michael D., Chad Compton, and Lyle Flint, "The Effects of Computer-Mediated Communication on an Individual's Judgment: A Study Based on the Methods of Ash's Social Influence Experiment," *Computers in Human Behavior, 4* (1988), 311–321.

Spears, Russell, and Martin Lea, "Panacea or Panopticon? The Hidden Power in Computer-Mediated Communication," *Communication Research, 21*, no. 4 (August 1994), 427–459.

Stefik, Mark, ed., *Internet Dreams: Archetypes, Myths, and Metaphors*, Cambridge, MA: The MIT Press, 1997.

Steuer, Jonathan, "Defining Virtual Reality: Dimensions Determining Telepresence," *Journal of Communication, 42*, no. 4 (Autumn 1992), 73–93.

Strauss, Judy, and Raymond Frost, *Marketing on the Internet: Principles of Online Marketing*, Upper Saddle River, NJ: Prentice-Hall, Inc., 1999.

Suarez, Fernando F., and James M. Utterback, "Dominant Designs and the Survival of Firms," *Strategic Management Journal, 16*, no. 6 (September 1995), 415–431.

Tapscott, Don, *The Digital Economy: Promise and Peril in the Age of Networked Intelligence*, New York: McGraw-Hill, 1996.

Taptich, Brian E. "Less Than Zero Margins," *Red Herring* (March 1999), 46–50.

Tax, Stephen S., Stephen W. Brown, and Murali Chandrashekaran, "Customer Evaluations of Service Complaint Experiences: Implications for Relationship Marketing," *Journal of Marketing, 62*, no. 2 (April 1998), 60–76.

Valacich, Joseph S. et al., "Communication Concurrency and the New Media: A New Dimension for Media Richness," *Communication Research, 20*, no. 2 (April 1993), 249–276.

Vassos, Tom, *Strategic Internet Marketing*, Indianapolis, IN: Que Corporation, 1996.

Vesely, Rebecca, "Kiddie Kash," *Business 2.0* (May 1999), 24–26.

Walther, Joseph B., Jeffrey F. Anderson, and David W. Park, "Interpersonal Effects in Computer-Mediated Interaction: A Meta-Analysis of Social and Antisocial Communication," *Communication Research, 21*, no. 4 (August 1994), 460–487.

"Web Security: A Matter of Trust," *World Wide Web Journal, 2*, no. 3, O'Reilly & Associates, Inc., Sebastopol, CA, 1997.

Widing, Robert E., II, and W. Wayne Talarzyk, "Electronic Information Systems for Consumers: An Evaluation of Computer-Assisted Formats in Multiple Decision Environments," *Journal of Marketing Research, XXX* (May 1993), 125–141.

Wilde, Louis L., "The Economics of Consumer Information Acquisition," *Journal of Business, 53*, no. 3 (1980), 143–165.

Winer, Russell S. et al., "Choice in Computer-Mediated Environments," *Marketing Letters, 8*, no. 3 (1997), 287–296.

Zeff, Robbin, and Brad Aronson, *Advertising on the Internet*, New York: John Wiley & Sons, Inc., 1997.

Zimmerman, Jan, and Michael Mathiesen, *Marketing on the Internet*, Gulf Breeze, FL: Maximum Press, 1998.

Index

Boldfaced page numbers indicate pages where boldfaced terms are defined.